1001 ACTIVITIES FOR A SMARTER CHILD

Consultant:
Susan Miller, Ed.D.

PUBLICATIONS INTERNATIONAL, LTD.

Louis Weber, CEO
Publications International, Ltd.
7373 North Cicero Avenue
Lincolnwood, Illinois 60712

Manufactured in China.

8 7 6 5 4 3 2 1

ISBN-13: 978-1-4127-1389-4
ISBN-10: 1-4127-1389-7

Susan Miller, Ed.D., is professor emerita of early childhood education at Kutztown University of Pennsylvania. She has written for more than 250 journals, magazines, and books, including Scholastic's *Early Childhood Today, Childhood Education, Early Childhood News,* and the weekend activities for their *Parent & Child* magazine. Miller is a frequent presenter at the National Associations for the Education of Young Children conferences and the Association of Childhood Education International Study conferences.

Contributors: Suzanne I. Barchers, Ed.D.; Susan Bloom; Marilee Robin Burton; Sandra Fisher; Susan G. MacDonald; Carole Palmer; Leslie Anne Perry, Ph.D.; Joyce Stirniman; Elizabeth C. Stull, Ph.D.; Beth Alley Wise

Cover Illustration: Lyn Martin

Illustrations: Kate Flanagan
Additional illustrations: Anne Kennedy, Lynn Sweat, George Ulrich

MIX FUN WITH LEARNING

◁▷◁▷◁▷◁▷

Young children are naturally curious about the world around them. They eagerly use all of their five senses to explore and experiment as they expand their knowledge and practice new skills. In *1001 Activities for a Smarter Child*, you and your child will find a vast array of wonderful, fun-filled educational activities to ignite these sparks of curiosity and give your child a head start in school.

Together, you'll discover and participate in exciting activities that will strengthen your child's total growth and development—socially, emotionally, physically, and intellectually. You'll have many opportunities to explore relationships through dramatic play and suggested conversations. By means of storytelling, art projects, and singing, your child will learn important skills for self-expression. Your child's hand-eye coordination, so necessary for success in reading and writing, and large and small muscles will become refined through hands-on activities such as making puzzles and playing games. With this book, your child will develop lifelong problem-solving skills by learning to gather information, analyze thoughts, and apply ideas as he or she enjoys constructing a city or investigating a nature project. Creativity will be stimulated through a myriad of open-ended activities that challenge your child to explore a variety of art media, design an invention, or produce an original play. You can select from a wealth of motivating language arts activities that will build the necessary skills involved in reading, writing, listening, and speaking (all of which contribute significantly to your child's reading development).

Each of these intriguing activities will strengthen important skills that will make your child more knowledgeable about a vast array of ideas.

As you read through the easy-to-follow directions, you will become aware that some of the activities in *1001 Activities for a Smarter Child* can be undertaken by your child independently, while others will require your assistance. Your role will often be that of a play partner. Sometimes you will help set up an activity, particularly if supervision is required. You know your child best; therefore, you know when he or she needs to be supervised closely. For safety reasons, when small or sharp objects are being used, or when activities take place around water or heat, direct supervision is usually necessary. These cautions will be indicated for you.

Some projects in this book call for paint or other materials (glue, flour, etc.) that can be messy. Protect your child's clothing, if necessary, with a smock or apron. You may also want to safeguard the work surface with newspaper or a plastic table covering.

Each activity has been rated with a difficulty level in the form of an owl. The number of owls will guide you:

 The activity is easy.

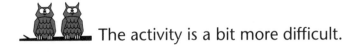 The activity is a bit more difficult.

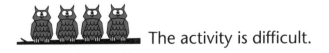 The activity is of intermediate difficulty.

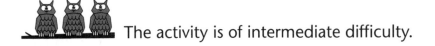 The activity is difficult.

 The activity is quite challenging.

These ratings are simply suggestions, however. Again, you know your child best. The activities should be fun and enough of a challenge so that they will be exciting for the child. On the other hand, you do not want to frustrate your child with activities beyond his or her abilities. With your guidance, your child can grow in both competence and confidence.

Various children learn in different ways. Even though one medium activity may be easy for your child, another medium activity could be quite hard. If your child, no matter what the age, does not have prior experience with the topic, concept, or skills involved, then he or she may need to gain some basic skills or concepts by trying some easier activities first.

As you and your child select an activity, discuss what you are going to do. Take time to talk with your child and allow questions while he or she is working on a project. Be patient, and encourage your child in the activity. Feel free to change the pace of an activity at any time. You can even modify the setting, as activities don't all have to take place at home—your child can learn about letters and sounds through a picnic in the park, or discover shapes on an outdoor scavenger hunt. You may also find it helpful and fun to repeat an activity from time to time. The projects are designed so that they can be enjoyed over and over again. Try repeating favorite activities by adding a new twist.

The activities included in *1001 Activities for a Smarter Child* cover a variety of themes and subject areas (math, language, science, social studies, music, movement, art, nutrition) to keep interest high. A detailed index is provided so that you can easily find the type of activities that you are looking for. Feel free to skip around— your child may learn best by doing, so he or she might really enjoy pasting together a collage or cooking "peanut butter roll-ups." At the same time, your child might be less motivated by listening to the reading of a poem or playing the game "Old MacDonald Had a Farm." However, even if your child does not necessarily learn as easily by listening, you should not skip these activities altogether. They may not be his or her favorites, but they may prove more exciting than you expect!

In his book *Frames of Mind,* Howard Gardner describes various types of learning abilities that are present in all of us. If your child seems to learn best by classifying and likes to explore patterns and relationships, he or she is probably a "logical/mathematical learner." Or, if the child is good at picking up sounds and likes to sing and play instruments he or she may be a "musical learner," learning through rhythm. While your child may have a favorite learning style, and some abilities may be stronger than others, it's possible to promote other areas of intelligence. Encourage your child to learn in different ways by trying a variety of the activities in this book. It's an intriguing, fun way to help raise a brighter, more interesting, well-rounded child. While it may seem that some activities are similar to one another, the presentation within them varies in order to appeal to the different ways children learn.

Some activities require various materials. Help your child gather them, providing whatever support or time is needed. Make places for the child to share his or her work with other family members. You may want to consider using a camera or video recorder to document the work. Sharing ideas with others helps your child to organize his or her thoughts, gain self-expression skills, and enhance self-confidence.

Let the child know that it's all right to take safe risks or to pull back if uncomfortable with any project. Most important, enjoy your time together as your child becomes intrigued, mystified, playful, and brighter! As you and your child work and play, he or she will become more confident. Remember, the activity is often more important than the product. Have a wonderful, pressure-free, exploratory time together!

MINGLE & MERGE COLOR SPLURGE

◁▷◁▷◁▷◁▷

Watching colors change is fun!

Color mixing can be fascinating to observe, but when mushing and mixing playdough is part of the process, it is doubly enticing. Cover the work surface with newspaper. Make 3 balls of playdough in the primary colors (red, blue, and yellow) as a base for mixing experiments. Invite the child to help make the dough. For each ball, mix together ½ cup cold water, ½ cup salt, 1 teaspoon oil, and food coloring. Then gradually mix in 1½ cups flour and 1 teaspoon cornstarch until dough forms. Knead the dough into a malleable ball. After the 3 balls are made, the child can experiment by mixing portions of the different colors together to see the results. To add challenge, encourage the child to make as many different colors out of the 3 original balls as possible. The child can then classify and group all the colors created or arrange them in a series!

What You'll Need
- newspaper
- bowl
- measuring cups and spoons
- water
- salt
- oil
- food coloring
- flour
- cornstarch
- clear plastic jars (optional)
- squeeze bottles (optional)
- eyedroppers (optional)

A simpler variation is coloring water with food coloring to make red, blue, and yellow water that the child can mix. The colored water can be placed in plastic squeeze bottles, allowing the child to squeeze combinations of colors into clear jars. Or the water can be put into jars, and the child can use eyedroppers to mix the colors into different jars.

BUILDING BIG BLOCKS FOR BIG BLOCK BUILDINGS

◁▶◁▶◁▶◁▶◁▶

Build big, tall towers with do-it-yourself grocery-bag blocks!

What You'll Need
- big brown grocery bags
- newspaper
- masking tape

The child can make giant blocks by wadding up old newspapers and stuffing them into large brown grocery bags. Put a second bag upside-down over a filled bag to seal off the open end. Secure the second bag with masking tape. The child can create a whole set of big blocks that can tower high but will tumble safely! Children may soon grow tired of making blocks, so adults should make this a project that spans a number of days, or adults can make most of the blocks before the child sits down to make a few. Add diversity by creating an additional set of smaller lunch-bag blocks.

Activity Twist

Construct some additional unique blocks from recyclables that you find around your house. Tape the ends shut on large boxes. Stuff cereal boxes with packing peanuts to create sturdy blocks. Washed-out milk cartons make wonderful castle towers, and empty oatmeal containers can function as barn silos.

ALL ABOARD!

◁▷◁▷◁▷◁▷

Kids are conductors and animals are commuters in this transportation game.

What You'll Need
- toy animals
- letter cards
- several shoe boxes or similar containers

Use children's love of imaginative play to help them learn how to recognize and identify the shapes of different letters.

Help the child create a train out of shoe boxes or some other convenient containers. Have her line up the toy animals and place a letter card by each one. Explain that the cards are the animals' tickets. In order to board the "passengers," the child must be the conductor and identify the letter on each animal's card.

TOP-NOTCH HOPSCOTCH

◁▷◁▷◁▷◁▷

Invent new twists (and hops) for an old hopping standby.

If the child isn't familiar with hopscotch, teach the game to the child and play it a few times. Then invite the child to invent a new hopscotch game using chalk to draw lines and boxes on a sidewalk or patio. Encourage the child to think about how the new game will be played, including how to move (jump, hop, step), which way to go, and how to win the game!

What You'll Need
- chalk

WHAT DO I SEE?

◁▶◁▶◁▶◁▶

*A keen eye and a good set of clues are valuable tools
for this game of seeing and saying.*

Begin by inviting the child to define an *adjective.* Explain to the child that adjectives describe nouns by telling how many or what kind. Some examples of adjectives are: A *tiny* kitten, a *blue* ball, a *cold* day.

Have the child think of an object in the room. It must be an object that is clearly visible. Ask the child to help you guess the object by offering clues that describe it. Point out that the clues should include adjectives that describe color, size, shape, or some other characteristic about the object (noun).

CEREAL TREAT

◁▶◁▶◁▶◁▶

Guess your cereal surprise while the child learns about character traits.

What You'll Need
- empty cereal box
- small object
- sandwich bag
- self-adhesive notes
- pencil

Begin by having the child put a small, clean object, or "prize," inside a sandwich bag, and place it in an empty cereal box. Make sure the child keeps the identity of the object a secret. Next invite the child to write words that describe the object on self-adhesive notes. Attach the notes to the box.

Now it's up to you to guess the prize after reading the descriptive labels. After making your guess, dig into the box, and pull out the prize to see if you are correct. For the next round, you can turn the game around and hide a treat for the child to find.

My Favorite Year

◁▶◁▶◁▶◁▶

Every adult has a favorite year when many special events occur.
This activity will preserve those memories.

Help the child prepare to interview an adult about a favorite year. Explain to the child how the following interviewing procedures are essential for a good interview: introducing oneself, having a list of good questions, allowing the adult to give complete answers, and thanking the adult when the interview is finished. Suggest that the child follow the five *W*'s used in newspaper reporting when planning the questions: who, what, when, where, and why.

After the interview is over, the child can listen to the tape and write down the favorite memories. Help the child create a small book or a birthday card that lists the highlights of the year. Save the tape for a permanent memory of the person interviewed.

What You'll Need
• tape recorder
• paper
• pencil

On Again, Off Again

◁▶◁▶◁▶◁▶

Here's a way children can learn to recognize 2 important words.

What You'll Need
• paper plates (one for game board and one for each player)
• paper fastener
• small piece of poster board
• pen or marker
• 6 construction-paper or plastic board-game markers for each player

Play a game that teaches simple word recognition. For the game board, draw 6 sections on a paper plate. Write "ON" or "OFF" in each section, alternating the words. Fasten a long spinner made out of poster board to the center of the plate with a paper fastener.

To play the game, write each player's name on a paper plate. Have the players take turns spinning the spinner. If the spinner stops at *ON,* the player puts a marker on her plate. If the spinner stops at *OFF,* she does not get a marker. Continue until one player has 6 markers on her plate.

WHAT DOES IT SAY?

◁▷◁▷◁▷◁▷

Every object has a name. Match words to objects in your room.

After letter sounds have been mastered and the capital and lowercase letters have been learned, the next step is to apply that knowledge to reading words.

Write simple words (for example, *ball, pen, desk, cup*) on index cards. Make sure the words correspond to objects found in the child's room. Give the child a card and ask her to sound out the word printed there. When the word is said, instruct the child to take the card to her room, locate the object matching that word, and place the card next to the identified object.

HAPPY ABOUT VERBS

◁▷◁▷◁▷◁▷

Clap, tap, stomp, laugh, and sing until you're happy about verbs!

Clap your hands and tap your feet as you join in the fun while singing the first verse of "If You're Happy and You Know It" with the child.

> **If you're happy and you know it, clap your hands. (clap, clap)**
> **If you're happy and you know it, clap your hands. (clap, clap)**
> **If you're happy and you know it,**
> **Then your face will surely show it!**
> **If you're happy and you know it, clap your hands. (clap, clap)**

Invite the child to write new verses for the song. Help the child think of new actions to replace clapping hands, such as stamping or tapping feet, or moving arms. Point out that the name for each action is a verb. Next, together sing the new verses the child has suggested, and sing until you're happy!

ALPHABET APPLES

◁▶◁▶◁▶◁▶

Get to the core of the "short" letter A.

Reward children with paper apples as they learn to identify the beginning sound of the "short" letter *A*.

Cut several apples out of red construction paper. Print *Aa* on each one. Say a series of word pairs such as *car/ant.* Have the child identify the word that begins like *apple.* Other word pairs to use are *add/bear, after/cup, fire/alley, attic/uncle, peach/alligator,* and *eat/at.* As an extra challenge, have the child draw items that begin with the "short" letter *A*.

NEWSPAPER LETTERS

◁▶◁▶◁▶◁▶

Use a newspaper to set up this letter-search activity.

This activity exposes the child to the newspaper, a medium in which letters and words are important.

Give the child a page from a newspaper, and ask her to search it for a particular letter. Every time that letter is found, have the child put a circle around it with a marker. You may limit this to capital or lowercase letters, or search for both. Try different letters, and have the child note the frequency of some letters (such as *E*) compared to others (for example, *X).*

BUILDING TOGETHER APART

◁▶◁▶◁▶◁▶◁▶◁▶

It's a challenge to build the same building as someone else without looking!

What You'll Need
• large cardboard box
• scissors
• set of blocks

Create a divider by cutting off the flaps on both ends of a large cardboard box and then cutting along a vertical corner fold. Set the divider up on a table or on the floor. Divide a set of blocks so that each person (an adult and a child or 2 children) has the identical number, size, and shape of blocks. Position 1 person on 1 side of the divider and the other on the other side, making sure that neither can see what the other person is doing. One person builds a building, describing each step of the building process: what kind of block is being used and where it is being placed. The other person tries to make the same building at the same time by listening to and following the directions. When the 2 buildings are finished, remove the divider and compare the buildings. Then take down the buildings, put the divider back up, and reverse the roles!

SOUP'S ON!

◁▷◁▷◁▷◁▷

A hot phonics lesson will have kids saying, "More soup, please!"

What You'll Need
- can of soup
- pot
- bowl
- spoon

Caution: This project requires adult supervision.

Here's an activity that teaches children important kitchen skills while helping them recognize beginning sounds.

Invite the child to choose a kind of soup to prepare. Read the directions aloud, and have the child help you follow each step. While you both eat the soup, give clues to a word that begins like the word *soup*, and have the child guess the word. For example: "This is something to eat for lunch. It is made with bread." (Answer: sandwich.) Then have her think of another word that begins with *S* and give you clues about it.

BEEP! BEEP!

◁▷◁▷◁▷◁▷

Investigate what makes common sounds and experiment with ways to write them.

Take a walk outside to record environmental sounds, such as a car horn honking, birds chirping, sirens blaring, the wind howling, dogs barking, and so on. Later, have the child listen to the recorded sounds and create words to describe them. Some examples might include: *beep! beep!, chirp! chirp!, woof! woof!,* and *wr-r-r-r!* Invite the child to paint the sound words in large letters on long pieces of butcher paper to create a vocabulary mural.

What You'll Need
- tape recorder
- butcher paper
- paint
- paintbrushes

MUSICAL WORDS

◁▶◁▶◁▶◁▶◁▶

Combine writing with music for this inspirational activity.

What You'll Need
- recording of theme-related music (such as scary, water, or cowboy)
- pencil
- paper

Choose a place where the child will not be disturbed. Explain that you will be playing some music that should make the child think of related words. For the beginning writer, you may want to tell the child what kind of music you will play. For the older child, let her try to determine what kind of music is playing.

Invite the child to listen to the music and write down all the words the music prompts. As the music continues, the child may want to take a second piece of paper and arrange the words in a new design that combines the words with an illustration. For example, water music may prompt a drawing of the ocean with words on waves.

MEMORY MADNESS

◁▷◁▷◁▷◁▷

Here's a simple activity that helps sharpen the child's ability
to remember details.

Invite the child to remember as many details as possible about a recent adventure, visit, or even a walk around the block. Then ask the child questions that challenge the child's memory skills.

What did the child hear, see, taste, smell, or touch? What was the weather like? Were there birds in the sky? Was a radio playing? What song was playing? Were people standing with their feet together or apart? Which hand petted the cat? This can be an ongoing activity for you to do periodically with the child.

BUTTON, BUTTON!

◁▷◁▷◁▷◁▷

A misplaced button leads to a game of beginning sounds.

Play this hiding game with a small group to give children practice with beginning sounds.

First, cut a "button" with a diameter of approximately 2" out of heavy paper or poster board. On each side of the button, write a letter. Have players sit in a circle on the floor and choose one player to be "it." The player hides her eyes while the other players pass the button around. After a minute or so, the player who is "it" says, "Button, button, who's got the button?" At this point, the player holding the button must hide it in her lap.

The player who is "it" then opens her eyes and tries to guess who has the button. If the guess is correct, the child who is "it" must identify the letter on top of the button and say a word in which that letter is the beginning sound. If she is correct, then the person hiding the button becomes "it."

What You'll Need
• construction paper or poster board
• blunt scissors
• marker or pen

CURTAIN'S UP!

◁▷◁▷◁▷◁▷

These ideas will encourage the child to act out a favorite story.

What You'll Need
- favorite picture book
- paper
- pencil

Read the book aloud together. Discuss with the child how to turn the book into a play. What parts will be the dialogue? What can be read aloud by a narrator? Help the child write a section of the book in script form. Then choose characters and read the script aloud together. To extend the activity, read the script into a tape recorder and share with others.

RED RAKES, PURPLE PIGS

◁▷◁▷◁▷◁▷

Here's a colorful way to learn beginning letter sounds.

Use children's knowledge of colors to help them learn beginning sounds.

What You'll Need
- paper
- pencil
- crayons or colored markers
- old magazines
- blunt scissors

First, help the child make a color wheel. Draw a circle, and divide it into 6 sections, like a pie. Color the sections in this order: red, purple, blue, green, yellow, orange. Make picture cards by cutting out a picture whose name has the same beginning sound as each color word—for example, a rake for *red,* a pig for *purple,* a blanket for *blue,* grass for *green,* yarn for *yellow,* and an orchestra for *orange.*

Ask the child to name each color on the wheel and then place the picture with the same beginning sound next to that color. Children who are more advanced can find their own matching pictures.

ABC Concentration

<⊳<⊳<⊳<⊳<⊳<⊳

Alike or different? Let kids decide in this game.

What You'll Need
• 10 letter cards

Recognizing whether 2 letters are alike or different is an important reading skill.

Shuffle 10 letter cards (5 pairs of matching letters), and lay them out faceup in 2 rows. Invite the child to put the 5 pairs of matching letters together.

As a variation, make 1 set of matching letters uppercase, the other set lowercase. You can also increase the number of cards used.

1-2-3 Surprise!

<⊳<⊳<⊳<⊳<⊳<⊳

Act out new endings for favorite 1-2-3 stories.

Act out a story with the child in which something happens 1, 2, or 3 times and then has a surprise ending. For added fun, you and the child can make up a new surprise ending. Here are some story suggestions:

"Goldilocks and the Three Bears"
"The Three Little Pigs"
"Jack and the Beanstalk"
"Three Billy Goats Gruff"

WEIGH AWAY

◁▷◁▷◁▷◁▷

Light, lighter, lightest—which is which?

What You'll Need
- hole punch or large nail
- 2 empty plastic margarine tubs of equal size
- yarn
- blunt scissors
- hanger
- assorted items, such as stuffed animals, toy cars, blocks

Let your child help you make a simple balance scale. First, punch or poke 3 holes equidistantly around the rim of the 2 plastic margarine tubs. Cut 6 pieces of yarn all the same size. Thread a piece of yarn though a hole, and tie one end of it to the tub; repeat for all holes and all pieces of yarn. Then tie the 3 strings of 1 tub on 1 end of a hanger and the 3 strings from the other tub on the other end. Now you have a balance scale! Hang the scale on a doorknob. Once the scale is set up, encourage the child to gather an assortment of items, predict which will be heavier or lighter, and then test those predictions by putting the items in the scale. To make the activity more challenging, the child can continue to compare a group of objects until he is able to put them in order from lightest to heaviest. He can also make predictions about how many of a lighter object it will take to equal the weight of a heavier one.

SIMPLE AS A SIMILE

As tall as a skyscraper or as strong as an ox, this simile activity is sure to be a big, big hit with children.

Have the child read poems that use similes. Point out the similes and explain that these phrases use the words *as* or *like* to compare two things. Next place several small objects in a bag. Let the child remove one object at a time from the bag and use a simile to describe or compare its size to another object. Use the following format to get the child thinking:

What You'll Need
• poetry collection
• bag
• several small household objects

_____ is as big as _____
_____ is as strong as _____
_____ is as wide as _____
_____ is as round as _____

ART GALLERY TOUR

◁▷◁▷◁▷◁▷

Create an art gallery, and give guided tours!

What You'll Need
- child's artwork
- tape
- twine
- clothespins

Set up an art gallery together with the child by displaying an assortment of the child's artwork. The work can be taped to a wall, clothespinned to a line, or set up on tables and shelves. The child can take family members on a tour of the gallery, telling about each work of art.

NATURE COLLAGE

◁▷◁▷◁▷◁▷

Collect and compare and collage!

The child can collect nature items in a bag, and then bring them home to look at and compare them more carefully. The child might want to use an egg carton to sort some of the findings. After observing and examining all the assorted items, the child can arrange and glue some of them onto cardboard to create a nature collage. For easier gluing, have the child put glue on the cardboard first, then place the items on the glue.

What You'll Need
- bag
- nature items (twigs, bark, leaves, petals, seeds, pine needles, pebbles, even a little dirt)
- egg carton
- cardboard
- nontoxic white glue

LOOP-DE-LOOP BALL

◁▶◁▶◁▶◁▶◁▶◁▶

Catch the loops—it is fun and easy!

What You'll Need
• 8 pairs of old clean pantyhose
• blunt scissors

This nylon loop ball is easy for young children to catch because it gives them handles that can be grasped and tossed easily. Because it is soft and flexible, it is excellent for younger children who need further development of the muscles of the hand, wrist, and arm. The ball can be washed in the washing machine and dried in the dryer.

Instructions to make the ball—let the child help you wherever possible:

1. Cut off each pantyhose leg at the top of the thigh and at the ankle. You should end up with 16 legs.

2. Roll each leg into a loop by inserting one of your arms into the stocking, and rolling the stocking back down to create a donut shape. Roll all 16 legs in this way.

3. Cut 3" pieces of yarn to use to tie the loops together.

4. Assemble the 16 loops by tying them to the other loops at 4 or 5 points, until all loops are tied together in the shape of a ball. If each loop is thought of as the face of a clock, all the loops will be tied together by securing them to each other at 3, 6, 9, and 12.

Alphabet Song

◁◁▷▷◁◁▷▷

An old song is a great way to begin the day—and learn the alphabet.

Teach the child the "Alphabet Song":
"A, B, C, D, E, F, G,
    H, I, J, K, L, M, N, O, P,
    Q, R, S,
    T, U, V,
    W, X,
    Y, and Z.
Now I know my ABCs,
Tell me what you think of me."

By singing this song, the child learns rhyming sounds and the sounds of the letters, while at the same time developing a frame of reference for alphabetical order.

For a variation, write the letters of the alphabet on a sheet of paper, and ask the child to point to each letter while singing. You can also record the child singing on a cassette tape that can be played again and again. For a second verse, replace the last line above with: "Won't you come and sing with me?"

Riddle Time

What appears once in a minute,
Once in a blue moon,
Yet never in one hundred years?
(The letter M)

FLOWER SCRUTINY

◁▷◁▷◁▷◁▷◁▷

So many flowers—how are they alike, and how are they different?

Flowers are a part of plants, and they come in all different sizes, shapes, colors, and smells! Invite the child to compare 4 different kinds of flowers and note all the similarities and differences. The child can use the magnifying glass to look closely. The blunt scissors and plastic knife can be used to dissect the flowers and look inside them. For a more advanced activity, have the child record the findings (or dictate them to you). The child can draw pictures of the different flowers, record their colors, or count how many petals each flower has. Additional flowers can be added to the study. (Flowers can be obtained from the garden or from a supermarket—yesterday's wilted bunch is often available at a discount!)

What You'll Need
- 4 different kinds of flowers
- blunt scissors
- plastic knife
- magnifying glass
- paper (optional)
- pencil (optional)
- crayons (optional)

The most effective kind of education is that a child should play amongst lovely things.

—Plato

CHARACTER TRANSPLANT

◁▷◁▷◁▷◁▷

Interesting situations prevail when a character is transported from its original story to new surroundings.

Choose a character from a favorite story together. Discuss what the character is like and how he, she, or it acts, reacts, solves problems, and so on. Then create a whole new story or situation, and put that character in it. Invite the child to talk about what the character would do and how the character would react in that entirely new setting.

What You'll Need
• storybook

YELLOW YES

◁▷◁▷◁▷◁▷

Yellow is an affirmative color in this word recognition activity.

Here's an activity that uses color recognition to reinforce the *Y* sound.

Print the words *yellow* and *yes* on a sheet of paper. Say the words, and ask the child to tell you how they are similar. Have the child print the word *yes* in yellow crayon, then collect several objects that are yellow. You may choose to have the child collect objects from both inside the house and outside.

Put the yellow objects in a cardboard box. Add several objects that have other colors. Pull one object at a time out of the box, and hold it up for the child to see. If the object is yellow, the child has to hold up the paper with yes printed on it and say, "Yellow—yes."

What You'll Need
• marker or pen
• sheet of paper
• yellow crayon
• yellow objects
• nonyellow objects
• cardboard box

PUPPET PROBLEMS

◁▷◁▷◁▷◁▷

Help perplexed puppets with their problems!

Make some simple puppets together by drawing faces on paper lunch bags with markers. (Or, cut out shapes from felt or paper scraps for the face and glue them on the bag.) Stuff the bag with crumpled newspaper, and insert a paper-towel tube in the bottom of the bag. Scrunch the end of the bag around the tube, and secure it by tying a piece of yarn around it. Use the tube as a handle for the puppet. When the puppets are finished, pose a problem that the 2 puppets might be having, and ask the child for help solving the problem. Either the adult can speak for the puppets and the child can act as an intermediary, or the adult can use

1 puppet and the child the other, with the 2 puppets talking to each other to work out the dispute. To make the activity easy, present problems that are not interpersonal; for example, one of the puppets might have trouble finding a lost toy or be afraid of sleeping with the light turned off—so it needs advice!

What You'll Need
- markers
- paper lunch bags
- blunt scissors
- felt or paper scraps
- nontoxic white glue
- crumpled newspaper
- paper-towel tubes
- yarn

GEOBOARD

◁▷◁▷◁▷◁▷

Make shape art, then take it apart!

What You'll Need
- piece of wood
- nails
- hammer
- large colored rubber bands
- ribbon (optional)
- yarn (optional)

Make a geoboard for the child by hammering large nails at equal intervals (about 1½") in rows on a board. The child can help (with supervision) with some of the nailing. When the board is complete, the child can then make geometric designs by looping the large rubber bands around the nails (be sure you are using rubber bands large enough so the child isn't frustrated and they are safe—the band won't pop off and hurt the child). For an easier, more freeform variation, nail 8 to 15 large nails randomly on a wooden base. The child can use ribbons and yarn and weave them around the nails to make designs.

ALLITERATIVE ANECDOTES

◁▷◁▷◁▷◁▷

Creating alliterative anecdotes enhances skills of working with initial sounds.

Make up and recite the beginning of a sentence in which almost all the words start with the same letter. Then invite the child to make up the end of the sentence, continuing to use words starting with that same letter. For example, you might start a sentence, "Seven silly sailors sang," and the child might end it with "seven salamander songs."

> Seven silly sailors sang

> seven salamander songs.

Start again with another new sentence. This time invite the child to start the new sentence with a new letter. Try to work through the entire alphabet. Be ready for some adventurous tongue-twisting.

Activity Twist

For a real challenge, create a short story with the first sentence by adding more sentences that start with the same letter. You may even want to try creating a story using all the sentences that start with different letters.

ANIMAL MOVES

◁▶◁▶◁▶◁▶◁▶◁

Wiggle, wriggle, romp, and stomp!

Invite the child to run, hop, creep, crawl, and "fly" like common animals and insects might. Encourage the child to wriggle across the room or yard like a slithery snake. Challenge the young athlete to jump like a hoppy frog or to trot like a frisky pony. Use descriptive language to help paint a movement picture. For a greater challenge, add more details to each animal story. For example: "Can you sneak along like a cat who has just spotted a butterfly and then show me what the cat will do next?"

WORD BALLOONS

◁▶◁▶◁▶◁▶◁▶◁

Put letters together and celebrate with colorful balloons.

In this activity, children can learn how to put letters together to make words using balloon shapes.

What You'll Need
- construction paper
- blunt scissors
- marker or pen
- index cards

Cut a balloon shape out of construction paper, and write the word ending *an* on it. Print the lowercase letters *c, f, t, m, p,* and *r* on index cards. Have the child put each letter card in front of the word ending on the balloon and say the new word. You can make other word balloons using the word endings *at, ell, op,* and *ot.* (Point out that not all letter combinations will form words.)

ALPHABET MEASURING

◁▷◁▷◁▷◁▷◁▷

Mix 1 measure of counting with 2 measures of letter identification.

Following your specific instructions, a child can master measuring skills while learning to recognize the shapes of different letters.

What You'll Need
- measuring spoon
- small container of sand (or flour)
- 3 plastic drinking cups (marked *A, B,* and *C*)

Show the child how to dip the measuring spoon into the sand (or flour), level it, and pour it into a cup. Have the child follow your directions and put specific amounts of sand in the letter cups. For example, you might say, "Put 2 tablespoons of sand in the *B* cup," or, "Put 3 tablespoons of sand in the *C* cup." For an added challenge, add more letter cups.

LETTER COLLAGES

◁▷◁▷◁▷◁▷◁▷

Cut it, glue it, paste it! This creative activity is sure to keep hands busy.

Read aloud a variety of ABC books with the child. Point out the pictures, the letters, and the corresponding beginning sounds as you read. Next give the child large paper letters that you have cut out in advance. Ask the child to cut out pictures of objects from old magazines that begin with the sound each letter stands for—for example, a cat and a car for the letter *c,* and a dog, a deer, and a door for the letter

What You'll Need
- ABC books
- heavy paper (precut into large letters)
- old magazines
- clear tape or glue
- blunt scissors
- hole punch
- string

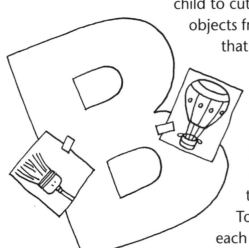

d. Encourage the child to tape or glue pictures over the entire letter to create a colorful letter collage. To complete the project, punch a hole in the top of each letter, and hang them in a room.

PAPER CAPER

◁▷◁▷◁▷◁▷◁▷

Paper is very light, but how far will it go if you blow?

What You'll Need
- several index cards or small pieces of paper (all the same size and kind)
- block or book

Challenge the child to estimate how far a small piece of paper can be blown. The child can place a block or book on the floor to mark the estimate and then test the estimate by putting the card on the floor and sending it off with a large puff of air. The child can mark the actual length it

moved and retest to see if the results are always the same. Encourage the child to think of ways to alter the paper to change the results. What happens if the paper is folded? Or crumpled? Are the results the same? Different? Why?

Activity Twist

Extend the fun! Tape a berry basket, open side facing out, to the floor. Crumple paper into different-size balls, and see if you can blow the balls—soccer-style—into the berry basket net. Which paper ball is the easiest to move? Why? Use this ball to play "soccer blow" with a friend. Keep score if you like.

OPPOSITES OBSERVATION

◁▷◁▷◁▷◁▷◁▷

Go ogling for opposites all around!

This search can take place outside or inside. The child looks for 2 things that display opposite attributes, such as something fast and something slow; something quiet and something loud; something big and something little. Encourage the child to come up with new categories of opposites! For a variation, look at magazines or picture books, and find opposites in the pictures together.

BOOKMARKS

◁▶◁▶◁▶◁▶◁▷

These decorative bookmarks will help the child keep her place when reading a favorite book.

What You'll Need
- favorite book
- card stock
- blunt scissors
- markers

Have the child read a favorite book. Then cut the card stock into the size of a bookmark (roughly 2" × 8"). Explain to the child that a bookmark not only marks a page but can also be used to summarize the book. Invite the child to draw a picture on the bookmark that summarizes the book. Once the summary has been drawn on the bookmark, discuss the picture with the child, using descriptive words.

FLOWING FOUNTAINS

◁▶◁▶◁▶◁▶◁▶◁▷

Water play is engaging, but it can be artistic, too.

Have the child experiment with simple fountains. Make water fountains with the child by punching holes in several plastic containers and then filling them with water. (Be sure to do this either outside or in the house inside a plastic tub!) The holes can be punched in a row vertically, around the bottle at the same level, or randomly around the container.

What You'll Need
- several empty plastic milk cartons or plastic bottles
- large nail
- measuring cups or water containers

Encourage the child to come up with different plans for hole-punching designs. The child can fill the containers and observe and describe how the water flow is different depending on where the holes are.

ROLL POLL

◁▷◁▷◁▷◁▷

Perform a rolling-down-a-ramp test!

Caution: This project requires adult supervision.

Gather up assorted items for the roll poll. The child can make a ramp by elevating one end of a piece of cardboard on a block or book. The child can then predict which of the assembled items will roll and which will not. The items can be tested one by one to check out the predictions. The child can then sort the items into 2 groups: things that roll and things that don't roll. Encourage the child to discuss and conclude what the difference is. (Adult needs to supervise—smaller objects can be choking hazards!)

What You'll Need
- block or book
- cardboard
- assorted items (marble, eraser, cotton ball, crumpled ball of foil, bottle cap, pencil, button, cork, etc.)

DOT PAINTING

◁▷◁▷◁▷◁▷

Dab with dots to create colorful painted point mosaics.

What You'll Need
- tempera paint
- fruit foam trays
- paper
- cotton swabs
- colored construction paper (optional)

The child can use cotton swabs to make dot pictures. Pour several colors of tempera paint into well-washed fruit foam trays for easy dipping. The child can dip the swabs into paint and then dab them onto paper to create dot pictures. For a variation, provide unusual color combinations. The child might explore dot painting using white dots on black construction paper, blue and yellow dots on yellow paper, various shades of pink on red paper, or any other combination you can think of!

PARACHUTE PLAYING

◁▷◁▷◁▷◁▷

Don't let the parachute touch you—run under and back before it falls to the ground!

What You'll Need
- large round tablecloth
- 4 or 5 small balls

This is such a fun activity your child will want to do it over and over. Place the round tablecloth on the floor. Kneel down and hold one side. Have your child kneel and hold the another side. Rise together at the same time, raising your arms as you rise, lifting the tablecloth over the child's head. Do this several times—up and down—to see how well the tablecloth is held up by the air beneath it. Then let it float to the ground. This is an activity, however, that lends itself to more than one child being involved. If there is more than one child, have one child at a time run underneath the tablecloth when it is held at its highest point. After the child understands how the parachute works, start using the balls. Both of you stand holding the sides of the parachute and toss balls into the middle of the cloth. Quickly toss the parachute up and down, trying to keep the balls in the center of the cloth. This is a challenge as the balls go everywhere.

Vision is the art of seeing the invisible.

—Jonathan Swift

MIRROR DANCING

◁▶◁▶◁▶◁▶◁▶◁▶

Watch me watching me in the mirror!

What You'll Need
• full-length mirror

Have the child stand in front of a full-length mirror and dance or move around using arms and legs. Point out how the arms and legs look as they move. Encourage the child to nod and wiggle and explore. When the child becomes aware that what she is watching is the reflection of what she is doing, place the child in front of you. Explain that you are going to be the mirror and will do exactly what you see the child doing. Copy the child's movement—then trade places and let the child be your mirror!

READING WITH EXPRESSION

Reading is always more fun when expression is added.

Read the book aloud with the child. Try to read the story by using as much expression as possible, such as whispering, shouting, dragging out words, building up suspense, and so on. Depending on the text, dialogue, or events, invite the child to read the

What You'll Need
• any book that has strong rhythm or dialogue

words in a loud, soft, fast, playful, or slow voice. For additional fun, have the child read the story into a tape recorder to share with others.

JACK-IN-THE-BOX

◁▷◁▷◁▷◁▷

Children will jump for joy when they learn the letter J.

Play an active game with the child that emphasizes the beginning sound J.

Ask the child to demonstrate the action of a jack-in-the-box. Say the words *jump* and *jack.* Have the child say additional words that begin with the *J* sound. Explain that you will say a word. If it begins with the *J* sound, like *jack-in-the-box,* the child jumps up. If it does not begin with the *J* sound, the child stays "in the box." Begin with the words *jar, sand, tree, jet, jelly, box, jeep,* and *pear.*

VANILLA OR CHOCOLATE?

◁▷◁▷◁▷◁▷

What flavor cone would you like?

Take some time out on a hot summer day, and visit an ice cream shop with the child.

On your way to the shop, ask the child, "What flavors of ice cream do you think the shop will have?" Upon entering the store, look together at the different pictures and advertisements for ice cream treats and the listings of ice cream flavors. Say, "I see a flavor beginning with a *V.* What do you think it could be?" (Answer: vanilla.) Repeat the game with other flavors.

SILENT SINGING

◁▷◁▷◁▷◁▷

Sing a song silently!

Choose action songs with plenty of gestures for silent singing. Together, sing the songs out loud the first time around, accompanying them with all the gestures. Then, "sing" the songs silently, using all the gestures but only mouthing the words. Songs can be silently "sung" together in a "chorus" or can be "sung" solo as adult and child take turns silently singing songs (with gestures) for one another to guess. Some good songs with many gestures to start with are "The Itsy Bitsy Spider," "Head and Shoulders," "Open, Shut Them," and "Five Little Ducks."

LETTER SCRAMBLE

◁▷◁▷◁▷◁▷

Spell a word—sound by sound and letter by letter.

What You'll Need
- index cards
- pen or marker
- picture cards

When the child has learned all of the capital and lowercase letters of the alphabet, you can help him take the next step in language development.

Show the child a picture card (for example, a hat), then give him a stack of randomly mixed index cards, each one containing one of the letters required to spell the pictured object (in this case, *T*, *H*, and *A*). First, have the child name the object in the picture. Then sound out each letter in the word, and have the child take the corresponding letter card and place it in the proper spelling order. Have the child say the word and spell it aloud. Continue in this manner with other picture cards.

WORD WALK

◁▶◁▶◁▶◁▶

Use the great outdoors to encourage good listening and the writing of words associated with all the sounds you hear.

Take a walk in your neighborhood. Have the child listen carefully to all the sounds you hear and write them down. Some may not really be words and have no regular spelling. In that case, have the child

What You'll Need
• clipboard
• paper
• pencil

try to make up a spelling that seems logical, such as *zwee* for a whistle or *fawish* for a breeze. Explain that sometimes these made-up words become real words (this is called *onomatopoeia*, which means the spelling of the word is based on the vocal imitation of the sound it describes).

LETTER TIC-TAC-TOE

◁▶◁▶◁▶◁▶

This game helps kids learn letters—up, down, and sideways.

What You'll Need
• 3 sheets of construction paper (including 1 red sheet and 1 yellow sheet)
• marker or pen
• blunt scissors

Play tic-tac-toe with a phonics twist. Make a tic-tac-toe board on a sheet of construction paper. Write a different letter on each of the 9 squares of the board. Next, cut 2 sets of square markers, 5 red ones and 5 yellow ones, that fit in the tic-tac-toe squares. Give each player 1 set of markers.

The first player chooses a square. In order to put a marker there, he must name the letter in the square. The game continues until one player covers a row across, down, or diagonally or until the board is filled.

ALL EYES AND EARS

⊲▷⊲▷⊲▷⊲▷

Take a close look around the room to find rhyming objects.

In this activity, use objects found in the home to help the child become accustomed to rhyming words.

Show the child an object found in the home (for example, a bat) and have him tell you what the object is and then think of a word that rhymes with it, such as *cat.* Compare and discuss the difference between the object you chose and the rhyming word selected by the child.

BUILDING BLOCKS

⊲▷⊲▷⊲▷⊲▷

*Wooden blocks become a motivating tool for the child to practice **ing** words.*

Set out blocks with letters on them. Have the child line up the blocks to form the word part *ing.* The child may gather the *s* block *(sing)*, the *k* block *(king)*, and other blocks to form words. It may be

necessary to remind the child that when a word ends in *e,* he should drop the *e* before adding *ing,* as in *skate* and *skating* or *smile* and *smiling.* Try other spelling patterns for continued practice.

COLORS AROUND ME

◁▶◁▶◁▶◁▶◁

Go color sleuthing up and down, all around town!

What You'll Need
- 8 to 10 white index cards
- crayons

Have the child use the crayons to mark a different color on each index card. Invite the child to choose one card for some neighborhood detective work. Then take a walk around the block, bringing the color card along to match colors. The child can carry the card and search for houses, cars, signs, flowers, and other things that are the same color as the mark on the card. For a variation, go shape, number, or letter searching. For each kind of search, help the child prepare the cards to carry along to help focus the detective work.

Activity Twist
Take a colorful walk! The adult can pop the lenses out of an old pair of children's sunglasses. Glue in pieces of colored cellophane. Let the child wear the colored glasses on a walk. How does the world look now?

SLEEPY TIME RECIPE

Getting ready for bed can be a sweet experience with this writing and sharing activity.

Discuss with the child the interesting things that happen at night. For example the stars come out, the fairies put stardust in the child's eyes, and the moon comes up. Talk about recipes and how ingredients can carefully be mixed to make a special treat. Have the child make a list of all the ingredients that would be perfect for a good night's sleep. Then invite the child to create a "recipe," deciding what amounts would be just right. For example, a child may want 2 cups of stardust to dust the whole room; maybe even just a pinch for the eyes. Is the whole moon necessary or just a slice?

What You'll Need
- paper
- pencil

After the child has written the recipe, have him read it at bedtime. For a variation, make a wake-up recipe using the same process.

NEW ENDINGS

Practice problem-solving skills while creating new endings for old stories.

Provide examples of how stories can have many different outcomes and endings. Then invite the child to retell a favorite story or folktale as accurately as possible, with one small exception: The child must make up a different ending.

THEME DOMINOES

◁ ◁ ▷ ◁ ▷ ◁ ▷

This version of dominoes is a matching activity based on the popular children's game.

What You'll Need
- tagboard
- old magazines
- blunt scissors
- clear tape or glue

Decide on a category, such as furniture, animals, or transportation, and make dominoes that depict several objects in the chosen category. The dominoes can be made by cutting and taping or gluing small pictures from old magazines on precut tagboard rectangles. Explain to the child that pictures of each object should appear on at least 3 dominoes. Then play dominoes using the following rules of the traditional game.

Turn dominoes facedown on a table. Each player picks 5 dominoes and places the pieces faceup in front of them. Players then take turns placing 1 domino at a time on the board. A domino may only be placed on the board if one of its halves matches a domino already on the board. For example, if the domino on the board has a picture of a moving van, a player can only place another domino that matches that picture on the board. Matching dominoes can be placed end to end or end to side. If a player does not have a match, he must pick from the remaining dominoes until a match is found. The first player to run out of dominoes is the winner.

IT SOUNDS LIKE THIS!

◁▷◁▷◁▷◁▷◁▷

Use your imagination and skill to imitate natural sounds.

Challenge the child to listen to the sounds all around and to invent sounds to imitate them. The child might try to imitate natural sounds, such as wind, rain, or thunder, or household sounds, such as running water or the broom when a parent sweeps the floor. For more of a challenge, play a sound-guessing game. Take turns imitating nature and household sounds for the other person to guess.

When two languages are spoken in the home, children initially are a little slow to reach the standard language development milestones in each language. But by 3 or 4 years of age, they usually are fluent in both languages.

WHAT WILL HAPPEN?

◁▷◁▷◁▷◁▷◁▷

As with all skills, making accurate predictions takes practice. Try it and see!

Before you and the child go shopping, run errands, or visit friends or family, discuss what you might see and hear and what might happen. Make a list of your predictions. After returning from your outing, check the list and see how many of the predictions were accurate.

What You'll Need
- paper
- pencil

For a challenging variation, help the child make a list of predictions for an entire week. See how many predictions come true.

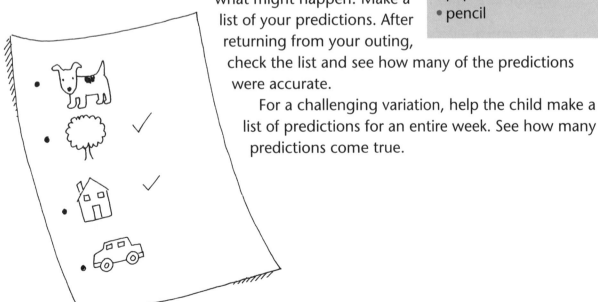

In, On, Under

Get those pesky prepositions straight—and learn to read them.

What You'll Need
- box
- book
- index cards
- marker or pen

Here's a word recognition activity that will also help children understand the meaning of prepositions.

Make word cards with the words *in, on,* and *under.* Place the box on the table. Place the book on top of the box. Hold up the *on* card, and say, "The book is on the box." Continue by putting the book inside the box and under the box, saying explanatory sentences and holding up the appropriate word cards. Then put the book in each position, and have the child hold up the preposition card that describes its location.

Spelling Volcano

Engage the child in this challenging activity of wits and vocabulary.

What You'll Need
- pen or pencil
- paper

Begin by drawing a set of boxes in the shape of a volcano, like the example shown here: 2 boxes at the top, followed by a row of 3 boxes, a row of 4 boxes, a row of 5 boxes, and so on up to 7. Then write a 2-letter word on the top row. Have the child add 1 new letter to that word to spell a new word. The new letter can be added to the beginning, middle, or end of the 2-letter word. Write the new word in the second row of the volcano. Continue in this way, adding 1 new letter at each row to make a new word, going as far down the volcano as possible. Can the child make it to the bottom with a 7-letter word?

Finding the "In Group"

◁▶◁▶◁▶◁▶◁▶◁

Create categories, then figure out what fits in and what doesn't.

What You'll Need
- 2 long lengths of yarn or string
- household objects such as: paper clips, bottle caps, crayons, buttons

Caution: This project requires adult supervision.

Make 2 large circles using the 2 lengths of yarn or string, and have the circles overlap so there is a middle section. This is called a Venn diagram. Explain to the child that you can use the 3 sections for creating categories. Discuss together the idea of categories and that each circle of yarn will contain a category of items, while the section where the yarn circles overlap will be used for any items that fit in both categories. Use some of the collected objects as an example (beware of a choking hazard with small items). One circle might be for buttons. Place all the buttons from the assorted objects into that circle. The other circle might be for blue things. The child can find all the blue things and place those in the second circle. That might include a blue crayon, a blue plastic animal, and a blue bottle cap. Ask the child if there are any items that are both buttons and blue. Explain that those items fit in both categories, so they go in the middle section. Next, remove all the items from the 2 circles and intersecting section and place them back in the group of assorted items. Invite the child to come up with 2 new categories for the items and to create a new Venn diagram. You can also sort pictures into the 2 circles.

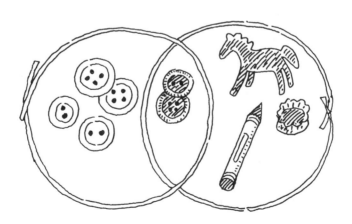

FITTING LETTERS

◁▶◁▶◁▶◁▶

Matching capital and lowercase letters will be fun with these puzzles.

Using index cards positioned horizontally, you can make several (or all 26) letter cards. Write a capital letter on the left half of each card and the corresponding lowercase letter on the right half. Randomly cut the cards between the letters (using notches, angles, zigzags, and curved cuts), then mix them up in a single pile.

What You'll Need
• index cards
• marker or pen
• blunt scissors

The object of this activity is for the child to match the capital letter to its lowercase partner. The child will know that he made a correct match when the 2 halves fit together. You can begin this activity with only a few letters and eventually work up to mixing and matching the entire alphabet.

ANTONYM ANTS

◁▶◁▶◁▶◁▶

Pretend you're on a picnic, eating words.
But you'll have to pick the ants out of your sentence first.

Explain to the child that antonyms are pairs of words that mean the opposite of each other, such as *hot* and *cold, day* and *night,* and *big* and *small.* The object of this activity is for the child to pick the ant (antonym) out of a sentence, think of its opposite, and give that opposite back to you.

For example, you say a sentence that has an antonym in it, such as "The soup is hot." Explain that the antonym the child has to work into a sentence is the opposite of *hot.* The child then takes the antonym of *hot* and works it into the sentence, such as, "The water in the pool is cold." The following examples will help get you started.

The soup is *hot.* (Antonym is *cold.*)
The river is *deep.* (Antonym is *shallow.*)
The hallway is *long.* (Antonym is *short.*)

BACKWARD BEE

◁▶◁▶◁▶◁▶◁

Spelling words backward is just as fun as spelling words forward. Try it and see!

Begin by providing a list of words for the child to spell. They may be words from a school spelling list or words the child wants to learn to spell. Then, just like in a regular spelling bee, give the child the words to spell. However, instead of spelling the word forward, have the child spell it backward. The child gets one point for each word spelled correctly—backward, that is!

LOOK, LISTEN, AND DO

◁▶◁▶◁▶◁▶◁

Play a clapping, snapping, stomping, jumping pattern game!

Make up 2-part patterns using clapping, patting, or other body movements. Demonstrate a pattern, such as clap-stomp-clap-stomp-clap-stomp, and then invite the child to repeat the pattern. As the child gains more experience, she can try a hand (or foot!) at making up her own 2-part patterns. Take turns making up patterns for one another to repeat and continue. Increase the challenge by including some 3-part patterns in the game. For an even greater challenge, take turns adding an action to one another's pattern. For example, the adult might make up the pattern: clap-tap. The child can repeat it, and then change it by turning it into the 3-part pattern: clap-tap-stomp. The adult can repeat it and then add one more: clap-tap-stomp-wiggle.

PEEKABOO

⊲▶⊲▶⊲▶⊲▶⊲▶

Wits will be sharpened with this brainteasing and thinking activity. Get ready!

Review a list of vocabulary words with the child. These may be words used in math, science, social studies, or reading. Write a sentence for each vocabulary word on the list. Then cover the vocabulary word in each sentence with a self-adhesive note. Invite the child to

Mike ☐ his bike to school.

read the sentences and try to determine which word is under the flap before lifting it and peeking to check.

What strategies did the child use to discover the word? Emphasize how listening to the other words in the sentence and thinking about words that will make sense in completing the sentence are good strategies for finding the missing word.

WHIMSICAL WORDS

⊲▶⊲▶⊲▶⊲▶⊲▶

Compose poetic nonsense!

Read the child poetry that uses made-up or nonsensical words. Explain that sometimes poets use pretend words to make a poem silly, fun, or different. Talk about the nonsense words you hear in the poems you read and why the poet might have used them. Then together create invented poetry using whimsical word sounds in place of real words. The poems can be all made-up word sounds or include just 1 or 2 nonsense words here and there for fun. For a challenge, have a pretend conversation using only made-up words!

WHAT'S THE LETTER?

◁▷◁▷◁▷◁▷

This guessing game is a simple phonics activity that can be done anytime or anywhere. It's great for traveling.

Begin by pointing to an object in the room or a picture in a magazine or book. Say the name of the object, and ask the child to name its beginning letter. Continue to offer the child new items for letter guessing, or invite the child to choose an object and give you a turn at guessing.

To increase the difficulty of the game, instead of naming the object, offer a 2- or 3-word description of it and ask the child to say the first letter of its name. The more unusual the items chosen for the game, the more interesting the game can be!

CREEPY CRAWLY EXPLORATION

◁▷◁▷◁▷◁▷

Explore the earth up close and personal!

What You'll Need
• plastic magnifying glass

Find a grassy area where the child can stretch out on the ground. Invite the child to choose one little attractive patch of earth and spend some time closely observing what goes on there! The child can use the magnifying glass and note what is there and what is happening. Encourage the child to describe the earthy discoveries by asking open-ended questions, such as: "What seems to be moving? How does it seem to move? What color is it?"

WALL HANGING

◁▶◁▶◁▶◁▶◁▶◁▷

A burlap wall hanging is just what you need for that empty wall.

What You'll Need
- 18" × 24" piece of burlap
- old ribbon and/or thick yarn

By going over and under burlap threads with some yarn, children can make a beautiful wall hanging—and learn a few letters as well.

With the burlap's finished edges at the top and bottom, prepare the piece of burlap by removing cross threads from along the unfinished edges. This will leave open spaces in the material for the child to weave in different materials.

Show the child the piece of burlap with the open spaces and the yarn, and then say, "I am thinking of two words, one beginning with an *O* and the other with a *U*, that explain how you fill the open areas of the burlap. How can you put some yarn in those places?" (Answer: over and under.) Have the child select some yarn, and try going "over" and "under" the lengthwise threads. Explain that this process, going over and under, is called weaving.

Ask the child, "What letter does the word *weaving* begin with?" As the child is weaving, have him say "over" and "under" during the weaving process. Even if a few threads are skipped, the effect will still be beautiful. Try different thicknesses and colors of yarn and/or ribbon for a distinctive weaving.

LETTER NECKLACE

◁▷◁▷◁▷◁▷◁▷

Help kids make a simple necklace they can wear with pride.

What You'll Need
- index cards
- marker or pen
- hole puncher
- 24" length of yarn
- old magazines (optional)
- blunt scissors (optional)
- glue or clear tape (optional)
- paper clip (optional)

In this activity, children can show what they've learned by wearing it around their necks.

Use 6 to 8 index cards. On the first card, write a letter. On each of the other cards, the child should make a picture of an item whose name begins with that letter. Or you can ask the child to cut out magazine pictures of objects that have the same first letter and glue or tape them on the cards.

When the child has completed the cards, punch 2 holes at the top of each one. String the yarn through the cards, keeping the letter card in the center. Have the child name the letter and the pictured items. Put the stringed cards around the child's neck so she can wear them like a necklace. Fasten the ends fairly loosely with a paper clip (to prevent a choking hazard).

Hinkie-Pinkie!

Why shouldn't you tell a cow a secret?
Because cattle tattle.

NUMBER SEARCH

Search for (and discover!) numbers in familiar territory!

What You'll Need
- index cards
- pencil

Send the child on a search for a number that can be found around the house. Provide the child with a number card to make matching easy. The child can look for one number at a time, carrying an index card with a number from 1 to 10 writ-

ten on it to help the child remember just what the number looks like. Challenge the child to find that number in as many places as possible! Numbers can be found on clocks, radios, calendars, books, magazines, clothing, and food boxes. For a variation, have the child listen for a number, too! Numbers can be heard on the radio, on TV, in songs, and in conversations.

BODY LANGUAGE

Kids need not look far beyond their own noses to learn to read their first words.

Here's a phonics activity that also tests a child's quickness and coordination.

What You'll Need
- marker or pen
- index cards

Write the words *head, neck, leg, foot,* and *toe* on separate index cards. Read each card with the child. Have the child identify the beginning sound in each word and touch the body part the word names. Shuffle the cards, and place them face down. Instruct the child to choose one card at a time, identify the body part named on the card, touch that body part, and then say another word with the same beginning sound. Remind the child to identify the initial sound in both words.

REPTILE FAMILY

Even squeamish kids will like these colorful snake puzzles.

What You'll Need
- construction paper
- pen or marker
- blunt scissors
- plastic container

Here's a personalized puzzle that helps children recognize various kinds of likenesses and differences.

Make several snakes by drawing and cutting out squiggly snake shapes from different colors of construction paper.

Along each snake, write the name of a family member or friend in large letters with space between the letters. Cut each snake into pieces with a letter on each piece. Put all the pieces into a container and mix them. Have the child put each snake back together by matching colors, letters, and edges.

VANILLA PUDDING

V stands for vegetable—but also for this very tempting treat.

Children can practice their *V* sounds while helping you make (and eat) vanilla pudding.

Print the letter *V* on a piece of paper. Ask the child to think of words that begin with that letter, naming *vanilla* if he doesn't. Make some vanilla pudding, having the child help you follow the directions on the box and mix the ingredients.

As you are eating the pudding, discuss other words that begin with the *V* sound, such as *vacuum cleaner, valentine,* and *vitamin.* Have the child display as many of these items as possible, or write the letter *V* on self-adhesive notes and label each item.

What You'll Need
- pen or pencil
- piece of paper
- box of instant vanilla pudding
- milk
- wire whisk or mixer
- bowls
- spoons
- self-adhesive notes (optional)

SHAPING UP

◁▷◁▷◁▷◁▷◁▷

Mold yourself into any kind of shape.

What You'll Need
• large towel

Do this activity on a large towel (or on a carpet). Have the child lie on the floor. Then give suggestions about how the child can move his body into different shapes. Here are some

suggestions for shapes: round, flat, wide, narrow, long, short, fat, thin, pointed, crooked, square, heart. Along with learning about the body, the child can begin building a vocabulary of descriptive words. To increase the difficulty of the activity, challenge the child to form letters of the alphabet with his body.

PREPOSITION CUE CARDS

◁▷◁▷◁▷◁▷◁▷

While retelling this story, the child will add flavor with cue cards and sounds while learning about prepositions.

Retell the story "The Three Billy Goats Gruff," emphasizing the words and phrases that tell where: *on the hillside, over the bridge, under the bridge, across*

What You'll Need
• construction paper
• markers

the planks, into the water, and others. Next have the child make cue cards that say *on, under, across,* and *over,* and decide on appropriate sound effects for each.

Retell the story again. This time have the child hold up the cue cards at the appropriate time and add the designated sound effect. Explain to the child that these words that tell when or where are called prepositions. Invite the child to make a list of all the prepositions he can think of.

FLASHLIGHT ART IN THE DARK

◁▷◁▷◁▷◁▷

Shine colored light to glow and gleam and blend and beam.

What You'll Need
- flashlights
- colored cellophane
- rubber bands

Cover the top of a flashlight with colored cellophane, and secure it with a rubber band. Cover the top of a second flashlight with a different color of cellophane. When the flashlights are turned on, the light that shines through will make a tinted reflection as it hits the wall or ceiling. The child can explore the colored reflections in a darkened room and can also experiment with color mixing using beams of tinted light. The child can use the 2 flashlights and direct them so the beams collide, or the adult and child can each shine a beam, dancing the lights together and apart.

Activity Twist

Add some music and jazz up your colored lights with some flashlight dancing. Move your flashlights rapidly to fast music and slowly to dreamy music. Try twirling and shining your colors on the ceiling, walls, and floor for a wonderful kaleidoscope effect.

STAY STILL & MOVE

◁▷◀▷◀▷◁▷

Frolic and bounce in one place in one space!

Challenge the child to find new ways to move while staying in one place. Give the child masking tape to create an × on the floor to mark the spot! The child can start off by sitting on the spot. Encourage the child to experiment with different ways to move or dance while

What You'll Need
• masking tape
• music

sitting. Help the child by offering some suggestions, such as swaying, twisting, or wiggling. After experimenting with a variety of movements while sitting, invite the child to explore movement possibilities while keeping contact with the spot using a foot, hand, or tummy. Add music to dance on the spot!

Activity Twist

Create a homemade game! Use a plain, old, clean plastic shower curtain or tablecloth. Trace the child's hands and feet with permanent marker in numerous places on the plastic surface and on large index cards. Now, hold up one card at a time so the child can match that hand or foot on the sheet. Then, stay still, or twist and move, to add the next body match shown on the selected card.

SCAVENGER HUNT

◁▷◁▷◁▷◁▷◁▷

A keen eye for detail will help the young detective when searching for items in this scavenger hunt.

Have the child number a piece of paper from 1 to 5. Then invite the child to draw the following pictures next to the corresponding number on the paper.

What You'll Need
- paper
- crayons or pencils
- bag with handle

1. desk
2. envelope
3. tree branch
4. kitchen drawer
5. sewing basket

Next have the child go on a scavenger hunt around the room, around the house, or in other safe locations to collect something that can be found in or on each object on the list. For example, the child's collection may include a pencil (from a desk), a stamp (from an envelope), a leaf (from a tree branch), a spoon (from a kitchen drawer), and a button (from a sewing basket). If necessary, have the child return the items after the scavenger hunt.

WALKING THE TIGHTROPE

◁▷◁▷◁▷◁▷◁▷

Keeping one's balance is necessary to walk the letter tightrope. Be careful.

What You'll Need
- Rope cut in lengths of 4'

The challenge of walking a tightrope is exciting to a child. The motor skills necessary for balancing have to be used in this activity.

Take a piece (or pieces) of rope, and outline a very large letter (capital or lowercase) on the floor. The goal of this activity is for the child to "tightrope-walk" this letter. Make sure that, as the child is walking this letter, he is moving in the way that the letter is properly formed (top to bottom and left to right). Also, arms can be extended sideways to simulate the moves of a tightrope walker.

For an additional challenge, the child can walk sideways, moving on one foot next to the other; or, the child can be asked to cross one foot over the other.

A CLOSE LOOK

◁▶◁▶◁▶◁▶◁▶◁▶

A picture is worth a thousand words. What do you see?

What You'll Need
• detailed ABC picture books

A beginning reader needs to develop the skill of observing and interpreting pictures. ABC books can help because they have illustrations that aid the child's understanding of the relationship between letters and their sounds. Some pages have one word, some have rhyming text, and some use alliteration (2 or more words in a row that begin with the same letter sound). These books are useful because they help develop the foundations of phonics. At the same time, they are visually stimulating, helping to maintain a child's attention.

Examine a variety of ABC picture books, then ask the child to take a close look at one of them. Encourage the child to observe as much detail as possible. Next, select just one page and say the word for an item depicted there. The child then needs to find something else on that page that begins with the same letter as the word you said. Alternate turns, paying attention to the letters and sounds as you go through the letters from *A* to *Z*.

HERO POSTER

◁▶◁▶◁▶◁▶◁▶◁▶

Making posters is a creative activity that encourages reading and writing.

What You'll Need
• book with a make-believe hero
• construction paper
• pencil
• poster paints or markers

Begin by having the child read a book that features a make-believe hero. Encourage the child to write down several interesting facts contained in it. Then help the child plan different components to include in a promotional poster for the hero of the book. For example, the poster might feature famous moments, heroic qualities, challenges the hero faced, photographs or drawings of the hero, and so forth. Be ready for some poster-creating fun!

MINI-PIZZA RECIPE

◁▷◁▷◁▷◁▷

Try these delicious little pizzas for lunch and learning.

Caution: This project requires adult supervision.

Not sure what to make for lunch? How about mini-pizzas? Preheat your oven to 425°, and place the ingredients on a table or counter.

First, split a muffin in half, and place the halves on a baking sheet. (You can toast the muffin first, if you want a crunchy crust.) Show the child how to spoon tomato sauce onto the muffins, followed by any vegetable toppings that he may like—onions and mushrooms, for example. Let the child put the cheese on the pizzas, then bake them for 10 to 15 minutes. As always, be careful that the child doesn't come into contact with the stove or heated baking pan.

What You'll Need
- tomato sauce
- English muffins
- shredded mozzarella cheese
- vegetable toppings (if desired)
- spoon
- baking sheet
- paper
- crayons

While the pizzas are baking, help the child make a recipe card using pictures and beginning letters. Arrange them sequentially to show how the mini-pizzas were made. For example:

1. Picture of a muffin and the letter *M.*
2. Picture of sauce on a muffin half and the letter *S.*
3. Picture of vegetable toppings, if used, along with their beginning letters.
4. Picture of cheese and the letters *Ch.*

Sounding Off

◁▷◁▷◁▷◁▷

Make lots of noise—all with your mom's or dad's approval!

Caution: This project requires adult supervision.

Exploring noise-making is natural for a young child, but listening takes practice and skill! Let the child experiment with sounds by putting different amounts and kinds of materials into a variety of containers and then closing them, shaking them, and listening. To simplify the activity, decrease the variables: The child can use containers that are all the same size and shape but filled with different materials. Or, he can fill containers of different sizes and shapes with varying amounts of the same material. To increase the difficulty, ask the child to line up the containers in order from the softest noise-maker to the loudest. (Supervise young children; small objects can be choking hazards.)

> **What You'll Need**
> • variety of empty containers with tops, such as coffee can, film canister, margarine tub, cereal box, oatmeal canister
> • fillers, such as uncooked rice or kidney beans, paper clips and buttons

HOW DOES AN ELEPHANT DANCE?

◁▷◁▷◁▷◁▷

Just imagine some silly things—elephants dancing and walruses waltzing!

The child can listen to a piece of music and imagine and act out how an elephant might move and dance to that piece of music. Ask the child to picture the elephant dancing! How would it move to the music? Would it take big steps or little ones?

What You'll Need
• music

Activity Twist

Use old, clean socks to create animal hand puppets! The child can use markers, buttons, and ribbon to decorate the socks with different animal faces. Once the puppet creations are complete, have fun dancing and acting out each animal's movements. For added challenge, find books on the animals and discuss how the animals move, what the animals eat, and where the animals live.

WHAT WEIGHS MORE?

◁▷◁▷◁▷◁▷

Compare weights with a simple sock test!

What You'll Need
- variety of small household objects and toys
- 2 large socks
- balance scale (see "Weigh Away" on page 20) or long block and a piece of heavy cardboard

The child can test the comparative weights of 2 objects using 2 socks to test by feel. The child chooses 2 different objects to test, predicts which is the heaviest and which is the lightest, and then puts each item into a separate sock. Standing up and holding a sock in each hand, the child tests the weight by feel. To check the results of the sock test, the child can use a balance scale or can make a simple balance beam by resting a piece of cardboard on a block. For a further challenge, the child can test 4 or 5 items to find out which is the heaviest. To determine the heaviest item, the child can test 2 items at a time, each time eliminating the lightest, and testing the heavier item with the next item from the group of 5. Through testing, the child will eliminate the 4 lightest items one by one and will end up with the heaviest item.

HOLEY LACES

◁▷◁▷◁▷◁▷

Make a lovely lacing by weaving in, out, around, over, and otherwise!

Caution: This project requires adult supervision.

Cut a square from poster board or a shoe box and randomly punch holes in the square. The child can use a piece of yarn (stiffen the end with glue for easier lacing) to lace in and out of the holes. Tie a knot in the end of the yarn to keep it from pulling through. The lacing can occur as randomly as the holes! To enhance the design, add small pieces of construction paper with holes punched in them, pasta with holes, and beads to the mix! (Beware of choking hazard.)

What You'll Need
- poster board or shoe box
- hole punch
- blunt scissors
- yarn
- nontoxic white glue
- construction paper
- pasta with holes
- beads

NATURE WALK

⊲►⊲►⊲◄⊲►⊲◄►

Take a woody walk, and predict what the sights might be.

What You'll Need
- marker
- pad of paper
- pencil

Plan a walk in the woods or through a park. Talk together first about what different things might be seen or heard. Make a picture list of all the predictions to take along. The list might include birds, squirrels, flowers, trees, rocks, ants, and people. The child can check off items along the way. When you return to the

house, check the list together to see how many of the predicted items were seen and also to note and add important observations that were not predicted beforehand! For a variation, take a walk and ask the child to predict how many of one kind of thing might be seen, such as how many birds sitting in trees, red flowers, dogs on leashes, and then count them together.

LETTER MOBILE

⊲►⊲►⊲◄⊲►⊲◄►

Collect 2- and 3-dimensional items for this mobile display.

A mobile is an interesting way to display a letter. Have the child choose a letter. Draw it on construction paper, and cut it out. Punch a small hole in the top, attach a piece of yarn or string, and hang it from the hanger.

What You'll Need
- construction paper
- pen or marker
- blunt scissors
- hole puncher
- string or yarn
- wire coat hanger
- old magazines
- collected items (see left)

Have the child collect items and pictures of items whose names begin with the same letter. For example, choosing the letter C, the child might find a paper cup, a cookie cutter, and a picture of a cat. Hang the items on the mobile with string or yarn of varying lengths.

ACROSTIC POETRY

◁▷◁▷◁▷◁▷

This easy form of poetry can be used whenever a special day, person, or event calls for a poem.

Perhaps it is Father's Day and the child needs to make a card. Or maybe a special friend or family member needs a comforting thought. To create an acrostic poem, have the child write a key word, such as *father*, vertically on the left side of the paper. Then, on each line, write a related word that begins with each letter, creating a poem such as the following:

Fun
Always helping
Terrific
Helpful
Exciting
Ready

As this poem demonstrates, not all poems have to rhyme, so the child doesn't need to be concerned about that.

For variety, the child can use 2 or more words for each line, creating a series of phrases.

PROVE IT!

◁▷◁▷◁▷◁▷

Challenge the child to use critical thinking skills to "show what you know."

Make a statement, and ask the child to think about the statement and then guess whether the statement is true or false. After the child has answered, ask him why he chose that answer. How did the child decide or know that your statement was true or false? How can the child prove that the statement was either true or false? Encourage the child to back up his statement.

WHAT IF?

◁▷◁▷◁▷◁▷

Imagine and invent right along with the story.

Share simple stories, and use them as springboards for creative thinking. Engage the child in discussion throughout the storytelling, stopping along the way to invite the child to share ideas. Ask questions like: What might happen if...? What do you think will happen next? What makes you think that? What would you do if you were in the story? How do you think the grandfather feels? What else could he do? What else could the little girl have done? What would have happened if the dog stayed outside? Can you think of another way the story could have ended?

What You'll Need
• storybook

Activity Twist

Look through magazines for interesting, silly, exciting, or scary pictures. Mount them on construction paper to serve as storyboards. Use them to generate ideas for the child to tell pretend stories or serious stories. For example, you might use one storyboard for a creative story starter and another for a unique ending!

TALL, SMALL, OR TAIL

◁▷◁▷◁▷◁▷◁▷

Did you know that all lowercase letters can be grouped into one of three categories?

Categorizing lowercase letters will help the child learn and recall these letters.

Spread the lowercase alphabet cards on the floor or table. Pick out an example of a "tall" letter (such as *b*), a "small" letter (such as *a*), and a "tail" letter (one that goes below the baseline, such as *g*). Use these letters to start 3 piles. Have the child place all of the other letters into one of those 3 piles.

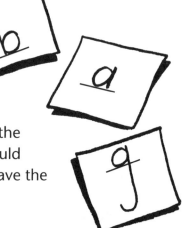

When the child is finished, the "small" pile should contain the letters *a, c, e, i, m, n, o, r, s, u, v, w, x,* and *z.* The "tall" pile should contain the letters *b, d, f, h, k, l,* and *t.* The "tail" pile should have the letters *g, j, p, q,* and *y.*

COPYCAT WORDS

◁▷◁▷◁▷◁▷◁▷

Copycat or oddball? Kids decide as they look at and listen to a series of words.

In this activity, children recognize both visually and aurally whether words are the same or different.

On a sheet of paper, write a series of 3 words, such as *cat/can/cat.* Read the words aloud. Ask the child to circle the word that is different. Write another row of words with-

out reading them aloud. Again, have the child circle the word that looks different. Read the words and ask the child to repeat them. Continue with other series of words, such as *pig/pig/big; dog/hog/dog; bed/red/red; pink/pink/sink; hen/ten/ten;* and *five/five/dive.*

TACO SURPRISE

◁▷◁▷◁▷◁▷◁▷

Learning about nouns was never as much fun as it is in this taco surprise!

Caution: This project requires adult supervision.

Help the child learn about nouns as you make tacos together. Begin by listing the materials you will need. Then have the child divide the materials into 3 noun groups: ingredients, cooking utensils, and serving materials. Using these lists as guides, carefully gather the necessary materials, and set them out on a table or other large work area. Take care to prepare the ingredients before you begin. To make the tacos, follow this simple recipe, adapting it to personal taste.

What You'll Need
- paper
- pen or pencil
- taco ingredients (sour cream, lettuce, tomato, green pepper, cooked beef or chicken, olives, shredded cheese, taco sauce, taco shells)
- cooking utensils (spoon, knife, cookie sheet)
- plates
- napkins

1. Fully cook beef or chicken, drain, and set aside.
2. Heat taco shells in warm oven for 3 to 5 minutes.
3. Spoon meat into bottom of heated taco shell.
4. Top with shredded lettuce, chopped tomatoes, chopped green peppers, sliced olives, shredded cheese, taco sauce, and sour cream.
5. Serve and eat!

INGREDIENTS	COOKING UTENSILS	SERVING MATERIALS
sour cream	spoon	plates
lettuce	knife	napkins
tomato	cookie sheet	
green pepper	oven	
beef	pot holders	
chicken		
olives		
cheese		
taco sauce		
taco shells		

LETTER DROP

A handkerchief and a group of friends add fun to this learning activity.

What You'll Need
• handkerchief

Give children practice identifying beginning sounds as they play "Drop the Handkerchief."

Have a small group of children stand in a circle. The child who is "it" takes the handkerchief, walks around the outside of the circle, and drops the handkerchief behind one player. That player must name a word and then tell the letter that makes its beginning sound. If the player is correct, he then becomes the player to drop the handkerchief. To make the game more challenging, you may want to give a category for the words to be named, such as vegetables, plants, or animals.

HINKIE-PINKIE

This activity challenges the child to use critical thinking, rhyming skill, and cleverness!

A *hinkie-pinkie* is a riddle in which the answer is a 2-word rhyme. If the rhyming words have 1 syllable, the riddle is a *hink-pink.* If the words have 2 syllables it is a *hinkie-pinkie.*

Begin by giving the child a clue as to whether the riddle is a hink-pink, or hinkie-pinkie. Here are 2 examples:

Hink-Pink: What is a chubby pet that meows? (fat cat)

Hinkie-Pinkie: What is a puppy that got all soaking wet in the rain? (soggy doggy)

DOODLE DRAWING

◁▷◁▷◁▷◁▷◁▷

Turn squiggles and lines into squirrels, lions, or designs.

What You'll Need
- paper
- markers or crayons

Draw a squiggle, line, or half shape on a piece of paper. Challenge the child to use the doodle on the paper as a picture starter. The child can turn the squiggle into a picture of something or into a design. For a variation, draw 2 or 3 shapes on the paper for the child to use as a picture starter.

Activity Twist

The child can use finger power to create doodle squeezings. Mix some flour, water, and salt in a bowl until it is the consistency of toothpaste. Place the mixture in a plastic squeeze condiment bottle. The child can slowly squeeze a fascinating array of doodle lines onto a cardboard surface. For more fun, let the doodles dry and color them with markers!

SWEET OR SOUR?

◁▷◁▷◁▷◁▷◁▷

Kids must get their taste buds working for this savory experience.

Show your good taste as you help a child review words that begin with the letter *S*.

What You'll Need
- snack foods as described below

Have the child taste several different food items and describe their tastes with an *S* word. Explain that many different kinds of tastes can be described with *S* words, such as sweet, sour, spicy, salty, sticky, and sugary. The word *soft* can also describe foods.

Prepare some snacks from among the following: potato chips, dill pickle, sweet pickle, salsa, white bread with peanut butter, pretzel, white bread with jelly, hot dog, or salami. The child can also taste lemon juice and other juices. Have the child taste each food and use one or more *S* words to describe it.

WHERE WOULD I LIVE?

Learning how to compare features of different places can be a useful skill. Start by comparing city and country.

Have the child make a chart by writing *country* on one side of the paper and *city* on the other side. Then have the child list the features of each area. Once the features have been listed, discuss the advantages and disadvantages of both areas. Follow this example.

What You'll Need
- paper
- pencil

Country	City
Quiet	Exciting
Fields	Streets
Trees	Buildings

FAIRY-TALE TURNAROUND

This fairy-tale turnaround will inspire imaginative thinking in the young reader!

What You'll Need
- favorite or familiar fairy tale

Read the fairy tale aloud together. Discuss its plot, and then talk about what would happen if one of the bad characters was good. How would that affect the plot? What would happen to the other characters? How would the changed events affect the ending? Retell the story together with the new ending.

LETTER LONDON BRIDGE

◁▷◁▷◁▷◁▷

London Bridge is falling down—unless kids can identify beginning sounds.

What You'll Need
- index cards
- old magazines
- blunt scissors
- glue or clear tape

Here's a new slant on an old singing game that will help children practice letter sounds.

Make picture cards by cutting out pictures of simple objects and pasting or taping them onto index cards. To play the game, sing "London Bridge Is Falling Down" with a small group of children.

The players walk one by one through the bridge formed by two other players holding hands above their heads. When the song ends, the players making the bridge drop their arms, leaving the child "caught" inside the bridge. In order to be "released," the child looks at a picture card, identifies it, and then gives a word with the same first-letter sound as the object in the picture.

Fun Fact
Toddlers are often inclined to use "telegraphic" speech, leaving out words that are not essential for meaning (as people used to do when sending telegrams). For example, it is not uncommon for them to abbreviate simple sentences, saying, "What doing?" instead of "What are you doing?"

RAINBOW MAKER

◁▷◁▷◁▷◁▷

***Kids won't care what's over the rainbow when they create
this colorful arc out of clay.***

This activity introduces the child to one of nature's
wonders while contemplating the letter *R*.

Discuss rainbows with the child. Talk about a
time when you saw a rainbow in the sky. Find a
picture of a rainbow in a magazine or picture book,
or ask the child to draw a picture of one.

Ask the child to identify the beginning sound in
the word *rainbow,* and say some other words with

What You'll Need
• picture of a rainbow (or
crayons and paper to draw
one)
• clay or playdough in several
different colors

the same beginning sound. Help the child make several long coils of clay or playdough
in several different colors. Show the child how to put the coils close together in arcs to
make a rainbow.

DIP AND DYE

◁▶◁▶◁▶◁▶◁▶

See what happens when you dip coffee filters into colored water.

Dipped and dyed coffee filters look beautiful and are an easy way for a child to learn some new *D* words.

Pour some water into small containers. Fill them about half full. Have the child add a different food coloring to each container. Discuss with the child the colors that were added and their beginning letter sounds—for example, *R* for red, *B* for blue, *G* for green, and so on.

Have the child fold a coffee filter into small sections. Ask her to think of a *D* word to describe a way to get the colored water on the folded coffee filter. Then have the child dip part of the filter into one of the colored water containers. Repeat dipping into the other colors using different parts of the filter. When the child has finished dipping the filter, open it up and place it on newspapers to dry.

Ask the child the following questions. "What *D* word did you do to the filter?" (Answer: dip.) "What happened to the white filter when it was dipped into colored water?" (Answer: It was dyed.) Have the child describe what colors she sees on the filter and what happened when some colors were mixed together. Ask her to name the beginning letters of those colors.

Hink-Pink!

Q: What does a full moon make?
A: A bright night.

MARK IT!

⊲▶⊲▶⊲▶⊲▶⊲▶

The child will enjoy reading with you while learning about beginning sounds. Pull up a chair!

Choose a favorite picture book with the child. Then help the child write 1 letter on each of 5 separate self-adhesive notes. While the child pages through the picture book, ask her to mark with a self-adhesive note 5 objects or words in the book that use the corresponding consonant. Invite the child to share the book with you, pointing out the words and pictures she has marked.

What You'll Need
• favorite picture book
• self-adhesive notes
• pen or pencil

PICK A NUMBER

⊲▶⊲▶⊲▶⊲▶⊲▶

All numbers are lucky when kids use them to learn letters.

What You'll Need
• paper
• 10 cards with numbers 1 through 10
• pen or pencil

This activity helps children recognize both letters and numbers.

On a sheet of paper, write the numbers 1 through 10 in a column, and write a letter by each number. Shuffle the number cards and place them in a stack.

Instruct the child to take the top card, match it to a number on the sheet, and name the corresponding letter.

If the child identifies the letter correctly, she keeps the number card. If the child is incorrect, the card is placed at the bottom of the stack. When all the letters have been identified correctly, make a list with different letters.

One Word Swaps

◁▶◁▶◁▶◁▶◁▷

Here's an activity that requires careful listening and thinking. Humor is a bonus!

Begin by making up a sentence and writing it on a piece of paper. Make sure the sentence has an interesting subject, contains an activity, and mentions a place. (Example: I walked to the park and saw a tree.) Before slowly reciting the sentence to the child, ask her to listen carefully in order to repeat it. Explain that after you say the sentence, the child should change one of the words to a different word and then repeat the sentence in its slightly altered form. Any word in the sentence can be changed, as long as the sentence still makes sense. (Example: I walked to the park and saw a dog.) The more the meaning of the sentence changes, or the funnier it gets, the better.

After the child has changed a word and recited the sentence revision, write the revision underneath the original. Then take another turn yourself and change a different word. (Example: I ran to the park and saw a dog). Continue taking turns, changing a different word each time. The game ends when every word in the original sentence has been changed.

Example:

I walked to the park and saw a tree

I walked to the park and saw a dog.

I ran to the park and saw a dog.

I ran to the beach and saw a dog.

Mom ran to the beach and saw a dog.

Mom ran to the beach and heard a dog.

Mom ran along the beach and heard a dog.

Mom ran along the beach and heard two dogs.

Mom ran along a beach and heard two dogs.

Mom ran along a beach then heard two dogs.

STRIKE!

◁▷◁▷◁▷◁▷

*Have a ball with this simple milk-jug bowling game,
designed to reinforce word recognition.*

Use permanent markers to write words on
the plastic milk jugs. Set up the jugs like
bowling pins in rows of 1, 2, 3, and 4,
as shown. Invite the child to roll a ball
down the "lane" and try to knock over
the pins. The child gets 1 point for each pin
she knocks over—but only after reading the word
on it! (Help the child recognize letters and sound out the words.)

What You'll Need
- 10 plastic milk jugs
  (½ gallon or quart)
- permanent marker
- rubber ball

ME BOX

◁▷◁▷◁▷◁▷

Create a box of items that together tell a personal tale.

What You'll Need
- box
- assorted items cho-
  sen by child: photos,
  stuffed animals, book

Challenge the child to assemble a "Me Box." The child can
choose 5 or 6 personal items to place inside the box.
Encourage the child to pick things that together will tell
something important about her. After the box is created,
the child can share it with family members and explain all
the choices.

Activity Twist

Help the child write a personal story! The child can draw pictures that
together tell a story about her. The drawings can be of the child, family
members, pets, favorite television shows, toys, or books. An adult can help
label the pictures. For added fun, the child can "read" the story into an
audio tape, including her name, family members' names, pet names, etc.
Send the audio tape to a relative who lives far away!

I'm on TV

◁▷◁▷◁▷◁▷

Talk on TV, and pretend the whole world can see!

What You'll Need
- cardboard box
- scissors
- paint
- paintbrush
- nontoxic white glue
- buttons or bottle caps
- paper-towel tube (optional)
- yarn (optional)
- foil (optional)

Make a TV out of a cardboard carton. The adult can cut a "viewing screen" out of the front and back of a box. The child can then paint and decorate the box. The child may want to paint the TV black or brown or create a rainbow or scenic TV box—honor all choices! Knobs can be painted on the box, or the child may want to glue on buttons or bottle caps. The child can also make a microphone by cutting a paper-towel tube in half, and then taking one of the halves, painting it, and

gluing a length of yarn to the bottom and a ball of foil to the top. When the box is dry, set it on its side on a table. The child should stand behind the box so her face is seen in the TV screen. The child can then use the microphone and broadcast news of the house.

COFFEEPOT

◁▷◁▷◁▷◁▷

In this activity, the child will coffeepot the word you're thinking of.

Begin by thinking of a verb (an action word) such as *walk.* Then think of a sentence using that word. For example, "The tiger walks in the jungle." Next say the sentence aloud to the child, but replace the chosen verb with the word *coffeepot.* The sentence now becomes, "The tiger coffeepots in the jungle."

Invite the child to guess your word. If the child is unable to guess, think of a new sentence. "I walk to school everyday," for example, would be "I coffeepot to school everyday." Keep making up new sentences until the child guesses the word.

BIRTHDAY FOR A BEAR

◁▷◁▷◁▷◁▷

Everyone deserves a birthday party, even bears and other animals!

What You'll Need
- stuffed animals
- paper plates
- party hats
- playdough
- crayons
- paper
- blunt scissors
- wrapping paper
- ribbon

The child can plan a party for a stuffed bear or another favorite stuffed toy. The child can make decorations, decide on games, create a playdough birthday cake, and even make and wrap a gift to give to the birthday animal. The child can also make party invitations to "send" to other stuffed toys and animals. Then it's time to have fun, play games, sing "Happy Birthday," unwrap presents, and enjoy the pretend cake!

CLIMB EVERY MOUNTAIN

◁▷◁▷◁▷◁▷

See who's king of the mountain when it comes to beginning sounds.

Give active children a goal to reach as they practice beginning sounds.

First, make letter cards by printing letters on index cards. Make a "mountain" by stacking blankets in a big mound on the floor. You may put cushions and pillows in the center of the mound to support the mountain. Put letter cards in folds of the blankets all the way up and around the mountain. Challenge the child to climb the mountain by identifying each letter on the way to the top and saying a word in which that letter stands for the beginning sound.

What You'll Need
- index cards
- marker or pen
- blankets

As children become better at identifying the letters and sounds, have them start over at the bottom if they give an incorrect answer. If you have a real hill or something else that can be climbed in your backyard, try this activity outside.

BUBBLE PICTURES

◁▷◁▷◁▷◁▷

Have double bubble fun indoors or outside!

What You'll Need
- pie tin or plastic bowl
- tempera paint
- water
- liquid detergent
- drinking straw
- straight pin
- paper
- glycerin (optional)

The child can use a straw to blow colorful painted bubbles and then create bubble pictures using the suds. This is a great outdoor summer project—it can get messy, but it's lots of fun! In a pie tin or plastic bowl, thin the tempera paint with water, and add a healthy portion of liquid detergent to make it bubble easily. If you add a few drops of glycerin (available at a drugstore), the bubbles will be bigger. Have the child practice blowing out with a straw before blowing into the bubble solution to avoid sipping any paint. Use a pin to prick a few holes around the top of the straw—this will also keep the child from sucking in the paint. Invite the child to blow into the soapy paint and experiment with bubble making. The child can make prints with the frothy suds by placing a piece of paper on top of the bubbles, gently pressing down, and then lifting the paper off.

Fun Fact
No other language has more ways to pronounce the same letters and letter combinations than English. Consider: heard/beard, low/how, paid/said, break/speak, five/give, four/tour, and ache/mustache.

TRUE OR FALSE

◁▶◁▶◁▶◁▶◁▶

Discriminating between truth and untruth can be a fun way to develop and practice reasoning skills.

Tell the child that you are going to make 5 statements, 4 true ones and 1 false one. Invite the child to listen carefully to all 5 statements and guess which is false. The statements can be very simple—cats like milk, the window is open, ducks have feathers, elephants swim in the ocean, we will have potato soup for lunch—or they can be more difficult—horses are mammals, the moon is a planet, bread is made from wheat, the neighbor's dog's name is Rusty, I made my bed this morning.

   After doing this activity several times, invite the child to make up 5 statements, 4 true ones and 1 false one, and try to stump you!

SHAPE WORDS

◁▷◁▷◁▷◁▷◁▷

Draw shape words that illustrate the meaning of nouns.

What You'll Need
• markers or crayons
• paper

Have the child choose words that are nouns, such as *insects, animals,* or *toys.* Encourage creative thinking as the child writes the words so that the letters conform to the shape of the object. For example, the letters *c-a-t-e-r-p-i-l-l-a-r* may be written to take on the curved shapes of the insect, as in the example shown, or the word *k-i-t-e* may be written with tall letters to create a diamond shape. What other words can the child decorate?

The interested child can take the project a step further and create a concrete poem. Explain that concrete poetry is when words in a poem are arranged to make a picture of what the poem is about.

Fun Fact

Although there are about 40 different sounds in English, there are more than 200 ways of spelling them. The long O sound can be spelled in several ways: stow, though, doe, sew, soul, and beau. The long A sound can be spelled as in rate, main, stay, freight, break, veil, ballet, and obey. The SH sound can be spelled in the following ways: shoe, sugar, special, passion, delicious, ocean, tissue, conscience, and nation.

FLIP, FLAP, FLOP

◁▷◁▷◁▷◁▷◁▷

The child will flip while uncovering directions in sequence!

What You'll Need
- 2"×18" piece of paper folded in half lengthwise
- blunt scissors
- crayons or markers

Invite the child to describe steps in a familiar process, such as preparing a bowl of cereal, building a wooden block castle, or brushing teeth. Help the child cut 3 or more flaps in the top half of the paper, depending on the number of steps in the process. (There should be 1 flap for each step.)

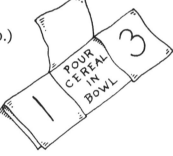

Cut from the edge of the paper toward the fold. Then have the child write the steps on the underside of the sheet, with one step underneath each flap. Write the corresponding numeral (1, 2, 3) on the covering flap to show the order of the steps. Have the child turn up each flap as she describes the sequence.

CHECKLIST

◁▷◁▷◁▷◁▷◁▷

Can you find what's on your list?

Children are naturally observant of their surroundings, so compose a checklist and make a game out of it. The list can be made of pictures, either line drawings or pictures cut from magazines and glued to the list, or it can be words for young readers. Items pictured might include a dog, bird, mailbox, stop sign, something orange, and something yellow. Tie a pencil to a clipboard with yarn, and invite the child to carry the checklist as you take a walk through the neighborhood. Let her check off each item she discovers.

What You'll Need
- check-off list
- clipboard or cardboard and large paper clip
- pencil
- old magazines
- nontoxic white glue
- yarn

COMPUTER COPYCAT

◁▶◁▶◁▶◁▶◁▶

E *is for* e-mail *and* **O** *is for* online *when you're a child of the computer age.*

What You'll Need
- computer
- pencil
- sheet of paper

Expose a child to a device she will have to master some day—the computer keyboard—while she practices identifying and copying letters.

Show the child where letters are located on a computer keyboard. Press the "caps lock" key so that only capital letters will be displayed. Tell the child to press any letter key, then have her copy the letter with a pencil on a sheet of paper.

Continue by having the child press as many as 5 letter keys, copying the series of letters on paper. More advanced children can be directed to press specific letters to spell a word they know.

ANIMAL PANTOMIME

◁▶◁▶◁▶◁▶◁▶

Act out animal movements for a beastly guessing game.

What You'll Need
- animal pictures
- index cards
- nontoxic white glue
- paper bag
- markers or crayons (optional)

Draw or glue pictures of various animals on index cards. Place cards in a bag, and take turns pulling one out. The person who has chosen a card peeks at it and then places it facedown outside the bag. That person then pantomimes the action of the animal for the other player to guess. If the other player is having trouble figuring out what the animal is, use animal sounds for clues!

LETTER FOR THE DAY

◁▶◁▶◁▶◁▶◁▶◁▶

Check your calendar to find out what special letter day it is.

Not sure what to do, say, wear, or eat on a particular day? Let this activity help you.

You will need a calendar. Ask the child to randomly pick a letter of the alphabet for each square that represents a day of the month. There aren't as many letters as there are days in a month, so some letters will repeat. Each night, ask the child to think of things that could be done the next day beginning with that particular letter. Using the letter *B* for an example, you could bounce a ball, bake, or blow bubbles. You could also eat butter, bread, or a banana, or wear something blue, brown, or black. Encourage the child to say all the *B* words she can think of. Have fun!

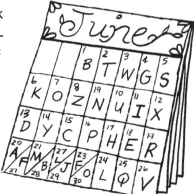

FARMER IN THE DELL

◁▶◁▶◁▶◁▶◁▶◁▶

When a "cat" takes a "cow," hi-ho the dairy-o!

Play a favorite singing game to help children practice beginning sounds.

Sing "Farmer in the Dell." Start with the traditional verse: "The farmer in the dell, the farmer in the dell, hi-ho the dairy-o, the farmer in the dell." For the second verse, begin by saying, "The farmer takes a cat." Have the child sing new verses, adding a new word beginning like the word *cat* each time. For example, the third verse might be "The cat takes a cow" and the fourth verse, "The cow takes a carrot."

After the child has sung several verses, change to a new letter, such as *D* ("The farmer takes a dog"), and continue.

READ MY BREEZEOMETER

◁▷◁▷◁▷◁▷

Your breezeometer will show how the wind blows!

What You'll Need
- dowel or stick
- duct tape or other heavy-duty tape
- yarn
- blunt scissors
- small items of various weights: paper, fabric scraps, plastic lid, cardboard, pencil, washer

It's easy to look out the window and notice whether the wind is blowing or to stand outside and comment on the breeze, but it's not as easy to compare one day's wind to another day's. Here's a useful tool to help the child compare a light breeze to a heavier wind. Start by locating a long dowel or have the child find a long stick outdoors to use as the breezeometer base. Then gather together a variety of small items of varying weights, and ask the child to arrange them from light to heavy. With adult help, the child can attach the items to the stick (in weight order, with lightest at the top) by taping a piece of yarn to each item with heavy-duty tape and then tying the yarn pieces to the stick, leaving each item dangling a few inches. The items should be tied at intervals of a few inches apart. Now the breezeometer is ready to test the wind! Take the stick outside and plant it in the ground so that it stands upright. The breezeometer can gauge wind strength by demonstrating which items blow in a breeze. In a mild breeze only the lightest items will blow, while the heavy ones remain hanging. A medium breeze will blow the light and medium-light items. In a strong wind, everything will blow!

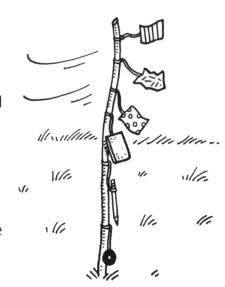

Hink-Pink!

Q: What do you call musicians on the beach?

A: A sand band.

PEEKABOO PICTURES

◁▶◁▶◁▶◁▶◁▶◁◁

This observation activity will encourage the child to see "the big picture"!

Create peekaboo pictures by cutting a picture from an old magazine and gluing or taping it onto a sheet of paper. Do not let the child see the picture. Next, cut a small circle or square in a second piece of paper. This will be the guessing page.

Take the guessing page and lay it on top of the picture. The small portion of the picture viewed through the peekaboo hole becomes the clue for the child to guess the identity of the bigger picture.

MAKE IT MODERN

◁▶◁▶◁▶◁▶◁▶◁◁

In this creative retelling activity,
the child brings favorite characters to life in modern times.

Invite the child to retell a familiar folk or fairy tale, such as "The Three Little Pigs" or "Cinderella," but to change the setting to the place where you live and to modern times. If the story took place today, for example, what would be the same? What would be different? If the three little pigs were building their house next door, what materials would they use? Who would they ask for supplies? Would they call each other on cell phones when the wolf was blowing down their houses? If Cinderella lived in your town, where would she live? What would she wear to the ball? Where would the prince live?

TINY TAPPING

◁▶◁▶◁▶◁▶◁

Tap a tiny tune with finger cymbals.

What You'll Need
- metal bottle caps
- hammer
- nail
- elastic
- blunt scissors
- tape or CD player

To make the cymbals, the adult punches a hole in the center of a metal bottle cap with a nail (be sure the bottle caps have no sharp edges). Cut a piece of elastic about 2" long, and thread one end through the hole in the cap. Tie the ends in a knot. Make another in the same way. The child can slip the cymbals onto thumb and forefinger and tap them together to make up a rhythm or to play along with a cassette or CD.

REAL OR MAKE-BELIEVE?

◁▶◁▶◁▶◁▶◁▶

Listen and ponder whether stories could really be real!

Share fiction and nonfiction books with the child. After reading a story or a section of a book, ask the child to determine whether the tale was real or make-believe. Encourage the child to explain the reasoning behind the determination. For a variation, look at magazine pictures together, and take turns making up real and make-believe statements about the pictures. One person makes a statement and the other guesses whether the information stated is real or make-believe.

Hink-Pink!
Q: Where can you take a cold swim?
A: In a cool pool.

PROPER NOUN DRILL

◁▷◁▷◁▷◁▷

*This simple activity based on proper nouns will teach the child
how to react in an emergency situation.*

What You'll Need
- pencil
- index card
- play telephone (or real telephone that is not connected)

Have the child write pertinent information on an index card so she knows how to answer the operator if a 911 emergency call has to be made. The information should include the child's name, address, and phone number. Explain that proper nouns are names of people, places, or things and begin with a capital letter. Have the child put the emergency information by the phone.

Using a play telephone or a real phone that is not connected, have the child role-play calls to 911. You should play the role of the emergency operator, asking the child the nature of the emergency, her name, and address. The child may refer to the emergency card by the phone as needed.

911 Information
Name-Jennifer Frank
Address-100 Your Street
Apartment 10A
Orlando, Florida
Phone-555-4888

SPLASH COMPARISONS

◁▷◁▷◁▷◁▷

Drop rocks in water and compare the splashes!

This is an outdoor activity! Draw concentric circles on a large piece of paper. Have the child gather big (but not too big!) and little rocks for splash testing. After the rocks have been assembled, place a large plastic bowl filled with water in the middle of the sheet of paper. The child can drop rocks, one by one, from the same height (arm straight out above bowl). After each rock is dropped, the child can mark the farthest splash of that rock by placing the rock on the splash. After all the rocks have been tested, the child can evaluate the splash capabilities by viewing how far each rock is sitting from the bowl. For a further challenge, the child can cut a length of yarn to represent the distance from the bowl to the farthest splash of each rock. Have the child compare the pieces of yarn to see which rock made the biggest splash.

What You'll Need
- large piece of paper
- marker
- large plastic bowl filled with water
- rocks of varying sizes
- yarn (optional)
- blunt scissors (optional)

CARD CLAP

◁▷◁▷◁▷◁▷

Match a pair of letters, and put your hands together.

What You'll Need
- 2 matching sets of letter cards

Use letter cards for this letter-recognition game. Begin by using only the *A* through *M* cards of both sets. Shuffle each set of cards. Place the 2 sets in side-by-side piles. Pick up and display the top card of each set. Tell the child to clap if the 2 cards show the same letter, in which case you put the matching cards aside. If the 2 cards do not match, place each one at the bottom of its pile. Continue until all matching pairs have been identified. Then put the cards back into their sets, shuffle each set, and repeat the activity. Add new matching pairs of cards to the sets when the child has mastered the first half of the alphabet.

EXPRESS MAIL

⊲▸⊲▸⊲▸⊲▸

Writing, mailing, and delivering these special phonics letters will keep the young mail carrier's hands full.

What You'll Need
- 3 shoe boxes with lids
- blunt scissors
- crayons
- 3"×5" index cards
- envelopes

Cut a 4½" slit in the lid of each shoe box. Write a letter or cluster of letters, such as *d, t, str,* or *m,* on the front of each box. Invite the child to pretend to be a mail carrier whose job is to sort and deliver the mail. With crayons, have the child draw pictures of objects that begin with each of the letters on the mailboxes on several 3" × 5" index cards. Then have the child place each picture in an envelope, address the envelopes, and deliver them to the correct mailbox.

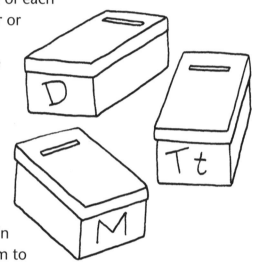

SING-ALONG FUN

⊲▸⊲▸⊲▸⊲▸

Inspire the young lyricist by using familiar songs.

Choose a simple song, such as "Skip to My Lou." Sing it with the child. Don't worry if you don't have a beautiful voice! Then discuss the rhymes in the song. Talk

What You'll Need
- simple songs
- paper
- pencil

about how to create new verses. Invite the child to write some new verses. Then read them, learn to sing them, and teach the song to others.

WHAT'S INSIDE?

◁▷◁▷◁▷◁▷

Predict what's inside fruits!

Caution: This project requires adult supervision.

Invite the child to look at different fruits and predict how many seeds are inside. Then cut open the fruit, and take a look. Encourage the child to make an estimate after viewing the seeds but before counting them. Then count to check! The child can count the seeds for fruits with single or only a few seeds. The adult and child can count higher numbers together. For fruits with lots and lots and lots of seeds (pumpkins), use paper cups to count by tens. Plant some of the seeds after counting. The avocado seed will sprout if you pierce it with 3 or 4 toothpicks and place it in a jar of water with the pointy side up. Refrigerate apple seeds for 6 weeks in a moist paper towel before planting so they will react as if winter has just ended. Instead of planting the pumpkin seeds, toast them and enjoy them as a treat!

What You'll Need
- variety of fruits (such as avocado, lemon, apple, pumpkin)
- knife (for adult use only)
- small paper cups

Tongue Twister!
Peter Piper picked a peck of pickled peppers;
A peck of pickled peppers Peter Piper picked;
If Peter Piper picked a peck of pickled peppers,
Where's the peck of pickled peppers Peter Piper picked?

STRING LETTERS

◁◆▷◁◆▷◁◆▷

String 'em up! Use common string to form letters.

What You'll Need
- pieces of string
- paper and pen (optional)

Manipulating string requires the child to practice fine motor coordination.

Using different thicknesses and lengths of string, a child can form letters of the alphabet. For example, the string can be swirled into the letter *S*, or it can be zigzagged to form a *Z*. Try to describe each letter the child makes using a word that begins with that letter. For example, point out the swirling *S*, the zigzagged *Z*, and the curved *C*. For younger children, it may be helpful to begin with sheets of paper that have letters drawn on them already.

DINOSAUR INFO

◁◆▷◁◆▷◁◆▷

This challenging, ongoing learning activity is a model for increasing the child's knowledge base.

What You'll Need
- 2 copies of dinosaur books

As scientists have made new discoveries, many older dinosaur books have become outdated. This gives you a good opportunity to show the child how learning never stops. Gather 2 books on dinosaurs from the library—1 old and 1 new. Then search for some examples of facts that have changed with new information and discoveries. List those facts, then discuss them with the child. For an ongoing activity, invite the child to watch the newspapers and children's magazines at the library for more dinosaur information to use for later discussion.

RHYMES FROM A TO Z

◁▷◁▷◁▷◁▷

Z *is for Zoo—and that rhymes with* boo, too, *and* moo!

Combine rhyming skills with a review of the alphabet and beginning sounds in this game. Display the alphabet. Point to the letter *A* and say, "*A* is for *and.*" The child must name a rhyming word (*band, hand, land, sand*). Continue with *B* is for *ball,* *C* is for *cat,* *D* is for *dig,* and so on. Challenge a more advanced child by having her give a letter and a word while you say a rhyme.

LOOPING INTO WRITING

◁▷◁▷◁▷◁▷

Looping helps get the brain working and provides a fundamental process for narrowing in on an idea.

What You'll Need
• paper
• pencil

Begin by inviting the child to do 3 minutes of freewriting, which involves writing any words or phrases that come to mind. Make sure the child keeps writing the whole time. Don't worry about the quality of the writing, punctuation, and so on. When the designated time is up, have the child reread the work and circle 1 good idea. Then encourage the child to write on that idea for 2 to 3 minutes. Again, when the designated time is up, have the child reread the work and circle 1 good idea. You may need to repeat this process 1 more time.

When finished, the child will be ready to begin writing on the topic and be happy with the starting point. Encourage the child to use this process as a writing technique, and you'll be developing a writer!

BREAK THE CODE

◁▶◁▶◁▶◁▶◁▶◁▶◁▷

The child becomes a spelling sleuth while trying to break secret codes.

What You'll Need
- paper
- felt-tip pen
- pencil

Help the child make a code breaker. Begin by drawing a wheel pattern, like the one shown here, with a felt-tip pen. Write the letters of the alphabet in sequential order in the spaces on the outer edge of the larger wheel, and write their corresponding numbers, 1-26, on the inner wheel as shown.

Next, write a secret message on a separate piece of paper in code; that is, substitute the corresponding number for each letter. Then the child can take on the role of a young sleuth and decode a secret message by using the code breaker. For example, a message in code might read:

13-5-5-20 13-5 1-20 20-8-5 6-15-18-20!

Using the decoder, the child could easily spell out the real words:

M-E-E-T M-E A-T T-H-E F-O-R-T!

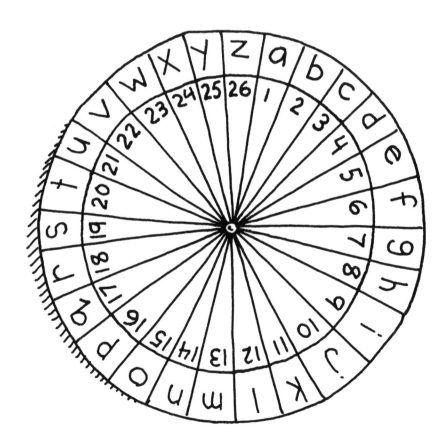

HOT/COLD

◁▶◁▶◁▶◁▶

They know the sensations. Now kids can learn to read the words.

This simple activity helps a child practice spelling and reading temperature words.

Print the word *hot* on 1 card and *cold* on another. Discuss each word with the child, asking her to identify the initial sound in each word, as well as the other sounds if possible.

Have the child copy the word *hot* onto 4 more cards and the word *cold* onto 4 more cards. Then ask the child to put the 10 cards on items around the house (and outside, if you wish), labeling items that are either hot or cold. For example, the child might put a *hot* label on the oven door or near a fireplace and a *cold* label on an ice chest or wading pool.

Riddle Time!

Q: What two letters did Mother Hubbard find in her cupboard?

A: MT.

A CLOSER LOOK

◁▷◁▷◁▷◁▷

Try this activity after you finish reading a story to a child.

What You'll Need
• storybook

You can never read to a child too often. A child will develop a love of reading by your reading aloud to her. This also helps develop the child's vocabulary, letter recognition, letter sounds, intonation and inflections, and comprehension.

After reading a book to the child, ask her to point to a certain letter on the page and to identify it (for example, capital *T*, lowercase *w*).

LETTER HEADBAND

◁▷◁▷◁▷◁▷

Stylish kids will enjoy making wearable art with letters.

What You'll Need
• construction paper
• blunt scissors
• stapler
• pen or pencil
• crayons or colored markers
• glue or clear tape

In this activity, the alphabet goes to children's heads!

Cut a long strip of construction paper about 3" wide. Put the strip around the child's head. Find a comfortable fit for the headband, and staple the ends of the band together.

On sheets of construction paper, draw outlines of letters and have the child color them in. Discuss the names

of the letters as he colors. You may want to focus on one letter or on several letters. Cut out the letters, and help the child glue or tape them onto the headband. The child can wear the headband or can take it off and name the letters. For a new challenge, have the child make another headband using the letters of his name.

TREASURE HUNT

◁▷◁▷◁▷◁▷

Find and follow clues to discover a treasure!

What You'll Need
- index cards
- pencil
- tape
- small treasure (see right)

Hide a treasure (two cookies in a bag, a card that says "I Love You," a book, or a toy) somewhere in the house. Then make clue cards that lead from one place to another. Write or draw the clues on index cards to make the clue cards. The clues can be simple sentences or pictures that tell where the next clue can

be found. For example, a clue card might say: "Go to a bed," "Bed," or have a picture of a bed on it. The child can go check all the beds in the house and discover the next clue card on one of them! Set each of the clue cards around the house, and tell the child where to find the first one. Use 3 to 6 clue cards to lead the child to discover the treasure.

ACHIEVING A BALANCE

◁▷◁▷◁▷◁▷

There's no fear of falling from this home balance beam!

Place a long strip (at least 10 feet) of wide masking tape on the ground or floor. Demonstrate walking along the tape, making sure your feet do not touch the ground or floor on either side of the tape. Invite the child to walk along the tape strip as well. Once he is comfortable crossing this "balance

What You'll Need
- masking tapes of different widths

beam" without "falling off," increase the challenge. Place a long strip of masking tape that is a little less wide on the ground or floor and ask him to try again. Keep using progressively narrower strips of masking tape. Then go back to the widest strip of masking tape and encourage the child to attempt running the entire length. Increase the running challenge by using progressively narrower strips of masking tape, too.

T Party

◄►◄►◄►◄►◄►◄►

This activity will definitely put the T into tea party.

Hold a real or "pretend" tea party that includes many foods and objects whose names have the beginning sound *T.*

With the child's help, identify tea-party items whose names begin with the *T* sound. Discuss each step with the child: Set the table with a tablecloth, dishes, teacups, and teaspoons.

Have the child create a centerpiece by making several letter *T*'s out of drinking straws or craft sticks. Put the *T*'s into pieces of clay to keep them upright, and then place the pieces of clay into a small flowerpot or bowl. Next, make "tulips" by drawing tulip-blossom shapes on various colors of construction paper, cutting them out, and gluing them to the craft sticks or straws.

Ask the child to help create the menu and serve some of the following real or pretend foods: tea, toast, tuna, and tarts.

What You'll Need
- dishes
- table
- tablecloth
- teacups
- teaspoons
- straws or craft sticks
- clay
- small flowerpot or bowl
- construction paper
- marker or pen
- blunt scissors
- glue

Expressive, Imaginative Play With Fabric

⊲▶⊲▶⊲▶⊲▷

Make-believe fun is found in new forms with fabric.

This open-ended, very expressive activity requires imagination on the child's part and guidance from the adult on how to work with the fabric. Have the child take one end of the fabric, with the adult taking the other. Try to make the fabric move,

What You'll Need
• 3 yards fabric

float on air, and turn as you both turn. Explore ways to make the fabric move. After the child has discovered some of the ways fabric moves, try the following activities:

1. Hold the fabric at each end and make waves, like the soft waves on a calm sea. Then make the waves like the huge waves on a stormy ocean.

2. Hold the fabric around each of you. Pretend you are in a boat on a calm sea moving gently with the waves.

3. Pretend you are like a flagpole and the fabric is the flag. Make it move with the wind—both a calm and a wild wind.

4. Pretend the fabric is like a sleeping animal by rolling it into a ball. The child can grasp one end of the fabric and shake it as if the animal is awakened as the fabric is unrolled. The child can also make sounds of an awakened animal.

5. Hold both ends to make the fabric into something like a mountain. Then let go to have the mountain crumble flat.

6. The child can wrap herself in the fabric and then spin out of the fabric like a top. (Be sure this is done in a safe place.)

7. Stretch the fabric over both of your heads and be like a Chinese dragon in a parade.

LIGHTS OUT STORIES

◁▷◁▷◁▷◁▷

Just what happens in the house when the lights go out at night?
Perhaps it isn't what we think!

What You'll Need
- paper
- pencil

We all know that sometimes toys appear to come alive and take on their own personalities. But what about those plain, ordinary items we find in other parts of the house? Have the child think about all the various items stored in the kitchen: blender, mixer, spoons, spices, coffeemaker, toaster, and so on. Would the knives be mean and the spoons be sweet? Would the bigger items try to control the little ones? Would they all get out and make special foods for the pets?

Think about different possibilities. Then invite the child to write a highly imaginative story about what really happens during those magical hours.

FLOWER BEADS

◁▷◁▷◁▷◁▷

Make scented beads from fragrant flowers.

Make a flower-flour dough by using crushed fragrant flower petals. Cut the flower petals with scissors into small pieces and then crush them with the back of a large spoon. The child can help cut and crush the petals before making the dough. To make the dough, have the child help you mix the flour, salt, and water until stiff. Then add the crushed flower petal pieces and mix until crumbly. The child can shape the dough into large beads and pierce them with a pencil. Set the beads outside to dry for several days, or use a wire cooling rack inside. When dry, the child can use a blunt darning needle to string them on yarn to make a scented necklace or bracelet. As a variation, the child can create scented sculptures with the flower-petal dough.

What You'll Need
- 3 cups fragrant petals (such as rose petals)
- blunt scissors
- large spoon
- bowl
- ⅓ cup flour
- 1 tablespoon salt
- 2 teaspoons water
- pencil
- wire cooling rack
- darning needle
- yarn

FISHING FOR RHYMES

⊲▷⊲▷⊲▷⊲▷

Practice identifying rhymes when playing this modified version of Go Fish.

What You'll Need
- 30 index cards
- crayons or markers

Use index cards to create a deck of rhyming cards. The deck should be made up of 15 rhyme pairs, such as *cat/hat, bug/rug,* and *car/star*—1 word for each card, 30 cards in all. When the deck is complete, pass out 4 cards to each player. Explain that the object of the game is to be the first person to get 2 pairs of rhyming cards.

Begin the game by asking the child for a card that rhymes with a card in your hand. For example, if you have a *hat* card, you would ask, "Do you have a rhyme for *hat*?" If the child has a card that rhymes, he must give up that card. If not, you may draw a new card from the deck. For every card picked from the deck, one must be discarded and placed at the bottom of the deck.

Once the game is finished, encourage the child to create sentences that use a pair of rhymes.

CIRCLE SEARCH

◁▷◁▷◁▷◁▷

Hunt through the house in search of circles!

Caution: This project requires adult supervision.

The child can go on a circle hunt looking for things that are circles and gathering circle objects. The child might note a circular window, the circle of a lamp shade, a globe, or the almost circle of a toilet bowl!

Objects the child can gather might include a penny, a paper plate, a washer, a button, a jar top, or a marble (watch carefully for choking hazards). Variations include scouting for squares and traversing for triangles!

Activity Twist

Continue your circle search on a walk outdoors. Bring along a camera to take pictures of your circular finds. When they are developed, put them in a photo album to talk about and share with others. No camera? Bring along a clipboard to make sketches and a list of your circular discoveries (bird's nest, tires, red traffic light).

APPLE TREE

<⊳<⊳<⊳<⊳<⊳<⊳

There is more to an apple tree when the child plays this version of Hangman.

What You'll Need
- masking tape
- paper
- pencil

Before play begins, make a ladder with masking tape on a tile floor or smooth surface. Make 5 rungs on the ladder. Then draw an apple tree on paper. Next think of a specific spelling word, perhaps one from the child's weekly spelling list or a word the child may want to learn to spell. Then draw a row of apples on the tree.

Next have the child stand on the bottom rung of the ladder and try to guess one letter that is part of the word. Every correct letter gets written in the appropriate apple. For every incorrect guess, the child must step up one rung on the ladder. The game ends when the child guesses the spelling of the word correctly or if he "steps off the top of the ladder." Ready to play again? Just erase the letters on the tree, and start the game over.

 # LETTER SCULPTURE

<⊳<⊳<⊳<⊳<⊳<⊳

Mold youngsters' minds with three-dimensional letters.

Making three-dimensional letters enables a child to experience the alphabet in a new way.

Put some moist sand in a shoe box. Help the child write letters in the sand. Let the child choose the letters to write, such as the initials of his first and last name. Make the letter shapes in the sand deep and wide. Mix the plaster of paris according to the directions on the package, and pour it into the letter shapes. Let the letters dry. Take the letters out of the box, and display your three-dimensional letters.

What You'll Need
- shoe box
- sand
- plaster of paris
- water

GET IN SHAPE

◁▶◁▶◁▶◁▶◁▶

Cookie cutters can be fun even if you aren't doing any baking.

Children will enjoy using cookie-cutter shapes to work on beginning sounds.

What You'll Need
- cookie cutters shaped like various objects
- paper
- pen or pencil
- crayons or colored markers
- blunt scissors

Find cookie cutters of various recognizable shapes, such as a tree, a bell, or a specific animal. Trace each shape on a sheet of paper, then ask the child to color and decorate each shape. Next, have the child name each shape and the letter that begins its name. Write this letter on each shape, then cut them all out. Have the child pick a shape, name the letter on it, and say a word that begins with the same letter.

BACK-TO-BACK PICTURES

◁▶◁▶◁▶◁▶◁▶

Find out how well a child can listen, draw, and describe in this challenging activity.

Set up a seating arrangement in which you and the child each have a piece of paper but cannot see the other person's paper. Choose a common object, and begin to draw a picture of it. As you are drawing, describe your picture, and

What You'll Need
- paper
- crayons

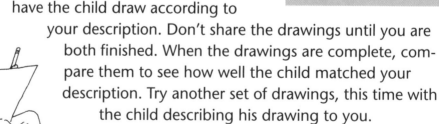

have the child draw according to your description. Don't share the drawings until you are both finished. When the drawings are complete, compare them to see how well the child matched your description. Try another set of drawings, this time with the child describing his drawing to you.

ABC STRIPS

◁▷◁▷◁▷◁▷

Children who master this game won't be puzzled about alphabetical order.

This activity helps children practice putting letters in alphabetical order.

Draw lines on a sheet of construction paper to divide it into 4 horizontal strips. Have the child write the letters *A, B, C,* and *D*—one on each strip. Cut the strips apart, and shuffle them. Then ask the child to put the strips back together in the correct order. Make other puzzles using other sets of 4 letters in alphabetical order.

What You'll Need
- construction paper
- marker or pen
- blunt scissors

RHYME-A-STORY

◁▷◁▷◁▷◁▷

By listening for rhymes, the child will practice comprehension while creating a story.

Make up a story together, but tell it in rhymes. Begin by making up the first sentence. For example, you might say, "The dog went for a walk." Then invite the child to make up a rhyming sentence, then another sentence for you to rhyme. Explain to the child that his second sentence does not have to rhyme with his first sentence. For example, the child would add "The dog began to talk. Then the dog began to run." Then you would continue with: "He wanted to get out of the sun. He found a tree to lay under." Continue until you and the child are satisfied with the ending.

DANGER! VOLCANO ERUPTION!

◁▷◁▷◁▷◁▷◁▷

Create bubbling, fizzy explosions for dramatic science play.

Caution: This project requires adult supervision.

What You'll Need
• sand or dirt
• empty can
• vinegar
• food coloring
• baking soda
• water (optional)
• milk (optional)
• lemonade (optional)

With the child, make a volcanic mountain out of sand or dirt that's in a sandbox, a large box, or an outside play area. Help him place an empty can, open end up, in the top of the mountain. The child can then fill the can halfway with vinegar and add a few drops of food coloring. Then have him add a spoonful of baking soda. Watch the eruption! Talk with the child about chemical reactions and explain that when baking soda is mixed with an acid it causes a reaction (creating the carbon-dioxide "explosion"). The child might want to experiment further (with adult supervision) to discover other liquids that will have the same effect when mixed with baking soda. The child can try different liquids, putting a spoonful of baking soda into ½ cup each of water, milk, and lemonade to see the results.

JOKING AROUND

◁▷◁▷◁▷◁▷

Consider "the source" when you need some laughter to liven up your day!

Staple several pieces of paper together to make a book. Go to the library, and check out some joke books. Then have the child write some of the favorite jokes she finds in the joke books. The child can also try creating original jokes or revising existing jokes to add to the collection. Share the new joke book with friends and family, and have a constant source of laughter.

What You'll Need
• stapler
• paper
• joke books
• pencil

RHYMIN' SIMON

◁▷◁▷◁▷◁▷

Saying the right words can earn applause in this game of rhyme recognition.

This game gets children to practice recognizing rhyming words.

Begin by saying, "Simon says clap if the words rhyme." Then say a word pair, such as *bell/well.* The child should clap because the two words rhyme. Continue with other pairs of words, not all of which will rhyme—for example, *snake/cake, cup/star, tree/see, red/bed, mop/top, book/hook, desk/chair, paper/shoe, fish/dish,* and *dip/clip.* Challenge children who master rhyme recognition to create their own rhyming and nonrhyming pairs of words. Then it will be your turn to clap.

PROLIFIC PUPPETRY

◁▶◁▶◁▶◁▶◁▶◁▷

Gloves, mittens, and old clean socks turn into puppets for friendly talks!

What You'll Need
- clean old gloves
- clean old socks
- blunt scissors
- nontoxic white glue
- felt scraps
- paper scraps
- yarn
- old mittens (optional)

Glove Puppets: The child can glue felt or paper scraps onto each finger of an old glove to turn them into 5 friendly fellows. Glue yarn to the tip of each finger for hair. The child can then wear the glove and create conversations among the 5 friends.

Finger Puppets: Cut the fingers off an old glove. The child can create a face for each finger (or 1 finger) the same as was done for the glove puppets. These finger puppets can be used individually. (The 5 fellows don't always have to stick together anymore!)

Sock Puppets: The child can create a face on a clean old sock by gluing on felt, paper scraps, and yarn. The child can then slip the whole sock on over a hand and use it as a hand puppet to talk and tell stories. (Mittens can also be used!)

Fun Fact

Fifteen capital letters are called stick letters and are made with horizontal, vertical, or diagonal lines—A, E, F, H, I, K, L, M, N, T, V, W, Y, X, and Z. Circle letters include O, Q, and C.

FROZEN ART

◁▷◁▷◁▷◁▷

Here's a new way to explore ice...paint on it!

What You'll Need
- manila or newsprint paper
- shallow pan
- water
- aluminum foil
- freezer
- watercolor paint
- brush
- sugar
- newspaper

The child can create frozen paper by dipping a piece of absorbent paper into a shallow pan of water. The child should then place the wet paper onto a sheet of aluminum foil the same size and put a second sheet of foil on top of the wet paper. Place the paper and foil in the freezer until frozen. Then take it from the freezer, and peel off both sheets of foil. Now it's time to paint! When the picture is finished, have the child sprinkle it with sugar to create a textured effect.

Then place the picture in the freezer to freeze the paint! (No foil is needed this time.) When frozen, remove the paper from the freezer and place on newspaper to dry.

NURSERY RHYME INTERPLAY

◁▷◁▷◁▷◁▷

Familiar nursery rhymes can inspire endless story creations.

Read aloud several familiar nursery rhymes that the child knows and enjoys. Then invite the child to read the nursery rhymes aloud. Discuss what might happen if the characters met each

What You'll Need
- favorite nursery rhymes

other. For example, could Jack and Jill have saved Humpty Dumpty from falling off the wall? What would happen if the little old lady who lived in the shoe left her children with Peter Peter Pumpkin Eater? Have the child create new versions and share them with others.

WOODWORKING

◁▶◁▶◁▶◁▶◁▶◁▶

Build your own creations out of wood.

Caution: This project requires adult supervision.

Woodworking is a classic activity, but it is often avoided with young children. However, properly supervised, woodworking is among the most enriching activities young children can do—it teaches many skills. Place the towel on the floor in a very low-traffic area (outside on a picnic table would also be a good spot). Fold the towel into a thick pad. Place the board on the towel. This is the child's workbench. Make sure the child understands what a workbench is—a place to work. Nails are not to be hammered into the workbench. On the workbench, the child can hammer roofing tacks into a wood scrap. In doing this, the child will be practicing hitting the head of the nail and developing fine motor skills. Roofing tacks are ideal because the head is large and the nail shaft is short. This makes it easier for the child to be successful. Next, give the child longer nails that allow her to nail pieces of wood together, creating various constructions from the wood scraps. It is not important that the constructions be anything—the goal is in the process of building, not in the final outcome!

LABEL IT!

◁▷◁▷◁▷◁▷

By using labels, the child will identify and learn new words.

What You'll Need
- poster board
- crayons or markers
- self-adhesive notes

Explain to the child that pictures make it easier for us to understand a story or any other information that we read. Also explain that some pictures have labels, or captions, next to them to name the parts of a picture. Invite the child to draw a picture of a favorite toy, then label the parts he knows with self-adhesive notes.

SUFFIX BINGO

◁▷◁▷◁▷◁▷

This twist on the familiar board game is a motivating way to apply knowledge of word endings.

Prepare and distribute bingo cards with a grid made of 9 squares. Have players randomly write the following word endings in the grid boxes: *s, es, ed, ing, less, ly, ful, er, est.* To play the game, say words that contain one of the suffixes. Then have players cover the appropriate suffix on their playing card. The first player to cover 3 suffixes in a row shouts "BINGO!" and is declared the winner.

Hink-Pink!
Q: What does a full moon make?
A: A bright night.

What's the Title?

◁▷◁▷◁▷◁▷

This inventive story-making game involves creative thinking, summarizing, and problem-solving skills.

What You'll Need

- pictures from books or magazines

Begin by looking at a picture in a book or magazine together with the child and discuss what you see. Pretend that one picture illustrates an entire story.

Invite the child to tell you what he thinks the story might be about. Discuss possible details of the story. Then have the child invent a title that would fit the story.

Alphabet Bouquet

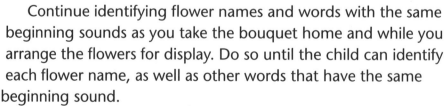

◁▷◁▷◁▷◁▷

What could be more beautiful?
A bouquet with a flower for each letter of the alphabet.

From a garden or flower market, such as the one at a grocery store, let the child choose and pick (or buy) one each of several different types of flowers, such as a rose, carnation, daisy, tulip, daffodil, and lily. As the child chooses a flower, name it. The child then has to say a word with the same beginning sound as the flower's name.

What You'll Need
- flowers—one each of as many different varieties as possible

Continue identifying flower names and words with the same beginning sounds as you take the bouquet home and while you arrange the flowers for display. Do so until the child can identify each flower name, as well as other words that have the same beginning sound.

I KNOW A PLACE

<><><><><>

Puzzle about places with a place-guessing game.

Take turns thinking up different places to use for puzzling one another. One person can think of a place and tell all about what kinds of things people do at that place (for example, the park, the circus, a church, a swimming pool, etc.). The other person can guess what the place is. For a variation, pantomime what people do at the place!

THUMBS-UP

<><><><><>

*Every kid can be a critic and vote "thumbs-up" for **U** words.*

Use hand motions to emphasize words that begin with the letter *U*.

Have the child demonstrate the gestures for "thumbs-up" and "thumbs-down." Explain that when you say a word, he should show thumbs-up if the word begins with the letter *U* or point thumbs-down if it does not. Words to use might include *apple, desk, ugly, under, off,* and *umbrella.*

ABC Go!

◁▷◁▷◁▷◁▷◁▷◁▷

Kids need quick hands and sharp eyes to play this fast-paced game.

What You'll Need
• pad of self-adhesive notes
• marker or pen

This activity is designed to sharpen a child's letter- and word-recognition skills.

Start with 8 self-adhesive notes. Select 4 simple words, writing each one on 2 separate notes. Words to start with are *car, big, top,* and *nut.*

Give the child one set of words, and keep the other set. Each player should attach one note to the front of each hand and one note to the back of each hand. Begin with the players putting their hands at their sides. One player says, "ABC Go!" and then each player displays the front or back of his right or left hand. The child looks at the words displayed by each player and decides whether they match. If they do, the words are removed. If they do not, the game is repeated.

Play until all notes have been paired and removed. Then new words can be written on new self-adhesive notes. Children with more highly developed coordination can put notes on index fingers and thumbs.

Shakin' up the Cream!

◁▷◁▷◁▷◁▷◁▷

Butter is easy to make with a little muscle power.

What You'll Need
- small clear jar
- ½ pint heavy cream
- cup
- plastic knife
- plate
- crackers

Cracker snacks spread with homemade butter are delicious! Have everyone wash hands, then let the child pour the cream into the jar and tighten the lid. (Adult should make sure lid is on tightly.) Take turns shaking the jar. Encourage the child to use muscles and shake hard. After 10 minutes, the cream will be turning to butter and the whey separating. Let the child observe the results during the process. The child can pour the whey into a cup and taste it if curious. The butter left in the jar will be soft and easy to spread. For more challenge, invite the child to compare the taste, texture, and color to store-bought unsalted butter and describe what is the same and what is different.

Step by Step

◁▷◁▷◁▷◁▷◁▷

While learning how to formulate questions, the child will enhance story comprehension.

Begin by having one player take on the role of a character from a favorite story both players have read. Next have the other player try to guess the identity of the character by asking a maximum of 10 questions that can be answered yes or no. For example, suggest the following: Are you a person? Are you an animal? Do you have fur? Did you ever blow down a straw house?

Take turns with different characters, and see how many questions it takes to guess the character. The player who correctly identities the character in the least amount of questions is the winner.

OBSTACLES OF COURSE

◁▷◁▷◁▷◁▷

You never know what obstacle might pop up on this course!

What You'll Need
- 3 cardboard boxes
- about 1 yard of fabric
- table
- masking tape
- construction paper
- blunt scissors

Make paper cones to place along the route to mark the course boundaries. Take a sheet of construction paper, and cut out a half circle. Roll the paper into a cone, and tape it. Cut off the top and bottom of 1 box, and turn it on its side. Leave 1 box open on top for the child to crawl in and out. Cut holes in adjoining sides of

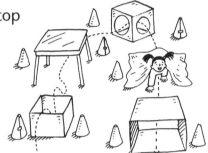

the last box. Now design the obstacle course, placing the cones to guide the child through it. The child will spend hours crawling around these obstacles!

 # WHICH ONE DOESN'T GO?

◁▷◁▷◁▷◁▷

Use logic to figure out what doesn't belong.

What You'll Need
- pictures cut from magazines

Provide the child with groups of 4 pictures in which 1 thing doesn't belong. For example, give her pictures of ice cream, donuts, cookies, and broccoli or pictures of sneakers, rain boots, ballet shoes, and an umbrella. Challenge the child to figure out which item doesn't belong and explain why. For further play, encourage the child to suggest a 4th item that would go with the group!

ROLLING THE DIE

◁▷◁▷◁▷◁▷

A simple roll of the die leads to learning letters—and words.

What You'll Need
- cube-shaped wooden block or box
- 6 pieces of paper small enough to be taped to the sides of the cube
- pen or marker
- clear tape

Find a cube-shaped wooden block or box. Choose any 6 letters of the alphabet, write them down on individual pieces of paper, and tape them to the cube (1 letter on each side). Roll the cube as you would a die, then have the child call out the letter that appears on the top and say a word that begins with that letter. Change the letters periodically to reinforce the recognition of other letters and sounds.

ROCK & ROLL

◁▷◁▷◁▷◁▷

Make, shake, and compare noises!

Caution: This project requires adult supervision.

Gather several cans and an assortment of objects to use for noisemakers. Invite the child to examine the objects and guess which would make the loudest or softest shaker noises. The child can then test out guesses, placing 1 object in a can at a time and comparing the noises different objects make. You can compare 2 cans with an object in each, or 3 objects in 3 cans can be compared at a time. If more cans are available, after initial comparisons, the child can place every object into an individual can and try to identify the content of each can by the noise each makes. (Small objects may pose a choking hazard!)

What You'll Need
- empty coffee cans and lids
- assortment of common objects (rock, button, cork, cotton ball, bottle cap, paper clip, magnet, eraser)

TAPE COLLAGE

◁▷◁▷◁▷◁▷

Tape away—create a picture with nothing but tape!

What You'll Need
- several kinds of tape (clear tape, masking tape, colored masking tape, electrical tape, bandage tape, painter's tape)
- blunt scissors
- paper

The child can experiment with a variety of different kinds of tapes. The tapes can be cut or torn and then stuck onto paper to make a tape collage. The child can compare the colors, textures, widths, and stickiness of the different tapes while using them to compose a picture. For a challenging variation, the child can

use the tape to make a picture instead of a collage. The child can "draw" a house, tree, or face using tape to make all the lines and dots.

KNOCK-KNOCK!

◁▷◁▷◁▷◁▷

Here's a word-matching game that will leave even the most talkative children speechless.

What You'll Need
- index cards
- marker or pen

In this game, children have to give a nonverbal signal to indicate whether words they are shown are alike or different.

Make a set of word cards with simple words. Make duplicate word cards for about half the words. Explain to the child that you will play a game in which 1 knock signals yes and 2 knocks signal no. Tell the child to knock on the table once to signal yes if you show 2 words that are alike and knock twice to signal no if they are not alike. Then show the child 2 word cards at a time.

CHARACTER INTERVIEW

◁▷◁▷◁▷◁▷

Encourage the child to interpret information and make predictions while pretending to be a favorite character.

Invite the child to pretend to be a favorite character from a favorite story. Explain that you are going to interview the character and the child should answer all your questions as the character would. Ask questions that wouldn't necessarily be found in the original story. For example, ask the character about favorite foods, what kind of stories the character likes to read, what the character wants to be when it grows up.

After you interview the child/character, choose another character together and switch roles. Now it's the child's turn to interview you!

FAVORITE FOOD FILE

◁▷◁▷◁▷◁▷

Put your recipe file in alphabetical order in this activity.

Use an alphabetical theme to make a recipe file of children's favorite foods.

What You'll Need
- index cards
- pen or pencil

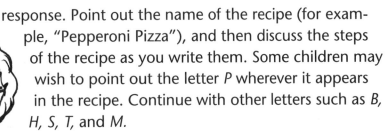

Start by asking the child, "What's your favorite food that starts with *P*?" Write a recipe card for the child's response. Point out the name of the recipe (for example, "Pepperoni Pizza"), and then discuss the steps of the recipe as you write them. Some children may wish to point out the letter *P* wherever it appears in the recipe. Continue with other letters such as *B*, *H*, *S*, *T*, and *M*.

PB AND J FUN

◁▷◁▷◁▷◁▷

Warning! This is only for brave adults! Be prepared to be messy!

What You'll Need
- paper
- pencil
- bread
- peanut butter
- jelly
- knife
- plate

Everyone thinks they know how to write good instructions. After all, how hard could it be to write instructions for something as simple as creating a peanut butter and jelly sandwich?

In this activity, invite the child to write instructions for making this favorite sandwich. The child can make as many steps as are necessary. Then you must follow the steps in the most literal manner possible. For example, if Step 1 says, "Spread the peanut butter on the bread," you

will have to use your fingers for spreading the peanut butter. Nothing was said about using a knife! After the sandwich has been made, discuss the importance of detailed instructions. Have the child rewrite the directions, and try again. Bon appétit!

DOCTOR'S VISIT

◁▷◁▷◁▷◁▷

Turn a routine doctor's visit into a learning experience by looking at X rays.

What You'll Need
- alphabet cards
- dictionary

Here's an activity that will help the child learn about the rarely used letter *X*.

On a routine doctor or dentist visit, ask the doctor or dentist (or an assistant) to show the child an X ray and discuss its creation and function. If time permits, let the child see an X-ray machine and how it works. This may help alleviate any fears the child may have about getting an X ray taken.

At home, show the letter *X* to the child, be it on an alphabet card or in the dictionary.

CHOCOLATE LEAVES

<|◁|◁|◁|▷|◁|▷|

Turn over a new leaf, and learn about the letter L.

What You'll Need
- mint leaves bought at grocery store
- chocolate chips or bars
- double boiler
- water
- food brush

Caution: This project requires adult supervision.

Children can work on beginning word sounds as they make and eat a beautiful and delicious treat.

Wash the mint leaves well. Melt some chocolate, either chips or bars, in the double boiler over boiling water, keeping the child at a safe distance from heat sources. When the chocolate has melted, use a food brush to coat the underside of each leaf with a layer of chocolate. Do not make the chocolate layer too thin, or else it will be difficult to peel off.

Put the leaves in the freezer for a few minutes to harden. Then carefully peel off each leaf. As you eat the chocolate "leaves," take turns naming other words that begin with the letter *L*.

PASS THE BEANBAG

◁▷◁▷◁▷◁▷

Beans, beans, can you throw the beans?

Caution: This project requires adult supervision.

The child can help make the beanbags. Fill each nylon leg with 1 cup beans. Tie the end of the nylon tightly,

What You'll Need
- 3 legs from old nylons
- small beans
- 3 old socks (without holes)
- bucket or 5-pound coffee can
- old belt

and cut off the excess. Place the nylon beanbag inside a sock and tie off the end of the sock tightly; cut off the excess. (Be sure sock material is thick and without holes—small beans can be a choking hazard.) Then find a spot that is out of the traffic area. Place the bucket on the ground. Take 3 giant steps away from the container and lay the belt down. The child can then stand behind the belt and toss the beanbags into the container. Increase the challenge by moving the belt farther away from the bucket.

GET IN THE ACTION

◁▷◁▷◁▷◁▷

A beloved Mother Goose rhyme becomes a foundation for teaching verbs.

Sing a few verses of "Here We Go Round the Mulberry Bush" with the child. Invite the child to pantomime the actions. Explain that a word describing action is called a *verb*. Then have the child create his own verse, following the examples below. Ask the child what verb(s) he pantomimed in the verse.

Here we go round the mulberry bush,
the mulberry bush, the mulberry bush.
Here we go round the mulberry bush,
So early in the morning.
Verse 2. This is the way we wash our hands.
Verse 3. This is the way we wash our clothes.
Verse 4. This is the way we go to school.

STACK-A-STORY

◁▷◁▷◁▷◁▷

Busy hands will love the challenge of this story-building activity.

What You'll Need
- 3 to 6 cardboard boxes
- poster paints
- paintbrush

Set out boxes and materials for painting. Discuss the main events in a favorite story or a story you and

the child have recently read together. Then assist the child in painting a story scene on each cardboard box. When the boxes are dry, have the child stack them in rows so they can be "read" from left to right. Invite the child to retell the story in sequential order.

STORY SWITCHEROO

◁▷◁▷◁▷◁▷

Tell a story in a mixed-up way!

What You'll Need
- crayons
- paper

The adult makes simple drawings to represent the 4 main events of a favorite story or well-known fairy tale. Draw each picture on a separate piece of paper. Lay out the pictures in order, and retell the story using the pictures as prompts. After you have finished telling the story in the traditional way, turn over the pictures and have the child

mix them up. The child can then turn them over in the mixed-up order and reinvent the story, telling it using the new sequence. For more of a challenge, the child can draw the pictures for the activity.

VISIT THE VET

◁▶◁▶◁▶◁▶◁▶◁▶

It is time for your pet's annual check-up. Visit your veterinarian, and have a learning experience.

A visit to the veterinarian can be a great learning experience for a child. It can help him to learn more about the family pet and the care that it needs.

On your ride to the doctor's office, discuss with the child what an animal doctor is called. (Answer: *veterinarian.*) Ask what letter is at the beginning of that word.

In the veterinarian's examining room, ask the child to name some things that he sees there—for example, a table, some cotton, a light, medicine, a stethoscope, and so on. Then, as you say a beginning letter, have him tell you the object that starts with that letter. Use the items that the child observed. While the veterinarian is examining your pet, ask her to tell the child what she is doing and why.

On your way home, talk about some of the different *V* words that you encountered during the trip to the vet.

BIRD-WATCHING

◁·◁·◁·▷·▷·▷·◁▷

Go birding with homemade play binoculars!

What You'll Need
- paper-towel tube
- blunt scissors
- nontoxic white glue

To make binoculars, the adult can cut a paper-towel tube in half and have the child glue the 2 halves together, side by side. Take a walk to the park or go outside in the yard to look for birds to observe through the "binoculars."

Encourage the child to describe any birds that are sighted while birding. The child can tell about the size and color of the bird, how it flies or walks, and where it lands. The child can also imitate the bird's movements and make guesses and hypothesize about what the birds are doing and why.

Activity Twist

For further bird study, check out a children's library book on backyard birds, and look at the pictures together to find out more about the birds you observed while birding.

Do You Remember?

◁▶◁▶◁▶◁▶◁▶◁

Sharing facts with the child is an interesting exercise to enhance listening and strengthen memory.

Begin by telling 10 things about yourself to the child. Your list may include such things as "I like dogs," "Yesterday I ate spaghetti for dinner," or "The red shirt I am wearing is the one Grandma gave me." Then invite the child to tell 10 personal facts as well.

After both of you have recited a list of 10 personal facts, take turns trying to remember and repeat as many of the statements from the other person's list as possible.

Snap! Tap! Hear That?

◁▶◁▶◁▶◁▶◁▶◁

The child will develop sequencing skills essential to reading comprehension while creating sound patterns.

Invite the child to use his body to create a sound pattern. The sound may include clapping, slapping your knees, snapping your fingers, or stamping your feet. Start off by demonstrating a simple pattern for the child with only 3 or 4 elements such as clap-clap-stomp, clap-clap-stomp, or snap-clap-snap-stomp, snap-clap-snap-stomp. Ask the child to listen to the pattern and repeat it. If the child has any difficulty remembering the whole pattern, repeat it again. Then invite the child to invent a pattern for you to follow. Make the patterns progressively longer as you continue to play the game.

BASKETBALL FUN

◁▷◁▷◁▷◁▷◁▷

Basketball fans can learn letters and words while they play their favorite game.

What You'll Need
- toy basketball hoop or empty ice cream container
- small rubber ball
- scissors (optional)

Children will enjoy playing basketball—and keeping score—in this beginning-sound game. If you do not have a toy basketball hoop, you can make one by cutting the bottom out of a large, empty ice cream container.

Hang the hoop on a door, and show the child how to score a basket with the rubber ball. Each time the child prepares to throw the ball, he must say a word that begins like *basketball* or like *fun.* The child receives 1 point for each basket he makes and 1 point for each correct word. Play until the child scores 5 points.

WORD DOMINOES

◁▷◁▷◁▷◁▷◁▷

Word matching is fun when it's done with dominoes.

Playing a domino game gives children practice in visually matching words.

What You'll Need
- index cards
- marker or pen

Make 10 word dominoes by placing each card horizontally and drawing a vertical line down the center. Write a simple word on either side of the line. Write each word on 2 different cards. Also, make cards that have the same word twice. For example, a set of cards might read *cat/dog, dog/pig, pig/ball, ball/run, run/cat, cat/cat, dog/dog, pig/pig, ball/ball,* and *run/run.*

Play the game by spreading out the cards face down. Take turns picking a card and placing it with one end or the other next to a card with a matching word. If you select a card that doesn't match any of the words displayed, put it on the bottom of the pile and select another card. Eventually, all of the cards should be connected.

TREE OF WORDS

◁▷◁▷◁▷◁▷

Try this activity when trees are colorful in the fall or when they are just beginning to sprout new leaves in the spring.

Begin by taking a walk with the child, talking about the trees in the neighborhood. Take along paper and pencil, and write down all the words related to tree that you use, such as *branch, leaves,* or *trunk.* Next, draw a big tree on a large piece of paper, including branches and leaves. Then help the child write the tree words in their correct location on the tree. After everything's labeled, suggest that the child color the picture.

Vary this activity by using all the words relating to flowers, such as *smell, petal, stem,* or *bug.*

SEEK AND SAY

◁▷◁▷◁▷◁▷◁

Find a toy and match it with the right letter card.

Children love finding hidden objects. In this game, they will find objects and identify the beginning sounds of the objects' names.

Lay the letter cards out in rows. Hide objects, such as a vari-ety of toys (ball, doll, teddy bear, car, top, jack-in-the-box, bat) around the room or yard. Have the child search for the toys. After finding a toy, he must locate the letter card that stands for the beginning sound in the toy's name in order to keep the card. Continue until all the objects are found and the beginning sounds of their names are identified. This is a good game for a group of children.

O, O, OPPOSITE

◁▷◁▷◁▷◁▷◁

Up and down, in and out. Here's a game of opposites.

Short vowel sounds are challenging for a child to learn, but if he can remember a key word, the task becomes easier. To help a child learn the short *O* sound, play "O, O, Opposite."

In this game, you say one word or do some action, and the child responds with the opposite word or action. For example, you sit down, and the child stands up. You walk forward, and the child walks backward. You point to something black, and the child points to something white. You touch the top of something, and the child touches the bottom. Continually stress the word *opposite* with its short *O* sound, to point out what the child is doing. This game also involves the concept of directional words.

ESTIMATING AT HOME

◁▷◁▷◁▷◁▷◁▷

Turn everyday experiences into estimating opportunities!

Challenge the child to make predictions or estimates around the home and then test them out. For example, ask the child to estimate how many steps it is from the bed to the closet, or to predict how many boxes of cereal are on the shelf or how many toothbrushes are in the bathroom. Then go with the child to check the estimates or predictions!

 # TISSUE PAPER PAINTING

◁▷◁▷◁▷◁▷◁▷

Create brilliantly colored collages from pieces of tissue paper.

Make a diluted glue mixture (1 cup of water with 2 tablespoons of glue mixed in). Cut or tear colored tissue paper into small pieces. The child can choose paper pieces and arrange them on light-colored paper. Then the child can paint over them with the diluted glue mixture to keep them in place. The colors will mix and blend as they are painted with the liquid. For a variation, the child can draw a picture on the paper first and then add the tissue paper to decorate the picture.

What You'll Need
- nontoxic white glue
- water
- bowl
- measuring cup
- multi-colored tissue paper
- light-colored paper
- brush
- blunt scissors (optional)
- crayons (optional)

DRIVING AROUND TOWN

◁▷◁▷◁▷◁▷

Add spice to running and jumping with a little bit of fantasy.

What You'll Need
- cardboard box
- blunt scissors
- paint
- paintbrush
- paper bag
- markers
- construction paper
- nontoxic white glue
- newspaper
- long wrapping-paper tube
- twine
- sock (optional)
- permanent marker (optional)
- felt pieces (optional)

Create cars for driving and horses for riding, and then let children go to town in a backyard or outdoor area with plenty of room to move around. To create a car, cut the bottom and top off a cardboard box. Cut a large armhole in opposite sides of the box. The car can be painted on the outside if the child wants, and car details (headlights, bumper) can be added. The child can then step into the car, put arms through the sides and, holding the bottom edge, drive around. To create a horse for romping, have the child draw a horse face on a paper bag. Draw ears on the bag or make construction-paper ears to glue on. (An old sock can also be used as an alternative for the horse's head. The horse's face can be drawn with a permanent marker or glued on with felt pieces.) Fill the bag with crumpled newspaper, and place it over the end of a long wrapping-paper tube. Securely tie the paper-bag head to the tube with a piece of twine. Tie the free ends of the twine together to make reins so the child can guide the horse when riding it!

To be what we are, and to become what we are capable of becoming, is the only end of life.
—Robert Louis Stevenson

WHAT'S THE MOOD?

◁▷◁▷◁▷◁▷

Share, discuss, and sort happy and sad pictures.

What You'll Need
- magazine pictures
- blunt scissors
- marker
- boxes

Label 2 boxes—draw a happy face on one and a sad face on the other. Gather an assortment of pictures of people and animals cut from magazines. Invite the child to sort the pictures into the happy and sad boxes. Encourage the child to tell about the choices she made. Later on, add other categories, such as angry and frightened. The child might want to suggest categories as well, such as excited or sleepy.

Activity Twist

Look at family or class pictures together. Ask how the child thinks the various people are feeling in the photos. See if the child can find clues in the pictures to help determine why the subjects are feeling that way. For example, grandmother is happy and smiling—she is sitting in front of a birthday cake.

ICE CUBE PAINTING

⬦⬦⬦⬦⬦⬦

Run out of tempera paint? Try painting with colored ice cubes.

What You'll Need
- foam egg carton
- water
- food coloring
- freezer
- craft sticks
- paintbrush
- white paper
- pen or marker

To make colored ice cubes, fill each section of an empty foam egg carton ¾ full of water. Have the child squeeze drops of different food coloring into the various sections. As the child is squeezing a particular color, ask her to name the color and to tell you what letter and letter sound is heard at the beginning of that color word—for example, *R* for *red, Y* for *yellow,* and so on. Encourage the child to mix some of the food colors to make new colors (blue and red make purple; yellow and red make orange). Place the egg carton in the freezer. When the colored water is nearly frozen, add craft sticks to serve as handles for painting.

Give the child a paintbrush and instruct her to brush water over a sheet of white paper while you are breaking the egg carton to remove the frozen colored ice cubes. Ask the child to select a colored ice cube, and have her again tell you the beginning letter sound of that cube's color. Have the child hold the cube by the craft-stick handle and "paint" on the wet piece of paper. Different letters and designs can be created. When these paintings are dry, you and the child can title them.

WEB WEAVING

◁▷◁▷◁▷◁▷

Web weaving is made easy with a little paint squeezing!

What You'll Need
- paper
- crayons or markers
- paint or nontoxic colored glue in squeeze bottles

Provide the child with a paper that has a large dot (approximately ½" in diameter) drawn anywhere on the paper. The dot is the start of a spider who needs a web! Encourage the child to draw legs for the spider. The child can then create the

spider's web by squeezing paint or colored glue in any kind of line design. To make the activity richer, read a story about a spider, fiction or nonfiction, before asking the child to weave a web for her imaginary spider.

RHYMING GOOD TIME

◁▷◁▷◁▷◁▷

Reading words that rhyme is an easy and entertaining way to introduce new words to the young reader.

What You'll Need
- any book that has rhyming text

Read the rhymes aloud to the child, emphasizing the rhymes as they occur. Read the book again, but this time hesitate just before a rhyming word. Encourage the child to predict and point to the rhymes during the reading.

On another day, reread the story and encourage the child to identify even more portions of the text, especially entire lines that repeat rhymes. Remember to have the child point to at least some of the words while reading them aloud.

FANCIFUL LISTS

▷◁▷◁▷◁▷◁

*Here is an imaginative and sometimes silly game
that fosters the ability to generate ideas.*

Begin by brainstorming unusual topics together or by taking turns suggesting topics to each other. Make a list together or separately containing items that might belong to a particular topic. The following are a few topics to begin with:

What are 5 things you'd want to be sure to take with you on a trip to the moon?

What are 6 unusual things you can think of to do with a paper bag?

What are 7 things you could give a hungry monster to eat?

SAVOR THE FLAVOR

▷◁▷◁▷◁▷◁

Take a taste test, and tell what tastes best!

Have everyone wash their hands first! Gather together food samples with a variety of sweet, salty, and sour flavors. The child can take a taste test blindfolded or with eyes closed. Invite the child to guess what each food is and also to describe how it tastes using flavor words. For a variation, the child can taste, compare, and describe foods with different kinds of textures (sticky, crunchy, smooth).

What You'll Need
• blindfold
• variety of food snacks with different kinds of tastes and textures: pickle, orange slice, potato chip, marshmallows

Activity Twist

As an alternative, ask the child to try smelling some of the food choices. Encourage her to use descriptive words (spicy, good, smelly) to tell about the fragrant samples. Challenge the child to group the foods by these descriptive categories.

PICTURE PUZZLES

◁▷◁▷◁▷◁▷

Make personalized puzzles to take apart and put together.

Have the child help choose the picture to be used. This can be a magazine picture, a photo that has been scanned and printed out at 8" × 11", or a drawing she has done. Glue the picture to a piece of stiff paper. When dry, cut the picture into 3 to 8 odd-shaped pieces (3 for a toddler, more for an older child). The child can fit the pieces together to complete the puzzle. Keep the puzzle pieces in the self-sealing bag.

What You'll Need
- picture
- stiff paper
- nontoxic white glue
- blunt scissors
- self-sealing plastic bag

Activity Twist

For added challenge, make giant puzzles! Have a photo of the child enlarged, use a colorful poster, or have the child draw a picture on poster board. Cut the picture into pieces (try 5 pieces for a toddler, more for an older child). Once the child masters the puzzle, cut the existing pieces in half to create more challenging puzzle fun!

WASH, RINSE, DRY

◁▷◁▷◁▷◁▷

Here's an alphabet game to make those tiresome bath time tasks lots of fun.

At bath time, try this beginning-sound chanting game. Start with the word *wash.* As the child washes each arm, each leg, his torso, and his face with soap and cloth, he chants, "w-w-wash my arms, w-w-wash my legs," and so on for each body part. Repeat the activity with the word *rinse* ("r-r-rinse") as the child rinses each body part. Finally, use the word *dry* ("d-d-dry") as the child dries each body part.

What You'll Need
- bathtub
- water
- washcloth
- soap
- towel

Lists, Lists, Lists!

◁▷◁▷◁▷◁▷◁▷

*Involve the child in writing a regular household task,
such as making a grocery list.*

Collect a variety of colorful grocery advertisements that include pictures and words. Have the child cut out the pictures of the grocery items you regularly purchase. Next, the child should glue or tape the pictures to the index cards—1 picture per card. Help the child write the word for each item on the other side of the card. Then invite the child to make up a grocery list on a separate card by copying the words from the front of the cards.

Just for fun, invite the child to make grocery lists for storybook characters, such as Mama Bear from "Goldilocks and the Three Bears" or Little Red Riding Hood. Another good activity is to create lists for special occasions, such as birthdays, holidays, picnics, and so on.

Past Tense Sense

◁▷◁▷◁▷◁▷◁▷

*The child will identify and use past-tense verbs while creating
a decorative scrapbook page!*

Find a photograph of the child, or have the child draw her own picture. Have the child tape or glue the picture or drawing on a piece of paper. Encourage the child to decorate the page using one or more of the following suggestions: paint a border, glue or tape a paper frame around the picture, use fancy letters to write a caption, add ticket stubs or other souvenirs associated with the picture. Invite the child to write a sentence at the bottom of the scrapbook page to tell what the picture is about. Remind the child to write in the past tense.

INVITE A BUG HOME

◁▷◁▷◁▷◁▷

Make a bug home so you can bring a bug home!

Gather up the materials with the child and take them outdoors. The child can scoop some dirt into the cup and then add a rock or pebbles, a twig, and a leaf to make a bug house. Add a spoonful of water for moisture. After the house is "furnished," the child slips the house inside the stocking. The child scoops the bug inside the cup and closes the stocking top with the twist tie. Observe the bug for an afternoon before setting it free.

What You'll Need
- plastic cup
- plastic spoon
- nylon stocking foot
- twist tie
- items from nature (dirt, pebbles, twigs, leaves, etc.)

Activity Twist

Become a bug detective. Use a plastic, unbreakable magnifying glass to check out small details—spots, wings, legs. What does the bug do with the water? With the leaves? You may want to try sketching your observations on a pad with a pencil or crayon. Use your sketches to help identify your bug in a field guide.

WOOD SANDING

◁▷◁▷◁▷◁▷

Keep young hands busy going around and around, up and down, and side to side sanding wood.

What You'll Need
- wood
- sandpaper

Need some help with a refinishing project? Ask the child to help you and at the same time develop the small muscles necessary for writing.

Select a piece of wood. Give the child a piece of coarse sandpaper. Show the child how to sand the furniture by using different motions—circular, up and down, and back and forth. Describe these motions as they are being done. These are the same motions that are used when writing letters.

DEAR WISE OWL

◁▷◁▷◁▷◁▷◁▷

Invite the child to get to the bottom of this puzzling letter about a mysterious box.

What You'll Need
- large piece of construction paper
- markers
- notebook paper
- pen or pencil

Read the following letter to the child:

Dear Wise Owl,

When I opened the front door this morning, there was a large box on my doorstep. It was wrapped in shiny red paper and had a giant bow. Just as I was about to open the box, it moved! What do you think is in the box? What should I do with it?

Please tell me what you think!

Brandon

Help the child write the letters of the alphabet down the left side of a large piece of construction paper. Ask her to suggest creative ideas for what may be in the box. Invite the child to think of a guess that begins with each letter, or as many of the letters as she can, and write each guess on the construction paper next to the appropriate letter. Have the child decide on one item from the list that she thinks is most likely to be inside the box.

PEANUT BUTTER ROLL-UPS

◁▷◁▷◁▷◁▷

Making these tasty, no-bake snacks is a great way for the child to practice following directions.

Have the child follow these simple directions to make an easy, nutritious snack.

1. Put 2 tablespoons of powdered sugar in a mixing bowl.
2. Add 2 tablespoons of powdered milk.
3. Add 4 tablespoons of peanut butter.
4. Add 4 tablespoons of pecan pieces.
5. Mix.
6. Roll the mixture into golf-ball-size circles, and place them on a plate.
7. Put the roll-ups in the refrigerator for a few hours until cold.
8. Take out of the refrigerator, and enjoy a tasty, nutritious snack.

What You'll Need
- measuring spoons
- mixing bowl
- powdered sugar
- powdered milk
- peanut butter
- pecan pieces
- wooden spoon
- plate

OUTSIDE ORCHESTRA

◁▷◁▷◁▷◁▷

Find musical instruments in nature, and play them!

What You'll Need
- sticks
- rocks
- acorns
- oatmeal box or paper bag

The child can use creativity to invent instruments from items collected from nature. The child can make rhythm sticks with 2 sticks, a drum and drumstick with a large rock and a stick, cymbals with 2 flat rocks (being careful of fingers!), or a shaker by placing acorns inside an oatmeal box or paper bag.

PIZZA PUZZLE

◁▷◁▷◁▷◁▷

There are many ways to cut a pizza—and to learn the alphabet.

Here's a puzzle to help children practice identifying letters.

Cut a circle out of the construction paper to fit the bottom of the pizza pan. Then cut that circle into several pieces of varying shapes and sizes. Write a letter of the alphabet on each piece. Invite the child to put the puzzle together in the pan, naming the letter on each piece she uses. Begin with a puzzle that has only a few pieces, and work up to more complex puzzles.

What You'll Need
- pizza pan
- construction paper
- blunt scissors
- marker or pen

To Rhyme or Not to Rhyme

◁▷◁▷◁▷◁▷◁▷◁▷

Here's a rhyming game that helps a child develop important language skills.

Being able to hear different sounds in a series of words is an important skill that can be developed in young children.

First explain what a rhyme is. Use a series of 2 words that sound alike, such as *bat* and *cat* or *dog* and *log.* Once that concept is clear, say 3 words—2 that rhyme and 1 that does not, such as *bat, cat, mop.* Ask the child to identify the word that doesn't rhyme. (Change the order of words occasionally so that the nonrhyming word isn't always the last word in the group.)

Next, try saying 4 words—3 words that rhyme and 1 word that doesn't, in any order (for example, *tree, bird, free, key*)—and ask the child if she can identify the word that doesn't rhyme. If the child is having difficulty picking the nonrhyming word, have her repeat all 4 words. If the child has trouble recalling all of the words, repeat the list yourself.

Rhyme Time!

Once I saw a little robin
go hop, hop, hop;
I asked the little robin
to stop, stop, stop.
He blinked his eye and turned around
with a peep, peep, peep,
and across the yard he went
with a leap, leap, leap.

BEAUTIFUL BEADS

◁▷◁▷◁▷◁▷◁▷

Transform everyday items into decorative beads!

What You'll Need
- playdough
- paintbrush and paint
- yarn
- dowel

Help the child make playdough, using the recipe provided on page 7. When the dough is pliable, show the child how to form beads by rolling little handfuls of the dough into balls. The child can make holes in the beads with the end of a paintbrush. Set the beads out to dry overnight. After they have dried, she can paint them. When the paint is dry, the child can string the beads on yarn for wearing or for decoration! For a decoration variation, tie several strands of beads to a dowel with yarn for a pretty mobile.

ELABORATE, EXAGGERATE

◁▷◁▷◁▷◁▷

*The child will delight in this exaggeration game
that cultivates descriptive language skills.*

Begin by making a simple statement, and invite the child to add some exaggerations to it. Explain that when one exaggerates, a lot of descriptive language, real or unreal, is added. For example, if you say, "The bear went to the store," the child might reply, "The big bear went to the honey store." After the child adds some descriptive words, take a turn yourself, and exaggerate the statement further. Continue taking turns until the original statement has become an elaborate, descriptive sentence that can be either funny or serious.

 # FACE IT!

▷◁▷◁▷◁▷◁

Get ready to "Face It!" as the child explores character expressions.

What You'll Need
- old magazines
- blunt scissors
- colored construction paper
- clear tape or glue
- crayons or markers

Invite the child to cut out pictures of faces from old magazines. The faces the child chooses should show specific expressions, such as happy, sad, angry, scared, excited, worried, or surprised. Help the child glue or tape the expressive faces on colored construction paper. Then help the child add speech or thought balloons with words the child thinks the people are saying or thinking.

To take this one step further, have the child glue 2 or 3 faces onto 1 sheet of construction paper, and together create a cartoon conversation between them.

SHE LOOKS HAPPY.

SIGN SYMBOLS

◁▶◁▶◁▶◁▶◁

Signs are everywhere. While traveling,
identify and interpret these signs and symbols.

Next time you take an automobile trip to visit grandparents or friends, ask the child to look for traffic and advertising signs and symbols and tell you what they are. Early reading begins by interpreting various signs and symbols and associating words, sounds, and meanings to them.

   One of the first signs that usually is recognized is the octagonal Stop sign. Also look for One Way, School Zone, No Crossing, and other signs and symbols during your trip. This activity expands the child's reading environment and encourages the use of beginning sounds.

CORK CREATIONS

◁▶◁▶◁▶◁▶◁

Create critters and other things with cork!

The child can construct people, animals, and other things and inventions by gluing corks together. Chenille stems can be used and inserted into the cork for arms, legs, or machine parts. Paper scraps can be glued on to make clothing, hats, animal ears, or decorations. Yarn can also be glued on for decoration, for hair, or to make a tail. The child can use markers to make eyes, ears, or noses where needed! To simplify, individual corks can be made into little cork people and used for play. Cut strips of colored paper that are half as wide as the corks. The child can glue the colored paper strips around the bottom of the cork for clothing. The child can then draw eyes, nose, mouth, and hair on the cork with markers.

What You'll Need
- corks
- chenille stems
- construction paper
- scissors
- nontoxic white glue
- yarn
- markers

STAMP IT!

◁▶◁▶◁▶◁▶◁▷

All the child needs to make and send this special birthday card is a little word study and a lot of love.

Invite the child to make a birthday card for a special friend or family member while practicing vocabulary skills. Begin by talking about the greeting "Happy Birthday." Write the words in a place where the child can see them, and then spell them together. Help the child cut out letters *H, A, P, Y, B, I, R, T,* and *D* from a sponge, corrugated cardboard, or polystyrene. Help

dip the letters into a shallow dish of paint, and then stamp the letters on folded cards to create the greeting *HAPPY BIRTH-DAY.* When the greeting has dried, invite the child to decorate the card further and sign it before delivering it.

What You'll Need
- pen or pencil
- paper
- sponge, corrugated cardboard, or polystyrene
- blunt scissors
- poster paints
- dish
- folded construction-paper cards

DIGIT LETTERS

◁▶◁▶◁▶◁▶◁▷

What letters can you make with your fingers?

Making letters with your fingers can be fun, yet challenging. It can also help a child who is having difficulty distinguishing between similar letters—lowercase *b* and *d,* for example.

With your left hand, use the pointer finger and thumb to form what will look like the signal for OK: The pointer finger and thumb form a circle, with the rest of the fingers lining up straight in a single row. When you have done that, a lowercase *b* has been made. Do the same finger formations with your right hand to make a lowercase *d.*

If you place these 2 letter formations side by side, they kind of look like a bed with 2 pillows. Seeing this, the child can then associate the beginning sound of *b* and the ending sound of *d* in the word *bed.* This helps her remember the differences between the 2 letters, and it reinforces the process of reading from left to right. See how many other finger letters the child can make.

WORD SQUARE

◁▷◁▷◁▷◁▷

Here's a head scratcher that will keep the child thinking long after it is put down.

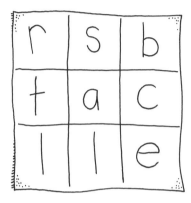

Copy a word square like the one shown here on a piece of paper. Begin by having the child choose any letter in the puzzle and start building a word. Explain that each letter in the word being built must touch another letter in the square. To accomplish this the child can move down, across, or diagonally around the square. Demonstrate by spelling the word *ball.* Encourage the child to spell as many words as possible using the letters in the square.

LEAF AND FLOWER PRESSING

◁▷◁▷◁▷◁▷

Press and preserve flowers and leaves for pictures and for saving.

What You'll Need
- leaves
- flowers
- paper towels
- newspapers
- telephone books or heavy books
- paper (optional)
- nontoxic white glue (optional)
- clear contact paper (optional)

The child can collect leaves and flowers for pressing. Let the child place the leaves and flowers between 2 sheets of paper towel. The child can place this paper-towel-and-flower sandwich on top of a stack of newspaper and then place more folded newspaper on top. Place heavy books or telephone books on top of the newspapers. The flowers or leaves will take about 3 to 4 weeks to dry out and flatten. The child can peek and check the progress regularly during that time. After the flowers have flattened and dried, the child can use them to make a collage, seal them between 2 sheets of clear contact paper, or save them in a box or in a book!

DUCK, DUCK, GRAY DUCK!

Using a traditional game in a new way encourages children to learn.

This adaptation of a traditional game focuses on the beginning sound of the letter *D*.

Invite several family members or friends to sit in a circle on the floor with you and the child. One player walks around the outside of the circle and taps each player, saying "Duck." She then stops behind one player and says, "Gray duck." That player must say a word that begins like the word *duck,* at which point she becomes the player who walks around the circle and chooses a "Gray duck."

TUNNEL HOLE ROLL

Make a bending, turning, long marble tunnel roll!

Caution: This project requires adult supervision.

What You'll Need
• cardboard tubes
• blunt scissors
• masking tape
• marbles
• blocks

Be sure this activity is supervised—marbles are choking hazards! Make the tunnel tube with the child by using cardboard tubes from wrapping paper and paper towels. Cut some of the tubes to make them shorter. Make slits in the end of 1 tube, and then slip another tube inside the first. The tubes can be angled and then taped together. Attach 5, 6, 7, or more tubes to make long, winding tunnels. The child can then set 1 end on a block or chair and roll a marble through. The child can experiment by placing the tube at higher or lower levels and also changing the angle of the bends. Invite the child to share findings and conclusions after experimenting.

C Is for Color

◁▷◁▷◁▷◁▷

The only thing more fun than matching letters is making lots of noise when you're finished!

Caution: This project requires adult supervision.

Here's a creative, colorful way to learn the letter C.

Use new or old crayons. Tear off 2 sheets of waxed paper measuring approximately 8½" × 11". Draw a large letter C on a sheet of paper, and tell the child that it stands for the beginning sound in the word *color*.

Have the child sharpen several crayons in a portable pencil sharpener. Take the shavings from the crayons and arrange them into the shape of a large C on 1 sheet of waxed paper. When the letter is finished, put the other sheet of waxed paper on top to cover it.

Next, put another sheet of paper on top of the waxed paper, and press the top sheet briefly with a warm iron. (Take care that the child doesn't touch the warm iron and get burned.) The shavings will melt to form a multicolored letter. Have the child display the picture and think of other words that begin with the C sound.

Touchable Fruit Salad

◁▷◁▷◁▷◁▷

Making fruit salad can be a touching experience.

Caution: This project requires adult supervision.

What You'll Need
- fruits as described at right
- scarf for blindfold
- large bowl
- knife (to be used by adult)
- cutting board

Help a child master beginning letters while making a healthy snack that both of you can enjoy.

Collect as many of these fresh fruits as possible: apple, orange, grape, pineapple, cantaloupe, peach, grapefruit, and banana. Have the child put on a blindfold, feel each fruit, and guess what it is. After each fruit is named correctly, take the blindfold off. Ask her to say another word that begins with the same sound as the name of the fruit.

Then ask the child to help you prepare each fruit for a fruit salad. Making sure the child is closely supervised, have her do as many steps as is safely possible, such as washing fruit, peeling the banana, and pulling grapes from their stems. Discuss the other steps, such as cutting up the fruits, as you do them.

Hamburger Harry

◁▷◁▷◁▷◁▷

Favorite foods come to life—and teach the sound of the letter H.

Creating a person from a hamburger box makes learning the *H* sound fun.

Next time you go out for a burger, hold on to the box. Using markers and pieces of construction paper, help the child make a face on the top of the hamburger box. Show the child how to open and close the "mouth" by opening and shutting the box. Then have the child use the hamburger person's voice to tell an *H*-word story.
For example: "A hamburger hopped to a house to help a hungry hippopotamus."

What You'll Need
- paper hamburger box
- markers
- construction paper
- glue or clear tape

SHAPE CONCENTRATION

◁▶◁▶◁▶◁▶

Play a concentration game and search for hidden shape pairs.

What You'll Need
• index cards
• blunt scissors
• markers
• stickers (optional)

Prepare a concentration game by cutting index cards into squares and then drawing pairs of shapes on separate cards. Make 8 to 16 cards (2 of each shape). To play shape concentration, mix up all the cards and spread them out facedown. One person turns over 2 cards, hoping to find a match. If the cards match, the person

takes the pair and gets a second turn. If the 2 cards do not match, the cards are turned facedown again, and the next person takes a turn. Play until all the pairs have been found. The person with the most cards is the winner. For a variation, make different kinds of concentration games using stickers (animal concentration, dinosaur concentration, butterfly concentration, etc.).

SPOON A BALL ALONG

◁▶◁▶◁▶◁▶

Try a tricky athletic feat with just a table-tennis ball and a spoon!

Challenge the child to carry a table-tennis ball in a serving spoon across a room without dropping it. This is not easy to do and may take some practice! After the child has mastered the task, make it even

What You'll Need
• table-tennis ball
• serving spoon

trickier. How fast can she carry the ball across the room without dropping it? Can she carry it while weaving around several chairs instead of straight across the room? Create a simple obstacle course with the child to test her ball-carrying skill!

SING A STORY

◁▷◁▷◁▷◁▷

Make a story musical, and sing it like a song.

Ask the child to think of a favorite story or fairy tale that she knows well and is fond of telling. Talk about the story together. Discuss who is in it and what the characters do. Then challenge the child to tell the story in song. Make up a tune, or use a familiar tune, and sing the start of the story as an example. Invite the child to continue the rest of the story in song, inventing the tune and lyrics as she goes along.

SAFE CITY

◁▷◁▷◁▷◁▷

Plan a town that will keep its inhabitants safe!

Share ideas about what makes cities safe. Encourage the child to give reasons for ideas. The child may come up with many unique suggestions as well as traditional ones. Support all ideas! Then invite the child to draw a town that incorporates some of the ideas for safety. The child can make signs, build special buildings, make parks far away from streets, etc.

What You'll Need
• paper
• markers

Activity Twist

Ask the child to draw pictures of the people who help to keep your neighborhood safe—police officers, firefighters, doctors, crossing guards. Next, discuss what the child can do to help safety officials: never play with matches, dial 911 in an emergency, only cross the street with an adult, etc. Teach the child her address and phone number.

Rock Person

◁▷◁▷◁▷◁▷

Make a rock character, and roll with the letter R.

What You'll Need
- rock
- yarn
- glue
- blunt scissors
- marker or pen
- construction paper
- clear tape

Reinforce the letter *R* with a "person" made from a rock. Help the child find a smooth, medium-sized rock. Cut lengths of yarn, and have the child glue them to the top of the rock to serve as hair. Have the child draw arms, legs, and facial features on construction paper. Cut them out, and glue or tape them to the rock. Ask the child to say additional words that begin with the letter *R*.

Fun Fact

English is a growing language. At the beginning of the twentieth century, words were added at the rate of 1,000 per year. Now, the increase is closer to 15,000 to 20,000 words per year. In 1987, the second edition of the Random House Dictionary included 50,000 words that did not exist for its first edition 21 years earlier and 75,000 new definitions of old words.

Poem Pyramids

◁▷◁▷◁▷◁▷

Practice learning initial sounds of words with these simple sound poems.

The structure for these sound poems is very simple. Each poem has only 4 lines. The first line has 1 word, the second line has 2, the third line has 3, and the fourth line has 4. Each line includes the words of the line before it and adds 1 new word. The tricky part is that all words must begin with the same letter! Take a look at the example below.

Begin by choosing a letter or inviting the child to choose a letter, and create a poem pyramid together. After finishing the first poem, invite the child to create a new poem, using a different letter.

Example:

Bee

Buzzy Bee

Big Buzzy Bee

Big Buzzy Bee Bumbling

Night Scenes

◁▷◁▷◁▷◁▷

Depict the deep of night with dark paper pictures.

Invite the child to draw nighttime (inside or outside) pictures using dark paper to inspire nighttime thinking. Chalk, pastels, and gel pens show up brightly on black paper, adding flash to working on a project about the dark. For a variation, add sticker stars to the materials.

PASTA PIZZAZZ

◁▶◁▶◁▶◁▶

This entertaining spelling project allows the child to analyze spelling patterns while creating wearable art.

Have the child paint uncooked rigatoni noodles. Once the paint is dry, write the following words on the noodles: *hen, pen, Ben.* String the noodles on a piece of yarn. Do the same for this next batch of words: *cake, wake, take.*

Next, ask the child to look at the words on each strand, identify the spelling pattern (in this case *en* and *ake*), and make new word noodles to add to each. Help the child tie the finished strands to create wearable spelling art.

For a challenging variation, invite the child to construct a sentence using as many words from the wearable art as possible. Expect some silly sentences!

What You'll Need
- rigatoni noodles (without ridges if possible)
- paints
- paintbrush
- felt-tip pen
- strands of yarn

SPORTSWRITERS

◁▶◁▶◁▶◁▶

For every sporting event, sportswriters need to be there to get the story. So grab your pencil!

Invite the child to be a sportswriter. Page through the sports section of a newspaper to familiarize the child with headlines, photo captions, and stories in the sports section. Then help the child collect the tools she will need for the next assignment, including a pencil or two, paper, and some newspapers. Explain that the child's task is to capture, in a single sentence, the main idea or most important moment of a sporting event. Explain how important this story is and how it might appear in the sports section of tomorrow's newspaper.

What You'll Need
- old newspapers
- pencil
- paper
- blunt scissors
- clear tape
- newsprint

First, have the young sportswriter cut out a picture of someone participating in a sport. Invite the child to write a caption or headline, such as the one pictured here, about the athlete. Tape the headline and picture on newsprint to resemble a newspaper.

THE MISSING D's

◁▷◁▷◁▷◁▷

*Become a detective and find the missing **D***'s.

Role-playing is an important way for a child to learn, and pretending to be a detective can be challenging and exciting.

Give the child a magnifying glass. The "detective" searches the home for things that begin with the letter *D*. Have the child collect the *D* things in a dishpan. (Hints: doll, stuffed dog, dime, dish, dice, domino, drum, diaper.)

What You'll Need
- plastic magnifying glass
- household items that begin with the letter *D*
- dishpan

STORY HANGER

◁▷◁▷◁▷◁▷

Hangers are not only for clothes!
They can also be used to tell about a favorite storybook.

Draw and cut a door hanger out of tagboard. Be sure to make it large enough to fit on a doorknob. Then encourage the child to write the title and author of a favorite book or story on the back of the hanger. She can then draw a picture or write a sentence about the book on the front of the tagboard hanger.

What You'll Need
- tagboard
- pencil
- blunt scissors
- felt-tip pen

Invite the child to place the hanger on a friend or sibling's door, desk, or coat hook to encourage that person to read the book, too.

CLIFFORD THE BIG DOG BY

CHART SMART

Need a spark for teaching adjectives? Try this simple sentence-building activity.

What You'll Need
- paper
- pencil

Look at the chart shown here. Invite the child to build sentences using 1 word from each row. Have the child choose a word from the first line and write it on a piece of paper. Then have the child choose a word from the second line to follow the first word. Continue in this manner for the third and fourth lines. Next have the child read the completed sentence aloud. Point out the words that describe size and shape. Explain to the child that descriptive words are called *adjectives*. Repeat the activity several times.

> One, The, Some
> bus, whale, volcano, flower, dinosaur, snowflake
> is, are
> big, little, giant, tiny, yellow, gray, red

ITTY-BITTY, TEENY-TINY ME

Pretend to be teeny-tiny for a little itty bit of fun!

Ask the child to make believe that he is very, very small and to do everything in an itty-bitty, teeny-tiny way. Here are some possibilities: Take itty-bitty, teeny-tiny steps when walking. Take itty-bitty, teeny-tiny bites of food when eating. Make an itty-bitty, teeny-tiny drawing on a teeny-tiny, itty-bitty piece of paper. Encourage the child to think of many different actions and activities to try out in a small way. Later on, the child can try doing everything in a GREAT BIG, GIANT WAY!

STORY FLIPS

◁▷◁▷◁▷◁▷

These story-building squares offer the child infinite imaginative narrative possibilities.

What You'll Need
- paper
- crayons or markers
- old magazines
- blunt scissors
- clear tape or glue
- 8"×10" cardboard squares

Build stories by flipping pictures the child has drawn or cut out of old magazines. The pictures should include animals, people, and objects. Help the child glue or tape each picture onto its own cardboard square. Once you and the child have assembled 12 to 20 pictures, ask the child to sort them into 4 random piles. Invite the child to turn over a square from each pile and then make up a story based on the 4 pictures. Continue with another set of 4 pictures for endless creative story-building fun!

> The woman went shopping to buy a dog to give to her cat.

POPCORN P'S

◁▷◁▷◁▷◁▷

Pop some popcorn and make some P's, if you please.

Make popcorn with the child. As the kernels pop, repeatedly say the word *pop*. After eating some of the popcorn, ask the child if she can arrange individual pieces of popcorn in the shape of the letter P. (For a young child, a large letter P can be drawn on a piece of paper, thus serving as a guide.) When the popcorn P has been made, spell out the word *popcorn* beneath it in popcorn.

What You'll Need
- popcorn
- popcorn popper
- paper (optional)
- pencil (optional)

HAT PARADE

⊲▪⊲▪⊲▪⊲▪⊲▪⊲

A hodgepodge of hats opens the door to delightful drama!

What You'll Need
- paper plates
- hole punch
- yarn
- nontoxic white glue
- ribbon
- tissue paper
- construction paper
- blunt scissors
- stapler
- markers
- newspaper
- masking tape

With adult help, the child can make an assortment of hats and then use them to invent stories and for other dramatic play.

Paper-Plate Hat: Use a hole punch to punch a hole on both sides of a paper plate. Thread and tie a piece of thick yarn through each hole. The child can decorate the top of the hat by gluing on ribbons, tissue paper, and strips of construction paper. When the hat is completed, the yarn strips can be tied to hold the hat on the child's head. For a variation, cut a large hole in the middle of the paper plate so that the hat is a brim only, and invite the child to decorate the brim.

Band-and-Strip Hat: Use a thick strip of construction paper to make a band that fits around the child's head. Staple the ends of the band together. The child can use additional strips of construction paper to make the crown of the hat by stapling them in arches from one side of the band to the other. The child can glue on decorations or use markers to color on the strips and arches.

Cylinder Hat: Bend a large piece of construction paper into a cylinder to fit on the child's head. The child can cut slits (approximately 1½" long) all around the bottom edge and then bend the cut paper out. Cut a hole the size of the cylinder in the middle of a paper plate, then let the child slide the plate over the top of the cylinder to where the slits begin. The child can glue the slits to the bottom of the plate to create a brim. The child can then decorate the hat.

Brimmed Newspaper Hat: Open several sheets of newspaper. The newspaper is placed over the child's head. A piece of masking tape is taped around the crown of the child's head to fit, and then the child can trim the brim. Decorate!

JUMP FOR J

⬦▸⬦▸⬦▸⬦▸⬦▸⬦

Recognizing the letter J is fun when you get to jump for it.

What You'll Need
- at least 57 index cards (or cards made from poster board)
- marker

You can use letter cards for a variety of fun phonics activities.

Make 1 set of 26 alphabet cards in capital letters—1 letter per card. Make another set of 26 cards using the lowercase letters—again, 1 letter per card. Make at least 5 extra cards for the letter *J,* some uppercase, some lowercase.

Show the letter *J* cards to the child, pointing out that in this activity the letter stands for the word *jump.* Shuffle the cards, and have the child crouch down as you show her the cards 1 by 1. The child has to jump up each time you display a letter *J.* Encourage the child to call out every letter that she recognizes.

MAKE A MAGNET

⬦▸⬦▸⬦▸⬦▸⬦▸⬦

Learning's a matter of attraction when you investigate and explore with magnets!

Invite the child to experiment with the magnet and see what it will pick up; then have the child try to pick up objects with the nail. The child can magnetize an iron nail and experiment again. Magnetize the nail by stroking it with the strong magnet 50 to 100 times. The strokes all need to be in 1 direction!

What You'll Need
- magnet
- iron nail (not galvanized)
- a variety of magnetic and nonmagnetic items (paper clip, button, penny, washer, screw, cotton ball, eraser, feather, brass fastener)

CHAIN OF LETTERS

⊲▶⊲▶⊲▶⊲▶⊲▷

Make a paper chain, and practice forming letters.

What You'll Need
- construction paper
- blunt scissors
- glue
- letter cards

In this activity, the child creates a long paper chain, which he can use to form any of the alphabet's letters.

Cut several strips of paper approximately 6" long. Help the child make a paper chain by gluing the first strip into a circle and then linking and gluing the strips inside one another to make a chain. When the chain is about 24" long, ask the child to lay the chain down in the shapes of letters that he copies from letter cards.

WORD SHOPPING

⊲▶⊲▶⊲▶⊲▶⊲▷

Go on an educational grocery-shopping spree in this let's-pretend game.

Familiar food names are a good starting place for learning to read words.

Using index cards, make word cards with food names such as *apple, cookie, meat, milk,* and *juice.* Have the child choose a card, and say the word together. Then invite the child to go grocery shopping. To "buy" a card and put it in the bag, the child must say the food name on the card.

What You'll Need
- index cards
- plastic or paper grocery bag
- marker or pen

For a variation, you might also use toy food items or even real fruits and vegetables with the word cards.

FUNNY FARM

⊲▷⊲▷⊲▷⊲▷⊲▷

Laugh and learn with this silly beginning-sound game.

What You'll Need
• paper
• marker or pen

Use children's love of tall tales to practice beginning sounds.

Start a Funny Farm story about an animal on your farm: "I have a gorilla who gulps guppies." Encourage the child to create another sentence. In each sentence, use a lot of words beginning with the initial sound in the animal's name. Take turns making up Funny Farm sentences. Then have the child draw a picture of the animals you have created.

MY BODY AND ME

⊲▷⊲▷⊲▷⊲▷⊲▷

Combine art and writing while the child learns his body size and parts.

Begin by placing a large piece of butcher paper, big enough for the child to lay on, on the floor. Then take a pencil and trace around the child. Next, use scissors to cut out the outline carefully. Have the child write the names of body parts on self-adhesive notes and then place the notes at the appropriate parts of the drawing.

What You'll Need
• butcher paper
• pencil
• blunt scissors
• self-adhesive notes

Vary this activity by having the child lay on the paper in amusing poses, such as that of a weight lifter. Have the child draw accessories that would go with the chosen pose. In the case of the weight lifter, the child could add barbells. Another variation includes adding clothes for different types of weather, such as a pair of shorts, a coat, or a hat. Lay the clothing on a clean sheet of paper, and trace its outline as well. The child can then label the clothing. "Dress" the body parts depending on the weather.

REBUS WRITING

◁▷◁▷◁▷◁▷

*Test the child's creative thinking, problem-solving skills,
and ability to translate pictures into words.*

Begin by creating rebus sentences for the child to translate. As you write the sentences, draw certain words, especially repeated words, as pictures. For example, if you wrote a sentence about a king, you could draw a picture of a crown as the symbol for the word *king*. The child can color the pictures in the rebus. Then challenge the child to translate the rebus sentences you have created. The following is an example to get you started.

What You'll Need
• paper
• felt-tip pen
• markers

Once upon a 🕐, the 👑 visited the 🏰.

It was the 👑's birthday. He ate .

Fun Fact

A syllable is a word or part of a word pronounced with a single vocal sound. Each syllable must have a vowel, but not necessarily a consonant.

SUN PRINTS

◁▷◁▷◁▷◁▷◁▷

Make shape tracings using dark paper and sunshine!

What You'll Need
• dark construction paper
• rocks
• assorted shape objects: comb, coin, spoon, key

On a sunny (not windy!) day, the child can place a dark piece of construction paper outside on the ground in a sunny place. Have the child weight the corners of the paper down with rocks. The child can choose objects to place on top of the paper for printmaking. After several hours,

the sun will fade the paper, leaving a darker impression of the objects behind. The child can make prints of individual items on single sheets of paper or can create a collage print that includes several items on one paper. Discuss the changes of the paper with the child.

CREATE A LOGO

◁▷◁▷◁▷◁▷◁▷

Create a design that represents a specific idea or image about the creator.

What You'll Need
• magazines
• markers
• paper

Explain that a logo is a picture or design intended to tell something about a product that a company wants you to remember. Logos are often accompanied by a few words. Look for examples in magazines or on items you have around the house: sports equipment, electronic equipment, clothing, food, drinks,

and so on. Invite the child to design a personal logo that he might want to use. The child may wish to use one or more letters in his name as part of the design. Each logo should be accompanied by a name the child has created to be used with it. Then think about practical ways the child can use logos, such as to mark possessions or as decorative imprints for clothing.

TOTEM POLES

◁▷◁▷◁▷◁▷

Learn about other cultures and traditions while building totem poles that reflect important images from a story.

What You'll Need
- story or article about nature
- cardboard boxes
- poster paints
- paintbrushes
- pictures of totem poles (optional)

Explain to the child that a totem pole is a tall pole on which animals and other images from nature are carved or painted. Explain that totem poles are symbolic and often tell a story. If possible, show the child examples of authentic Native American totem poles from picture books.

Invite the child to read a nonfiction story or article about animals or nature. Then help the child paint cardboard boxes depicting important images from the story. Allow plenty of time for the boxes to dry before moving them. Finally, have the child stack the boxes so that they resemble a totem pole.

TRADE PLACES

◁▷◁▷◁▷◁▷

***You be me for a while, and I'll be you! Trade places with the child for
15 minutes of interesting conversation.***

This challenging activity is an intriguing way to practice critical thinking and interpretive skills. Pretend that you are the child, and invite the child to pretend to be you. When you speak, say the things you think the child might say, and use the expressions the child would use. Encourage the child to express words and ideas as you would. Then choose a topic together and have a conversation.

PICTURE DETAILS

◁▷◁▷◁▷◁▷

Look carefully at a picture and you'll see all kinds of things.

What You'll Need
- detailed "action" picture
- paper
- pencil

As a child learns to read, interpreting pictures becomes a big part of the language process.

In this activity, the child is asked to look very closely at a detailed action picture and describe what he sees. A child who cannot read will name specific objects that are seen—for example, a ball, a girl, a flower. A beginning reader is often able to describe what he sees with greater detail. As the child is telling you what object he sees, ask him what the beginning letter is. Then write the word down for the child to see.

BUBBLE RUN

◁▶◁▶◁▶◁▶

Long, longer, longest—how far will bubbles fly?

What You'll Need
- bucket
- liquid detergent
- water
- glycerin
- plastic 6-pack ring or plastic berry basket
- string (optional)
- tape measure (optional)

This is an outdoor activity for a day that is not too windy. Mix 3 parts liquid detergent and 1 part water in the bucket. Add a few drops of glycerin to make bubbles stronger. Locate a runway—a spot free of trees, gardens, and fences—where the child can chase bubbles. Using the 6-pack ring or the berry basket as a wand, dip ring or basket in detergent mixture, and blow soap bubbles into the air. Encourage the child to run after and catch as many bubbles as he can before the bubbles touch the ground. Encourage the child to guess what happened to the bubbles that went up in the air and blew away. Why did some go higher? To make this activity more challenging, use long pieces of string or a tape measure to measure the distances the bubbles traveled. Have the child compare the distances and figure out why a few bubbles went only a short distance while some others went farther.

BIOGRAPHY BOOK JACKET

⊲▶⊲▶⊲▶⊲▶

*Writing words for a book jacket is a creative exercise
that teaches the child summarization skills.*

Explain to the child that a biography is a book written about someone's life, and an autobiography is a book written by someone about his own life. Tell the child that a book jacket protects the book but sometimes also contains a summary of the book. Look at other book jackets together, and see how those summaries were written. Then have the child read a biography or autobiography, or read the book together. After the child has finished,

What You'll Need
• biography or autobiography
• paper
• pencil
• crayons or markers

discuss the key events in the person's life that were discussed in the biography. Invite the child to write a summary. Use the summary to create a book jacket for the biography or autobiography. Encourage the child to be creative in designing and coloring the front of the book jacket.

For an added challenge, invite the child to write a summary that might appear on the book jacket of his own biography.

WIND DETECTIVE

⊲▶⊲▶⊲▶⊲▶

Test the wind's strength with outside items.

What You'll Need
• nature items of assorted weights (feather, stick, rock, leaf)

On a breezy or windy day, the child can gather together an assortment of natural items and then predict which ones the wind will be strong enough to blow away. The items can be placed

on a table or bench one at a time to observe the results. For more challenge, have the child place all the items in a row and test them all at once!

GARDENING IN A TIRE

◁▷◁▷◁▷◁▷

Plant a seed, and help it grow into your very own plant.

What You'll Need
- old tire
- garbage bag
- potting soil
- trowels
- seeds
- watering can

This activity is best kept simple—plant one kind of seed at a time. Help the child select a plant that you know is hardy and easy to tend. Beans and squash both grow well. Choose an out-of-the-way place in the yard that gets sunlight half the day. Place the tire on top of the garbage bag. Have the child help you fill the tire with potting soil using the trowels. The child can plant 3 seeds, according to the package directions. Water the seeds as instructed. When there is about 4 or 5 inches of growth, remove 2 of the plants, leaving the most healthy one. Set up a schedule for watering and weeding with your child. Supervise these activities. Your child will be delighted when the plant bears fruit (or squash!).

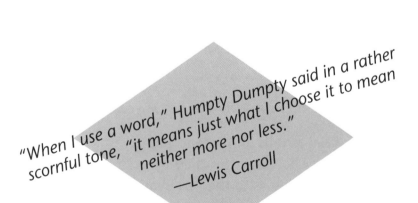

"When I use a word," Humpty Dumpty said in a rather scornful tone, "it means just what I choose it to mean neither more nor less."
—Lewis Carroll

POSTER POWER

◁▷◁▷◁▷◁▷

Any child who loves movies or videos will enjoy creating this colorful poster.

What You'll Need
- newspapers or magazines
- paper
- pen or pencil
- poster paper
- paints and paintbrush
- markers or crayons
- blunt scissors
- other decorating materials

Invite the child to choose a favorite recent movie or video. Collect information about the star or the movie itself from newspaper or magazine articles, and provide the child with a list of people that includes the stars, the director, the writer, and others involved in the production. Also include other information, such as reviews, that would encourage someone to buy a ticket to see the show. Have the child write a few simple sentences telling what he liked about the movie or video.

Next, help the child design the poster. Use paints, crayons, magazine pictures, or other materials to make the poster colorful and appealing. Display the finished poster in a prominent location.

MIRROR, MIRROR

◁▷◁▷◁▷◁▷

Look at me, and tell me what you see!

Stand together in front of a full-length mirror, and take turns describing what you see. Challenge the child to continue to add more and more details to the observations. For more fun, make a tape recording of the observations. Then, later the same day, return to the mirror and play back the tape. Note if anything has changed or if there are additional observations that were not noticed and recorded during the earlier viewing.

What You'll Need
- full-length mirror
- tape recorder
- blank tape

ALPHABET TRAIN

◁▷◁▷◁▷◁▷

Get on the right track with the alphabet train.

If possible, collect 26 small boxes and 1 larger box. Leave the open side of each box facing up. Line up the boxes end to end, like the boxcars of a train, then punch a hole in the center of the front and back of each "car." Thread yarn through the holes to connect the boxes. Make a knot on each end of the piece of yarn so that the yarn will not slip out.

What You'll Need
- boxes of various sizes and shapes
- yarn
- objects beginning with the different letters of the alphabet

When all 26 "cars" and 1 "engine" (the bigger box) are hooked together, write the alphabet on each of the small boxes—1 letter per box in alphabetical order. When the train is assembled, ask the child to find some object that begins with each letter and place it in the appropriate "car."

For a variation, if you can't find enough boxes, you can assign 2 or more letters per box.

OPENING A CAN OF WORMS

◁▷◁▷◁▷◁▷

The child will wiggle and giggle while learning about main ideas and supporting details.

Begin by wrapping a tin can (with a smooth edge) with construction paper and securing it with tape. Write the main idea of a familiar story on the outside of the tin can, turning the can around so the child will not see it. On each paper worm, write a supporting detail of the story, such as "The bear walked into the forest." Then place all the worms in the can. Explain that supporting details are pieces of information that work together to help tell the main idea. You may also want to discuss how each story has a beginning, a middle, and an end. Invite the child to pick worms from the can, read the sentences on them, and identify the main idea of the story.

What You'll Need
- empty tin can
- construction paper
- blunt scissors
- clear tape
- felt-tip pen
- worms made from construction paper or tagboard

The Bear Saw Lots of Animals

SENTENCE SPROUTS

◁▶◁▶◁▶◁▶◁▶◁▶

*Sentences are one of the fastest growing things on this planet.
You'll see why in this activity.*

Begin a story by saying a short phrase, such as "once upon a time" or "I know a person (or animal) named..." Then have the child write down the phrase and add the necessary words to complete the sentence. When the sentence is completed, offer another phrase. Continue the activity until both of you are satisfied with the ending.

What You'll Need
- paper
- pencil

IF/THEN CARDS

◁▶◁▶◁▶◁▶◁▶◁▶

*Challenge the child's thinking skills with this game of
cause-and-effect relationships.*

What You'll Need
- 10 index cards (3" × 5")
- blunt scissors
- markers
- basket

Cut 10 index cards in half. On one half of each card write the word *IF.* Write the word *THEN* on the other half of each card. Give the child all the sets of cards. Invite the child to write or draw pictures on each card, using the if/then formula. Suggest using ideas from a familiar story or rhyme. You may wish to create one set of cards for the child as an example, such as:

  "IF I jump in the puddle"
  "THEN I will get wet"

To play the game, have the child scramble all the cards, mixing the *IF*s with the *THEN*s, and put them all together in a basket. Challenge the child to match the top *IF* half of a card with its corresponding *THEN* half to show a complete, reasonable idea.

GLUE DROPS

⊲▸⊲▸⊲▸⊲▸⊲▸⊲▷

Turn glue blobs into unique individual thingamabobs!

The child can squeeze glue out into various large, odd-shaped globs on waxed paper. Put the waxed paper in a safe place to allow the glue to dry. (Depending on how big the glue blobs are, they can take up to a day or more to dry.) When dry, the child can decorate the blobs with markers. The hard, decorated blobs can then be easily removed from the paper. An adult can punch holes with a nail so the child can string the glue drops on yarn to make a necklace or a window hanging!

What You'll Need
- nontoxic white or colored glue
- waxed paper
- markers
- nail
- yarn

Activity Twist

For a colorful effect, try coloring the glue ahead of time by adding some food coloring. Then for more razzle-dazzle, sprinkle glitter on top of the wet glue globs and let dry. The child can then arrange these sparkly shapes on construction paper to create little imaginary scenes to describe.

PASTA MOSAIC

⊲▸⊲▸⊲▸⊲▸⊲▸⊲▷

You can never have too much pasta, right?
How many different kinds of pasta do you know?

What You'll Need
- index cards
- pen or pencil
- variety of dried pasta
- large piece of card-board or poster board
- glue

Choose a variety of words that relate to pasta. Some possibilities might be *sauce, cheese, tomato, spaghetti,* and *macaroni.* Write the words on index cards for the child to see. Invite the child to use the pasta to create the words, using different shapes, colors, and types to make the words look interesting. Experiment with the placement of the pasta on the cardboard before gluing it into place.

GELATIN ALPHABET

◁▷◁▷◁▷◁▷

Here's an activity that makes learning the alphabet easier to "digest."

In this game, children can learn their letters and eat them, too! Ask the child to help you make a gelatin dessert in any favorite flavor. Chill the gelatin in a long, flat pan. When it has solidified, use cookie cutters shaped like letters to make as many different letter shapes as possible. Use a spatula to pick up the letters and put them on a plate. Have the child name each letter before eating it.

What You'll Need
- gelatin dessert mix (and listed ingredients)
- flat pan
- letter cookie cutters
- spatula
- plate

Children with more advanced reading skills can arrange the letters to spell their names or another word before they eat the letters.

STEPPING INTO A STORY

◁▷◁▷◁▷◁▷

Become a character in your favorite tales!

What You'll Need
- favorite story or fairy tale
- paper
- pen or pencil

Read a favorite story or fairy tale with the child. Discuss the characters and events in the plot. Then challenge the child to put himself in the story and write a fairy tale of his own!

The child can replace one of the characters already in the story, or he can add himself as a totally new character. How will the story change as the child takes part in the action? How will the other characters react toward the child? Help the child come up with ways the child's character might affect the plot and the characters. Validate the child's ideas by writing them down in a new story. You might even want to add this story to the favorites that you read together.

CATEGORY CHALLENGE

◁▶◁▶◁▶◁▶◁▶

Sharpen your pencil and your wits for this word-category game.

What You'll Need
- paper
- pencil

Draw a grid on a piece of paper, 6 squares across and 4 squares down. Next, help the child choose 4 consonants and 1 vowel, and write them in squares 2 through 6 across the top. Think of categories, and list them down the left side. Start with only a few categories, and add more as the child gets used to the game. The object is for the child to come up with a word that begins with each letter in the top row and is part of the category listed on the side. Help the child to fill in and complete the game board. For a more challenging activity, give the child a designated amount of time (3-10 minutes) in which to complete the game.

	B	G	S	R	A
ANIMAL	bear	goat	snake	rat	ape
FOOD	banana		soup	radish	apple

WHO'S TALKING?

▷◁▷◁▷◁▷◁▷◁

In order to guess who's telling a story, the child will need to analyze information while listening.

Retell a story or folktale that both you and the child are familiar with. This time, however, pretend that you are one of the characters in the story as you are telling it. Don't tell which character you are, but tell the story from that character's point of view! Then challenge the child to guess which character is telling the story.

CLIFF-HANGER STORIES

▷◁▷◁▷◁▷◁▷◁

Promote story writing with this favorite form of story—the old-fashioned cliff-hanger.

Explain to the child what a cliff-hanger story is. If possible, rent some old movies that have cliff-hanger episodes, or share a story that leaves the reader wanting more at the end of each chapter. Help the child write a cliff-hanger story, with cliff-hangers at the end of each chapter. Write the cliff-hanger event on a piece of paper, and clip it to a hanger. See how long the child can keep the story going, cliff-hanger after cliff-hanger.

What You'll Need
- paper
- pencil
- hanger
- clothespins

GO FLY A KITE

◁◁▷◁▷◁▷◁▷

The child will enjoy practicing the ite *spelling pattern while flying a kite.*

What You'll Need
- paper kite
- paper
- markers
- stapler

Set out a paper kite. You may wish to make the kite from paper and wooden crossbars, or use a purchased model. Talk about kites with the child and explain how kites work with the wind to fly. Discuss the importance of the tail.

Then have the child write the word *kite* on the body of the kite. Point out the letters *ite* in the word, and explain that many other words are spelled with this pattern. Next have the child write other words that end with *ite* on pieces of paper, 1 word for each piece. Some *ite* words include: *bite, site, excite, invite, quite, recite, white,* and *polite*. Staple the paper pieces to the tail to make a high-flying kite. Then, if it's a windy day, go outside with the child and fly the kite together.

WHERE IS IT?

◁▶◁▶◁▶◁▶◁

*How many objects can you find in your home starting
with a particular letter of the alphabet?*

What You'll Need
• alphabet cards

An important step in learning to read is to be able to match a letter to its letter sound and to objects whose names have such sounds.

Hand the child an alphabet card (for example, the letter *D*). Ask him to look around the home for an object whose name begins with that letter (for example, a doll). Have the child say the letter and name the object to verify the match.

20 SECONDS

◁▶◁▶◁▶◁▶◁

The spotlight is on verb tenses in this memory-teasing activity.

What You'll Need
• several small items (buttons, pens, beads, spools of thread, etc.)
• tray

Play a memory game for the child to practice correct usage of the verbs *was* and *were*. Place 1 to 3 items on a tray directly in the child's view. Remove the tray from view after 20 seconds, and have the child describe what the objects looked like. Encourage the child to use the words *was* or *were* in the sentence.

Nuts and Bolts

In addition to nuts and bolts, what else can you find at a hardware store?

On your next trip to the hardware store, have the child accompany you and discover the various letters and letter sounds of the materials found there.

As you and the child stroll down the aisles of the store, stop and say, "I see something beginning with the letter *P*. What could it be?" (Answer: paint.) See how many different beginning letters you can find and name. Some items to look for are bolts, file, hammer, ladder, mailbox, nuts, rope, sandpaper, tacks, and wallpaper.

On your way home, talk about the many items that you saw at the hardware store and the different beginning-letter sounds of those things.

Animal Sounds

Who says animals can't talk? Listen carefully to what they are saying.

Exposing a child to the sounds that animals make is another way for him to be able to identify the sounds of different letters.

Make a sound that an animal makes, such as *moo*. Ask the child to tell you the first letter of that sound. Continue with other animal sounds, having the child identify the beginning letter of each one. Reverse roles. Other sounds you can use: *quack, tweet, meow, baa, hee-haw, woof.*

You can also sing "Old MacDonald Had a Farm" to reinforce the animal sounds. If you have any interactive books that have recorded animal sounds, you can play those with the child as well.

"Moooo"

LIKES & DISLIKES

◁▶◁▶◁▶◁▶◁

Create a collage chart to spark discussion of likes and dislikes.

Divide a large piece of paper in half, and label one side with a happy face and the other side with a sad face. The child can look through magazines for pictures of things she likes or doesn't like. The pictures can be cut or torn out and then glued onto the happy or sad side of the paper. The child can share the finished picture and tell about the things on each side and why she likes or dislikes each of them. For a simpler variation, look through a magazine together and take turns finding pictures of things that you each like or don't like and telling why. For added challenge, try looking for pictures in certain categories, such as foods, colors, weather, toys. Then, you can have fun discovering things about each other within the classifications. For instance, you may learn that you both like spaghetti but really dislike rainy days!

What You'll Need
- paper
- marker
- old magazines
- blunt scissors
- nontoxic white glue

Activity Twist

For added enjoyment, mount the pictures of things liked and disliked on index cards. Create a deck of cards with these. With markers, make happy and sad faces on paper plates. When a card is turned over with something you like (carrots), hold up the happy face. If you don't like what's on the card (spinach), hold up the sad face.

It's for the Birds!

◁▷◁▷◁▷◁▷

Make a bird feeder and watch the birds!

What You'll Need
- empty washed bleach bottle
- knife (to be used by adult)
- twine
- sticks
- glue
- birdseed

Caution: This project requires adult supervision.

Create a bird feeder by cutting holes in an empty washed bleach bottle or milk jug. Make 2 small holes at the top for twine to hang the bird feeder, 1 big hole in the middle for the bird to slip in and out, and several small holes around the bottom to insert twigs for perches. (Make sure the knife is used by an adult rather than by a child.) The child can find and collect the perch sticks, fit them into the holes, and glue them to make them secure. Fill the bottom of the container with birdseed, and hang the feeder in a tree. The child can watch the bird feeder and report observations. (Parents and child should clean out the feeder periodically to keep birds from getting sick.) For more challenge, the child can keep track of sightings, noting how many birds are seen at the feeder at different times during the day or at the same time on different days.

Simon Says

◁▷◁▷◁▷◁▷

Simon Says that children and adults alike will love this silly version of the popular game.

Remind players of the rules for Simon Says. Explain that you will play the game as it is normally played, with the following exception: The players should only follow a command if it begins with a *W* (or another target letter). For example, players can walk, wave, waddle, and wiggle but never hop, clap, or sing.

PAPER WEAVING

◁▶◁▶◁▶◁▶◁▶◁▷

Create woven art with colorful paper strips and a paper loom.

Make the paper loom with construction paper by cutting 8 parallel slits starting 1" from 1 edge of the paper and ending 1" from the opposite edge. Prepare the weaving strips by cutting strips of construction paper in different colors. The child can weave the strips over and under the rows on the paper loom. For a more decorative weaving, cut the weaving strips from a wallpaper sample book. (Many wallpaper stores will give away books that contain samples of discontinued papers.) To make the weaving more challenging (and to give it a pop art effect), cut curvy lines on the loom instead of straight ones.

What You'll Need
- construction paper
- blunt scissors
- ruler

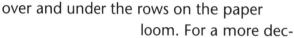

Activity Twist

Instead of weaving with paper, go on a scavenger hunt, and see what other intriguing materials you can find. Thick strands of bright yarn, fuzzy chenille stems, and satiny ribbon all provide for interesting textured weavings. For added excitement, you might wish to try fence weaving outdoors—manipulate sticks and tall dried grass through fence slats or chain links.

CHANGE IT!

◁▷◁▷◁▷◁▷

Sneaky things can happen in this alphabet memory game.

Memory games can help children develop the visualization skills essential to reading.

What You'll Need
• set of letter cards

Shuffle the cards, and lay down 3 cards in a row faceup. Have the child study the cards so that he will remember them. Ask the child to turn around. Then add 1 card or take 1 away. Ask him to turn back around and tell you what has changed. As the child becomes more adept at the game, make more complex changes, such as replacing 1 card with another.

TALL WALKING, ON SPONGES

◁▷◁▷◁▷◁▷

Walk like a robot!

What You'll Need
• 2 thick car-washing sponges
• string

Tie a sponge to the bottom of each of the child's feet, under the shoes, using the string. Have the child walk on the sponges. Model how the child should pick up her knees while walking so the sponges come off the ground. Encourage the child to "tall walk" by standing up straight (as opposed to bending over) when taking steps. Do this activity over a safe "fall zone" clear of furniture and with thick carpeting. This can also be done outside, but look for a place with soft grass cleared of rocks and other debris.

Activity Twist

Have fun walking other ways. Use your imagination! Walk as "tall" as you can (on tiptoes or with hands raised high in the air), or as "small" as you can (crawl or duck-walk). Try silly ways of walking, too. Pretend to be a spinning top or a giant dinosaur.

SAME SENTENCE STARTERS

◁▷◁▷◁▷◁▷

How many sentences can the child write that start with the same word?

Begin by choosing a word. Then invite the child to make up as many different sentences as possible that all start with the chosen word. By thinking of many possibilities, the child will be developing the skill of fluent thinking.

For example, if the word chosen is *dogs,* the child may suggest the following sentences:

Dogs like to run.

Dogs like to bark.

Dogs are the favorite animals in this family.

Dogs have fur and tails.

Dogs are sometimes walked on leashes.

DECORATING ME

◁▷◁▷◁▷◁▷

Put a painting on a face!

What You'll Need

- cornstarch
- water
- cold cream
- food coloring
- measuring spoons
- paper cups
- newspaper
- hand mirror
- shower cap
- smock
- cotton swabs

Make face paint together! Mix 1 teaspoon cornstarch, ½ teaspoon water, ½ teaspoon cold cream, and a drop of food coloring in a paper cup. Make several colors. Cover the table with plastic or newspaper. Set a hand mirror on a table. The child can put on a shower cap and smock and sit at the table along with the adult. Let the child use the cotton swabs to paint her face while looking in the mirror. For more creative fun, challenge the child to sing a song, tell a story, or put on a little act when all painted up! (Warn the child not to wipe the paint on clothing or other objects. Remove paint by using cold cream, soap, and water.)

INITIAL SANDWICHES

⊲⊳⊲⊳⊲⊳⊲⊳

Kids get to personalize these sandwiches in more ways than one.

What You'll Need
- bagel
- 2 slices of bread
- bread knife
- toppings (such as cream cheese, peanut butter, mustard, cut-up bits of ham, turkey, lettuce)

Teach a child his initials while preparing sandwich treats. Toast 2 bagel halves and 2 slices of bread. Cut each bagel half into quarters, then cut each slice of toast into 4 strips. Lay out the curves and strips along with toppings.

Ask the child to use bagel and toast pieces to form the initials of his first and last names on a paper plate. Let the child top each bread bit with various ingredients, and share a fun snack.

WHAT HAPPENED LAST?

⊲⊳⊲⊳⊲⊳⊲⊳

For fun and challenge, retell a story from the end to the beginning!

Invite the child to retell a favorite story, but to tell it backward, starting with the end first! The child tells the ending, then what happened just before that, and then just before that. Prompt the child with questions that help guide the storytelling back to the start . . . which is the end! To simplify the backward retelling, ask the child to tell the ending, 2 things that happen in the middle, and then the beginning.

Rhyme Time!

Sing a song of sixpence,
A pocket full of rye;
Four and twenty blackbirds
Baked in a pie!
When the pie was opened,
The birds began to sing;
Wasn't that a dainty dish
To set before the king?

RHYMING CIRCLES

Find some time to rhyme fun rhymes.

The child will be able to learn and review new rhyming words with this activity.

What You'll Need
- lightweight cardboard
- scissors
- marker or pen
- brad fastener

Cut a circle measuring approximately 8" in diameter from a sheet of lightweight cardboard. With a marker or pen, divide the circle into 8 equal segments, as if it were a pie. At the outer edge of the circle, write a different, frequently used consonant (for example, *S, P, T, C,* etc.) in each segment. Make 8 circles with 3" diameters. On each circle write 1 of the following letter pairs: *at, an, in, on, un, ap, op, ad.* Put a hole in the center of each circle. Place 1 of the smaller circles on top of the 8" circle. Connect the 2 circles with a brad fastener.

Have the child turn the big circle and line up the different consonants with the letter pair on the smaller circle. See what words can be created by doing this. Note, however, that not all of the combinations work. Point this out to the child. Try new centers for new words.

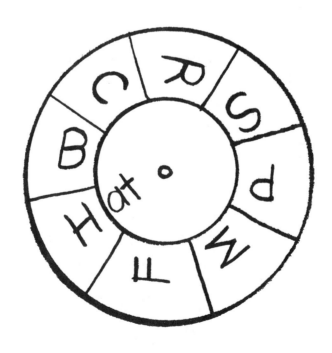

Go Fish

⊲⊳⊲⊳⊲⊳⊲⊳⊲⊳

Catch your favorite fish!

What You'll Need

- a 24" to 30" stick or dowel rod
- string
- tape measure
- 6" hook-side hook-and-loop-fabric fastener and ½ to 1 yard loop-side hook-and-loop-fabric fastener
- scissors
- needle
- thread
- fabric glue
- hula hoop
- marker (optional)

Have the child help tie 24" of string to 1 end of the stick. (Let the child help measure the length with a tape measure.) Cut and fold 6" of hook-side hook-and-loop-fabric fastener with the hook-side facing out, then sew the ends together. Have the child help tie the hook-side hook-and-loop-fabric fastener circle to the string on the stick. Use the pattern at right to make the fish, enlarging it if you wish. The child can help trace the fish onto the loop-side hook-and-loop-fabric fastener. Cut out 2 pieces of hook-and-loop-fabric fastener for each fish you wish to make. Glue the 2 sides together.

Place the fish on the floor (you can use a hula hoop on the floor for a lake). Have the child use the fishing pole to catch fish. Make the activity more challenging by writing numbers on the fish and/or making the fish different colors. This will add number recognition and color recognition to the game. The child can catch the red number 6 fish or the green number 2 fish.

Alphabet Quilt

◁ ▷ ◁ ▷ ◁ ▷ ◁ ▷

No sewing is necessary in this quilting bee.

Because making an alphabet quilt takes time, finishing one gives a child a real sense of accomplishment. Besides reinforcing letter recognition, this activity gives a child a strong introduction to two-dimensional letters.

Draw lines to divide 1 sheet of poster board into 30 squares. Then write the letter Q and the word *quilt* on a sheet of paper. Explain that a real quilt is made of cloth; display one if available, or find a picture of one in a book or magazine. Point out that quilts have interesting patterns that are sewn together.

Tell the child that he will make an alphabet pattern on paper that can be used to make a cloth quilt. On another poster board, draw and cut out a pattern for each letter of the alphabet, sized to fit inside the quilt squares. (Since the alphabet has only 26 letters, repeat any 4 letters to fill the extra squares.) Instruct the child to trace the letter patterns within the quilt squares and then color them. This can be an ongoing project if you do a few letters each day.

What You'll Need
- marker or pen
- 2 sheets of poster board
- sheet of paper
- blunt scissors
- crayons or colored pencils

Fun Fact
Hidden-camera studies have revealed that although "sibling rivalry" behaviors may be extremely intense when the parents are present, siblings tend to be far more friendly and play well together when they are alone with each other.

MAGNETIC MELODRAMA

◁▷◁▷◁▷◁▷◁▷◁▷

Use magnets to keep paper actors on the move!

The child can create a stage for paper actors by setting a piece of tagboard across 2 stacks of blocks or books. Next, the child can make the "actors" by folding back the bottom third of an index card and drawing a picture of a person, an animal, or an imaginary creature on the top portion. The child should then glue a paper clip to the bottom of the folded-back portion. When the glue is dry, the child can place all the actors on the stage and start making up stories about them. To enhance the storytelling, the child can pull a magnet underneath the tagboard stage to move the characters around.

What You'll Need
- tagboard
- books or blocks
- index cards
- crayons or markers
- glue
- paper clips
- magnets

For a melodramatic magnet variation, the child can make refrigerator magnet faces! You can find round magnets (approximately 1" across) at a hardware or hobby store. Cut circles the same size as the magnets out of tagboard or other stiff paper. The child can draw faces on the stiff paper with markers and then glue the faces to the magnets.

PEEKABOO WINDOWS

◁▷◁▷◁▷◁▷

Open windows of opportunity to practice beginning sounds.

In this activity, children create windows that they can open to identify the pictures inside and make their beginning sounds.

What You'll Need
• construction paper
• blunt scissors
• drawing paper
• marker or pen

Fold a sheet of construction paper in half, from top to bottom. On 1 half, draw 2 large squares. Cut 3 sides of each square and fold the paper back to form a flap. Fold a sheet of drawing paper in half, also from top to bottom. Make a "book" by folding the construction paper, flap side on top, over the drawing paper.

Mark the positions of the construction paper squares on the paper. Ask the child to draw a picture of an object in each square on the drawing paper. Put the construction paper cover back on the paper. Ask the child to open each flap and identify the object in each window, along with the object's beginning sound. Continue by creating new pages of pictures to put inside the construction paper cover.

VERSES AND MORE VERSES

◁▷◁▷◁▷◁▷

You don't have to be a trained singer to have fun with this singing and writing activity.

Sing a favorite song together, such as "Hush Little Baby," "Itsy Bitsy Spider," or "I Know an Old Woman Who Swallowed a Fly." Show and explain how new verses are sometimes written just for fun to be shared with others. Explain how

What You'll Need
• paper
• pencil

most simple songs rhyme, and discuss what a rhyme is. Then try creating some new verses, singing them together. Have the child write the new verses on a piece of paper. Encourage the child to share with others, inviting them to add verses to the song, too.

How Many Will Fit?

◁▷◁▷◁▷◁▷

1, 2, 3—how many can there be?

It's common to look at a group of items and estimate how many there are. Here's a backward way to estimate! Ask the child to look at a small container and a group of objects and estimate how many of the objects will fit inside the container! The child can then check the estimation by counting the objects while placing them inside. For easy estimating, use a small clear jar and objects large enough so that only 5 to 10 will fit inside. To increase the difficulty, use larger jars and smaller items!

What You'll Need
- small clear plastic jar
- multiples of various items, such as cotton balls, marbles, peanuts, pennies, or poker chips

Red, Yellow & Green

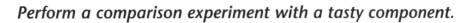

Perform a comparison experiment with a tasty component.

Caution: This project requires adult supervision.

Compare red, yellow, and green apples. Provide the apples, or visit a local market and pick them out together. Have everyone wash their hands, and be sure to wash the apples. Ask the child to compare their shapes. Then, cut the apples open and compare their insides. Invite the child to notice if the inside colors are also different or the same. Together, count the seeds of each apple. And finally, take a bite and talk about how the different apples taste. Encourage the child to use descriptive words, such as *tart, sweet,* and *crunchy.* For more challenge, the child can survey family members and find out which color apple is most popular.

What You'll Need
- red, yellow, and green apples
- plastic knife
- plate
- paper towels

TACTILE ALPHABET

◁▷◁▷◁▷◁▷

Make an alphabet book containing textured letters.

There are some things children can learn just by using their sense of touch. In this activity, the child will make a "tactile" alphabet book.

For each letter of the alphabet, write the capital and its matching lowercase letter on a sheet of construction paper. Make the letters reasonably large. Outline the letters in glue—spread wide is best. (Do 1 letter at a time so the glue will not dry before you can finish.) Help the child place any textured material that begins with the same letter (such as glitter for *G* or peanut shells for *P*) on the glue-outlined letters.

Additional suggestions for textured materials you can use for specific letters (feel free to use substitutes) are:

- apple seeds for the letter *A*
- buttons for the letter *B*
- cotton for *C*
- dots (left over from hole punch) for *D*
- eggshells for *E*
- feathers for *F*
- glitter for *G*
- hay for *H*
- ink for *I*
- "jewels" from old costume jewelry for *J*
- old keys for *K*
- lace for *L*
- magnetic strips for *M*
- nutshells for *N*
- oatmeal for *O*
- peanut shells for *P*

What You'll Need
- 26 sheets of construction paper
- marker
- glue
- textured materials found around the house (see below)
- hole punch
- O-rings

- quarters for *Q*
- rubber bands for *R*
- sand for *S*
- tape for *T*
- plastic utensils for *U*
- velvet for *V*
- wallpaper for *W*
- alphabet cereal *X*'s for *X*
- yarn for *Y*
- zippers for *Z*

When all 26 textured letters are made, punch holes on the left sides of each sheet of paper and connect the pages with O-rings. When the book is completed, ask the child to trace and feel the letters, name the letters, and then tell you what was used to make the letters. Help the child design a cover for the book.

Tongue Twisters!

Marvin Moose made many more messy mud pies.

Fifty-five funny farmers found forty-four fancy forks.

SHOPPING LIST

◁►◁►◁►◁►

Get ready for a trip to the store by making this shopping list.

What You'll Need
- food advertisements and circulars
- blunt scissors
- glue or clear tape
- paper

Many advertisements and circulars for food appear in newspapers. This is another source of both printed words and pictures that convey meanings.

Have the child cut out pictures of items that she would like to buy at the grocery store. Group the foods into categories (fruits, vegetables, meats, dairy products), then paste the pictures on a sheet of paper to form a visual shopping list. Go over the list with the child. How many *F* words are there? *V* words? *M* words? *D* words? Stress healthy foods when working on this project. Use this list for "Grocery Store Adventures" on the next page.

GROCERY STORE ADVENTURES

◁▷◁▷◁▷◁▷◁▷

Take this shopping list to the grocery store on your next visit.

What You'll Need
- grocery advertisements
- paper
- marker or pen

Turn grocery shopping into a learning experience with this activity.

Have the child make a shopping list from grocery circulars and advertisements. The child can do so by "reading" pictures and/or printed words and circling desired items. Help the child sound out and write down the names of the selected items.

On your next trip to the store, the child can shop for her items. As the item is found and placed in the cart, have the child cross it off the list. Emphasize the beginning sound of each item. Make sure the item selected is the same as the one on the list. The child will become more aware of categories of foods and will have to discriminate among the different brands of an item.

DISH-WASHING TIME

◁▷◁▷◁▷◁▷◁▷

*Discuss **D** words while you do the dishes.*

The child will learn all about the letter *D* in this kitchen activity.

Cut up a new kitchen sponge into strips about 1" wide. Help the child glue them onto construction paper to make three-dimensional versions of the letters *D* and *d*. Display the

What You'll Need
- new kitchen sponges
- blunt scissors
- glue
- construction paper
- dirty dishes

letters in the kitchen near the sink. Emphasize the *D* sound as the child helps you wash dishes. Discuss the

process using a variety of *D* words: *dirty dishes, draining, drying, dishwasher, dishrag,* and *dish towel.*

RECORDING STAR

◁▷◁▷◁▷◁▷

Every child will feel like a "star" hearing her own voice on a tape recorder.

Tape-recording helps reinforce recognition of beginning sounds by using the child's own voice.

Say a simple sentence that includes 2 words that begin alike. For example, "Mom put the jelly in the jar." Turn the tape recorder on, and have the child repeat the sentence, then say the 2 words that begin alike. Play the recording for the child. Then continue with new sentences.

ALPHABET OF YOU

◁▷◁▷◁▷◁▷

In this writing activity the child learns how to use adjectives in an alphabet poem.

Have the child begin by listing the letters of the alphabet. Talk about what an adjective is—a word that describes. Brainstorm a variety of positive adjectives that fit the child: *smart, curly-haired, inventive,* and so on. Have the child try to write 1 word for each letter of the alphabet. You may have to be inventive for *X: eXcellent* or *eXciting.* This is a great time to practice using a children's dictionary or pictionary to look for appropriate words. Repeat this process another time using a different topic.

Hink-Pink!

Q: What is a happy ending for a story about a lost dog?
A: The hound is found.

GREETING CARDS

⊲▶⊲▶⊲▶⊲▶⊲▶

Build an understanding of an author's purpose, audience, and main idea while creating a friendly greeting.

Discuss a list of greetings with the child, such as *hello, get well, congratulations, happy birthday,* and *I love you.* Invite the child to write a greeting on a piece of construction paper and decorate it with art scraps to make a card. Then have the child explain who the card is for (audience), why it was made (author's purpose), and what greeting was written (main idea). You may want to assist the child with addressing and stamping the envelope to mail.

What You'll Need
- colored construction paper
- felt-tip pens
- art and craft scraps
- glue
- envelope
- stamp

Activity Twist

For a fun twist, have the child describe the kind of greeting card she would enjoy receiving. Then have the child design and write it and then mail it to her own home!

WHAT KIND OF CAT IS THAT?

⊲▶⊲▶⊲▶⊲▶⊲▶

Fashion a family of felines from precut paper parts.

What You'll Need
- large index cards folded and cut as shown
- blunt scissors
- markers or crayons

Provide the child with precut cat bodies, heads, and tails as shown. The cat body should be cut from an index card folded in half so that the cat can stand upright. Cut a slit at the front end and back end of the top of the cat body for the head and tail. The child can decorate the cat's body, tail, and head.

Then the child puts a cat together by slipping a head and tail into slits at the front and back of the body. The child can make 1, 2, 3, or more cats, depending on interest. Invite the child to describe and tell about the finished cats.

SOUNDS AROUND

◁▶◁▶◁▶◁▶◁▶

Investigate sounds around by listening carefully with your eyes closed!

Start by playing a guessing game together. While the child's eyes are closed, the adult makes sounds with common items (shaking a key ring, flipping the pages of a book, tapping a spoon on the table). The child can guess what makes the sound and can also take a turn making sounds for the adult to guess. Then, to add challenge, the child can again close his eyes, this time listening to the sounds around. After sitting quietly for several minutes, the child can name everything he heard. This game can be played inside or outside. The child can also identify whether the sounds were made by people, animals, nature, or machines.

What You'll Need
• common household items: keys, book, spoon

ONE BOWL OF ICE CREAM, PLEASE!

◁▶◁▶◁▶◁▶◁▶

Mix up a simple recipe of ice cream for one!

What You'll Need
• ½ cup whipping cream
• 2 tablespoons powdered sugar
• ½ teaspoon vanilla
• measuring cups and spoons
• spoon
• cup
• plastic wrap

Wash hands before beginning! The child can measure the whipping cream, powdered sugar, and vanilla into a cup, stir the mixture with a spoon, cover it with plastic, and put it in the freezer. After a few hours the ice cream will be ready to eat!

I DID SPY

⊲▶⊲▶⊲▶⊲▶

Play a variation of the traditional "I Spy" game.

This game can be played indoors or out. Taking turns, one person starts by taking a look all around and then closing her eyes. The second person, with eyes open, asks questions about things in the room that the first person tries to answer while keeping her eyes closed. The questions are quick-take observation questions, such as: Is your blue sweater on the bed or the chair? How many books are on the table? What color is the towel that's hanging on the line?

READ TO ME

⊲▶⊲▶⊲▶⊲▶

For a change of pace, ask a child to read you a story.

What You'll Need
• children's picture books

Pretending to read helps children prepare to do the real thing.

Ask the child to read you a book. Read the title together. Then show the child how to turn the pages from the beginning to the end of the book. Encourage the child to tell you the story in the book by looking at the pictures. Ask her to find 2 words that look alike. Say the 2 words to the child, pointing out letters that are the same.

CIRCLE KITES

◁▶◁▶◁▶◁▶◁▶◁▶

Tell kids to go fly a kite—and learn about the letter K.

What You'll Need
- kraft paper
- blunt scissors
- ruler
- crayons
- tissue paper or crepe paper
- glue or clear tape
- string

This activity helps children become familiar with *K*, a rarely used beginning letter.

Cut a circle with a diameter of about 12" to 18" from the kraft paper. Ask the child to write the upper- and lowercase letter *K* on the paper circle then identify 3 things that begin with the *K* sound—for example, a kangaroo, key, and kettle.

Make 8 or 10 streamers, approximately 1" × 18", out of colorful tissue paper or crepe paper. Help the child glue or tape the ends of these streamers around the edge of the paper circle. Next, punch 2 small holes in the center of the kite, then put a string approximately 24" long through the holes, tying it so that the string is on the opposite side of the kite from the streamers. As the child runs outside, pulling the kite with the string, the streamers will float behind.

DRY & SPY

◁▷◁▷◁▷◁▷

Investigate evaporation!

What You'll Need
- variety of household materials (cotton ball, paper towel, sponge, fabric swatches, piece of cardboard)
- twine
- clothespins
- bowl
- water
- paper (optional)
- pencil (optional)

Gather together a variety of materials for testing, and set up a twine drying line. The child can soak each of the materials in a bowl of water and then clip each to the line with a clothespin. The child can make predictions about which things will dry first and last, and how long they will each take. The child can also test the drying time for the same item inside and outside—do the objects take the same time to dry inside and out? If not, which dries first, the outside item or the inside one? Are the results the same on a windy day as on a day with no wind? On a sunny day and a cloudy day? The child can observe the results and make conclusions about discoveries. For a greater challenge, the child can also chart the results.

SALT AND PEPPER

◁▷◁▷◁▷◁▷

Kids who practice this game can become seasoned players.

Children can learn letters by associating them with everyday items.

Make a deck of 20 construction-paper cards that has 10 cards of various colors plus 5 white cards and 5 black cards. Have both players use sheets of red paper to make scorecards, writing *S* in white crayon and *P* in black crayon at the top of the page.

What You'll Need
- construction paper (various colors, but including 1 sheet each of white, red, and black)
- scissors
- white and black crayons

Shuffle the 20 cards, and then take turns choosing one. Each player should write an *S* in the *S* (for *salt*) column in white when a white card is chosen or the letter *P* in the *P* (for *pepper*) column in black when a black card is chosen. Continue until 1 player has written 5 of either letter, going through the cards a second time if necessary.

POPCORN POETRY

◁▷◁▷◁▷◁▷

Popcorn Poetry is a contagiously funny way to review spelling patterns while writing poetry.

What You'll Need
- index cards
- markers
- construction paper

Invite the child to help you make word cards for words that are spelled with the spelling pattern *ot*, such as *not, hot, got, pot,* and *dot.* Then copy the poem shown here on construction paper, leaving the spaces blank. Place the word cards randomly next to each line in the poem. Have the child read the *ot* words in the order they are listed.

Using the cards, invite the child to select the words so the poem makes sense, and place the word cards next to the appropriate sentences. Let the child have the honor of reading the finished poem aloud.

Pop! Pop! Pop! Pop the corn into the _____. [hot]

Pop! Pop! Pop! Take and shake it 'til it's _____. [got]

Pop! Pop! Pop! Lift the lid. What have we _____? [pot]

Pop! Pop! Pop! POPCORN! That's what!

CARROT COINS

◁▷◁▷◁▷◁▷

Carrots are the coin of choice in this counting and beginning-sound activity.

Caution: This project requires adult supervision.

Children will enjoy pretending to buy things with carrot coins.

Make the coins by slicing carrots into thin, round slices. Ask the child to help you think of—and gather—household items whose names begin with the same sound as the word

What You'll Need
- carrots
- knife
- household items described below

carrot. For example, you might collect a cup, a can, corn, coffee, a toy car, a candle, and a camera. Have the child name the item she wishes to purchase. Give a price in carrot coins. Have the child count out the appropriate number of carrot coins.

LETTER LION

◁▷◁▷◁▷◁▷

Make friends with a lion that only eats letters.

Younger children will enjoy practicing beginning sounds by feeding a hungry lion.

On brown wrapping paper, draw a large lion's head. Cut a large round hole for a mouth. Put the lion's head on a box with a hole cut in the position of the lion's mouth. You might also hang the lion on a door. In order to feed the lion, the child must take a letter card, identify the letter, and say a word that begins with the sound the letter stands for. If the child gives correct answers, she drops the card into the lion's mouth.

What You'll Need
- large sheet of brown wrapping paper
- marker or pen
- blunt scissors
- box
- letter cards made from index cards

ICE CREAM CONE CAKES

◁▷◁▷◁▷◁▷

Here is a great treat for a child.

What You'll Need
- boxed cake mix (and listed ingredients)
- canned frosting
- sprinkles or other toppings (optional)
- flat-bottom ice cream cones
- hot pads
- cake pan
- mixer
- mixing bowl
- ladle

Instead of making cupcakes, try these ice cream cone cakes.

With the child's help, pick a boxed cake mix recipe, and assemble all the ingredients, measuring according to the directions. Have the child put the ingredients in a bowl and stir. As you beat the mixture with a mixer, the child can place flat-bottom ice cream cones on a baking sheet. Preheat your oven. Give the child a ladle and have her fill the ice cream cones not quite full with the mixed batter. Place the cones back on the baking pan. While the cakes are baking, decide on the frosting to be used and if any special toppings are desired when icing the cakes. Review with the child the sequence of making these cakes, and point out the long *I* sound that is heard in the words *ice cream* and *icing*.

PRINT MATCHING

◁▶◁▶◁▶◁▶◁▶

Match assorted objects to their telltale prints!

Caution: This project requires adult supervision.

Create an inkpad by setting the sponge in a shallow pan of paint. Press objects such as a large button, quarter, penny, key, comb, bottle cap, etc., into the sponge, and "print" each object on a separate card. Gather all the items together, and share the prints with the child. Challenge the child to match each item with its print. (Supervise the child—small objects can be choking hazards.) To continue the exploration, invite the child to make more prints!

What You'll Need
- sponge
- paint
- shallow pan
- index cards
- assorted objects (large button, coins, key, comb, bottle cap)

CHARACTER CHARADES

◁▶◁▶◁▶◁▶◁▶

The child will growl like a big wolf or scold like a mother hen while acting out favorite story characters.

After reading a favorite story together, invite the child to choose a character from the story to pantomime. Have the child focus on the character's actions, feelings, emotions, specific physical traits, and role within the story. Invite the child to use a particular scene from the story when pantomiming. Try to guess what character is being pantomimed.

WORD BY WORD

◁▶◁▶◁▶◁▶

Roll the dice, and see who reads the next part of the story!

Take turns reading aloud a short story with the child, sentence by sentence. A roll of the dice determines how many sentences each player will read per turn. Begin by rolling the dice to see who goes first—high roll wins. The first player rolls the dice to determine how many sentences she should read. The next player rolls the dice and reads the number of sentences that are shown on the dice, starting where the last player left off. This technique helps with vocabulary building, word recall, and patience!

What You'll Need
- dice
- short story

Activity Twist

For a challenging twist, try writing a story together, word by word. Roll the dice for each turn to determine how many words of the story a player must contribute.

WHAT KIND OF CREATURE ARE YOU?

◁▶◁▶◁▶◁▶

Imaginary creatures come to life while molding with modeling clay!

The child can use plasticine clay to create and invent creatures. Cover the work surface with aluminum foil or a plastic mat. The child can model and shape the clay into a creature and then use accessories to make impressions in the clay or for animal parts. Encourage the child to describe the animal. To make the activity more challenging, invite the child to talk about how the animal moves, what it likes to eat, where it lives, and other zoological details of its pretend existence.

What You'll Need
- plasticine clay
- aluminum foil or plastic mat
- toothpicks
- buttons
- yarn
- ribbon
- pebbles

TALL TALES

◁▶◁▶◁▶◁▶◁▶

Everyone loves to exaggerate and embellish stories,
especially when retelling tall tales.

Tall tales tell about American heroes who helped settle our country. They built the railroads, cleared the forests, and planted the apple trees. Some stories, such as "Johnny Appleseed," have developed from the lives of real people.

Read a few tall tales to the child. Discuss all the exaggerations and embellishments in the tales. Can Pecos Bill's horse, Widow Maker, really bounce to the sky? What is real and what isn't? Discuss what makes these tales "tall," and list them on a piece of paper. For an additional challenge, try writing a tall tale together.

 # OUTDOOR ART WALK

◁▶◁▶◁▶◁▶◁▶

Find everything from A to Z when you go outdoors and look carefully.

This activity takes the child outside of the home to find things that begin with different letters of the alphabet. Besides expanding the scope of the child's environment, it reinforces the idea that objects outside the home also have beginning sounds.

Bring a notepad on which you have written the alphabet, 1 letter per line, down the left side. Use as many pages as you need to complete the alphabet. As a certain object is identified by the child, have her tell you what the first letter of the word is. For example: *acorn = A; bird = B; vine = V; tree = T.* Write the object's name next to the corresponding letter on the notepad.

Note: If you can't find an *X* but still want to make use of the letter, put an *X* over every letter for which you find an object.

IMPROMPTU INTERVIEW

◁▷◁▷◁▷◁▷◁▷

Interview a child about the secret of his success!

What You'll Need
- clipboard
- paper
- pencil
- tape recorder
- blank tape

Pose as a journalist with a clipboard and a tape recorder. Ask the child questions about something he does well. The interview might center around a single achievement, such as making a playdough sculpture or learning to tumble upside down. Or it could center on a special area of interest or expertise, such as drawing pictures of bugs, singing, or running! Ask for background information as a journalist on a news story would, such as the child's age, what other kinds of things the child likes to do, what the child likes to eat for breakfast, etc. Ask about the specific reason for the interview, how the child became interested in it, prior experience, and the secret of the child's current success. Ask the child for any advice for others as well. Take notes and also tape-record the interview. When the interview is over, listen to the tape together. Ask the child if there is anything further that needs to be added to the story. If the story is complete, play it again for other family members to hear. The child can then answer any additional questions that come up.

 # OH WHERE? OH WHERE?

◇▷◁▷◁▷◁▷◁▷

Help find a lost pet with this vocabulary-building activity about descriptive words.

Sing the following familiar song with the child. For fun, invite the child to add body movements and sound effects, such as barking. Ask the child to describe what the dog looks like. Follow up by having the child change the words in the song to reflect another lost pet. Encourage the child to use descriptive words that may help others know what the lost pet looks like.

Oh where, oh where has my little dog gone?
Oh where, oh where can she be?
With her ears cut long and her tail cut short.
Oh where, oh where can she be?

WATCH A WATERWHEEL WORK

◁▷◁▷◁▷◁▷◁▷

Construct a waterwheel that works, and watch the water turn it around!

What You'll Need
- washed yogurt cup
- scissors
- plasticine clay
- 2 toothpicks

Cut strips of plastic from the side of a yogurt cup. The child can create a waterwheel by placing the plastic strips in a row around a ball of plasticine clay. Place toothpicks on either side of the ball. The child can then hold the waterwheel loosely by the toothpicks under a faucet of running water and watch the water make the ball spin around (toothpicks will turn as the waterwheel turns). The child can experiment further by changing the size and shape of the ball of clay, the distance between the paddles, the size of the paddles, how the water hits the paddles, etc.

DIAMOND POEM

◁▶◁▶◁▶◁▶◁▶◁▷

While composing this poem about a favorite pet, the child will use words that are real gems!

Invite the child to write a poem about a favorite pet. The poem should be in the shape of a diamond. Help the child write the poem by following these line-by-line instructions and writing the words described.

What You'll Need
• poster board
• markers

Line 1—Kind of pet

Line 2—2 adjectives that describe the pet's shape or size

Line 3—3 verbs that end with *ing* and tell what the pet does

Line 4—4 nouns that name what the pet likes

Line 5—3 verbs that end with *ing* and tell what the pet does, different than those in Line 3

Line 6—2 adjectives that describe the pet's personality

Line 7—Name of the pet

Invite the child to share the poem with you. Then look at the poem again with the child, pointing out the nouns. Look again for verbs and then for adjectives. You should find an abundance of each.

Hamster
tiny, chubby,
hiding, running, chewing,
carrots, lettuce, apples, oats,
gnawing, nibbling, squeaking,
sweet, shy
Furball

BE STILL AND SMELL

◁▶◁▶◁▶◁▶◁▶◁▶

With this little nose I smell...?

What You'll Need
- rubber cement
- stiff paper squares
- variety of spices (such as garlic, cinnamon, oregano)
- hole punch
- reclosable plastic bags

With your child, make spice cards by spreading rubber cement on a paper square and sprinkling it with a spice. Make 2 cards for each kind of spice. When the cards have dried, punch several holes in each one so fragrances will waft through for easy smelling when they're facedown. (Be sure the cement has dried before the child smells the cards.) Ask the child to turn all the cards facedown, mix them up, and try to match mates. Encourage him to pick the cards up and sniff them, keeping the cards facedown while doing so! For easier sorting, the child can turn over all the cards and use visual cues on them to help make the matches. Keep the spice cards in reclosable plastic bags, 1 kind of spice per bag, when they are not being used.

DON'T LOOK NOW

◁▷◁▷◁▷◁▷

Pin the tail on the...alphabet?

What You'll Need
- poster board or butcher paper
- marker
- tape
- scarf to be used as a blindfold

Here's a twist on an old party favorite, "Pin the Tail on the Donkey." Use a marker to print the letters of the alphabet in random order on the poster board or butcher paper. Tape this letter chart to the back of a door.

Cover the child's eyes with the scarf, and turn her around 2 or 3 times. Tell the child to locate and put a finger on the chart. Take off the blindfold, and have the child iden-

tify the letter she is touching. Repeat until several different letters have been identified.

TONG, TONG, TONGING

◁▷◁▷◁▷◁▷

See how quickly you can pick up objects using tongs.

If you have a dog, you may want to close it out of the room before beginning this activity. The dog may interpret the child's movement of the dog biscuits as teasing, which could be dangerous.

Before beginning, make sure to wash the double-sided dog dish thoroughly. Or, better yet, use a new, unused dog dish. Place a few of the objects (all the same kind) in 1 side of the dog dish. Have the child use the tongs to pick up the objects on 1 side of the dog dish and move them to the other side, one at a time. Then have the child move the objects back. Each time you get out the dog dish and tongs, choose a different object to move. As the child gets better at the activity, choose smaller objects to make it more difficult.

What You'll Need
- a double-sided dog dish
- tongs
- everyday objects: dog biscuits, large marbles, rocks, large buttons, leaves, paper clips

LETTER WINDOWS

Open your window and pull in a letter.

Children can improve their fine-motor coordination by helping cut and paste the pieces for this activity.

Have the child help you make a house by gluing a sheet of light-colored construction paper to the poster board. Make a triangular roof out of another sheet of construction paper and glue it on top of the house shape. Draw 3 rows of square windows on the house, with 3 windows in each row. From another sheet of construction paper, cut squares the size of the house windows plus a 1"×2" flap on top. Put glue on the flaps and glue 1 over each window. With a pencil, write a letter on each window (not each flap).

After the child has studied the letters on the windows, cover each 1 with its flap. Remove the letter cards for the 9 letters you wrote on the windows, and shuffle the 9 cards. Have the child pick a card and then try to choose the window with the matching letter. If the child chooses correctly, she puts the letter card aside. If not, the child puts the card at the bottom of the card pile and goes on to the next letter card. Continue until all the letters have been correctly chosen. To play again, erase the letters on the windows, and write new ones.

MAGAZINE PICTURE PUPPETS

◁▶◁▶◁▶◁▶

These simple puppets offer an easy way to engage the child in language expression and development.

Begin by helping the child cut out pictures of people and animals from old magazines. Glue the pictures to cardboard for sturdy backing, and cut around the picture shape. Next, glue a craft stick to the back of the cardboard. The craft stick will be the puppet's handle. When the glue on the picture puppets is dry, the child can use them to act out and tell made-up stories.

What You'll Need
- old magazines
- cardboard
- blunt scissors
- glue
- craft sticks

BAG IT!

◁▶◁▶◁▶◁▶

The child will "Bag It!" while learning about vowel sounds.

What You'll Need
- 5 paper bags with handles
- marker
- small common household items

Write the vowels—*A, E, I, O,* and *U*—on each bag. Find a small household item with one of the vowel sounds in its name, and place it inside the corresponding bag. Then place the bag on the back of a child's chair. Invite the child to find another item with the same vowel sound and place it in the corresponding bag. Now it's your turn to find an item with a different vowel sound and place it inside the corresponding bag. Continue taking turns placing items in the bags until all vowel sounds have been used.

PLASTIC GROCERY-SACK KITE

◁▷◁▷◁▷◁▷

Let's go fly a kite!

Caution: This project requires adult supervision.

What You'll Need
• plastic grocery sack
• string

Bring together the 2 handles of the plastic grocery sack, and tie them together with a long piece of string. Leave 3 feet of string tied to the handles. Tie a large loop on the other end of the string for the child to hold while flying the kite. Have the child take the kite outdoors and run while holding the string close to the bag handle. As the bag fills with air, the child can slide her hand down the string to the loop end. Grocery bags make terrific kites, and when one tears, you can just tie on a new one! But be careful—plastic bags can be a suffocation hazard.

Activity Twist

Try out some other kite designs, and see which ones work best. Cut shapes out of large pieces of heavy construction paper (diamond, heart, gingerbread man). Or, use a brown paper lunch bag. Then, decorate a paper plate with taped crepe-paper streamers. Staple 3 feet of string to these experimental kites, and try them out!

SHAPE WIND CHIMES

<⊳<⊳<⊳<⊳<⊳<⊳

Listen to the wind when it blows these "chimes."

What You'll Need
- clay
- waxed paper
- rolling pin
- plastic knife
- pencil
- string
- 6" dowel rod or stick

Small hand muscles will be used as the child kneads and squeezes clay to make it pliable.

Give the child a ball of clay to knead and soften. As she is squeezing and "working" the clay (on a piece of waxed paper), ask her, "How does it feel, and what shape does it have?" Look around the room and find other shapes—for example, a rectangle, a square, a triangle, and a diamond. Talk about them and identify their beginning letter sounds (the letter *R* for *rectangle,* *S* for *square,* and so on).

When the clay is softened, have the child roll it with a rolling pin to make it flat. Help her cut out shapes from the clay with a plastic knife. Give directions as follows: "Make a shape that begins with an *R.*" Continue with the other beginning letters (*S, T, D*) to create different shapes.

Carefully lift the clay shapes, and put them on another sheet of waxed paper. Using a pencil, make a hole at the top of each shape. When the clay is thoroughly dry, ask the child to help you tie 1 end of string to each shape (through each hole) and the other end of the string to a stick or dowel rod. Tie another piece of string to the rod so the shapes can be hung as wind "chimes."

As you and the child are hanging these chimes where the wind can blow them, ask her to name the *W* word that causes the chimes to make sounds. (Answer: *wind.*) Review the beginning sounds of the suspended shapes.

WHAT IS IT?

◁▷◁▷◁▷◁▷

*Increase vocabulary and strengthen listening skills by playing
this descriptive word game.*

Describe a familiar person, place, animal, or object using only single descriptive words—no sentences. List 4 or 5 descriptive words that relate to the item, and then challenge the child to guess what it is. If you were thinking of a pet rabbit, for example, you may describe it as "furry, white, soft, small, and friendly."

Once the child has guessed what the object is, encourage the child to create a sentence using the name of the object and as many of the descriptive words as possible.

"I REMEMBER" POEM

◁▷◁▷◁▷◁▷

*This activity is perfect for sharing an unforgettable memory
with a favorite relative or friend.*

When a special occasion is approaching, such as a birthday, Mother's Day, or Father's Day, have the child think of all the memories she can recall about time shared with the person to be celebrated. Invite the child to write down a word or two about

What You'll Need
• paper
• pencil or markers

each memory. Then have the child create a series of sentences. Most of the sentences should begin with "I remember..." Arrange the sentences into a poem.

I remember when I loved to read in my dad's office.

I remember that there was just enough room between his bookshelves for me to curl up.

I remember that it was always quiet there.

But most of all

I remember that the heater kept me warm!

Activity Twist

Suggest that the child write other poems following this format. You might use sentences beginning, "I love...", "I wish...", "I'm happy when...", or other combinations.

PRETTY PASTA PATTERNS

◁▶◁▶◁▶◁▶◁▶

Make radiant rainbow necklaces from colored pasta pieces.

What You'll Need
- assorted pasta with holes
- plastic self-sealing bags
- food coloring
- rubbing alcohol
- aluminum foil
- yarn
- masking tape
- construction paper (optional)
- cardboard (optional)
- nontoxic white glue (optional)

Caution: This project requires adult supervision.

The child can help color the pasta and then use it to make patterned necklaces and decorations. Invite the child to place a handful of uncooked pasta in a plastic bag and add a few drops of food coloring. The adult adds a small amount of rubbing alcohol. (The alcohol will help create brilliant colors and will also help the pasta dry evenly.) Seal the bag and ask the child to shake it so all the pasta pieces get colored. Spread the pasta out on aluminum foil to dry. Make several different colors of each of the pasta shapes. When all the pasta has dried, the child can create necklaces or decorations by stringing the colored pasta in different patterns on the yarn. (Wrap the end of the piece of yarn with masking tape to make stringing easier.) For a variation, the child can make patterned pictures by gluing the colored pasta in pattern rows on construction paper. The child can also create exciting pasta mosaics by gluing pasta designs on cardboard.

TONGUE-TWISTER TIME

◁▷◁▷◁▷◁▷

Kids are never too tired to tell tall tongue-twister tales.

Many children have tried the tongue twister "Peter Piper picked a peck of pickled peppers." In this activity, let the child have fun with alliteration and develop a new tongue twister.

It can be challenging to think of a sentence (or phrase) with words that all have the same beginning sound. ABC books, poetry books, and picture books that focus on alliteration can be read to the child. This is an enjoyable exercise and serves as a model.

After the child has developed her own tongue twister, see how fast it can be said by both the child and you. Then, test it with the rest of the family.

> **What You'll Need**
> • pencil
> • paper

She sells seashells by the seashore.

Peter Piper picked a peck of pickled peppers!

SHOE SOCK SHOE SOCK SHOE SOCK

◁▷◁▷◁▷◁▷

Lay out a pattern for all to see!

Invite the child to create patterns using household items. Make suggestions about items you can use to make the patterns; encourage the child to think up what else could be used for this activity. Patterns can be made with shoes and socks across the living room floor, spoons and forks around the kitchen table, or hats and mittens on a bed. To increase the challenge, the child can make three-part patterns.

> **What You'll Need**
> • household items: shoes and socks, spoons and forks, hats and mittens

Activity Twist

Be pattern detectives on a walk through your neighborhood! You can find patterns everywhere—in the bricks of houses, in flower beds, on people's clothing, in the windows of stores. See who can identify the most patterns! This is also a great game to play in the car or in a restaurant.

WATER MELODIES

◁▷◁▷◁▷◁▷

Be the composer of your own "water music"!

What You'll Need
- glasses and glass jars
- plastic tub
- water pitcher and water
- spoon

Here's a simple way to create pretty sounds. Help the child place glasses and glass jars in a plastic tub and fill them with different amounts of water. The child can then gently tap the glasses with a spoon to make sounds. The sound of each jar or glass can be modified either by adding more water from the water pitcher or by removing some water from the containers. Encourage the child to explore altering the sound of each "instrument" as well as creating her own tunes. To make this more difficult, ask the child to place the glasses in order from the highest pitch to the lowest, according to the sound scale. If the glasses are different sizes and shapes, the child will need to rely on listening skills in order to complete this task. To simplify, use fewer glasses that are all of the same size and shape. For an added challenge, ask the child to figure out how much water to add to 2 differently shaped glasses in order to get the same sound when each one is tapped.

LEGACY

◁▷◁▷◁▷◁▷◁▷

Passing a legacy on to a friend or sibling can be a memorable and loving gift.

Explain to the child that a legacy is something that is passed on from person to person. It need not be money but could be a favorite book, a beloved toy, or something that you had painted, drawn, or written. At an appropriate time (birthday or New Year's Eve) have the child create a legacy for a sibling or friend. Share the legacy with the recipient.

WHAT'S THE QUESTION?

◁▷◁▷◁▷◁▷◁▷

Reveal the answer, and guess the question!

Turn questioning and answering backward, and make it into a game. Take turns making up and reporting "answers" to each other. After one person makes up an answer, the other person comes up with a question for which the answer given could be true. To make the game more challenging, try coming up with 3 different questions for which the answer could be true! To simplify, choose answers that the child commonly uses in replying to questions, such as the child's name, the child's age, or "fine."

Lights, Camera, Action!

◁▶◁▶◁▶◁▶◁▶◁▶

While taking part in dramatizing a favorite story,
the child will focus on story comprehension.

What You'll Need
- hats
- masks
- costume props

Begin by choosing a favorite story together that has lots of action. Then act the story out with the child, or invite the child to play all the parts in the story. Use hats, masks, or simple costume props such as scarves and oversize shirts to depict the different characters.

Match Me

◁▶◁▶◁▶◁▶◁▶◁▶

Try the magazine letter challenge. Locate lowercase letters
to match capital letters.

A subscription to a children's magazine can be very exciting for a child. She may come to anticipate each issue and the opportunity to learn new things. Save back issues of any children's magazines that you purchase or subscribe to. Ask the child to find a lowercase letter in the magazine that

What You'll Need
- several children's magazines
- alphabet cards (capital letters)
- blunt scissors

matches each capital letter on the alphabet cards, which you randomly present to her one card at a time. As each letter is found in the magazine, the child cuts it out and places it on the letter card next to its corresponding capital.

LITTER PATROL

◁▶◁▶◁▶◁▶

Kids can be good citizens while they learn about the letter L.

Children can spruce up the neighborhood and learn the letter *L* at the same time.

Make a litter collector by cutting the top off an empty cereal box. Punch a hole in each side of the box near the top, then put the yarn or cord through the holes. Tie the 2 ends together to form a loop.

On a piece of felt, draw a two-dimensional capital letter *L*. Cut out the letter and paste it on the litter collector. Explain to the child that *L* stands for the word *litter*.

As you walk through the neighborhood or a park, have the child put on gardening gloves and pick up paper, wrappers, and other litter that you find along the way, putting them in the litter collector. Dispose of this in a proper container to show the child where litter belongs.

What You'll Need
- empty cereal box
- blunt scissors
- hole punch
- yarn or cord
- piece of felt
- paste
- marker or pen
- gardening gloves

BEGINNING, MIDDLE, OR END?

◁▶◁▶◁▶◁▶

Like the best stories, most words have a beginning, a middle, and an end.

What You'll Need
- piece of poster board
- blunt scissors
- tape measure
- marker or pen
- letter cards

In this activity, children who have mastered beginning sounds can practice listening for letter sounds in other parts of a word.

Cut a piece of poster board approximately 18"×6". Divide it into 3 sections. Choose a letter card. Say some words that have that letter at the beginning, middle, and end. For example, for the letter *S*, you might slowly say the words *syrup, messy,* and *bus.* Have the child place the letter card on the beginning, middle, or end section of the letter strip to indicate the *S* sound's position in each word. Select a new letter, and repeat the activity.

FOLDING ALPHABET

◁▷◁▷◁▷◁▷

Folding fans is a fabulous way to form flexible fingers.

What You'll Need
- blunt scissors
- construction paper of various colors
- large piece of poster board
- glue

Working with colorful strips of paper can make learning letter shapes a lot more fun.

Cut construction paper into 10 strips measuring approximately 1"×12" and 10 strips measuring approximately 1"×6". Use a variety of different paper colors. Show the child how to fold the strips like a fan, making folds about 1" apart.

After the child has folded several strips of each size, have her arrange them in the shape of letters on the poster board. The child may make random letters, specific names, or begin the alphabet. The strips can be attached to the poster board with a few spots of glue. Cut more strips if the child wants to make the whole alphabet.

THIRD-PERSON TALES

◁▷◁▷◁▷◁▷

This activity stretches the child's ability to relay experiences from a new perspective.

Invite the child to tell you about an event in his day. Explain that you want the child to tell it to you in the third person—in other words, the child should tell about an event that happened to him during the day as if it happened to someone else.

For example, instead of the child saying "I got up early today," the child would begin by saying "He got up early today."

UPPITY UPPITY

◁▶◁▶◁▶◁▶◁▷

Play Uppity Uppity—don't let the balloon touch the ground!

Caution: This project requires adult supervision.

Blow up 2 balloons ¾ full—this will make accidental popping less likely. (Always supervise young children around balloons!) In this game, the adult and child each get 1 balloon, and they must keep their own balloon in the air as long as possible. For a variation, make balloon rackets to bat the balloon back and forth. For a racket, bend a wire coat hanger into a diamond shape, and straighten out the hook. Pull an old nylon stocking over the diamond, wrap the end of the stocking around the straightened hook, and tape it in place.

What You'll Need
- balloons
- wire hangers (optional)
- pliers (optional)
- old nylon stocking (optional)
- masking tape (optional)

REFRIGERATOR WRITING

◁▶◁▶◁▶◁▶◁▷

The refrigerator is not just for keeping things cool. Use it to encourage writing, too.

What You'll Need
- magnetic letters or word sets
- notebook
- pencil

Fill the front of the refrigerator with the magnetic letters or words. Create some simple words on the refrigerator for the child to read, and then copy them in a notebook. Then

encourage the child to create words. Have the child copy these words in the same notebook. Invite the child to form sentences with words created. Use this as a time to reinforce spelling skills, as well.

SHOE SOLE WORD

◁▷◁▷◁▷◁▷

By matching these shoe soles, the child will practice "stepping into" words.

What You'll Need
- heavy paper precut in shoe-sole shapes
- felt-tip pen
- list of spelling words
- several pairs of shoes

On pairs of precut paper soles, write words such as *man, car,* and *door*—the same word on each half of the pair. Place 1 "sole" of each word inside 1 shoe from each pair so that the card stands on end and the word is clearly visible. Set out

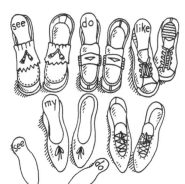

the remaining soles, and invite the child to place them in the empty shoe of the pair that matches the one with the same word.

LOOK! A BOOK!

◁▷◁▷◁▷◁▷

Add to a private library by making a personal book!

What You'll Need
- construction paper
- blunt scissors
- hole punch
- chenille stems
- markers

Cut construction paper into equal-size squares. Ask the child to count out 5 sheets of paper and punch a hole in the corner of each of the squares. Then the child can loop a chenille stem through the holes and twist the ends. Another way to fasten the books is to punch several holes along one edge and weave a chenille stem through the holes.

The child can draw a story in the book and share it. Make blank books ahead of time for just the right moment—when the author is ready to write or draw!

For a fun variation, create blank books with different shapes. Cut out pages into apple, animal, or house shapes that can be combined into a book.

Young authors can create stories to fit the different shapes.

FUN FOLDERS

◁▷◁▷◁▷◁▷

Make a collage of items that begin with the letter F.

What You'll Need
• file folders
• marker or pen
• old magazines
• blunt scissors
• glue or clear tape

A file folder makes an excellent organizer for pictures illustrating beginning sounds.

Print the letters *Ff* on the front of a folder. Have the child look through magazines for pictures of objects whose names begin with the letter *F.* Cut out the pictures and arrange them in an

interesting layout across the middle of the opened folder. Glue or tape the pictures in place. You can make additional folders for other letters of the alphabet.

MORE TASTING AND TELLING

◁▷◁▷◁▷◁▷

Taste some more, and tell about more than taste!

Have everyone wash hands first! Gather several different kinds of bread together to taste and compare. The child can look, touch, and taste each kind of bread. Invite the child to share observations about the size, shape, color, and texture of the different breads.

What You'll Need
• variety of breads (whole wheat, corn tortilla, bagel, croissant, challah)

How are they the same? How are they different? Encourage the child to describe the taste of each of the breads using descriptive words, such as *sweet, chewy, dry,* or *soft.* To explore breads further, go on a shopping excursion to the market or bakery, and choose a new kind of bread together to buy and try!

SUIT UP FOR OUTER SPACE!

◁▷◁▷◁▷◁▷

Turn paper bags into space suits, and take off!

What You'll Need
- large brown paper bags
- masking tape
- blunt scissors
- markers
- thick yarn (optional)

The child can create space shoes by putting a large paper bag over each shoe and crumpling up the ends to make them snug on the ankles. Tape the shoes at the ankles with masking tape. For space sleeves, cut the bottoms out of 2 large bags. Crumple the bags and tape at the wrists and upper arms. For a helmet, cut a large window out of a bag and place it over the child's head. The child can decorate the space suit before it is donned. To make the suit reusable, substitute thick pieces of yarn for the masking tape. To extend the space play, provide a space snack for the child: Pour juice into a plastic bag, insert a straw, and seal snugly with a twist tie.

 # NAME THAT CARD

◁▷◁▷◁▷◁▷

*Playing cards aren't just for playing.
They can also be used to teach beginning sounds.*

In this game, children can learn the basics of playing card games as they work on beginning sounds.

Shuffle the cards. Show the child 1 card at a time, and say its number or name (jack, queen, king, ace). Have the child say a word that has the same beginning sound. If the answer is correct, give the child the card. Continue until the child has won several cards. As the child learns the names of the cards, he can say the name of each card as well as a word with the same beginning sound.

What You'll Need
- deck of playing cards

A Gorgeous Gift

<◁ ▷ ◁ ▷ ◁ ▷ ◁▷

A surprise awaits you when you open this gorgeous gift.

What You'll Need
- box
- ribbon
- gift item that begins with the letter G

People enjoy giving gifts almost as much as they enjoy receiving them. This activity lets the child select a gift to give to you, making the exercise an educational experience as well.

Give the child a box. Ask him to search in or around the home for a special item that begins with the letter G to serve as a gift for you (for example, gloves, golf balls, a game, grapes, etc.). Ask the child to put the object in the box without telling or showing you what it is. Have the child use ribbon to tie around the box (if he knows how to do so). When the child gives you the gift, he must provide you with clues (for example, "you use this outside") until you are able to guess what it is. After you guess what the item is, open it, then review all the G words talked about in this activity (*gift, give, guess,* etc.).

SYLLA-BALL

◁▶◁▶◁▶◁▶

The child will roll with laughter while playing this build-a-syllable, word-making game.

What You'll Need
• softball

Begin the game by sitting on the floor facing each other. Start by saying the first syllable of a familiar word, such as *mon,* while rolling the ball to the child. Once the child catches the ball, he must repeat the first syllable and quickly add the second syllable, such as *ster,* to make *monster.* If the child finishes the word, 1 point is given. Play continues until the child reaches 10 points.

BANANA BOATS

◁▶◁▶◁▶◁▶◁▶

*Kids can navigate the beginning **B** sound with these yummy snacks.*

Children can have fun helping with each step of this fun and simple recipe, which includes a review of *B* words.

First, spread peanut butter on a slice of bread. Slice a banana lengthwise, and place one half in the center of the bread. Fold the sides of the bread up to make a boat. Fasten the boat by poking 3 or 4 pretzel sticks through both sides of the bread on top. Have the child name words that begin like *banana boat.* Then dig in!

What You'll Need
• white bread
• peanut butter
• banana
• pretzel sticks
• butter knife

COUNTING ALONG

◁▶◁▶◁▶◁▶

In this activity the child will combine counting with reading and writing.

Read and compare a variety of counting books together. Discuss what goes into a good counting book. Are accurate illustrations important? Does a story make the counting book more interesting? Plan to make a counting book together. You may choose to make a book that goes from 1 to 20 or one that counts by 5's to 100. Then on each page of the new book, write the words and numerals. Invite the child to illustrate the book, too.

What You'll Need
• several counting books
• paper
• pencil
• crayons or markers

READ THE LABEL

◁▶◁▶◁▶◁▶

Take a closer look at the words that are part of our everyday life.

In this activity, children learn to recognize the words that name objects they see every day.

Make word cards with the names of objects in a room. For example, in the kitchen, you might write the words *chair, table, sink, floor, stove, window.* Help

What You'll Need
• index cards
• marker or pen
• tape

the child match each card with the object it names, and tape the card to the object. Have the child walk around the room and "read" the label on each object. Try other rooms, such as the bedroom (*bed, desk, lamp, closet*) and living room (*couch, chair, TV, shelf*).

MY MAGIC SEED

◁▷◁▷◁▷◁▷

Plant an imaginary picture seed, and water it with words!

What You'll Need
- story about a magic seed
- paper
- lima bean
- nontoxic white glue
- crayons

Read a story together that is about a magic seed or about any kind of seed planting ("Jack and the Beanstalk" is a good choice). Then give the child a piece of paper that has a lima bean glued at the bottom. Tell the child that the bean on the paper is a magic seed that can grow into anything. Explain that the way the seed grows is by drawing. Invite the child to draw a picture that shows what the seed grows into and to tell a story about it. For a simpler variation, after reading a story about seed growth, invite the child to curl up into a small seed and dramatize the seed's growth into a plant. Add music to further inspire plant growth!

Do Birds Make Birds' Nests Best?

◁▷◁▷◁▷◁▷◁▷

Take a bird-nest test, and try to build a better bird's nest!

What You'll Need
- twigs
- leaves
- yarn
- cotton
- feathers
- string
- grass and weeds
- dirt
- water
- modeling clay (optional)

Gather together common items that birds use to build nests. Challenge the child to use the materials to create a bird's nest. The child can mold the items and try gluing them together using mud! The child might also enjoy making a bird out of modeling clay to sit in the hand-made bird's nest!

Two of a Kind

◁▷◁▷◁▷◁▷◁▷

Have you noticed that the letter B looks like 2 bumps on a stick?

What You'll Need
- paper
- pen

Here's a simple activity that helps children practice seeing likenesses and differences between letters but does not require letter identification.

Write a row of letters on a sheet of paper. For example: *C, E, C, D*. Point to each letter, and ask the child to describe it. When you point to the letter *C*, the child might say, "It looks like a circle with an opening." Then have the child point to the 2 letters that are the same.

FINGER FUN

◁▷◁▷◁▷◁▷

Pointing to pictures helps kids practice their letter sounds.

Play a picture game to help children learn the beginning sound of the letter *F*.

Using pictures cut from old magazines, make several picture cards that show objects whose names begin the same as the word *finger,* such as *fence, fox, fish,* and *fountain.* Make additional picture cards using objects that begin with other letters of the alphabet, such as a *cat, toaster, bicycle,* and so on. Mix the cards.

Point to a picture with your finger. If the picture name begins like the word *finger,* the child should say, "You put your finger on a _____," naming the pictured item. If the picture name does not begin like *finger,* the child should say, "No fingers here."

CHARTING THE WEATHER

◁▷◁▷◁▷◁▷

Keep track of the weather with a weather chart!

Make a chart for recording the weather. Use a long strip of paper, and mark off squares. The child can keep track of the weather by observing what is happening outside each day and then drawing a symbol in that day's square for sunny, rainy, cloudy, or snowy

or pasting a weather picture or sticker on the chart. For more challenge, the child can record the weather for a month and then count up and compare how many of each kinds of weather days there were in that month.

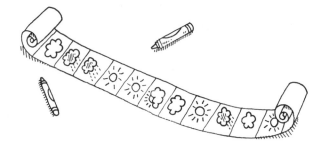

STORY CHORUS

◁▶◁▶◁▶◁▶◁▷

Creating sound effects to represent a story character is a wonderful way to engage the child in a favorite story.

What You'll Need
- favorite book or story
- sound-makers (key chain, whistle, jar of beans, musical instrument, etc.)

Begin by helping the child choose a story that has several major characters. Invite the child to choose a sound-maker for each one of the characters. The sound-makers may include musical instruments, a jar of beans, a whistle, or even a stomping foot. After each character's sound has been determined, read the story to the child. Each time the name of a particular character is mentioned, the child should make the appropriate sound.

FLIP-FLOP WORDS

◁▶◁▶◁▶◁▶◁▷

The child will flip over this spelling puzzler!

Did you know that some words, when spelled backward, spell another word? Try it and see. Begin by having the child spell *top*. Then invite the child to write the word again with the last letter first and the first letter last. What word did it spell? (*pot*) Try it again with *bus* (*sub*), and *pan* (*nap*). Continue by searching for new flip-flop words. Use a children's dictionary, if necessary.

BERRY DELICIOUS

◁▷◁▷◁▷◁▷

Here's a science, phonics, and nutrition lesson—all in one small cube.

What You'll Need
- berries (blueberries, rasp-berries, or strawberries)
- ice-cube tray
- water or juice

Children will be fascinated by berries frozen in ice cubes in this beginning-sound activity.

Pour water or fruit juice into an ice-cube tray. Have the child drop a blueberry, raspberry, or cut-up strawberry into each ice-cube section. Freeze the tray. When the treats are frozen, the child can put them into a drink. Have the child explain how the ice cubes were made and then think of words that begin or sound like the word *berry*.

GO, TINY TOE BALL, GO

◁▷◁▷◁▷◁▷

Make a tiny table-tennis ball go using only a toe!

What You'll Need
- table-tennis ball

With shoes, socks, or bare feet (all to different effect!) the child uses only toes to get a table-tennis ball to go just where it's supposed to go. The goal can be an easy one, such as to get the ball from one side of the room to the other. Increase the challenge by creating an obstacle course with a goal box at the end. The child can experiment with ways to get the ball to move using only toes. The ball can be kicked, tapped gently, or rolled along.

OCEAN IN A BOTTLE

◁▶◁▶◁▶◁▶

Make an ocean, and watch the waves tumble and twirl.

Caution: This project requires adult supervision.

The child can use a funnel to carefully fill a clean, clear, empty plastic bottle approximately ⅓ full with salad oil. The child can then use the sink or a plastic pitcher to add water almost to the top. Have the child add a few drops of food coloring. Glitter and fish charms can also be included to make the ocean more lively! Screw the top on and tightly secure it (adult can add some superglue so the ocean won't accidentally overflow). Now the ocean is ready to roll! The child can place the bottle on its side and gently roll it back and forth to watch the waves form and dance.

What You'll Need
- clear plastic bottle
- funnel
- salad oil
- water
- food coloring
- superglue
- plastic pitcher (optional)
- glitter (optional)
- fish charms (optional)

MUSEUM DISPLAY

◁▷◁▷◁▷◁▷

Here's an activity that lets the child create a mini-museum while learning about nouns.

Discuss the art, science, or history museums you or the child have visited and the kinds of things you each saw there. Also explain to the child that a noun is a word that names a person, place, or thing. Then help the child create a museum display of nouns by labeling exhibit areas as "People," "Places," and "Things." You may want to use empty shelves in a bookcase as your display area. Other good display areas include windowsills, cardboard boxes, and tabletops.

What You'll Need
• heavy paper
• markers
• 3 shelves or tables
• assorted household objects

Next have the child arrange collections of appropriate objects, such as stuffed animals and pictures, for each shelf in the display. It might be fun to set hours for museum tours and invite family members or friends to visit the museum. The child may want to act as a museum tour guide during the visits. Tell the child that a tour guide is someone who explains the exhibits to the visitors and answers their questions.

HANGING IT OUT TO DRY

<▷◁▷◁▷◁▷◁▷

The child can retell a favorite story while hanging homemade socks on a clothesline.

String a clothesline across one corner of the room, and clip several clothespins to it. Next have the child cut out 3 to 6 sock shapes from tagboard and, using the markers, illustrate a scene from a familiar story on each. You may wish to provide a copy of the book or story for the child to refer to while working. Then have the child hang the completed socks on the clothesline in sequential order while retelling the story.

As a fun, bet-I've-got-you-thinking variation of this activity, mix up the socks and hang them in random order on the clothesline. Challenge the child to find the mistake and correct it, or make up a new story with the events in the new order.

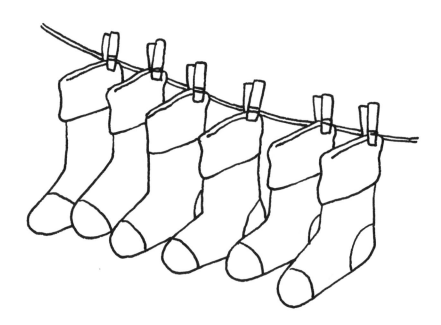

FINGERPRINT LETTERS

◁▶◁▷◁▶◁▷

Paint with your finger, and discover the curves and lines in letters.

What You'll Need
- tempera paint
- white construction paper
- clean foam meat tray

In this activity, the child uses paint and his finger to create letters.

Place some tempera paint on a clean foam meat tray. Have the child select one of his fingers (the pointer finger is probably best) and lay it down lengthwise in the paint. Ask the child to press the painted finger against the construction paper, making a fingerprint.

Next, help the child form a letter of the alphabet out of a series of fingerprints. Let him dip the selected finger back into the paint as needed. When the letter is dry, examine it together. Point out the different types of curved lines that appear in fingerprints.

WRAPPING-PAPER STORIES

◁▶◁▷◁▶◁▷

Create wordless books from wrapping paper, and read the books!

What You'll Need
- construction paper
- stapler
- wrapping paper with large patterns
- blunt scissors
- nontoxic white glue

Make a blank booklet by folding several sheets of paper in half and stapling them along the fold. Then invite the child to make a wordless book by cutting pictures out of the wrapping paper and gluing them into the book. When the book is finished, the child can make up a story and "read" the book by telling a story to go with the pictures.

SING ALONG

◁▷◁▷◁▷◁▷

Sing along as the child uses imagination to act out songs that tell a story.

What You'll Need
• tape player and cassettes of familiar songs (optional)

Sing along with familiar songs that tell a story, such as "The Farmer in the Dell," "There Was an Old Lady Who Swallowed a Fly," "In a Cabin in the Woods," "Five Little Ducks," "On Top of Spaghetti," and "Little Bunny Foo Foo." Invite the child to act out a character in the song while singing. Point out that most songs tell a story with special events or actions that happen at the beginning, the middle, and the end. Some of the songs end with an event that will make you laugh.

Activity Twist
Using the song "The Farmer in the Dell," have the child create new verses about the farmer. Then invite the child to act out those new verses while singing the words.

# WOODEN ALPHABET BLOCKS

◁▶◁▶◁▶◁▶◁▶◁

Build the entire alphabet using traditional wooden blocks.

Give the child a set of alphabet blocks, and ask him to arrange them in alphabetical order. As the

What You'll Need
• wooden alphabet blocks

blocks are being arranged, have the child say each letter. Some blocks have pictures. For a variation, have the child match the corresponding letter block to the picture block.

JACK AND JILL

◁▶◁▶◁▶◁▶◁▶◁

Rhyme at will with Jack and Jill.

What You'll Need
• paper
• marker or pen

Listening to and creating rhymes helps children begin to read and spell.

Say the first 2 lines of the nursery rhyme "Jack and Jill." Ask the child to name the rhyming words: *Jill* and *hill.* Write *Jill* and *hill* on a sheet of paper, and help the child think of additional rhyming words by changing the beginning sound: *bill, fill, pill, spill, still, will.* Write each word, and ask the child to point out how the words are alike and different.

POUND, PUSH, PULL & PUNCH PLAYDOUGH

◁▶◁▶◁▶◁▶◁▶◁▷

Pound out sharp shapes with your own homemade playdough!

What You'll Need
- large bowl
- measuring cup
- salt
- warm water
- all-purpose flour
- large spoon
- large plastic place mat
- container with lid
- food coloring (optional)
- cookie cutters (optional)
- plastic knife (optional)

To make a large amount of playdough, have the child help you measure and mix 1 cup of salt in 1 cup of warm water until it is partially dissolved. Add this mixture to 4 cups of flour. Mix with the spoon until well blended and the particles stick together. When the mixture forms a ball, knead it for 5 to 10 minutes. The child may tire of kneading after a few minutes—if so, the adult will need to finish. You can also add food coloring to the balls while you are kneading them if you want different colors of playdough.

When you have finished kneading, allow the child to roll, punch, push, pull, and pound using the place mat as the workspace. Not only is this play good for developing the child's hand muscles, but it is also a good outlet for a child's frustration! After each use, store the playdough in the container, keeping the lid on tight when it is not being used. After the newness of the activity has worn off, let the child use some of the optional tools listed to work with the playdough.

FAIRY-TALE SPIN

◁▷◁▷◁▷◁▷◁▷

Did the wolf in "The Three Little Pigs" get a fair deal? This activity lets other fairy-tale characters be heard.

Read or tell a familiar fairy tale to the child. Good examples include "The Three Little Pigs," "Cinderella," "Little Red Riding Hood," and "Jack and the Beanstalk." After sharing the fairy tale, talk about how people sometimes are misunderstood. Relate the stories to misunderstandings the child may have experienced, perhaps a disagreement with a sibling or friend. Discuss how the fairy-tale characters who seemed bad maybe didn't mean to be bad. For example, perhaps the wolf in "The Three Little Pigs" just wanted to be friends with the pigs.

After thinking of many possibilities for new ways of looking at a story from a different character's point of view, have the child write a new story spinning off from the old story.

What You'll Need
- fairy tale
- paper
- pencil

T PICTURE

◁▷◁▷◁▷◁▷◁▷

Kids can cross their T's with lots of different materials in this letter collage.

What You'll Need
- 2 drinking straws
- 2 pieces of uncooked spaghetti
- 2 pretzel sticks
- 2 chenille stems
- 2 cotton swabs
- 2 craft sticks
- glue
- sheet of poster board

Common items found around the house can be arranged to make letter forms—and a work of art.

Have the child arrange each pair of objects—drinking straws, spaghetti, pretzel sticks, chenille stems, cotton swabs, craft sticks—to make a capital or lowercase *T.* Then help the child glue each *T* onto a sheet of poster board using glue. Find a place where you can put the *T* picture on display.

This activity can be repeated with other capital letters that have straight lines—for example, *A, E, F, H,* and so on.

MASKING-TAPE TRAIL

◁▷◁▷◁▷◁▷

Tiptoe where the tape trail leads!

What You'll Need
• masking tape

The child can help the adult use masking tape to make a tape trail on the floor—the trail can wind or be straight. The child can then walk, tiptoe, hop, or go backward along the tape trail, trying to stay on the line! For a variation, make masking-tape "stepping stones" by creating round shapes, a foot apart, leading in a trail. The child can follow the stepping-stone trail by hopping or jumping from "stone" to "stone."

WEB WORDS

◁▷◁▷◁▷◁▷

This chip-flipping activity provides lots of practice for spelling words with the short e sound.

Before beginning, help the child draw a large web on a piece of poster board like the one shown here. In each section of the web, have the child draw a pic-ture of an object pronounced with a short *e,* as in *web.* (Give the child several words to choose from, such as *pen, bed, hen, egg,* and *net.*)

What You'll Need
• poster board
• markers
• flat plastic chips

To play the game, set 2 chips on a hard surface, such as a table or tile floor, next to the web game board. Instruct the child to bounce the chip off the surface to make it "jump" or "flip" into the air and then land on the web. The child may want to take a few practice flips. Then have the child say the name of the picture that the chip has landed on. Continue until the child has identified all the pictures.

Seeds on the Up-and-Up!

◁▷◁▷◁▷◁▷

Perform an experiment to see if seeds know which way is up!

What You'll Need
- 4 lima beans
- clear plastic jar or cup
- potting soil
- black construction paper
- tape
- plastic wrap
- rubber band
- paper (optional)
- pen or pencil

The child can fill the jar with potting soil and push a bean into the soil right next to the edge of the jar where it can be seen. The other 3 beans are also pushed in around the jar. The child can moisten the soil and check it daily (keeping it moist) until the seeds begin to sprout. Once the seeds have sprouted, wrap and tape the black paper around the jar. Make a greenhouse lid with plastic wrap and a rubber band. This will keep moisture in and prevent soil from spilling. Have the child place the jar on its side for 3 days; then turn it upside down for 3 days. For the next 3 days, place it on its side again; for the final 3 days set it right side up. (Keep checking the moisture level throughout the process, and add water when needed.) After the 12 days of rotation, the black paper is removed, and the child can note that the beans kept changing their growth pattern so they were always heading up. Encourage the child to draw conclusions about the reason for this. The adult and child can also keep track of what they have done by drawing pictures of how they placed the jar. The adult can mark each picture with dates of when the jar was placed in that position.

WORD WHEEL

◁▶◁▶◁▶◁▶◁▷

Get rolling with word play in this activity, and explore words that move.

Draw a picture of a wheel, using the example shown here as a guide. Be sure to include spokes and a round area in the center. Invite the child to think of something that moves, such as a bicycle, roller blades, or a wheelbarrow. Write the chosen word in the center of the word wheel. Talk about all the words the child can think of that relate to that word. For example, a bicycle may include handlebars, brakes, seat, gears, and so on. Write the related words between the spokes as demonstrated below.

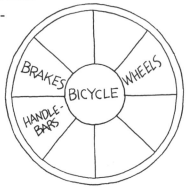

BLAST OFF!

◁▶◁▶◁▶◁▶◁▶◁▷

10-9-8-7-6-5-4-3-2-1 . . . BLAST OFF into reading comprehension with this rocket-construction project.

Cut a 6" circle out of blue construction paper, and cut a pie-shape wedge from it. Then wrap and tape the paper circle to make a cone. Cut the paper-towel tube to about half its length, and tape the cone to the top of one of the halves.

Next, invite the child to write the main idea of a favorite story on the body of the cardboard-tube rocket. If you prefer, the child can use a personal experience as a basis for the main idea. Help the child write supporting details on the strips of white paper. Then have the child tape the strips of paper to the bottom of the rocket.

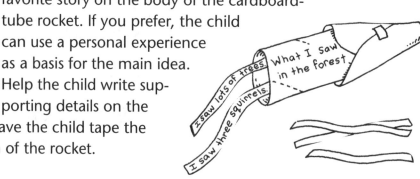

RIDDLE RHYMES

◁▷◁▷◁▷◁▷◁▷

Rum-tum-tiddle, tell me a rhyming riddle!

Take turns making up riddles that have rhyming hints for one another to guess. For example: "I'm thinking of something that purrs, and it rhymes with *hat*"; "I'm thinking of something you put on your foot, and it rhymes with *blue*." For a more challenging rhyming riddle variation, tell a riddle without a rhyming clue, for which the answer must be a rhyme. For example, what's a furry pet that purrs and is very large? (A fat cat.)

MAKE A MENU

◁▷◁▷◁▷◁▷◁▷

What goes with chicken and chili? In this game, cheddar cheese.

What You'll Need
• 7 paper plates
• canned goods
• blunt scissors
• marker or pen

This activity allows children to help plan lunch menus as they review beginning sounds.

Put 7 paper plates in a row. Write a day of the week on each plate. Invite the child to help you plan a week's worth of lunch menus by planning each day's menu around a different beginning sound. To illustrate each menu, have the child find canned goods and boxed goods in the kitchen, or find and cut out pictures of food. For example, you might start with the beginning sound *M* (macaroni, meat, milk). The child might find a box of macaroni and cheese and cut out a picture of a glass of milk. Other menu letters are *S* (soup, sandwich), *T* (tuna, toast, tomatoes), *P* (peanut butter, pear, potato salad), *H* (hot dog, hamburger), *B* (banana, beans), and *F* (fish).

Fuzzy, Bristly Words

The child may feel itchy or bumpy all in the name of learning adjectives.

Place several common household items (no sharp edges), each with a different texture, in a bag or box. Before beginning the game, explain that adjectives are words that describe nouns. Then draw a word web (see page 244) and write the sentence "It feels _____." in the center. Blindfold the child, and instruct him to place one hand inside the bag or box. Ask the child to describe what the objects feel like. Write the words the child uses on the web. Can the child guess what objects are in the bag?

What You'll Need
- common household materials with different textures
- large bag or box
- poster board
- markers
- blindfold

Activity Twist

To add a new angle to this activity, put several pairs of textured objects in the bag or box. Invite the blindfolded child to grab an object, describe how it feels, and then, only by touching, find its match.

Word Search

Track down and recognize words all around!

When you are walking around the house or the neighborhood, challenge the child to find words that she can read. These might be words that the child can sound out  and read or words that she recognizes (such as *stop*). As a variation, the child can start a collection of pictures and labels of recognizable words. The saved words can be kept in a box or used for a word collage. You can also start a "Word Wall," where you list all the words the child can read. As the list grows, the child will feel a great sense of accomplishment!

PEANUTS TO PEANUT BUTTER

◁►◁►◁►◁►◁►◁►

Homemade peanut butter is delicious.
Just shell some nuts, and follow the directions.

Caution: This project requires adult supervision.

This activity exercises the fingers and is especially good for a child with a high energy level. In addition to associating the letter *P* with peanuts, the child learns how to make peanut butter.

Give the child some unshelled peanuts, and ask him to crack and clean them. You may need to show the child how to crack the peanuts' shells, remove the peanuts, and skin them. When the peanuts are shelled and skinned, put a tablespoon of oil—and salt, if desired—in a blender and let the child add the peanuts. Put the lid on (only an adult should operate the blender), and process the oil and nuts. When the peanuts are blended, scoop the peanut butter from the blender with a spatula, and place it in a jar that has a lid. Have some toasted bread ready to taste this delicious treat. Refrigerate the leftover peanut butter when finished.

As an added activity, you and the child can make a label to put on the jar. Use a piece of paper, crayons or markers, and clear tape.

What You'll Need
- peanuts in shells
- blender
- 1 tablespoon vegetable oil
- salt (optional)
- lidded jar
- spatula
- toast
- paper (optional)
- crayons or markers (optional)
- clear tape (optional)

VESTED INTEREST

◁▷◁▷◁▷◁▷◁▷

This activity will give the child a vested interest in beginning letters and sounds.

Turn a large paper bag upside down, and cut it straight up the middle. Make a neck opening by cutting an oval shape in the top (formerly bottom) of the bag. Make armholes by cutting circles in the sides of the bag. Invite the child to choose a letter of the alphabet to paint on the newly created vest. Then suggest the child look through old magazines to find pictures of objects that begin with that letter, cut them out, and tape or glue them to the vest.

What You'll Need
- paper bag
- blunt scissors
- paint
- paintbrush
- old magazines
- clear tape or glue

STRING PAINTING

◁▷◁▷◁▷◁▷◁▷

Use a common object to create uncommon art!

What You'll Need
- newspaper
- lengths of string
- several colors of tempera paint
- paper
- containers

The child can achieve a variety of different effects using a string dipped in paint as a painting tool. Spread newspaper on the work area. The child can place a piece of string in one of the paint containers and allow the string to soak up the paint. The child can then arrange the string on the paper, fold the paper in half, and pull the string through the folded paper. Pulling the string will create a design. Through experimentation, the child will discover that the design result can be varied by how the string is placed on the paper and also by how it is pulled. A second and third string soaked in different colors can be used on the same paper to create blended effects.

POTATO-PRINT LETTERS

▷▶◁▶◁▶◁▶◁▷

You can bake them, cook them, mash them, and fry them.
You can also paint with them.

Caution: This project requires adult supervision.

In this activity, the child will stamp letters using potatoes.

Cut a potato in half. Using a letter stencil and marker, trace a letter onto the cut surface of the potato. The adult can use a knife to shave down the potato around the letter. The letter will then be raised, which will allow it to be printed more clearly.

Hint: Unless the letter you choose is symmetrical (such as capital letters *A, H, I, M, O, T, V, W, X,* and *Y*), it will need to be stenciled backwards so that the letter print will not be reversed. Pour some paint into the meat tray. Have the child take the potato, dip it into the paint so that the raised letter is covered, and then make several letter prints on a sheet of paper. Additional letters may be cut for different letter prints.

What You'll Need
- potato
- knife (used only by adult)
- letter stencils
- marker
- tempera paint
- paper
- clean foam meat tray

WHO AM I?

◁▶◁▶◁▶◁▶◁▷

In this guessing game, the child collects information
and draws conclusions from verbal clues.

Choose a character from a favorite story or fairy tale that both you and the child are familiar with. Then tell the child to pretend that you are one of the storybook characters. Invite the child to determine who you are by asking you yes or no questions for clues. Before the child begins asking questions, you may want to provide 1 or 2 clues to get started.

BUILDING BREAD

◁▷◁▷◁▷◁▷

Bake dainty delicious little loaves of beautiful bread.

What You'll Need
- 1 cup lukewarm water
- 1 teaspoon sugar
- 1 package yeast
- measuring cups and spoons
- bowl
- 2 cups flour
- 1 teaspoon salt
- 1 tablespoon oil
- wooden board
- extra flour
- clean towel
- cookie sheet
- oven
- pot holders
- timer
- loaf pan (optional)

Caution: This project requires adult supervision.

Wash hands first! Collect all the ingredients in a clean working area. The child can help measure the water, sugar, and yeast into a bowl and mix it. After the yeast has dissolved (a couple of minutes), the child can measure and add 1 cup of flour and mix again. Add the salt, oil, and second cup of flour, and mix; the bread is ready for kneading. Sprinkle a wooden board or clean working area with flour and take turns kneading the dough (about 5 minutes). Then put the dough back in the bowl, cover it with a clean towel, and set it in a warm corner to rise (about 45 minutes). Encourage the child to peek under the cover every now and again to observe the rising. When the dough is ready, it can be divided into small balls to be molded and baked on a cookie sheet (about 15 minutes at 400°F). Or the child can model one small ball into a personal loaf for quick baking, and the rest can be put into a greased loaf pan and baked for 45 minutes at 375°F.

FOOT PAINTING

◁▶◁▶◁▶◁▶

Fancy paint-dipped feet make toe painting nifty and neat!

What You'll Need
- newspaper
- tempera paint
- cornstarch
- water
- child-size chair or stool
- large paper
- large shallow pan
- pail of soapy water
- towel

The child can explore painting with feet and toes using finger paint placed in a large shallow pan or tray and a big sheet of paper on the ground.

First, spread plenty of newspapers on the floor. Make the homemade finger paint by mixing tempera paint with cornstarch and water. Place a child-size chair or stool on the newspaper and a large sheet of paper in front of the chair. Put a shallow pan of finger paint (big enough for feet) next to it. (Have a pail of soapy water and a towel nearby for cleanup!) The child can sit in the chair, dip feet into the paint, and then experiment painting with toes and feet. For a variation, tape together several large pieces of paper to make a very large painting surface. Invite the child to paint standing up! The child can walk across the paper, drag feet, and make toe lines and other large paint strokes.

THE MORAL OF THE STORY

◁▶◁▶◁▶◁▶◁▶

What better way to teach a lesson than through a little story?

Fables are short stories, usually involving animals, that teach lessons. Many are attributed to Aesop, the famous Greek writer of fables. Find several fables and take turns reading them. How many have people in them? Animals? What is the most common animal? For an additional challenge, make a list to keep track of the number of foxes, crows, and other animals found in the fables. Then, most important, discuss what lessons are to be learned from each story.

What You'll Need
• collection of fables

SOUND SORT

◁▶◁▶◁▶◁▶◁▶

Sorting pictures by beginning sounds is great exercise for hands and minds.

What You'll Need
• old magazines
• blunt scissors
• 2 shoe boxes
• tape

Sorting pictures can help children practice identifying letter sounds.

Cut pictures of objects out of old magazines. Tape a picture of an object (for example, a table) on the front of one of the shoe boxes. Have the child look through the other pictures you have cut out, putting into the box the pictures whose names begin with the same sound as the word *table.* Then change the picture on the first box, and tape a picture on the second box. Have the child sort through the pictures again, putting them into the 2 boxes according to beginning sounds.

This activity will work best if you find 3 or more pictures of things that begin with the same letter. For a variation, have the child sort actual objects.

ABC Star

⊲▷⊲▷⊲▷⊲▷⊲▷

Follow the letter dots and see what shines.

To help a child learn the sequence of the alphabet, ask her to connect a series of dots to form a picture.

The child will have to draw a line from letters *A* to *B*, *B* to *C*, and so on until an object appears. As the child masters the alphabet, the pictures can be made more complex.

Start by drawing (or tracing) a simple, easily recognizable object on a sheet of tissue paper. Transfer this image by placing the tissue paper on top of a regular sheet of paper and pressing dots along the object's outline at regular intervals. Mark these dots on the paper with a sequence of letters beginning with *A*, and have the child connect the dots by following the sequence of the alphabet.

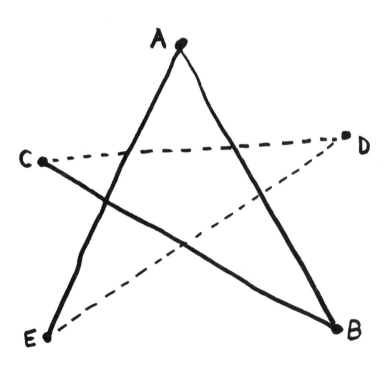

BODY CARDS

◁▶◁▶◁▶◁▶◁▶◁▶

Make up and perform easy or imaginative body tasks!

Create a simple deck of body-parts cards. Using 10 index cards, the adult can make simple line drawings to depict different body parts: eyes, nose, mouth, head, arms, hands, legs, knees, feet, toes. Mix up the cards, and then take turns picking the top one. After picking a card, make up a task for the other person to do with that body part! The tasks can be simple, for example: Clap your hands, stamp your feet, wiggle your nose. Or the tasks can be more challenging: Pick up a teddy bear with your feet, make a sound with your hands. For a variation, take 2 cards at a time and challenge each other with a task that involves both body parts: Put your hand on your knee, touch your arm to your nose.

What You'll Need
• index cards
• markers

NEWS REPORT INTERVIEWS

◁▶◁▶◁▶◁▶◁▶◁▶

Get the "scoop" while practicing research and organizational skills.

Invite the child to be a news reporter and report on an event that happened at home or while on a family outing. Choose a topic together for the interview. It may be something as ordinary as dinner last night or a little more unusual, such as what happened when the dog got out. Encourage the child to ask you questions that will uncover as many details as possible and to write down the answers on a piece of paper. Invite the child to give a news report as if reporting the story on the evening news.

TUBE ART

◁▷◁▷◁▷◁▷◁▷

Tiny or tall, big or small—tubes are the building blocks for a tower town.

What You'll Need
- cardboard
- cardboard tubes
- scissors
- nontoxic white glue
- paint
- brush
- construction paper (optional)
- tape (optional)

Provide the child with a piece of cardboard to use as a base and an assortment of long and short cardboard tubes. (The adult can cut the tubes into different sizes to increase the variation.) The child can create a tower town by arranging and gluing the tubes onto the cardboard base. When the glue has dried and the towers are secure, the town can be painted. To increase the challenge, the child can use construction paper to make additional tubes with greater size variation. Help the child cut the paper into different lengths and then roll them into fat and skinny cylinders. Use tape to secure the tubes.

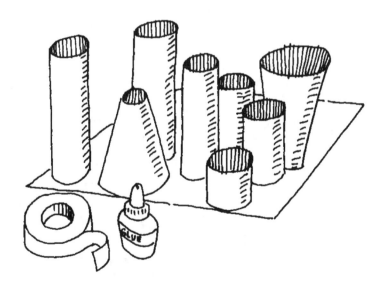

LIBRARY VISIT

◁▶◁▶◁▶◁▶◁▶◁▷

A trip to the library is a perfect activity for a rainy day.

Have an enriching experience by taking a child to a library. This visit exposes the child to the concept of alphabetical order and the purpose and use of a library. It will also help her develop an appreciation for books by showing how they are an invaluable source of information.

Give the child a topic such as animals. Ask her to name an animal that begins with the letter *H.* If the child says *horse,* look for an easy informational book about that animal, such as an encyclopedia or encyclopedic dictionary.

Use the library's computerized card catalog (if possible) to identify specific book titles, then show the child how to find the books on the shelves. Select several books, and check them out. Read the books to the child.

FAVORITE STORY CASSETTE

◁▷◁▷◁▷◁▷

Listen to a favorite story again and again and again and again!

What You'll Need
- tape recorder
- cassette
- favorite book
- bell

Make a cassette recording of one of the child's favorite stories. The child can listen as you read the story. Signal the child whenever it is time to turn a page. The child can then ring a bell. This will be the signal for the child to turn a page when looking at the book and listening to the tape independently.

 # NURSERY RHYMES

◁▷◁▷◁▷◁▷

Where did Jack and Jill go, and what happened to Humpty Dumpty?
Fill in the rhyming words.

Simple nursery rhymes help a child acquire rhyming and listening skills.

Read or say a nursery rhyme to the child. Repeat the rhyme, but this time do not say the rhyming word. Have the child add the missing word. Ask her which words sounded alike and if she can think of any other words that sound like those words.

I'm in Character

◁▷◁▷◁▷◁▷◁▷

Stepping into character is fun, and it enhances the child's ability to understand a different point of view.

Invite the child to choose a character from a favorite story. Then have the child perform some daily activities, acting and reacting as the character would. Encourage the child to imagine how the story character might eat lunch, clean up toys, or pet the dog. What might the story character say when the phone rings? How would the character wash her face? Encourage the child to think about how the character would react to a certain situation and then to speak or act out that reaction.

PUDDLE TESTING

◁▶◁▶◁▶◁▶◁

Puddles disappear—let's find out how!

Rain is mysterious. It falls out of the sky, then it disappears. How does it happen? The child can begin to make sense of some of nature's mysteries through careful observation. Here is a simple activity for a puddle study.

Invite the child to find a puddle on a cement area on a sunny day after a rainfall. The child can draw a chalk line around the puddle right at the water's edge. Ask the child to predict what might happen to the puddle now that the rain has stopped. Will it dry? How fast? Return to the puddle with the child several times during the day to check and see what has happened. If it is still there but has gotten smaller, the child can draw a new chalk border. Encourage the child to think about where the water went and what helped it dry up. As a variation, the child can take an old plate outside on a sunny day and pour water into it to create a puddle. The child can mark the puddle on the plate with a wax pencil to record the evaporation.

> ### What You'll Need
> - chalk
> - old plate (optional)
> - wax pencil (optional)

Activity Twist

Brainstorm! What else can you do with a puddle? Can you make it bigger? (Stand in it, put rocks in it.) Can you move it? (Stomp and splash in it, blow the water.) Can you play with it? (Float leaves, see your face in it.)

Spin and Win

◁▷◁▷◁▷◁▷

Even phonics wizards will need some luck to win this fast-moving game.

This spinning game requires both luck and knowledge of beginning sounds.

On the poster board, draw a large circle and divide it into 6 sections. Write a letter on the edge of each section. Cut out a long spinner, and attach it to the center of the circle with a paper fastener. Next, make a set of 6 picture cards (pictures cut from old magazines glued or taped to index cards). Each card should show an object that has a name beginning with 1 of the letters on the circle. Shuffle the cards and put them in a stack.

To play the game, a player spins the spinner and takes the top picture card from the pile. If the name of the picture begins with the letter sound she has spun, the player keeps the picture. If not, the next player spins. Continue taking turns until all the picture cards have been won.

Silly Willy

◁▷◁▷◁▷◁▷

Have fun with nonsense rhymes. See how many rhyming words you can use.

Young children get enjoyment from listening to and making up nonsense rhymes.

Begin by giving the child a word, such as *tall*. Ask her to think of a rhyming word, such as *ball*. Continue alternating back and forth with the silly rhyming. Even though the word pairs you create may not always make sense, it is important that the child recognizes and responds to the rhyming concept.

WHAT CAN SHAPES MAKE?

◁▶◁▷◁▶◁▷

Turn triangles, circles, squares, and rectangles into houses, horses, or bears!

What You'll Need
- construction paper
- blunt scissors
- paper
- nontoxic white glue
- crayons or markers

Provide the child with a piece of paper, glue, and an assortment of construction paper circles, squares, triangles, and rectangles cut in different colors and sizes. The child can choose shapes and arrange and glue them to make pictures—creating animals, people, vehicles, trees, houses, and assorted other things from the shapes. Give

the child crayons or markers to add extra details to the picture. For a variation, make stencils of small, medium, and large circles, squares, rectangles, and triangles for the child to explore and draw with, or cut cardboard shapes for the child to trace!

Activity Twist

Create stamps for circle and square shapes! Place different colors of tempera paint on glossy paper plates. Assemble cans and boxes of different sizes to use as your stamps. Dip the bottoms of your boxes and cans in the paint, then stamp out your shape creations on white paper. Try overlapping different colors to make new colors! See if you can design funny circle snow people and playful robots!

SHADOW PLAY

⊲▶⊲▶⊲▶⊲▶⊲▶⊲▶⊲

The child will enjoy imaginative storytelling through these shadow puppets.

What You'll Need
• bright flashlight

Cast a bright light against a light-colored wall. Sit between the light and the wall, and demonstrate how to make shadow puppets by manipulating your hands to create the desired shadow images. For example, form a rabbit using your thumb to hold down the last 2 fingers on the same hand and having the pointer and middle fingers straight up, slightly apart.

Invite the child to use her imagination to create other shadow puppets on the wall. Then encourage the child to make up a story about these shadow characters and to perform the show for others.

Hink-Pink!
Q: What happens when ghosts fall down?
A: They get boo-boos.

LETTERS ONLINE

⬦⬦⬦⬦⬦⬦⬦

It's never too early to join the computer age.
Kids can do just that while they learn letters in this simple activity.

What You'll Need
- computer

This activity can be done at home or school, if there's a computer available. Otherwise, try the library. Even the library's online catalog computer would work for this exercise.

Have the child type any letter on the keyboard. When it appears on the screen, ask the child to name it. If possible, use larger type and decorative fonts to keep the child's interest. For a more advanced child, name a letter and ask the child to find it on the keyboard and type it in.

CHEERY CHAINS

⬦⬦⬦⬦⬦⬦

Strengthen the child's vocabulary chain by learning new words associated with a familiar topic.

What You'll Need
- 1½" × 8½" paper strips
- crayons or markers
- clear tape or glue

Decide on a topic, such as food, animals, household objects, or a current social studies or science theme at school, and make a list of associated words. Then write the words on strips of paper. The child may draw illustrations to go with each word.

Next, invite the child to assemble the strips, or links, using tape or glue to make chains. Take a strip of paper, and form it into a loop. Tape the ends together. Continue adding loops of paper, stringing each new loop onto the previous one before taping it shut. Chains can be strung across a room, made into individual necklaces, wrapped around bushes or trees, or draped around a doorway. To reinforce learning, invite the child to review the words daily.

CHARACTER MOBILE

⬦⬦⬦⬦⬦⬦

The child will become familiar with characters in a favorite story when creating a character mobile.

Begin by inviting the child to draw pictures of various characters from a favorite story. Help the child label the pictures. Cut out different shapes (squares, circles, triangles) from the tagboard, and have the child mount each picture on individual tagboard shapes using glue. Punch 1 hole in the top of each shape and enough holes around the outside edge of a polystyrene plate for each of the shapes. Have the child thread yarn strands through the shapes and plates and then tie the yarn so the shapes dangle from the plate. Hang the finished mobile in a room for all to see.

To take this activity further, help the child add a word to each label describing a trait that character has.

What You'll Need
- favorite book or story
- paper
- markers
- tagboard
- blunt scissors
- clear tape or glue
- hole punch
- 10" to 12" polystyrene plate
- yarn

CREEPY CRAWLIES

◁▷◁▷◁▷◁▷

Using an interest in insects is a great way to inspire the reading of nonfiction books.

Nonfiction books often have bright, colorful pictures, charts, and boxes containing special information. Together, choose a particular creepy crawly, such as the ant, found in the book. Invite the child to read everything in the book about ants. Then look for ants outside together. Have the child make notes about the ants and compare them to the information found in the book. This process can be repeated several times during different seasons to see the changes that occur in the behavior of the chosen creepy crawly.

What You'll Need
- any nonfiction book with photographs or drawings of ants, beetles, or other insects
- notebook
- pencil

SPINNING WHEEL

◁▷◁▷◁▷◁▷

Kids can increase their vocabularies by taking a spin around the playroom.

Children can use pictures to learn to read the words for their favorite toys.

On a sheet of construction paper, draw a large circle and divide it into 6 or 8 sections. Ask the child to name several favorite toys. Write 1 of the toy names in each section of the circle. Have the child draw a picture in each section that matches the word.

Meanwhile, make a spinner out of heavy paper such as poster board. Attach it to the center of the circle with a paper fastener. Take turns spinning the spinner and reading the word in the section in which the spinner stops. When the child has mastered the toy words, make circles for animal words, food words, and so on.

What You'll Need
- construction paper
- pen or pencil
- small piece of poster board
- blunt scissors
- paper fastener

HOOPING IT UP

◁▶◁▶◁▶◁▶

Jumping through hoops—for a purpose!

What You'll Need
• hula hoop

There are lots of ways to play with a hula hoop. Young children find it extremely difficult to use as it was designed, but it is a fun toy to use in many ways! Here are some ways younger children will enjoy playing with it:

1. Lay the hoop on the ground and have the child crawl over one side, through the center, and under the other side.

2. Hold the hoop perpendicular to the ground and have the child walk or jump through it. (The hoop can rest on the ground or be held slightly above it.)

3. Lay the hoop on the ground, and have the child lie down in the middle. Have the child place his head on one side of the hoop and try to pick up the other side with his feet. Does the child find this easier when lying on his back or his side?

4. Encourage the child to roll the hoop and run alongside it, giving the hoop periodic pushes to see how far it will roll.

5. See if the child can spin the hoop.

LETTER FEELINGS

◁▷◁▷◁▷◁▷

Reach inside a grab bag to feel and identify letters.

This activity focuses the child's attention on the formation of letters, which is necessary for letter recognition.

Place all the capital or lowercase letters in a bag. Have the child reach inside the bag, feel a letter, and describe it so that you can guess what letter it is (for example, the letter *A* might be described as 2 long diagonal lines with a smaller line connecting them). Then reverse roles. You pick and describe a letter, and the child can try to guess its identity.

ALL I KNOW!

◁▷◁▷◁▷◁▷

Tell everything!

Pick one topic and challenge the child to tell all she knows about it. Some topic ideas are dinosaurs, dogs, trees, cookies, pizza, or shoes. The child's ideas can be written down and read back for review. Another list can also be made of things the child would like to know about the topic. After the second list has been made, encourage the child to come up with some ways to find answers to some of the questions on the second list. Make a research plan together. The plan might include observation, asking an expert, or getting a book from the library. Then put the plan into action!

YARN CYLINDERS

◁▷◁▷◁▷◁▷

*Round and round and round you go,
making a variety of brightly decorated containers.*

Collect an assortment of clean, empty, unbreakable cylindrical containers (oatmeal boxes, plastic juice bottles, salt boxes). Wrap each one from top to bottom with double-sided tape. Cut many colors of yarn into strips of different lengths. Show the child how to decorate the container by sticking the yarn to the tape. Start by wrapping yarn completely around the container horizontally. Next, go vertically, from top to bottom. Then place strips of yarn at interesting angles. Ask the child to decorate the other cylinders. In addition, invite her to make a special project out of the largest container. Tell her to start at the bottom and make one complete circle with blue yarn, then two complete circles with red yarn, three with green, and so on until she reaches the top. Help her count the total number of circles she has made when she is finished.

What You'll Need
- cylindrical containers of various sizes
- blunt scissors
- double-sided tape
- yarns of different colors

ICE POPS, PLEASE

◁▷◁▷◁▷◁▷

On a hot day, there's nothing as refreshing as this special treat.

Most children will enjoy helping out in the kitchen, especially if you're preparing something they like. In this activity, the child will make her own ice pops.

Let the child decide what flavor of ice pops to make, then pour the selected juice into a measuring cup, which will be easier for the child to control. Ask the child to pour the juice into small paper cups, but only about ¾ full. Place these cups in the freezer until the liquid begins to freeze slightly. At that point, remove the cups from the freezer and have the child push a craft stick or plastic spoon (handle end out) into the thickened liquid. Put the cups back in the freezer.

What You'll Need
- fruit juice
- measuring cup
- small paper cups
- plastic spoons or craft sticks

After the juice has frozen completely, it's time for a taste test. Peel the paper cup from the ice pop. As you and the child enjoy your snack, review all of the *P* words in this project: *pop, please, pour, place, push, peel, plastic, put, paper.*

HUNTING FOR SOUNDS

◁▷◁▷◁▷◁▷

Seek sounds that are all around to catch and collect!

What You'll Need
- tape recorder
- blank tape
- paper (optional)
- crayons or markers (optional)

Go on a sound search, taking a walk outside or a listening walk through the house. Invite the child to listen to all the sounds around and to choose several to collect. The sounds can be collected by imitating and repeating them or by recording them. After the sound search is over, the child can share the saved sounds by repeating the remembered ones or playing the tape and telling about what made the sounds that were recorded. The child can also draw pictures of the people, animals, or things that made the sounds that were collected!

POP-UP PUBLISHING

◁▷◁▷◁▷◁▷

Bring books to life with pop-up people and more.

What You'll Need
- paper
- blunt scissors
- crayons
- glue

The child can help make a pop-up book by creating the pop-up pictures and inventing the story!

To make the pop-up pages for the book, fold a piece of paper in half. Then cut two 1½"-long slits approximately 1½" apart in the middle of the folded edge of the paper. Push the paper between the two cuts to the inside of the fold in order to form a pop-up section. The child can draw a picture for the pop-up on another piece of paper, cut it out, and glue it onto the pop-up section. The child can then draw the background on the original pop-up page. Depending on the length of the story the child makes up, it can be contained within one pop-up page, or several pages can be pasted together to make a pop-up book.

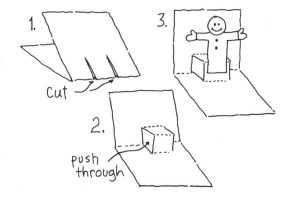

TOM TURKEY

◁▷◁▷◁▷◁▷◁▷

***Kids don't have to wait until Thanksgiving to make
and display this fine feathered friend.***

Teach a child to make a turkey—and master the letter *T*.
First, ask the child to identify the beginning sound in
the words *Tom Turkey* and then name other words with
the same beginning sound. Next, draw a pattern for a
feather on a sheet of construction paper, and cut it out
with blunt scissors. Have the child trace the pattern onto
several different-colored sheets of construction paper,
cutting them out as you did. Help the child glue or tape
the feathers to a paper plate (the turkey's body) so that
their tips extend past the outer edge of the plate and fan
out next to each other, like the feathers of a real turkey.

What You'll Need
• pencil
• different-colored sheets
  of construction paper
• blunt scissors
• glue
• clear tape
• paper plate
• chenille stems

Tape a chenille stem to the other side of the plate, extending it beyond the top
(feathered) edge to form the turkey's neck. Bend and twist 2 more chenille stems,
taping them to the bottom of the plate to make feet. Finally, cut out a round piece of
construction paper for the head, gluing or taping it to the end of the neck. Have the
child write the capital letter *T* twice (for *Tom Turkey*) on the turkey's "body."

QUICK DRAW!

<⊳►<⊳►<⊳►

This observation and classification activity will amuse the child endlessly.

What You'll Need
- markers
- large sheets of paper

Have the child draw 4 animals (or other objects) on a piece of paper, making sure that 3 have similar characteristics. The child may want to start with pictures of a zebra, a tiger, a coral snake, and a rabbit. Let the child decide which 3 are alike and in what ways. You'll notice in the example shown that 3 have stripes. It is also true that 3 of the animals shown have 4 legs.

Challenge the child to "fix" the fourth animal or object to make it like the other 3. Be prepared for some silly drawings!

 # ONE-WORD DRAMA

►<⊳►<⊳►<⊳►

Take a word, and act it out!

Take turns making up actions to dramatize single words. Start with simple action words, such as *hop, wiggle, laugh.* Feeling words can also be part of the game (*happy, sad, sleepy, grumpy, excited*). Choose words to act out for the others to guess! Other variations include using position words (*inside, around, under, through*) and action words (*sleep, read, eat, cook, drive*).

Fun Fact
The most widely used letters in written English are e, t, a, o, i, n, s, r, h, and l.

ALPHABET SALAD

<⊳<⊳<⊳<⊳<⊳<⊳<⊳<

If you've never had a radish and jalapeño pepper salad, try this recipe.

What You'll Need
- letter cards containing the letters *A* through *T*
- box or bowl
- various vegetables
- pen or pencil
- paper

This activity tests a child's memory as well as her vocabulary.

Put the letter cards in a box or bowl, and mix them up. Ask the child to choose 7 letters and name them. Then have her name vegetables that could be put into a salad whose name begins with each letter. Point out that some letters may have several items and others may have none. You can also help name items for difficult letters.

Keep the following ingredients in mind: asparagus, avocado, beans, broccoli, cabbage, carrots, celery, cucumber, garlic, green pepper, jalapeño pepper, lettuce, mushrooms, olives, onions, parsley, peas, radish, red pepper, spinach, and tomato. You may also suggest other salad items, such as apples, eggs, and nuts.

Write down each vegetable the child names. Edit the list together, choosing several items for a real salad. Shop for the items together. Discuss each vegetable as you prepare it and add it to the salad.

FOLD AND SEE, SYMMETRY!

◁▷◁▷◁▷◁▷

Make symmetrical paint pictures.

Help the child fold a paper in half and then open it up. Next, put several different colors of paint into separate containers. The child then scoops 1 or 2 small spoonfuls of paint into the middle of the paper and folds it in half again along the crease. The child gently pats and smooths the closed paper before opening it once more to discover the symmetrical design. After observing the colorful design, encourage the child to notice and talk about the 2 identical shapes that have been created. For a variation, the child can make symmetrical picture designs by using 2 or 3 colors at one time!

What You'll Need
• construction paper
• tempera paint
• small containers
• spoons

Activity Twist

Try a symmetry trick! Cut out some small pictures (catalogs are a great source) of symmetrical things (face, shirt, plate). Cut each picture in half. Give the child a small unbreakable rectangular mirror. Ask the child to place the long edge of the mirror upright next to the cut edge of the picture. Watch the symmetrical surprise image appear in the reflection!

GREAT & GRAND KITCHEN BAND

◁▷◁▷◁▷◁▷◁▷

Rap and tap and beat along while the music plays a rhythm song!

What You'll Need
- assorted kitchen tools (pot covers, wooden spoons, pans, chopsticks, etc.)
- cassette or CD with a strong beat

Gather together an assortment of cooking utensils for the child to create kitchen band music. The child can explore the different items and how to make musical sounds with them. Two pot covers can be used as cymbals. A pot can be beat like a drum with a metal spoon or chopsticks. Two wooden spoons can be tapped together like rhythm sticks—let the child use whichever end he wants. After the child has explored the musical possibilities of the utensils, one instrument can be chosen (to start with!) to play along with a music cassette or CD. The child can sit and listen to the music, paying attention to the rhythm and the beat, and play along. For more challenge, the child can march around the room playing the instrument along to the music!

LETTERS EVERYWHERE

◁▶◁▶◁▶◁▶

Making a collage of letters is a wonderful way to learn the alphabet.

As a child reads, many different sizes and types of print will need to be recognized. This activity will call attention to the variety of fonts and print sizes.

Give the child old magazines. The challenge will be to locate and then cut out large, single letters,

both capital and lowercase, from advertisements. After many letters are cut, have the child paste them on a piece of white construction paper in a collage format, covering the paper and overlapping the letters. Have the child read you the letters.

DANCING WITH ELBOWS, NOSES, OR TOESIES

◁▶◁▶◁▶◁▶

Dance and prance with different body parts!

Play lively music from a cassette or CD, and invite the child to dance to the music using just 1 body part! Allow child to stand or sit. How many ways can the child move to the music using only 1 body part? Two parts? Challenge the child to dance with just 1 toe,

with a toe and an elbow, with just a nose, etc. For added challenge, make simple pictures of body parts on index cards, and make the dance into a game. Have the child draw 1 or 2 cards to select which body parts to do a dance with.

PEEKABOO PLAYHOUSE

◁▷◁▷◁▷◁▷

Puppets and other people have fun peeking in and out!

What You'll Need
- construction paper
- blunt scissors
- nontoxic white glue
- old magazines
- craft sticks
- crayons

Create a peekaboo playhouse using 2 different colored sheets of construction paper. Cut a door in 1 sheet of paper, cutting it on 3 sides so the flap can be opened and closed. Glue the 2 papers together just along the sides and the top. Puppet creatures can be made by gluing pictures of people and animals cut out of magazines onto the end of craft sticks. The child could also  draw the pictures instead of cutting them out of magazines. The child can then use the puppets by slipping them through the bottom opening between the 2 sheets of the playhouse so the puppets pop in and out of the door. You can also help the child make a larger playhouse with a door and some windows so the puppets have more places where they can pop out!

CARDBOARD CRITTERS

◁▷◁▷◁▷◁▷

Construct creatures from a conglomeration of cardboard boxes.

The child can choose just the right boxes and cardboard tubes and glue them together to turn them into animals. The animals can be painted, and

 pieces of construction paper can be glued on to create ears and tails. To make the activity simpler, reduce the variables! Provide the child with 2 differently sized boxes and a few cardboard tubes to create a unique animal.

What You'll Need
- empty cereal and food boxes
- cardboard tubes
- nontoxic white glue
- paint and brush
- construction paper
- blunt scissors

BEANBAGS

◁▷◁▷◁▷◁▷

Turn those old worn-out jeans into something new.

What You'll Need
- old jeans
- ruler or tape measure
- marker
- scissors
- needle and thread
- beans
- 3 or more shoe boxes
- paper

Caution: This project requires adult supervision.

Not only are beanbags an ideal project for recycling old jeans, but what better way for the child to learn about the letter *B* sound than with *beans* and *bags*?

Put the jeans on a flat surface, and trace two 4" × 4" squares on top of a pant leg with a marker. Cut out the squares. (Since jean material is heavy, an adult should cut the material.) After the squares have been cut out, ask the child to put the squares together like a sandwich, with the finished sides touching. Stitch around 3 sides of the squares, creating a pocket with a 1" × 4" seam, then turn the pocket inside out. (The seam will be inside the pocket, and the finished side will be showing.)

As the child puts beans into the pocket, or "bag," she can count them. Fill the bag about ¾ full, emphasizing the word *bean* several times, then turn in the top edges of the open side and sew them together. Ask the child to tell you what was made, the steps taken to make the beanbag, and the *B* words used (*bean, bag*).

Assign a letter to each shoe box. A simple way to do this is to place a small piece of paper on which the chosen letter has been written inside each box. Place the boxes next to or near each other several yards away, and see if the child can toss the beanbag into one of the containers. Finally, name a word (or several words) that begins with that letter of the box where the beanbag lands.

MAKE PAPER

◁▶◁▶◁▶◁▶◁▶◁▶

Use old paper to make new!

What You'll Need
- paper towels
- bowl
- hot water
- powdered starch
- tablespoon
- eggbeater
- shallow pan
- screen
- newspaper
- rolling pin
- colored tissue paper (optional)
- glitter (optional)
- leaf pieces (optional)
- flower pieces (optional)
- ribbon (optional)
- dryer lint (optional)
- small flowers (optional)
- coffee grounds (optional)
- embroidery floss cut in small pieces (optional)
- spices (optional)

Caution: This project requires adult supervision.

Paper is not made just from trees. It's easy and interesting to create new paper from old paper! Invite the child to tear up several paper towels into small pieces and put them in a large bowl. Cover the towel pieces with hot water, and add a tablespoon of starch. With adult supervision, the child can beat up the mixture until it turns to mush and then pour the mush into the shallow pan. The screen is slid into the bottom of the pan, and the child "mashes the mush" around to cover the screen! The child can then lift the screen and allow some of the water to drip out back into the pan before setting the screen down on a stack of newspapers. The child can put more newspaper on top and use a rolling pin to squeeze out more water. Remove the newspaper on top, and gently lift the paper off the screen and set on dry newspaper to dry fully. For a variation, colored tissue paper can be added to the paper mix before blending to make colored paper. For more unusual papers, after the paper has been blended

to mush, try adding glitter, leaf pieces, ribbon, flowers, or the other optional materials mentioned in What You'll Need. Spices can also be added to make fragrant papers. If the child really enjoys this activity, extend it by having the child experiment using different kinds of paper for the original torn paper base. Try paper bags, notebook paper, holiday cards, newspaper, Sunday funnies, and any other paper you think would be interesting—then observe the results.

PHONETIC FOOTBALL

◁▶◁▶◁▶◁▶◁▷

Colorful football cutouts help kids score with beginning sounds.

What You'll Need
- construction paper
- blunt scissors
- marker or pen

Encourage sports lovers to practice beginning sounds.

Cut 6 football shapes out of construction paper. Print a different letter on each football. Place the footballs in a row. Have the child start at the left end of the row and say a word that begins with the sound of the letter on the football. Explain to the child that, to score a touchdown, she must reach the other end of the row by saying a word for each football's letter. Play again by adding new letters.

DIRT DETECTIVE

◁▶◁▶◁▶◁▶◁▷

There are amazing things to find in everyday dirt!

What You'll Need
- newspaper
- small shovel
- dirt
- sieve or strainer
- magnifying glass
- paper (optional)
- pen or pencil (optional)

Spread some sheets of newspaper on a table or on the ground outside. Ask the child to dig up a shovelful of dirt and spread it out on the newspaper—or have him strain the dirt through a sieve or strainer. He can search for rocks, pebbles, insects, seeds, roots, and other interesting finds. Give him a magnifying glass so he can zero in on the objects and see them better. Then ask the child to sort the underground discoveries into categories. You may also invite the child to make a record of his discoveries through drawings.

PEASE PORRIDGE WHAT?

◁▷◁▷◁▷◁▷

An old nursery rhyme becomes the spark for a study of antonyms.

Repeat the following Mother Goose rhyme, "Pease Porridge Hot." Help the child write down the words to the rhyme. Underline the words *hot* and *cold.* Ask the child how these words are related. (They are opposites.) Invite the child to substitute different pairs of word opposites, or antonyms, to make a silly version of the rhyme.

> Pease porridge hot,
> pease porridge cold.
> Pease porridge in the pot, nine days old.
> Some like it hot,
> some like it cold.
> Some like it in the pot, nine days old.

Why do we remember nursery rhymes and other poems? Because of the rhyme! Have the child decipher the rhyme scheme (the order of the rhymed words) in this and other favorite nursery rhymes. (The rhyme scheme here is ABBABB.)

SMELLS GOOD!

◁▷◁▷◁▷◁▷

Let kids' noses lead them through this initial-letter activity.

Children put their noses to work in this beginning-sound activity.

Collect several foods and other items with interesting smells, such as a slice of apple sprinkled with cinnamon, a lemon, an orange slice, a bar of soap, a bottle of perfume, toothpaste, a sprig of mint, a tea bag, an onion slice, and a banana.

Blindfold the child and let her smell an item and try to identify it. Then the child must say another word that begins with the same sound. For an added challenge, ask the child to write the letter that begins the name of the item.

WORD COLLAGE

◁▷◁▷◁▷◁▷

Words take on a personality all their own when they are artistically arranged in a collage. Get creative!

What You'll Need
• old magazines
• blunt scissors
• paper
• glue

Choose a topic. Good examples include food, fashion, sports, and music. Then have the child look through magazines to find all the related words she can in headlines or advertisements. Look for words in a variety of type styles, colors, and artistic treatments. Have the child cut out the words. Then invite the child to place the words on a large sheet of paper to create new sentences, phrases, or interesting arrangements. Glue all the words in place. If there is room, the child can add related pictures.

VERY PUNNY

◁▷◁▷◁▷◁▷

In the mood for a chuckle? Then jump right into this "punny" activity that focuses on homophones.

Explain to the child that homophones are words that sound the same but are spelled differently, such as *to, two,* and *too.* Begin by making a list with the child of familiar homophones, such as *bear* and *bare.* Then invite the child to write and illustrate some puns. For example, the child may write "The boy has bear feet." Explain the difference between "bear feet" and "bare feet." Discuss which sentence is funnier and why. Invite the child to share his work with others.

STRIKE UP THE BAND!

◁▷◁▷◁▷◁▷

Create and play your own musical instruments.

What You'll Need
- empty long tissue box
- rubber bands of different thicknesses
- two 4"×4"×2" blocks of wood
- sandpaper
- scissors
- nontoxic white glue
- thin elastic
- jingle bells
- needle
- thread
- wire coat hanger
- metal bottle tops
- hammer
- nail
- radio or tape player (optional)

Caution: This project requires adult supervision.

Guitar: The child can stretch 3 or 4 rubber bands over the oval of the tissue box. The child can strum the rubber bands.

Sandpaper Blocks: Cut the sandpaper to fit the blocks of wood. Have the child glue the sandpaper to the bottom of the blocks. Allow the glue to dry. The child can rub the sandpaper blocks together to make a scratchy musical sound. (Caution: Child should not hold the blocks above her head while rubbing them together. The grit from the sandpaper can get into eyes.)

Bracelet Bells: Cut 8 to 10 inches of elastic. Have the child thread the bells along the length and tie them in place. Sew or tie the ends of the elastic together. Have the child wear the bracelet on a wrist or ankle and shake it to the music.

Shaker: Make a shaker by opening a wire coat hanger near the hook. Using a hammer and a nail, make holes in the bottle tops, and slide them onto the hanger—arranging them back to front—on the bottom of the coat hanger. (Most of this the adult will do, but the child can help slide the bottle tops on the coat hanger when the holes are punched.) Reclose the hanger. The child can shake the hanger to the music.

Each of the instruments can be played alone or with music from the radio or tape player, or the whole family can get into the swing of it and become a band.

ABC—What Do You See?

◁▶◁▶◁▶◁▶

Children need to be observant to play this game successfully.

Children enjoy solving riddles, and this activity will help a child to become aware of objects in the environment through riddles.

This game may be played in the home or anywhere. Begin by saying: "ABC, what do you see? I see something beginning with *T*." Have the child solve the riddle by saying something that she sees beginning with the letter *T* (for example, *table, teaspoon, tree*). You can give additional clues as needed, such as color, size, shape, function, or location. You can also ask the child to touch the object that she identifies. Reverse roles, and have the child choose a letter and start the riddle.

RIDDLE GAME

◁▶◁▶◁▶◁▶

Share jokes and riddles with the child in this rib-tickling activity about letter sounds.

Tell the child that you are going to ask for an answer to a riddle. Explain that there may be more than one answer to the question, or riddle, but the correct answer must have a designated long vowel sound either in the middle or at the end of the word. See the following examples:

Long *e*—What insect makes honey in its hive? (bee)
Long *e*—Which bee rules the worker bees? (queen)

WHAT PAINTS HOW?

◁▷◁▷◁▷◁▷

Put down your paintbrush, and try these unusual painting tools!

What You'll Need
- feather
- twigs and leaves
- cotton ball
- cotton swab
- sponge
- paint
- paper
- paintbrush

Here's an artistic way for the child to experiment with a variety of improvised paint tools and have fun noticing the different results that can be achieved using them. Give the child a wide variety of paint tools, including a traditional paintbrush and some nontraditional tools, such as those listed at left. Let her experiment with the items and draw conclusions about how different tools paint. To make the activity more difficult, include the child when you choose the tools to be used, and continue to add new implements for further testing. To simplify, allow the child to experiment with only 2 or 3 very different kinds of implements at a time.

MENU SPECIALS

◁►◁►◁►◁►

Waiting for your food to be served? This menu game helps time pass by quickly.

What can you do in a restaurant to involve a child until dinner is served? Keep your menu, and play this game.

Ask the server if you may keep the menu until dinner is served. Give the child the menu, and have him locate a menu item beginning with a certain letter. You can be specific and state that it must be a capital or lowercase letter. When the child finds a word beginning with that letter, have him point to it and say the letter. Ask the child to look at all the letters in the word and, by sounding out the letters, try to determine what the menu item is.

LETTER RATTLES

◁▷◁▷◁▷◁▷◁▷

The only thing more fun than matching letters is making lots of noise when you're finished!

What You'll Need
- masking tape or adhesive labels
- marker or pen
- 5 empty coffee cans with plastic lids
- set of alphabet blocks

Children will compare uppercase and lowercase versions of letters in this activity.

Choose any 5 letters of the alphabet. Write the capital letter version on 1 piece of masking tape (or label) and the matching lowercase letter form on another. Put the capital letters on the empty cans and the lowercase letters on the detached lids, which should be placed nearby.

Lay out the blocks. Ask the child to find the blocks with the letters indicated on each of the cans, then put them inside the containers. Next, have the child find the lids with the matching lowercase letters and put them on the appropriate cans. Note that cans with blocks in them can be used as rhythm instruments.

ALPHABET WORD CHALLENGE

⊲▶⊲▶⊲▶⊲▶⊲◀

How many words can you think of that begin with a certain letter?

What You'll Need
• alphabet cards

After the child learns the alphabet and its letter sounds, this activity will provide a good review.

Show the child a letter of the alphabet. The challenge is for the child to name as many things as he can beginning with that letter. If a letter has different sounds (for example, the letter *G*, which can be hard or soft), encourage the child to use words with all the possible sounds of that particular letter.

BEGINNING JOURNAL

⊲▶⊲▶⊲▶⊲▶⊲▶

Keeping a journal is a creative way to document events. Try this easy journal for the beginning writer.

What You'll Need
• notebook
• pencil or markers

Begin by inviting the child to draw pictures of things that happened during the day. Then have the child add a few key words under the pictures so the events are remembered. Be sure each entry is dated. As the writing skills improve, help the child create complete sentences. You can also add a sentence or 2 each day. Turn this into a creative end-of-the-day activity.

WALDORF SALAD

◁▶◁▶◁▶◁▶

The child will enjoy learning about verbs while you chop, slice, and mix a Waldorf salad.

Caution: This project requires adult supervision.

Set out an apple, a stalk of celery, and some nuts. Ask the child to use simple words to explain what someone might do to each of the foods before eating them. Make a list of the action verbs suggested by the child. Then carefully prepare the ingredients according to the following recipe for a Waldorf salad. (When you chop up the ingredients, be sure to remind the child that he should always be very careful around knives.)

Mix together:
1 chopped apple
1 sliced celery stalk
½ cup chopped nuts
½ cup mayonnaise or salad dressing
Serve on a bed of lettuce.

What You'll Need
• apple
• celery
• nuts in shells
• mayonnaise or salad dressing
• lettuce
• nutcracker
• knife
• bowl
• spoon

SHARED WORD STORIES

◁▶◁▶◁▶◁▶

Combine groups of unrelated words to spur story narration. Expect some creative results.

Begin by writing 5 words on a sheet of paper. Invite the child to do the same on another piece of paper. Then, by using the words from both your list and the child's list, take turns making up and reciting a short story that includes all 10 words.

What You'll Need
• pencil
• paper

FELT-BOARD BACKDROPS

◁▷◁▷◁▷◁▷

The child's sequencing skills will be enhanced through this creative storytelling activity.

What You'll Need
- cardboard
- felt
- clear tape or glue
- paper
- markers or crayons
- old magazines
- blunt scissors
- sandpaper

Help the child make a felt board by gluing or taping a large piece of felt or felt squares onto a large piece of cardboard. Invite the child to draw or to cut out pictures of people and animals from old magazines. Then make those pictures sturdy by taping or gluing them onto small pieces of cardboard. Glue a small piece of sandpaper to the back of the cardboard so the story piece will stick to the felt board. Place the pictures on the felt board, and invite the child to use the characters to dramatize and tell a made-up story or to retell a favorite one.

ALPHABET HUNT

◁▷◁▷◁▷◁▷

Using a clipboard will add to kids' fun as they conduct this official alphabet search.

Here's a great way to brush up on all of the letters in the alphabet.

What You'll Need
- letter cards
- legal pad or paper and clipboard
- marker or pen

Remove any 1 letter card from a set of letter cards representing the entire alphabet. Place the remaining 25 cards around a room in plain sight, but in random order, then help the child write the letters of the alphabet in proper order down the page on a legal pad.

Instruct the child to go around the room and put a check mark on the pad beside the appropriate letter as he finds each card. When the child has finished this task, ask him to identify the letter on the pad that does not have a check mark. For beginners, use only the first 10 letters of the alphabet.

PIZZA PARTY!

◁▶◁▶◁▶◁▶

***Here the budding young chef learns descriptive words
while making a gigantic pizza!***

To perk up a child's appetite, tempt him with this activity—making a gigantic pizza. Show the pizza crust (large cardboard circle), and have the child suggest ingredients to use for making pizza. (Use the example provided for suggestions.) Invite the child to list suggestions on the recipe card. Provide assistance with spelling as needed. The child will enjoy following the recipe, cutting and pasting or taping paper replicas of the ingredients, of course!

What You'll Need
- cardboard circle 24" to 36" in diameter
- large recipe card
- pen or pencil
- paper scraps
- clear tape or glue
- blunt scissors

  20 slices of pepperoni
  2 green peppers
  1 pineapple
  2 hams
  30 tomatoes
  50 cups of cheese
  1 giant pizza crust
  10 sausages
  2 onions
  25 mushrooms
  5 anchovies
  100 olives
  12 cups of tomato sauce

Share recipes for making pizza from real cookbooks with the child. Compare the ingredients and the amounts used in the cookbook recipes to the recipe shown above.

Did you forget any essential ingredients? If possible, follow the cookbook recipe to make a real pizza.

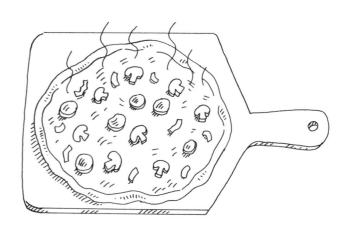

HARD C/SOFT C

⊲▶⊲▶⊲▶⊲▶

Is it hard or is it soft? How many C words can you think of?

The English language can be difficult for a young child. Some of the letters make a variety of different sounds, so it is important that the child be exposed to them.

Collect objects (or pictures of things) that begin with the letter C. The purpose of this activity is for the child to divide these materials into 2 groups: those with a hard C sound, as in *cake*, and ones with a soft C sound, as in *celery*. (Sample objects: *cup, cookies, ceiling, carrot, circle.*)

What You'll Need
- objects (or pictures of objects) that begin with a C

PRONOUN BINGO

⊲▶⊲▶⊲▶⊲▶

The child will have fun playing this familiar game of wits, luck, and learning about pronouns.

What You'll Need
- cardboard
- felt-tip pens
- game markers (beans, paper squares, bottle caps)

Before beginning the game, make a cardboard bingo game board. Write a pronoun—such as *he, she, we, they, it*—in each square. (The example shown is only a partially completed board.) Make sure that every board is differ-

B	I	N	G	O
HE	SHE	THEY	IT	WE
ME				

ent. To play the game, call out names of people, objects, or animals, both singular and plural, and have each player cover the square containing the corresponding pronoun. The first player to cover 5 squares in a row is the winner.

GIVE ME A RING

⬦⬦⬦⬦⬦⬦

This ring-toss game makes it fun to practice one of the more difficult letters.

What You'll Need
- poster board
- blunt scissors
- 12" to 24" pole
- paper
- pen

Active children can prepare to write by playing all kinds of physical games.

To make a ring toss game, cut several rings from poster board or cardboard. Make the hole of each ring about 6" in diameter. Put the pole in clay or sand to hold it upright. Invite the child to throw the rings around the pole. Each time he succeeds, have the child say the word *ring* and write the letter *R* on a scorecard. Continue until the child has scored at least 5 rings.

A DAY AT THE RACES

⬦⬦⬦⬦⬦⬦

It could be a photo finish when kids who know beginning sounds play this board game.

What You'll Need
- poster board or wrapping paper
- marker or pen
- letter cards made from index cards
- die and markers from a board game

Try this racetrack board game to practice beginning sounds. First, draw a large oval racetrack on poster board or a large sheet of wrapping paper. Write *Start* and *Finish* at the appropriate places. Mark the track with small squares, and place a letter card in each one. Place game markers at the beginning of the track.

Players take turns rolling the die and moving their markers along the track. When a player lands on a square, he must identify the letter and say a word that begins with the sound the letter stands for. If the player gives an incorrect answer, he goes back to Start. Play until someone reaches the Finish line.

RUN, WALK, JUMP, AND HOP

Hop for happiness and jump for joy in this beginning-sound activity.

Play an active game that focuses on the beginning sounds *H, R, W,* and *J*.

Say the word *hand,* and ask the child to demonstrate hopping. Point out that the words *hand* and *hop* begin with the same sound. Tell the child that you will say words that begin like *hop* and also some that begin like *run, walk,* and *jump.* He should perform the activity (hop, run, walk, or jump) whose name has the same beginning sound as the word you say. Words to use might include *rope, wet, jar, head, win, jet, red,* and *hat.*

SNACK FACE AT MY PLACE

Smile at a snack that will smile back!

What You'll Need
- plate
- plastic knife
- peanut butter or cream cheese
- rice cakes
- toppings (olives, carrot slices, apple slices, raisins, walnut halves)

First, have everyone wash their hands. Put a plate, a plastic knife, and the food items on a table. Invite the child to make faces out of them. Have him start by spreading peanut butter or cream cheese on a rice cake (or any round cracker or bread). Mouths, noses, and eyes (and ears and eyebrows and mustaches, if desired!) can be created by placing assorted toppings on the spread. The child can tell you about the face snack and then eat it as a treat. To make the activity more unusual and intriguing, invite the child to create 3 or 4 different faces. Then carefully cut each of the faces in half. The child can mix and match the faces before eating them!

CATCHING RAINDROPS

◁▶◁▶◁▶◁▶◁▶◁▷

Here's a way to catch a raindrop!

What You'll Need
- bowl
- measuring cup
- flour
- salt
- flat tray
- rain
- fork
- plate
- water (optional)

Raindrops fall so quickly it's never easy to see them individually or compare the size of one to another. The child can prepare a mixture in which to capture the falling raindrop shapes by mixing in a bowl 2 cups of flour and 1 cup of salt. The mixture is then spread out in a flat tray. The child should set the tray outside in the rain for a moment or two and then bring it back indoors. If there's no rain, the experiment can still be performed by gently dripping water from a wet hand over the mixture. Let the rain-catching mixture sit for a few hours. After that time, the flour and salt mixture will have created a mold around the shape the water made on impact. The shapes can be carefully scooped out with a fork and set on a plate in a warm place to harden. The child can then compare the sizes and shapes of the drops and ponder how and why hitting the ground makes them change. To extend this activity, encourage the child to repeat the experiment in different kinds of rain.

THAT'S CHEESY!

◁▶◁▶◁▶◁▶◁▶

You can eat the letters in this tasty alphabet game.

What You'll Need
- American cheese slices or block of cheese
- knife

Caution: This project requires adult supervision.

In this activity, children can make letters out of cheese strips or sticks.

Cut slices of American cheese into strips, or slice a block of any firm cheese such as mild cheddar, mozzarella, or Monterey Jack into sticks. (Be careful with the knife around the child.) Make the sticks approximately 2" long and ½" wide. Have the child wash his hands, then show him how to form the cheese sticks into letters. Start with letters that are easier to form, such as *E, F, H,* and *L.* Have the child form and identify several letters before eating them.

INSTANT SPEECH

◁▶◁▶◁▶◁▶◁▶

Speaking on the spur of the moment is a great way to develop organizational and expressive skills.

What You'll Need
- watch or timer

Begin by choosing common topics together, such as dogs, trees, or the weather. Then take turns challenging one another to do a 1-minute speech about what you know of the topic. As the child gains more knowledge about a topic, change the time to 2 minutes.

I Spy

◁▷◁▷◁▷◁▷◁▷◁▷

I Spy something red, yellow, blue, green, and purple in the sky.
The name has long a sound. What is it?

This game is played using long *a* words, such as *cake, page,* and *rainbow.* Look around the room until you find an object with a long *a* sound in its name. Give 1 or more clues to help the child identify the object. Then have the child spell the name of the object. Once the child has correctly spelled the name of the object, encourage him to use the name of the object in a sentence.

For a challenging variation, identify objects using other vowel sounds such as short *a,* short *e,* long *e,* and so on. Use as many vowel sounds as possible.

Seeds, Roots, and Shoots

◁▶◁▶◁▶◁▶

Besides seeds, what else will grow?

What You'll Need
- lima beans
- sweet potato
- potato
- carrot top
- plant cutting
- jars
- soil
- water
- toothpicks

Planting seeds isn't the only way to grow plants. New plants can also grow from roots, tubers, leaves, and stems. For many plants this ability is a form of self-preservation, in case their seeds cannot sprout because of conditions in the natural environment. Invite the child to experiment with different forms of plant growth! A lima bean can be planted in a glass jar. With adult supervision, the child can fill a glass jar with soil and push several beans down inside the jar along the edge. Set the jar in a sunny place, and keep the soil moist. The child will be able to watch the sprouting and growth of roots.

For sweet potato growth, the child can pierce the sweet potato with 3 or 4 toothpicks around its middle and set it in a jar so the toothpicks sit on the edge and the rounded end of the potato peeks out of the jar. The sweet potato, narrow end down, should be placed in the jar. The child can add water to the jar nearly to the top and set that jar in a sunny place also. For potato growth, the child can prepare the potato in the same way as the sweet potato, making sure to place the potato with the "eyes" on top.

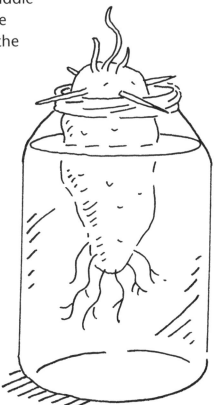

To grow a carrot plant, the child can cut off the top of a carrot, set it in a jar, and cover it to the top with water. Set the carrot in a sunny place, too!

Leaves cut from plants, such as philodendrons, and set in water will sprout new roots. They can then be replanted in a pot of soil to grow a new plant.

PUDDING PLAY

⬦◁▷◁▷◁▷◁▷

*Finger painting was never as much fun as it is with this pudding project.
And cleanup is as easy as 1-2-3!*

What You'll Need
- premixed pudding
- kitchen sponge
- dishpan
- soapy water

Begin by pouring a cup of premixed pudding on a clean, flat work surface. Invite the child to spread it around with his fingers. Then review final consonants by saying a word and helping the child figure out the final letter. Ask the child to write the final letter in the pudding. The child can "erase" the letter by rubbing over it with his fingertips. Continue by having the child write and erase final consonants and words for as long as the pudding lasts. (Pudding inevitably gets licked off fingers and out of the bowl, so it will not last too long.) For easy cleanup, use a sponge and a dishpan filled with soapy water.

SIMILE POEMS

◁▷◁▷◁▷◁▷

Once the child understands similes, they become easier to create!

This form of poetry is perfect for honoring a family member, creating a special card, or delighting a friend. The simile poem uses several sentences that have similes, which are 2 unlike thoughts that are compared to each other. The key words that identify a simile are *like* and *as*. The poem can be as short as 2 lines, as in the following examples, or as long as the young poet prefers. For an extension, have the child consider making a "simile book" to keep favorites that are heard or read for use in later writings.

What You'll Need
- paper
- pencil
- examples of similes from poetry books for young children

Mother is like a soft pillow
Her lap is as soft as a cloud.
My cat is like a ball of fur.
Her paws are as soft as velvet.

Silhouette Spray

◁▷◁▷◁▷◁▷

Paint around to see the shape!

What You'll Need
- newspaper
- leaves
- rocks
- twigs
- flowers
- construction paper
- tape
- thinned tempera paint
- plastic spray bottles

Create a nature painting of silhouette shapes. The child can collect nature items and tape them to construction paper. Spread newspaper over the work space for easy cleanup later. The child can tape 1 item on each piece of paper or can make a nature medley, taping several items on a large sheet of paper. Use the tape sparingly so it will lift easily from the project once it has been painted. Help the child roll the tape pieces to stick to both the underside of the object and the paper (you don't want the tape to be part of your silhouette!). After the items are taped in

place, the child can spray the entire paper with paint using the spray bottle filled with thinned tempera paint. When the paint is dry, the child can remove the items to reveal their silhouette shapes.

Under the Lens

◁▷◁▷◁▷◁▷

Look at the environment with this magnificent magnifying lens.

What You'll Need
- plastic magnifying lens
- notebook
- pen or pencil

Have the child practice using the verbs *see* and *saw* correctly. Then go on a walking field trip. Walk around the block, through a park, into a forest or wooded area, on the shore, or in another natural area. Invite the child to look through a magnifying lens to help observe, or see,

the surrounding environment. Encourage the child to use the words *see* and *saw* correctly while describing new discoveries. Then have the child record the discoveries, or what he saw, in a nature journal or notebook.

Topsy-Turvy Words

◁▷◁▷◁▷◁▷

*Use a spinning top to help youngsters recognize the letter **T**.*

Make word cards by writing simple words that begin with the letter *T* on index cards. Words to use include

ten, tap, tag, Tom, toe, tar, tax, tent, tall, tape, tail, and *tell.* Have the child spin the top. Hold up a card, and ask the child to read the word on

the card before the top stops spinning. If the child cannot read the word cards, draw a simple picture or other hint (such as the numeral 10 for the word *ten*) on each card before the game begins.

What You'll Need
• index cards
• marker or pen
• toy top

Morning, Afternoon & Evening

◁▷◁▷◁▷◁▷

Make a times-of-the-day collage.

The child can create a sequence collage to show the different kinds of activities that happen at different times of the day. Tape 3 different colored pieces of construction paper together to make a long piece of paper with 3 sections. Explain to the child that the first section of the collage is for pictures that show things people do in the morning when a day begins. The middle paper is for activities people do in the middle of the day. And the last section of the paper is for things that happen at the end of the day. Ask the child to tell you about different kinds of things he does in the morning, in the middle of the day, or during the evening when the day is ending. Then invite the child to find pictures in magazines to cut out that illustrate morning, afternoon, and evening activities and glue them to the collage.

What You'll Need
• construction paper
• tape
• old magazines
• blunt scissors
• nontoxic white glue

BALANCING ACT

◁▷◁▷◁▷◁▷

Keep cool and steady, and balance that bag!

Challenge the child to explore balance. With a beanbag on top of his head, can the child walk, tiptoe, or run without the bag falling? Can the child walk backward without dropping the bag? What about sideways? Can the child crawl without dropping the bag? The child can also experiment with balance by trying to walk steady with the bag placed on a shoulder, an outstretched arm, a foot, or one bag on each foot! Then try the same activities with the other objects.

> **What You'll Need**
> • items for balancing: bean-bag, sponge, paper plate

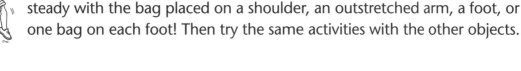

HOOP IT UP

◁▷◁▷◁▷◁▷

Hoop it up with this sockball-tossing game of skill, poetry, and real or make-believe story events.

Before beginning, mark a line on the floor with masking tape. Place 2 small wastebaskets about 12 feet from the line. Tape labels marked "REAL" and "MAKE-BELIEVE" on the sides of the wastebaskets. Set out a pile of balled-up socks by the masking-tape line.

To play, read favorite passages from books or poems the child recently read or enjoyed. Ask the child to decide whether the events and characters are real or make-believe. Allow time for the child to answer. Once an answer is given, have the child stand behind the line and toss a balled-up sock into the appropriate basket. When all the socks have been tossed, count them to see how many characters or events the child thought were real and how many were make-believe.

> **What You'll Need**
> • masking tape
> • 2 small wastebaskets
> • paper labels
> • markers
> • balled-up socks
> • storybooks

PICNIC IN THE PARK

◁▷◁▷◁▷◁▷

It's a perfect day for a picnic, but first you have to pack.

What You'll Need
- picnic basket
- foods beginning with the letter *P*

It is a beautiful day outside, so why not enjoy a lovely picnic in the park?

Have the child help you plan what to take on this picnic. However, only things that begin with the letter *P* may be taken. As you are talking, emphasize *P* words. Ask the child to think of foods that you can bring: peanut butter sandwiches, peaches, pineapple juice served in a paper cup, potato chips, pretzels. Prepare those foods, pack the picnic basket, and have a great time at the park.

POEM PICTURES

◁▷◁▷◁▷◁▷

Capture with colors the pictures that poems paint with words!

Share a favorite poem with the child. Invite the child to describe what and whom the poem is about and the scene where it might take place. The child can then draw a picture to illustrate the poem as imagined. For a variation, the child can create different illustrations for the poem (or for other poems) using different media, such as finger paints or watercolors.

What You'll Need
- paper
- crayons
- finger paints or water-color paints (optional)

SCARF DANCING

⊲▶⊲▶⊲▶⊲▶

Groove to the music!

What You'll Need
- radio
- scarves (or long pieces of ribbon or crepe-paper streamers)

Before beginning this activity, find a variety of music stations on your radio. Make a list so you can tune them in quickly. Give the child several scarves, and invite him to move to the music. Change the radio station frequently to provide examples of different types of music. As the music changes, talk to the child about body movement (how different parts of the body can be used to make slow or fast movements). Have the child create a self-expressive dance that incorporates different kinds of music.

Activity Twist

Manipulate your small finger muscles, too. Create unique designer scarves for expressive dancing. Together, cut or tear strips of fabric. Mix up some tempera paint and use lots of interesting objects to create print designs on the material. Or, try some exciting squiggles with nontoxic glitter glue. And now, let the dance begin!

Touching the Outside

◁▷◁▷◁▷◁▷◁▷

Turn a nature collection into a touch-and-guess game.

What You'll Need
- nature items with different textures (tree bark, pine needles, dry grass, pebbles, twigs)
- cardboard
- nontoxic white glue

Take a walk outside together, and collect a variety of nature items. Collect 2 of each item! When you return, have the child glue each item to an individual piece of cardboard. After the glue has dried, with eyes closed, the child can touch each item and guess what it is by feel. The child can also match the pairs, finding the same items using touch only.

Tool Printing

◁▷◁▷◁▷◁▷◁▷

Create kitchen art using cooking utensils for artist's tools.

What You'll Need
- newspaper
- common kitchen and household tools: potato masher, fork, garlic press, whisk
- shallow pan
- tempera paint
- paper

To begin, cover the work surface with newspaper. The child can experiment with printmaking using common utensils. The child can dip the utensil into a shallow pan of paint and then press it on paper to make a print. The child can explore and observe the different print each kind of tool makes and then create designs and pictures by printing. If the child enjoys printing activities, on another day, gather together a different assortment of common items to experiment with. Other good items to start with are a comb, keys, a large paper clip, and a plastic lid.

FOLLOWING DIRECTIONS

⊲▶⊲▶⊲▶⊲▶

*Here's an activity for the child to practice learning
how to follow directions while being creative!*

Decide on a craft project to make. Remember to explain to
the child the importance of carefully following directions.

When finished, have the child reread the directions.
Did the child follow them? If there were illustrations,
did the child need to rely on them to understand the
written directions? Try the same process with another
project to reinforce the importance of following directions for craft projects.

What You'll Need
• simple craft book
• various craft materials to
  complete chosen projects

ROCK, PAPER, SCISSORS

⊲▶⊲▶⊲▶⊲▶

*Rock crushes scissors, scissors cut paper—
but kids are the big winners in this activity.*

What You'll Need
• marker or pen
• 3 index cards
• small rock
• sheet of paper
• blunt scissors

Teach a child to distinguish between the letters *R, P,* and *S*
using a classic hand game.

Write the letter *R* on one index card, *P* on another, and
S on the third. Hold up a rock, and ask the child to identify
the beginning letter in its name. Do the same with the
paper and scissors.

Show the child how to play "Rock, Scissors, Paper" with
your hands: Make a fist for the rock, hold up the first 2 fin-
gers for the scissors, and hold the hand flat for the paper. Remember, rock beats scissors, paper beats rock, and scissors beat paper. Tell the child
you will hold up a card with a letter on it. The child
should respond by making the hand signal for
rock, scissors, or paper, depending on which
of those words begins with that letter.

CLAY POTTERY

A handmade piece of coiled pottery will be perfect for your table.

What You'll Need
• clay
• waxed paper
• small container of water

A child's hands will get a lot of exercise as clay is softened and then rolled into coils to form a piece of pottery.

Have the child "work" a ball of clay by kneading it to soften it. When the clay is soft, tell the child to pull off some clay from the ball and press that piece into a flat circle shape with his hand. It's best to do this on a sheet of waxed paper. Tell the child, "I am thinking of a word that begins with the same sound as the word *red*. This word describes what you can do to the rest of the clay to make long thin strips. What word is it?" (Answer: *roll*.) As the child is rolling the clay, ask, "What other *R* words can you think of?" (*Rub* and *round* are two possibilities.)

When the clay has been shaped into several rolls (coils), have the child take one and wrap it around the edge of the clay circle. Continue placing the other coils on top of the previous ones. When all the coils are on the base, forming a pot, ask the child to gently rub the inside of the coiled rolls to smooth and seam them together. If the clay is too dry, the child can dip his finger into some water and then smooth the inside of the pot.

Discuss with the child what *R* words were used in making this coiled pot. After a few days of drying and hardening, the pot is ready for a special spot in your home.

Assorted Assemblage of Paper

◁▷◁▷◁▷◁▷

Be a paper detective, and search for a multiplicity of paper types.

Challenge the child to find different kinds of paper around the house. How many different kinds can the child find? The child can start a collection of samples of each type of paper, such as writing paper, construction paper, newspaper, wrapping paper, paper bag, paper towel, toilet paper, cardboard. The child can categorize the papers, choosing the classification system (shiny or rough, printed or blank, etc.). The activity can be ongoing as the child continues to discover more and different kinds of paper all around.

I Like Ice Cream

◁▷◁▷◁▷◁▷

A tasty homemade treat helps children put the I in the alphabet.

What You'll Need
- large bowl
- eggbeater
- measuring cups
- measuring spoons
- egg substitute
- sugar
- vanilla extract
- salt
- evaporated milk
- whole milk
- freezer

Children can consider the long *I* sound as they help make homemade ice cream. Discuss the following steps as you and the child work together.

Pour enough egg substitute to equal 4 eggs in a large bowl. Beat in 1¾ cups of sugar, 1½ teaspoons of vanilla extract, and ¼ teaspoon of salt. Add 1 cup of evaporated milk and 1 quart of whole milk. Stir. Place the mixture in the freezer.

Ask the child to think of additional words beginning with the long *I* sound, such as *idea, icicle,* and *ivy,* as you work. You can also emphasize the beginning sounds of

vanilla, salt, and *milk* as you mix the ice cream.

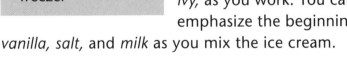

TOOL TIME

⊲◆⊲▷⊲◆▷⊲◆▷⊲◆▷

Every good cook knows the importance of using the right utensils.

What You'll Need
- ingredients and utensils needed for baking cookies
- baking pan
- oven
- concentrated juice drink
- water
- bowl
- rotary eggbeater
- spatula
- plates
- strawberries or apple slices
- tongs

Snack preparation helps a child develop small motor skills through the use of kitchen tools. Explain that you will prepare a snack that requires the use of several different kitchen tools.

First, prepare a refrigerated cookie dough roll, or make cookie dough using a mix or recipe. While waiting for the cookies to bake, let the child use a rotary eggbeater to mix water with concentrated juice mix in a bowl.

When the cookies are done, remove them from the pan and place them onto plates, using a spatula. Then let the child add a strawberry or apple slice to the plates using tongs. Discuss all the steps, utensils, and ingredients involved in making the snack, emphasizing the beginning sounds of each.

REARRANGED RETELLINGS

◁▷◁▷◁▷◁▷

Here is a wacky way for the child to communicate information in sequence.

What You'll Need
• paper
• markers or crayons

Help the child draw 4 or 5 separate pictures depicting 4 or 5 major events of a traditional or favorite story. Have the child lay out the pictures in sequential order and tell the story. Then randomly rearrange the pictures, and challenge the child to make up and tell a new version of the story in which the events occur in the new order. Expect some hilarious results!

CREATING A TIME CAPSULE

◁▷◁▷◁▷◁▷

In this activity, the child will have the opportunity to create his own legacy.

Discuss what a time capsule is and how people enjoy seeing what life was like in the past. Find a container that will be safe for at least 10 years: an airtight plastic container or a small fireproof box. Talk about what is important in the child's life right now. Have the child collect various items represent-

What You'll Need
• airtight container
• 3" × 5" index cards
• pencil

ing these times. For each item, help the child write a description on a card, including information about its use. Place the items in the box. Put a label on it that says "To be opened on __." Fill the blank with a date that is 10 years in the future. Then put the time capsule in a safe place to be opened 10 years later!

WHIRLYBIRD

⊲▶⊲▶⊲▶⊲▶

Make a paper copter and watch it whirl.

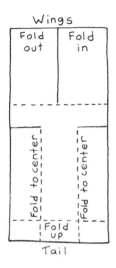

Wings

Fold out | Fold in

Fold to center | Fold to center

Fold up

Tail

Using the diagram shown, help the child create a whirlybird. After enlarging and copying the diagram onto paper, have the child help you cut on solid lines and fold on dotted lines. After folding in the sides of the bottom section, fold the tail section up. The child can then experiment dropping the whirlybird from high and low places and watching how it spins to the ground. The child can also make bigger and smaller whirlybirds to experiment with.

What You'll Need
- paper
- pencil
- scissors

WHAT'S THE OPPOSITE?

⊲▶⊲▶⊲▶⊲▶

Play a contradictory challenge game!

Take turns changing each other's words and statements into their opposites! Start off with easy words to think of opposites for, such as *hot (cold), rainy (sunny), happy (sad)*. Then try to turn simple sentences around! For example: A little girl ran home. (A big boy walked to the store.)

SEQUEL STORIES

Imagine what happens after the story ends!

Encourage the child to think about what happens after a favorite story ends. What do the people and animals do next? Do they have any other problems? Adventures? Funny experiences? Do they stay in the same place, move far away, or go on a vacation? Do they meet any new people? After reading or retelling a favorite story, invite the child to make up and tell a story about what happens after the story ends!

For a variation, the child can think of a "prequel" rather than a sequel, imagining and making up what took place just before the story in the storybook began.

What You'll Need
• favorite folktale or story

Rhyme Time!
Sammy the snake is sleeping,
when suddenly he awakes.
S-s-s
is the soft little sound he makes.
Sammy the snake is crawling,
over the leaves on the ground.
S-s-s
Sammy makes a soft
little sound.

LETTER ORDER

◁▷◁▷◁▷◁▷

CBA or ABC? When kids know their letters, they can put them in order.

What You'll Need
- set of letter cards with capital letters
- set of letter cards with lowercase letters

Children can manipulate letter cards to learn alphabetical order.

Remove the capital letter cards *A* through *F* from the first set of cards. Mix the 6 cards. Ask the child to lay the cards out in alphabetical order. When he is ready for more challenging activities, use additional capital letters and then lowercase letters.

PLEASE DROP IN

◁▷◁▷◁▷◁▷

While kids drop clothespins into a bottle, they learn different letter sounds.

What You'll Need
- plastic container (such as a 1-gallon milk container) with the top cut off
- plastic clothespins

Have the child practice the letter *P* sound by playing a variation of an old party favorite. Put the container on the floor, and have the child stand an arm's length away from it. Give the child 5 clothespins and instruct him to stand straight while attempting to drop each clothespin into the container. After dropping a pin into the container, the child must say a word that begins with *P.*

After the child drops the 5 clothespins, start over using words that start with a different first letter.

Fun Fact
Letters *I, T, L,* and *X* are the easiest letters to make.

DO AS I SAY!

◁▶◁▶◁▶◁▶

*This direction-following activity is fun and challenging,
and it enhances listening skills.*

Following directions involves several different skills, including listening, comprehending, remembering, and translating words into action. Begin by explaining that you are going to list several directions for the child to follow, and that each direction should be followed exactly in the order given. Start by giving only 3 or 4 directions at a time for the child to follow. For example, you may say "jump 6 times, turn all the way around, then touch your toes." After the child has shown that 3 or 4 directions can easily be followed, increase the difficulty by giving 5 directions in a series, and then 6.

READING THE SIGNS

◁▸◁▸◁▸◁▸◁▸

Don't waste a minute of learning while running errands.
Information is everywhere!

Opportunities to read exist all around us. While running errands, going to school, or just walking around the neighborhood together, take notice of all the different signs. Then have the child read the signs with you. Discuss how the words start and end. Encourage the child to read them independently.

RIDDLE DEE DEE

◁▸◁▸◁▸◁▸◁▸

The child strengthens comprehension skills while hopping through riddles.

What You'll Need
- 3 to 5 hula hoops
- riddle book

Lay the hula hoops on the floor, one in front of the other, as shown in the illustration. Read a riddle, and invite the child to solve it. For a correct answer, the child can hop into the first hula hoop. If the child is unable to answer the riddle, however, he cannot advance and must wait for the next riddle. Keep asking riddles until the child has reached the last hula hoop. Once the child does reach the end, switch roles and allow the child to ask the riddles while you progress through the hoops.

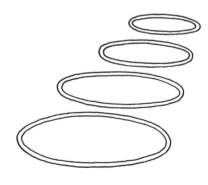

DIALING FINGERS

◁▶◁▶◁▶◁▶◁▶

Little fingers that are itching to use the phone like grown-ups will be satisfied with this pretend activity.

What You'll Need
- pen or pencil
- paper
- toy telephone with push buttons containing letters

Here's a spelling exercise that introduces a child to one of the wonders of modern technology—the telephone.

Explain to the child that, with real telephones, people must use specific numbers when they want to call someone. Tell the child that you will play a game in which he pretends to call friends and relatives by pressing the letters in their names instead of telephone numbers.

Ask the child to name someone, such as "David," whom he will pretend to phone. Print the name on a piece of paper. Have the child say the letter that stands for the beginning sound in the name and then press the button on the phone that has that letter.

See if he can finish spelling the name this way. If not, you can help by saying the letter and having the child find and press the correct button on the telephone.

QUILT MAKING

◁▷◁▷◁▷◁▷

Keep warm by wrapping yourself up in a beautiful quilt.

The letter *Q* is a difficult letter for a child to identify and learn because there are so few *Q* words. Tell the child that *Q* is so quiet that it needs a *u* standing next to it to make words.

Help the child make a quilt. Cut out 16 pieces of material measuring 10" × 10". The child can then take the squares and arrange them on the floor in 4 rows of 4.

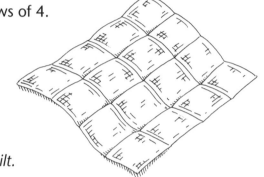

Using thread and a plastic needle, sew the squares with a simple up-and-down stitch. Keep adding squares. It is best to sew 4 squares together into a panel and then sew the panels together. Talk with the child about a quilt—how it may be used, why people make quilts, and the beginning letters and letter sounds in the word *quilt*.

LISTEN CAREFULLY

◁▷◁▷◁▷◁▷

One word in a group is not like the others. Which is it?

Select a letter of the alphabet, and think of some words that begin with the sound of that letter. Tell the child that you will be saying 3 words—2 words that begin with the same sound and 1 word that begins with a different sound. Say the 3 words—for example, *cat, ball, bird.* Have the child listen carefully and then tell you which word begins with the different letter sound.

To make this activity more challenging, say 4 or 5 words with the same beginning letter sound and 1 that is different. You can also reverse roles and have the child think of words that begin similarly and differently.

MUSICAL ALPHABET

◁▷◁▷◁▷◁▷

Here's a letter-recognition game that will be music to kids' ears.

The child's listening skills will get a workout in this activity.

Make a letter card for each letter of the alphabet. Lay the cards in a big circle on the floor, spaced about one child's step apart.

Tell the child to walk around the outside of the circle, one step per letter, when the music starts playing. When the music stops, the child must stop and name a word that begins with the sound represented by the letter she is standing next to. Repeat until many different letters have been used.

> **What You'll Need**
> • 26 index cards
> • marker or pen
> • radio (or cassette or CD player)

FOLLOW THE LEADER

◁▷◁▷◁▷◁▷

Can you do what I do? I can do what you do!

Follow the child around the house or yard, doing exactly what the child is doing— including running, flapping arms, waving, and hopping. When it is the adult's turn to be the leader, lead the child in some of the following ways: Use facial expressions, such as smiling, frowning, wiggling the nose, or winking; use head movements, such as nodding, twisting, or rotating the head; use finger and hand movements, such as wiggling fingers, snapping, waving, and clapping; use toe and foot movements, such as wiggling toes, tiptoeing, stomping, and sliding feet; and use body movements, such as bending at the waist, squatting, standing on one foot, and wiggling. To add more challenge, repeat combinations of moves, such as winking-waving-stomping-jumping.

Better to have education than wealth.
—Welsh proverb

SOAK IT TO ME

<><><><><><><>

What soaks in and what won't?

What You'll Need
- eyedropper
- cup of water
- paper towel
- cardboard
- polystyrene foam
- cork
- sponge
- waxed paper
- cotton ball
- plastic spoon
- aluminum foil
- button
- eraser
- rock

The child can make predictions about which items will absorb water and then test them by using an eyedropper to drip water on them. Have the child drip water on the paper towel first to show what *absorb* means. Then have the child drip water on the other items listed at left. After testing, the child can sort the objects into categories and describe the discoveries.

ALPHABET AVENUE

<><><><><><><>

Kids can walk the walk and talk the talk on this educational street.

What You'll Need
- butcher paper
- marker

On a large sheet of butcher paper, print a large letter with a marker. Make the letter approximately 2' high. You might start with the vowel *A, E, I, O,* or *U* or with the consonant *B, D, P, S,* or *T.* Put the sheet on the floor, and ask the child to walk on or around the letter while saying its name. After the child has mastered this letter, make a new sheet. You can also use a larger sheet to write several letters together at a time.

TACTILE LETTERS

◁▷◁▷◁▷◁▷◁▷◁▷

Here is a "sense-ational" way to learn letters.

What You'll Need
- burlap
- blunt scissors
- alphabet stencils
- glue
- lightweight cardboard

Children learn by using their senses, and touching is part of such learning. This activity is very good for a young child.

Cut out 26 pieces of burlap measuring approximately 5" × 5". Use alphabet stencils to transfer letters onto the burlap squares. Cut out the burlap letters. Glue them onto square pieces of cardboard. Make a set of capital or lower-case letters—or both. The object is for the child to close her eyes and feel the burlap letters, tracing the letter formations. Have the child tell you which letter it is.

For a variation, put the letters in a bag and have the child reach inside and feel the letter. Then have the child tell you what the letter is before pulling it out to see if the answer is correct.

WHERE CAN IT BE?

◁▷◁▷◁▷◁▷◁▷◁▷

Need two grocery items of the same thing? This is the activity for you.

Grocery shopping can be unpleasant for a young child, but by involving her in the process, it can become more interesting.

Return to an aisle where you have already selected an item—for example, the cereal aisle. Ask the child to find another box of the same cereal. This is great when you need two of a certain item, although you can always put one of the boxes back on the shelf. In this activity, the child will need to focus on the label (picture and writing), the size, and the shape of the item in order to make a correct match. Be sure that when you select an item it is on a shelf at or below the child's eye level so she can reach it.

Phonics Go Fish

◁▷◁▷◁▷◁▷◁▷

Do you have a picture of something that begins like the word **bed**? *Go fish!*

What You'll Need
- 10 pictures of objects cut from magazines
- blunt scissors
- clear tape
- 10 index cards

The card game "Go Fish" is ideal for identifying words with the same beginning sounds.

Cut 10 pictures from magazines and tape each one to an index card. Each picture name should have the same beginning sound as another picture name; for example, *bed/boy, cookie/car, lamp/lake, house/horse, roof/refrigerator.*

Shuffle the cards, then deal 5 cards to the child and 5 to yourself. First, lay down any pairs with matching sounds that either of you have. Then take turns asking each other for a card that will make a pair when combined with a card you already have. For example, "Do you have a picture whose name begins like *boy*?"

TELL IT BACKWARD!

◁▷◁▷◁▷◁▷

Here's a twist on storytelling—start with the ending first!

This challenging backward storytelling activity helps develop sequence understanding, comprehension, and story recall. Take turns retelling a favorite story with the child, only tell the story in reverse. You might want to have the book handy while retelling.

Begin telling at the end of the story. Then invite the child to tell the part that happened just before the ending. Take another turn and tell what happened before that. Continue taking turns until the whole story has been told, event by event, from end to beginning.

MAGIC WAND

◁▷◁▷◁▷◁▷

Make a magic wand and make magic!

Transform a piece of newspaper into a magic wand. Help the child roll the paper up into a skinny tube and secure it with masking tape. The child can decorate the wand with markers. Help the child cut fringe all around the top and tape the top of the strips together to create a bauble at the end. The child can then use the wand and invent magical consequences when the wand is waved or when someone is tapped by the wand. For a more brilliantly colored magic wand, use the Sunday funnies and colored masking tape.

What You'll Need
• newspaper
• masking tape
• markers
• blunt scissors
• colored masking tape (optional)

SECRET WORD

⊲▷⊲▷⊲▷⊲▷

Listening for verbal clues helps determine the meaning of unknown words.

Choose a word and keep it a secret. It must be a common word that is used often, such as water or a pet's name. Then, together with the child, agree on a sound for the secret word—for example, tapping your foot or whistling. Each time the word comes up in conversation, you will perform the signal. The game can take place during other activities such as preparing lunch, cleaning the house, or taking a walk. How long does it take the child to determine what the secret word is?

CAN YOU FIND IT?

⊲▷⊲▷⊲▷⊲▷

This hide-and-describe game allows the child to practice using descriptive verbal clues.

Choose 2 small objects together. Begin by hiding 1 of the small objects while the child has her eyes closed or has gone into another room. Once the object is hidden, give the child verbal clues that describe where the object can

What You'll Need
• 2 household objects small enough to hide

be found without actually revealing its exact whereabouts. Once the object has been found by the child, it is your turn to close your eyes or leave the room. This time the child will hide the second object and give you verbal clues that describe where the object can be found, without revealing its exact whereabouts.

FEED THE BIRDS

◁▷◁▷◁▷◁▷◁▷

What lovely treats for our feathered friends!

What You'll Need
- pinecones
- 2 plastic dishes
- peanut butter
- birdseed
- plastic spoon
- yarn

Find some pinecones, and as you are collecting them with the child, talk about the types of trees that have pinecones and needles. See what different sizes and types of pinecones you can find.

When you return home, tell the child that you will make a bird feeder from the pinecones. Ask, "Do you know what birds like to eat that begins like the word *sun*?" (Answer: seeds.) Put some peanut butter in one dish and birdseed in another. Have the child take a plastic spoon and spread peanut butter on a pinecone. Then have the child roll the peanut-butter-covered pinecone in birdseed. The peanut butter will make the birdseed stick to the pinecone.

When several bird feeder pinecones are made, take pieces of yarn and help the child tie a knot around the top of each one. Then make a loop at the other end of the yarn, and hang the pinecones on a tree branch. As you are hanging the bird feeders, ask the child, "What two things did you use to make this that began like the word *pat*?" (Answer: pinecone and peanut butter.) "What did you put on the peanut-butter-covered pinecone that begins like *sun*?" (Answer: seeds.)

Watch the tree, and see how many different birds come to eat these treats. Use a bird book to help identify them.

SNIP & CUT

◁▷◁▷◁▷◁▷

Cut! Cut! Cut! All for the fun of cutting!

What You'll Need
- blunt scissors
- paper plate
- variety of items to cut: construction paper, newspaper, plastic straws, fabric scraps, clean foam trays from fruit or vegetables, paper towels, yarn, ribbon
- clothespins (optional)

Provide the child with an assortment of materials to explore. Encourage the child to cut big pieces, little pieces, fat pieces, and skinny pieces. All the snippings can be collected on a paper plate. If desired, the child can create a collage with all the cut pieces, but no end product is necessary. The child will find cutting for its own sake enticing.

Activity Twist

It can be difficult for a young child to hold the paper still while cutting it. To make this easier, you can create a "cutting box" by cutting down the front of an open-top cardboard carton. Use clothespins to hold the paper steady on the high inside top of the box while the child holds the bottom edge of the paper and cuts with the scissors. The snips collect neatly on the bottom of the box.

PHONICS SALAD

◁▷◁▷◁▷◁▷

Toss some phonics in your recipe for a healthy, educational salad!

Begin by listing all of the ingredients you might put into a salad. Next, make a real salad using only ingredients that have a short vowel sound. Help the child sound out the words to hear the short vowel sounds. A short-vowel salad might have any or all of the following ingredients: lettuce, radish, celery, mushroom, egg, asparagus, olive, ham, and bell pepper. Top the salad with a favorite dressing, and enjoy the finished product! (If you do not want to make a real salad, you can easily adapt this activity to writing the ingredients on a recipe card.)

What You'll Need
- pencil
- index card
- salad ingredients
- large bowl
- salad spoons
- salad dressing

FINGER-PAINT FOLLIES

◁▶◁▶◁▶◁▶

This tasty substitute for finger paint provides an easy-to-clean-up and fun-to-use method to paint predictions.

Invite the child to spread the whipped cream on the top of a clean kitchen table, preferably one with a surface that can be cleaned easily with sponges and water.

What You'll Need
- whipped cream
- smock
- nursery rhyme
- kitchen sponge

Make sure the child is wearing a smock so she can be easily cleaned as well. Then read a nursery rhyme that is unfamiliar to the child. At some point in the rhyme, pause and ask the child to finger-paint a picture showing what she predicts will happen next.

Repeat this activity with other nursery rhymes. Have the child "erase" the previous drawing by rubbing over it with her hands. When finished, the child can sponge the excess whipped cream off the table.

BUILD A WORD

◁▶◁▶◁▶◁▶

Letters become the building blocks of words in this letter-recognition game.

What You'll Need
- index cards
- marker or pen

Putting 2 cards together to make a word will help children understand word construction.

Make 2 sets of cards. One set has a card for each of the following consonants: *B, C, D, F, S.* The other set has a card for each of the following word endings: *at, et, it, ob, ut, an, ell, ip, ot, un.*

Lay the consonant cards on a table, and put the word-ending cards in a pile. Have the child take a word-ending card and put it next to each consonant card that the word ending can be combined with to make a word. Have the child read each word. Continue through the set of word-ending cards.

INVENTING AROMAS

◁▷◁▷◁▷◁▷

Create personalized plant perfume!

What You'll Need
- plant materials: onion, leaves, flower petals, lemon peel
- waxed paper
- rolling pin
- jars
- water
- strainer

The child can choose any of a variety of plants, flowers, fruits, or vegetables and try to capture their scents. Extract the aroma by placing pieces of 1 plant, fruit, or vegetable between 2 sheets of waxed paper and then crushing them with a rolling pin. Place the crushed pieces inside a jar, and add water to cover the pieces. Leave the jar overnight to allow the water to absorb the scent. After a day, with adult help, the child can pour the scented water through a strainer into a new jar, straining out the crushed pieces. Then test the fragrance. For a more advanced exploration, the child can create several scents. The strained, scented water can be poured into jars, and the child can smell each of them to figure out which scent is which. Or each fragrance can be poured into 2 jars so the child can try to match the scents that are the same.

TABLE-TENNIS ART

◁▷◁▷◁▷◁▷

Paint table-tennis pictures!

What You'll Need
- pie tin
- construction paper
- blunt scissors
- table-tennis balls
- tempera paint
- paint containers
- spoon
- brownie pan (optional)
- liquid starch (optional)

Use a pie tin, paper circle, table-tennis ball, and paint to create circle designs. Cut a construction-paper circle the size of the pie-tin base, and place it in the pie tin. The child can dip the table-tennis ball into the paint, use a spoon to lift it out, and drop the ball into the pie tin. The child can then jiggle the pie

tin to create a design with the rolling ball. For a variation, use a brownie pan for square designs. Add a second table-tennis ball and a second color of paint for more fun! For thicker paint consistency, add some liquid starch to the paint.

FOOD RIDDLE

◁▷◁▷◁▷◁▷

Describing food characteristics will enhance the child's descriptive vocabulary—and make your mouth water!

What You'll Need
- foods that have distinctive characteristics (orange, apple, banana, squash, and so on)
- paper
- pencil

Have the child choose a food and make a list of all its characteristics without telling what the food is. For example, suggest that the list for an orange include words such as *bumpy, round, skin, sweet,* and so on. Invite the child to try to stump you by reading all the characteristics of a particular food without telling its name.

SALLY SINGS AND SHOUTS

◁▷◁▷◁▷◁▷

Children will love this action-packed verb game,
and it will strengthen their imagination.

What You'll Need
- paper
- pencil

Have the child write the first letter of her name. Then invite the child to think of verbs, or action words, that begin with that same letter. As a follow-up to the activity, see how many nouns—names of people, places, or things—the child can list beginning with that letter.

MASK MAKING

◁▷◁▷◁▷◁▷

Take part in making masks, then masquerade while playacting!

What You'll Need
- large paper bags
- markers or crayons
- blunt scissors
- glue
- construction paper
- fabric scraps
- yarn
- ribbon
- paper plate (optional)
- cardboard (optional)

Caution: This project requires adult supervision.

Turn large paper bags into masks of the child's favorite story characters! Place the paper bag over the child's head, and carefully mark holes for the eyes. Remove the bag, and cut the holes or invite the child to cut them. Recheck the eyeholes for good visibility, and adjust them for the child's best viewing. The child can then decorate the bag to resemble her favorite character by coloring it or gluing on pieces of construction paper, fabric scraps, yarn, and ribbon. Use fabric scraps or paper to create animal ears, and glue ribbon and yarn on the top of the bag to create hair. When the mask is complete, invite the child to act out scenes from a story or fairy tale.

For a simpler mask, cut eyeholes in a paper plate and decorate it. Glue a strip of cardboard to the bottom of the plate to use as a handle to hold the mask.

WRITING TO A TEE!

◁▶◁▶◁▶◁▶◁▶◁▶

This T-shirt will always be a child's pleasant reminder of a special event.

What You'll Need
- white T-shirt
- indelible markers
- 3" × 5" index cards
- cardboard

Choose a theme with the child, such as color words or a special event like a birthday. Think of a list of words together that relate to the theme or event: *cake, candles, gifts, cards, balloons, party, friends, ice cream,* and so on. Encourage the child to arrange the words on a T-shirt by writing the words on index cards and laying them on the shirt. Then place a piece of cardboard between the layers of the shirt. Invite the child to write words or draw illustrations on one side of the shirt with indelible markers. Let dry thoroughly. Turn it over, and repeat process. Let dry and wear.

 # WEATHER BAND

◁▶◁▶◁▶◁▶◁▶◁▶

Listen to the outside sounds and play that tune again!

The child can listen to the sounds that weather makes and try to re-create the natural sounds using handmade instruments and common household items. The child can use a paper-towel tube maraca to imitate rain sounds. Two pencils used like drumsticks might imitate rain dripping sounds. The wind might be imitated by humming into a kazoo, blowing through a paper-towel tube, or sweeping with a broom.

What You'll Need
- instruments from activities on pp. 276 and 284
- household items: broom, cardboard tubes, unsharpened pencils

The child might want to record the weather sounds created or make up a story to tell with the weather sound effects.

ANIMAL BINGO

◁▷◁▷◁▷◁▷◁▷

Play bingo and try for 3 animal matches all in a row!

What You'll Need
- tagboard or cardboard from cereal boxes
- scissors
- ruler
- markers
- animal stickers
- large buttons
- paper bag

Bingo boards can be made by cutting squares (approximately 8" × 8" each) out of tagboard or empty cereal boxes. With markers, draw grids on the boards to create 9 squares. Use animal stickers, and place a picture of a different animal in each square except the middle one. Draw a star or sun or happy face in the middle square—it is a free space. Make the game cards by cutting smaller individual cards and placing 1 animal sticker on each card. Use large buttons for the place markers. To play, place all the game cards in a bag. Each person starts off by putting a place marker on the free middle square. The caller then starts the game by taking a card from the bag. The caller looks at the picture and names the animal. Players check their boards to see if they have a picture of that animal. If the animal is there, the player puts a place marker on the picture. The first person to get 3 markers all in a row shouts "BINGO!" and is the winner. To make the game more challenging, instead of naming the animal on the card, the caller makes the sound of that animal!

JUST FOR THE TASTE OF IT!

◁▷◁▷◁▷◁▷◁▷

The child will eat adjectives with this tasty activity.

Display common foods that include a wide variety of tastes, such as jelly beans, lemons, pretzels, marshmallows, peanuts, raisins, sour apples, or sweet banana peppers. Let the child sample the foods and describe how they taste. Record the words the child uses. Did she use words such as *sour, sweet, tangy, spicy, salty, delicious,* or *tasty*? Explain that these descriptive words are called adjectives. Invite the child to add more adjectives to the list. See how many she can think of.

For an additional challenge, set out several foods with strong aromas, and invite the child to record words that capture their smells.

MANY MOVES

◁▷◁▷◁▷◁▷◁▷

Trek, tramp, and traipse to get from here to there!

Challenge the child to imagine, describe, and demonstrate as many ways as possible to move from one side of the room to the other! The child can hop, skip, jump, crawl, dance, and move from here to there in a myriad of ways. Add variety by giving the game a new twist. How fast can the child move across the room? How slow? What about how low?

MAKE A SIMPLE SOUP!

◁▷◁▷◁▷◁▷

Shop, prepare, and cook up a simple, sumptuous soup!

Caution: This project requires adult supervision.

Use the vegetables listed at right or make preferred substitutions! Discuss, shop for, and choose the vegetables for the soup together. To prepare the soup, have everyone first wash their hands, and then wash the vegetables. The adult can cut up some vegetables while the child is washing the others. Add the vegetables to the broth, and simmer until tender. Then add the noodles to the soup, and cook several minutes more. When the soup is ready, scoop it into bowls, and share the finished product. Discuss how the soup smells as it cooks, and discuss how it tastes when it's finished!

What You'll Need
- pot
- 1 can chicken or vegetable broth
- 2 cups water
- 1 cup tomato juice
- ½ teaspoon salt
- vegetables (1 carrot, 1 celery stalk, 1 small potato, 1 onion)
- 1 cup thin noodles, cooked
- cutting board
- knife
- pot holders
- large spoon
- 2 soup bowls
- 2 soup spoons

BIG BROWN BAG

◁▶◁▶◁▶◁▶

Better be bright-eyed for this big bag of B's.

Give the child a big brown bag, and pretend that she is going shopping in the home to find things that begin with the letter B. (You may specify a certain number of items if desired.) As the child finds an object, she should place it inside the bag. When the "shopping" is completed, ask her to tell you what she found and then discuss the objects, emphasizing the *B* sound. (Hints: *ball, balloon, basket, bathrobe, bag.*)

BOX TOWN

◁▶◁▶◁▶◁▶

Build a box town!

The child can use an assortment of boxes in different shapes and sizes to make the town. Spread newspaper on the ground where the town will be set up. The buildings can be made of separate boxes or from several boxes taped or glued together. The finished buildings can be painted. Milk cartons can be painted successfully if a little glue is added to the paint. Streets and parks can be painted onto the newspaper. When the town is finished, the child can

What You'll Need
• newspaper
• wide assortment of boxes (including empty food boxes and washed milk cartons)
• masking tape
• nontoxic white glue
• paint
• brushes

then name and describe the town. For more challenge, the child can make a map of the box town showing each of the buildings and any streets or parks.

FOIL SCULPTURE

◁▸◁▸◁▸◁▸◁▸

Transform junk into textured foil art!

What You'll Need
- piece of cardboard
- little items of household junk (screws, washers, paper clips, buttons)
- nontoxic white glue
- water
- brush
- aluminum foil
- soft cloth

Caution: This project requires adult supervision.

The child can start the sculpture by gluing assorted items with interesting shapes and sizes onto cardboard. (Be sure to supervise; small objects are choking hazards.) After the glue has dried and all the pieces are secured onto the cardboard, make a diluted glue solution. The child can paint the whole sculpture with the diluted glue. When the sculpture is covered with the diluted glue, have the child spread a sheet of foil over it, crunching it down to fit snugly over all the shapes—then rubbing over the pieces with a finger to highlight the forms underneath. Let the child decide whether to put the shiny side up or down. The child can then glue the edges of the foil over the cardboard with undiluted glue. Polish the sculpture with a soft cloth when fully dry! If the child enjoys working with the foil, another activity to experiment with is foil sculpture. The child can use the foil itself as the sculpting material. Sheets of foil can be crumpled and bent into different shapes, abstract or symbolic. The child can use tape to attach or hold the foil parts together.

I hear and forget.
I see and remember.
I do and understand.
—Chinese proverb

KEEPING TRACK OF A TREE

◁▷◁▷◁▷◁▷◁▷

Adopt a tree to visit and observe.

What You'll Need
- paper
- crayons
- pencil
- disposable camera (optional)

The child can choose a nearby tree to visit and watch for a long period of time—a season or even a year. The child can visit the tree weekly or biweekly. On each visit the child can draw a picture of it and note changes in appearance, dictating observations to an adult or writing in a journal. The child can also use a disposable camera to document the changes over the year.

CREAMY CREATIONS

◁▷◁▷◁▷◁▷◁▷

Let luscious letters add pizzazz to an ordinary dessert.

Children will have fun watching you form letters using a can of whipped cream.

First, invite the child to help you mix the ingredients to make a gelatin dessert. Put the gelatin in a long, wide pan, and chill. When the dessert is ready, write letters on it with the whipped cream. Talk about the formation of each letter as you slowly make it. Have the child name each letter and give a word that begins with that letter.

What You'll Need
- gelatin dessert mix (and listed ingredients)
- long pan
- can of whipped cream

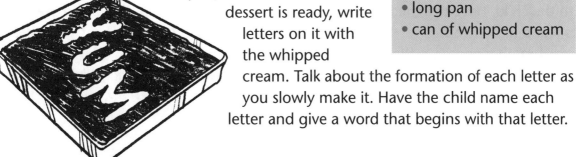

CONTRACTION MATCH

◁▷◁▷◁▷◁▷

Practice recognizing contractions with this simple matching activity.

What You'll Need
- 3" × 5" index cards
- markers

Begin by making 10 sets of contraction cards. Each set should consist of the contraction on one card and the words that make the contraction on another. Use these example sets to get started: *they'll* and *they will; can't* and *cannot; don't* and *do not; I'll* and *I will.* Next mix up the cards. Then invite the child to match a contraction with its correct counterpart words. When a match is found, have the child say what's on each card. After all the cards have been matched, invite the child to copy the contractions and the counterpart words cards into a personal dictionary.

LETTER INSERTS

◁▷◁▷◁▷◁▷

Turn a cat into a cot in this letter-substitution game.

Teach children to make new words by changing 1 letter at a time.

What You'll Need
- paper
- 2 different-colored markers or pens

On a sheet of paper, write "c__t" 3 times. Using a different-colored marker or pen, write the lowercase letter *a* in the blank in the first word form to make the word *cat,* and read the word with the child. Have the child explain what the word means. Write the lowercase letters *o* and *u* in the other "c__t" word forms to make the words *cot* and *cut.* Read the words together and have the child explain them. Review all 3 words. Then continue with new word forms such as "p__t" (*pot, pat, pet, pit*) and "h__t" (*hat, hit, hot, hut*).

I HEAR WHERE YOU ARE!

◁▷◁▷◁▷◁▷

Play a listening and locating game.

Invite the child to sit in the middle of a room with eyes closed. Explain that you are going to tiptoe to some part of the room and then make a sound. When you make the sound, the child should point to the place the sound is coming from—still with his eyes closed. The child can then look to check. Play again or trade places! You may also want to try hiding a kitchen timer. Ask the child to walk, with eyes closed, toward the ticking sound and locate the timer before it rings.

Activity Twist

Select an item located in the room (or car if you are traveling). The child's listening powers can help her guess where and what it is. Ask the child to guess where the secret item is located. If the child's guess is far away from the location, clap softly several times. If it's close to the spot, clap loudly as a guide. Keep clapping until the child figures out the item's location.

ALPHABET STAMPS

◁▷◁▷◁▷◁▷

It's as easy as 1, 2, 3: All you have to do is dip, press, and print.

In this activity, the child uses small muscles in the hand to hold a letter stamp and print letters while learning letter recognition.

What You'll Need
• alphabet stamps
• stamp pad
• paper

Get a stamp pad. Have the child take an alphabet letter stamp, press it onto the pad, and stamp the letter onto the paper to make a print of the letter. As each letter is printed, ask the child what letter it is. Discuss the lines of the letter. Are they curved or straight, or does the letter have both?

Continue printing letters. Ask the child to try to spell her name or other simple words. Have the child read what she has printed.

RAIN WALKING

◁▷◁▷◁▷◁▷

It's fun to be outside—in any kind of weather!

When there is a light rain on a spring day and the temperature is not too cold, take the child for a rain walk. Both of you will need an umbrella, because sharing one is difficult. Wear rubber boots or shoes you don't mind getting wet. As you walk, invite the child to do the following activities:

What You'll Need
- 2 umbrellas
- rain gear

1. Stomp in puddles.
2. Twirl the umbrella.
3. Talk about where clouds and rain come from.
4. Stick out her hand to try to catch a raindrop.
5. Stick out her tongue to taste the rain.
6. Listen to the rain hitting the umbrella.
7. If there is wind, talk about how the wind moves the rain and what the wind is doing to the umbrella.
8. Watch water running down the street; talk about why the water moves.
9. Make up a rain and umbrella song.

CHARACTER COMPARISONS

◁▶◁▶◁▶◁▶

Compare and contrast characters who live in different stories.

What You'll Need
• 2 stories

After reading 2 different stories, invite the child to talk about the main characters from each of them. Encourage the child to describe ways in which the people or animals were similar and ways in which they were different. The child can also talk about how their situations, their problems, their families, where they lived, or what they liked to eat were similar or different. For a more challenging activity, the child can imagine and describe what each character might have done if they were placed into the middle of the other character's story!

 # PICTURE THIS!

◁▶◁▶◁▶◁▶

The child takes on the role of a photographer while "taking pictures" of similar household objects.

Cut a 3½" ring from a cardboard tube. Cut 4 slits, 1" long, around one end of the tube. Bend the slits out. Place the cardboard box on the table with the open side facing away from you. The open side is the back of the camera, and the bottom of the box is the front. Tape the tube to the bottom of the box (the front of the camera), with the slits flush against the box. Cover the box with aluminum foil, still leaving the back open. Draw shutters, lenses, and buttons on construction paper, cut them out, and glue them to the front and sides of the camera.

What You'll Need
• cardboard tube
• scissors (adult use only)
• 4"×6" cardboard box
• tape
• aluminum foil
• construction paper
• crayons
• glue
• 3"×5" index cards

Next invite the child to "take photos" of pairs of household objects that are similar, such as objects that are the same shape. (The child can draw pictures on index cards and place them inside the camera.) At the end of the activity, remove the "photos" from the camera, and display them for others to see.

TAKING A MESSAGE

◁▷◁▷◁▷◁▷◁▷

Taking a phone message is an important skill and can be taught using this fairy-tale activity.

Together with the child, brainstorm several creative phone messages that might have been left by characters from certain fairy tales, such as "Little Red Riding Hood," "The Three Little Pigs," or "The Gingerbread Man." Write these messages on a message pad or on sheets of notepaper. For example, a message from Little Red Riding Hood's mother might read:

What You'll Need
- fairy tales
- notepaper or pink telephone message forms
- pencil

To: Red
From: Mom
Wolf seen in woods near Grandmother's house. Be careful!

Discuss the difference between the message above and a message that says simply, "Red: Your mom called." Invite the child to come up with new endings to the fairy tales based on what might have happened if the characters had received these telling phone messages. Emphasize the importance of writing down important details and information, such as time of call and return telephone number!

Activity Twist
To further this activity, encourage the child to practice writing down "messages" as you tell them to her.

Nursery Visit

⬦▶◀▶◀▶◀▶

Time to do some planting. Take a trip to a nursery and learn about plants.

Building one's vocabulary is a necessary part of language development. Visits to businesses offer valuable opportunities for a child to learn new words.

Visiting a garden nursery, the child learns that the word *nursery* does not always mean a place where babies or very young children are cared for. Upon arriving at a nursery, show the child the different types of plants, flowers, trees, shrubs, and other items that are available there.

Have the child select and purchase a plant to take home. Make sure the plant is suitable for a child and is not poisonous. On your way home, discuss what the child saw at the nursery and how to take care of the new plant. Discuss what the plant needs for it to grow. This can be done by saying, "I'm thinking of something that a plant needs for it to grow that begins with the letter *W*. What is it?" (Water.) Or: "I'm thinking of something that a plant needs for it to grow beginning with the letter *S*. What is it?" (Sun.)

SAME AS ME

<>─<>─<>─<>─<>

Make measuring meaningful by measuring with me!

What You'll Need
- yarn
- scissors

The child can use her own height as the unit of measure! Measure the child with yarn, and cut a piece the same length as the child's height. Then challenge the child to use the yarn to find something the same height as the yarn length, something shorter than the yarn length, and something taller than the yarn length. The activity can be done both indoors and out. For a variation, cut yarn the length of the child's foot, arm, or hand.

Activity Twist

Invite the child to try out lots of other arbitrary measures. See how many footsteps it takes to cross the room. Count how many hands it takes to measure the height of the TV. How many arms does it take to hug the jungle gym?

ALPHABET EATING

<>─<>─<>─<>─<>

Learn new words and try new foods while you create a menu for many meals to come.

Read the alphabet book together. Then read the book again, but this time have the child point to and read the words. Next list all the foods illustrated and organize them from *A* to *Z*. Some letters will have more than one food, other letters will have none, but include all of them.

What You'll Need
- alphabet book that deals with food
- pen and paper

Now plan what foods to eat over the course of a week, with the intention of eating through the alphabet. Use the letters with several choices to provide a series of menus that are balanced and interesting. Write up a menu for each meal, and have the child read the food words. At the end of the week, evaluate the process. Was it fun? Did the child learn some new words and try some new foods?

LONG VOWEL HUNT

◁▶◁▶◁▶◁▶

In the cupboard? In the toy box?
Who knows where the child will find objects needed for this vowel hunt.

What You'll Need
- construction paper
- markers

Fold a large piece of paper into 5 columns. Write these headings at the top: "Long *A*," "Long *E*," "Long *I*," "Long *O*," "Long *U*." Review these sounds together. Next have the child walk around the room, the house, or outside in the yard in search of objects that contain one of these vowel sounds. Ask the child to find at least 3 objects for each long vowel. Write the name of each object the child finds in the appropriate column on the paper.

WACKY WEEK

◁▶◁▶◁▶◁▶

Kids can "fry fish on Friday" and "sell socks on Saturday"
in this silly song activity.

Use song and pantomime to practice beginning sounds in words. Sing an "action" song about the days of the week to the tune of "Here We Go Round the Mulberry Bush." For example:

This is the way we wash our windows,
Wash our windows, wash our windows,
This is the way we wash our windows
So early Wednesday morning.

Have the child think of an action using words that begin with the same letter as the name of each day of the week. For example, "munch our meat on Monday" and "tickle a tiger on Tuesday." Encourage the child to pantomime each action as she sings the song.

RAIN DANCE

◁▷◁▷◁▷◁▷◁▷◁▷

*Defining main ideas becomes a lively performance
when a little song and dance is done.*

Sing the song "The Itsy Bitsy Spider" together. Discuss the main idea of the song. Then work with the child to create a dance showing the spider going up and down the water spout. Have the child perform the dance while the song is being played or sung. Repeat this activity using other familiar songs such as "Frosty the Snowman," "I'm a Little Teapot," and "Oh Where, Oh Where Has My Little Dog Gone?"

For added fun, invite other children to add details to the song by dancing or pantomiming the parts of the sun shining, the rain falling, flowers opening, and so on.

INVISIBLE WORDS

▷◁▷◁▷◁▷

*Spies and detectives have used this clever writing trick for years.
Here's the secret recipe!*

What You'll Need
- saucer
- lemon juice
- cotton-tip swab
- white paper
- towel
- iron

Pour some lemon juice into a saucer. Invite the child to dip a cotton-tip swab into the lemon juice and write a sentence, or message, on white paper. Perhaps the child can use new spelling words in the sentence. Then watch. As the juice dries, the writing becomes virtually invisible! Next, have the child give you the invisible message to see if it can be read.

Top secret tip for adults only: To make the words reappear, place the message face-down on top of an old towel or rag. Iron the back of the paper with a warm iron. Share the encoded message with the child, and see how many words are spelled correctly.

CROSSWORD BLOCKS

◁▷◁▷◁▷◁▷

*These simple crossword puzzles require only the addition
of one new letter to complete them.*

Set out wooden letter blocks of consonants to form crossword puzzles like the one shown here. Ask the child to place 1 block in the center of the puzzle to complete the spelling of 2 different words, one going across and one going down (such as using the letter *e* to spell *bed* and *hen*). Encourage the child to create her own 3-letter crossword puzzles.

What You'll Need
- wooden letter blocks

SNAP TO IT

◁▷◁▷◁▷◁▷◁▷

Use clothespins to avoid "hang-ups" when practicing the alphabet.

In this activity, children find and display the letters of the alphabet.

Place the alphabet cards in a stack or spread them out on a table. Put the box on the floor or on a table with the open side up. Name a letter. Have the child find the card with the letter you named and attach it to the edge of the box with a clothespin. Continue with other letters.

You might use the entire alphabet or choose only a few cards, depending on the child's skill level. As a variation, make one set of cards with only capital letters and another with only lowercase letters. Have the child find and match the letter pairs and clip them together on the edge of the box.

COMPOUND CATERPILLARS

◁▷◁▷◁▷◁▷◁▷

The child will enjoy this interesting take on compound words while making construction-paper caterpillars.

Explain that a compound word is made up of two separate words that are combined to make one word. Take turns naming compound words. Write the words you've named on a chart. Then set out precut paper caterpillars, similar to those shown here.

The child can fold the left and right ends of the caterpillar cutouts so that they meet at the middle. Have the child take a particular compound word from the chart and write the smaller words that are a part of it on the outside flaps of the cutout—1 word for each flap. Next, have the child unfold the flaps and write the compound word on the inside of the caterpillar. Invite the child to share the finished work with others.

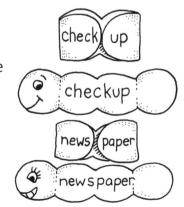

AUTHOR! AUTHOR!

◁▶◁▶◁▶◁▶

The child will learn about an author while you help him do an author study.

What You'll Need
- several books by a favorite author
- pencil
- paper

Collect a variety of books by one author and read them with the child. This part may take several days. Then discuss the kind of writing the author does. Does the author retell folk tales, write about nature, or write fantasies? Then discuss the style of writing. Is the writing humorous, simple, or complex? Make a list of the author's characteristics.

Vary this activity by using the same process for an illustrator study.

SUN/RAIN

◁▷◁▷◁▷◁▷

Meteorologists need not apply.
This activity focuses on the simple pleasures of the day's weather.

What You'll Need
• paper
• crayons or coloring pencils

Here's an activity that helps a child learn and compare two simple words whose meanings—and spellings—couldn't be more different.

Take the child for a walk on a sunny day, and talk about what you see. When you come in, print the word *sun* on a sheet of paper. Have the child draw a picture of the sunny day. Ask the child to think of other words that begin like *sun*. Repeat the activity on a rainy day, writing the word *rain* on a sheet of paper. Display the two pictures together, and discuss how they are alike and different.

REFLECTING RAINBOWS

◁▷◁▷◁▷◁▷

A mirror can create a magical rainbow!

What You'll Need
• small unbreakable mirror
• glass of water

Creating rainbows and dancing them around the room is magical as well as scientific. With adult supervision, the child can create a rainbow with a small mirror and a clear glass of water. Have the child carefully place the glass of water in direct sunlight and then submerge a small mirror halfway in the water (half of mirror should be below and half should be above water level). By tilting and rotating the mirror the child will catch the sunlight, which will then be refracted through the water to create the rainbow colors.

MY PRIVATE PLACE

◁▷◁▷◁▷◁▷

An old sheet is all that's needed to create a private suite!

Drape a sheet over a table to make a tent area underneath. The cozy corner can become a cave, barn, garage, or just a cozy place to play. The child can supply the cozy corner with stuffed animals, books, paper, crayons, and favorite toys to use and play

with in that private space. A private spot outdoors can also be created for a shady place to get away on a sunny day. Drape the sheet over a backyard table or over a rope tied between two trees.

What You'll Need
• sheet
• table
• stuffed animals
• books
• paper
• crayons
• cars
• rope (optional)

Activity Twist

Invite the child to create a private place for a miniature character collection. Use a shoe box with a lid so the child can easily transport this special play spot (to bed, on a car trip, outdoors). Encourage the child to decorate the special spot with soft cotton-ball clouds, crumpled tissue-paper hiding places, and felt-tip marker scenery. Have fun acting out little pretend scenarios over and over again!

TASTE, TOUCH, SMELL

◁▷◁▷◁▷◁▷

Learning the **S** sound can be **sweet, soft,** and **silky.**

Play a sensory game that emphasizes the beginning sound *S*. First, help the child name the 5 senses: sight, sound, touch, taste, and smell.

Begin by asking for a sense-related question that uses an *S* word. For example: "What can you find that feels soft?" Have the child find or name things in the house that answer the question. Then continue with other sense-related questions that contain *S* words, such as *silky, soapy, sour, sticky, sweet,* or *salty.*

LETTER HOPSCOTCH

◁▷◁▷◁▷◁▷

Hop to it, and enjoy a new way to play hopscotch.

Here's a letter game that's good for active children.

On a sidewalk or safe driveway, mark off a hopscotch game. Put a capital letter in each box as illustrated in the accompanying drawing. The child tosses the beanbag into

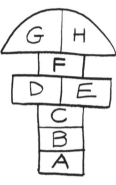

letter square *A,* then hops over letter *A,* landing on each of the other hopscotch grid letters in succession. The child then turns around and hops into the letter squares in reverse order. From letter *B,* however, the child picks up the beanbag in letter square *A,* hops into that square, and then hops out of the grid.

On the next turn, the child throws the beanbag to letter *B* and hops from letter *A* to *C,* and so on, repeating the procedure as before. The child always hops over the box that has the beanbag in it, until picking up the bag on the return trip and hopping out of the grid.

HEART PUZZLE

◁▷◁▷◁▷◁▷

Take time to solve this puzzle, and mend a broken heart.

Make a big heart shape on lightweight cardboard, and write the letters *H* and *h* on it in as large as possible. Make a puzzle by cutting the heart into a number of

pieces. The child takes the puzzle pieces and puts the puzzle together so that a heart is formed and the letters *H* and *h* are formed as well. The letters assist the child in assembling the heart puzzle and also in associating the *H* sound with the word *heart.*

MARSHMALLOW MINARET

⬦▷⬦▷⬦▷⬦▷⬦▷⬦▷

Build towers and castles with easy-to-use (and eat!) materials.

Invite the child to build structures with miniature marshmallows, using the toothpicks to hold joints together. She can make any type of structure, including towers or castles, people, creatures, or abstract objects. For a variation, combine large and small marshmallows, use white or colored marshmallows, or use peanut butter instead of toothpicks for glue!

What You'll Need
- miniature marshmallows
- toothpicks
- peanut butter
- plastic knife

CEREAL TIME

⬦▷⬦▷⬦▷⬦▷⬦▷⬦▷

Hot cereal can be both nutritious and educational.

What You'll Need
- hot cereal mix
- milk or water
- bowls
- spoons

Caution: This project requires adult supervision.

Practice beginning sounds as you make a hot breakfast with the child.

Use any hot cereal mix. Microwaving the cereal allows the child to participate in all steps. Follow and discuss each step together. As you prepare the cereal, ask the child to name words that begin like *cereal* (*ceiling, city, celery, circus*) or *oatmeal* (*open, okay, over*). Cereals may also have flavors such as cinnamon, peach, and maple syrup that can provide beginning-sound practice.

ADVICE FOR MOTHER GOOSE

◁▷◁▷◁▷◁▷◁▷

Help Mother Goose with her plentiful perplexities and problems!

What You'll Need
• Mother Goose nursery rhymes book

Share one or two nursery rhymes with the child. After the child listens to a rhyme, have him describe the difficulties the characters are involved in. Encourage the child to suggest ideas that the different characters might try (if they could) to solve each of their problems. If it's too late for the characters, let the child suggest what the characters might have done to prevent the problems that occurred!

EXPLORE THE DARK

◁▷◁▷◁▷◁▷◁▷

What does the dark look like?

If you turn on the light, can you see the dark? Do things look different in the dark and in the light? Answer these questions and more. The child can use a flashlight to explore the dark. Encourage the child

What You'll Need
• flashlight

to turn the light on and off, to notice how objects look in the dark and in the light, to explore the light trail the light makes, and to talk about and describe all that is seen and unseen! Then play a game of "Follow the Leader" with light. Take turns shining the beam around the room, inviting the other person to "follow the light!" Another variation is light tag. One person moves the beam around, and if the other can tag the beam, the flashlight changes hands.

SAY A SONG

◁▷◁▷◁▷◁▷

*Retelling song stories is a simple way to develop comprehension
and practice paraphrasing information.*

Sing a song that has a story in it, such as "Mary Had a Little Lamb." Then encourage the child to retell the story using narrative form, but without repeating the verses as sung in the song.

BUILDING WITH BOXES

◁▷◁▷◁▷◁▷

A box is not just a box, a box can be anything at all!

What You'll Need
- variety of large and small cardboard boxes
- paper plates
- cardboard tubes
- buttons
- spools
- string
- plastic bottle tops
- nontoxic white glue
- paint (optional)
- paintbrush (optional)
- water container (optional)
- markers (optional)

Provide an assortment of boxes in various sizes and then challenge the child to invent ways to use them. The boxes might become a vehicle for riding in, a computer, the control panel of a spaceship, a stove, etc. The child can glue boxes together or glue accessories to the boxes. The boxes can also be painted or decorated with markers.

INSECTS AND SPIDERS

◁▶◁▶◁▶◁▶◁▶◁▶◁▶

Make playdough bugs with lots of little legs.

Caution: This project requires adult supervision.

What You'll Need
- playdough
- chenille stems
- toothpicks
- buttons
- beans

The child can create insects and spiders by shaping the playdough and counting the body parts (2 for spiders, 3 for insects). Chenille stems or toothpicks can be used for legs. The child can count just the right number of legs to make accurate bug replicas—insects have 6 legs and spiders have 8—or children can invent many-legged creatures. Buttons or beans can be used for eyes, dots, and decorations. (Smaller children need supervision—buttons and beans are choking hazards!) Instead of familiar insects and spiders, the child can use the playdough to create amazing imaginary bugs!

If children grew up according to early indicators, we should have nothing but geniuses.
—Johann Wolfgang von Goethe

YES OR NO?

◁▷◁▷◁▷◁▷

Play a cooperative "Could it be?" guessing game.

Take turns making up true or silly statements to report to each other. One person makes a factual or funny statement, such as "I'm wearing blue shoes," "There's a giraffe in our backyard," "Uncle Pete loves baseball," or "We're going to have baked hats for dinner." Then the listener thinks about whether such a thing could be true and answers yes or no. For more challenge, encourage the child to give reasons for each yes and no answer.

FILL IT UP!

◁▷◁▷◁▷◁▷

*Gas tank empty? Stop at the next gas station
and fill both the tank and a child's mind.*

Letters and letter sounds can be learned anywhere, even at a gas station. See how many different letters can be found there.

As you and the child drive into a gas station, ask him, "What do you see?" When the child names an object (for example, a pump), ask what beginning letter that word has. Point to other objects (tires, a hose, a windshield, a car), and talk about their beginning sounds.

On your drive home, talk about the different things the child saw and the beginning sounds of those objects.

PICTURESQUE PATTERN

◁▶◁▶◁▶◁▶◁▶◁▶

This activity helps the child develop the colorful language necessary for clear commentary.

Begin by making a simple observation, such as "There's a bird in the tree." Then invite the child to add a descriptive word to give more information. For example, the child might say, "There's a small bird in the tree." Then you might say, "There's a small bird in the large tree," and so on. Take turns and continue adding more and more descriptive words to the original statement, giving the sentence as much vivid meaning as possible.

To extend this activity, help the child create an imaginative short story by adding more descriptive sentences.

BUTTON SORT

◁▶◁▶◁▶◁▶◁▶◁▶

Two-holed, four-holed, skinny, or stout, look at buttons and sort them out!

Caution: This project requires adult supervision.

What You'll Need
• large buttons
• egg carton

Gather together a variety of loose buttons. (Supervise carefully if buttons are small; they could be a choking hazard.) Spread the buttons out and invite the child to sort them. An egg carton can be used for sorting compartments. Encourage the child to choose the sorting categories and then describe them. The child might sort by color, by number of holes, by size or shape of the buttons, or by pretty and not pretty! If buttons are not available—or for variety—any kind of collection can be used for a sorting activity. The child can sort clean socks from the laundry before they are paired and put away; nuts, bolts, washers, and screws from the hardware drawer; a stack of photographs; and so on. To add challenge to the game, after the child has sorted a collection into groups, the child can invent new categories and re-sort the same collection a different way.

WHAT WAS THAT SOUND?

◁▶◁▶◁▶◁▶◁▶◁▶

This simple game enhances the child's listening skills and can be played anytime.

Have the child close her eyes and listen carefully. Then make a sound by using a common household item: shake a key chain, switch a light off and on, open and close a drawer, or rapidly flip through the pages of a book. After you have made the sound, ask the child to guess the name of the object making the sound.

CLAY PLAY DAY

◁►◁►◁►◁►

Every child is a sculptor in this easy letter-formation activity.

What You'll Need
- water
- salt
- measuring cups
- pot
- stove
- salad oil
- powdered alum
- measuring spoons
- flour
- paper
- marker or pen

Caution: This project requires adult supervision.

Forming three-dimensional letters allows children to experience the alphabet with their sense of touch as well as their sense of sight.

To make claylike dough at home, heat a mixture of 1½ cups of water and ½ cup of salt until it is almost boiling. Remove the mixture from the heat. Add 2 tablespoons of salad oil and 2 tablespoons powdered alum (available in the spice aisle in the supermarket). Cool the mixture for 5 minutes. Work in 2 to 3 cups of flour with your hands. The dough can be stored in plastic bags at room temperature and can be used for about a month.

Show the child how to roll small balls of clay into coils about 6" long. Or you may choose to cut strips from a flat sheet of clay. Write a letter on a sheet of paper. Have the child form the letter with clay strips. Start with simple letters, such as *T* and *L,* and continue with more complex letters such as *A* and *B.*

WEATHER REPORT

◁▷◁▷◁▷◁▷

Amateur weather forecasters take over the weather reporting for the day in this adjective-based activity.

Allow the child to take on the role of weather forecaster for the day. As she prepares to report the weather, help her make a list of adjectives describing different weather conditions, such as *sunny, rainy, windy, cloudy, snowy, hot, cold,* and so on. Use the construction paper to make props, such as pictures to represent the weather symbols, maps, and photographs. Also look through old magazines for weather pictures you can use. Encourage the young forecaster to use a pointer with the props to make the presentation more visual.

What You'll Need
- paper
- pencil
- construction paper
- markers
- old magazines
- pointer

Activity Twist

Review verbs by having the child name activities she likes to do on sunny, snowy, rainy, or windy days.

WHAT IS MISSING?

◁▶◁▶◁▶◁▶

Now you see it, now you don't. What could be missing?

What You'll Need
- tray of items with different beginning sounds

Try this activity to enhance a child's visual awareness and beginning-sound recognition.

On a tray, place a collection of various items, each beginning with a different letter (for example, boat, pencil, apple, cup, and sock). Begin with 5 items. Show the child the tray of items, and name them. Then ask the child to turn around so he cannot see the tray. Remove one of the items, and place it behind your back. Have the child turn around. Ask the child to identify the missing item. Give a clue by telling the child that the missing item begins with a certain letter (for example, *S*).

To make this activity more challenging, you can start with more objects; for younger children, you can start with as few as 3 objects. Reverse roles, and have the child remove an item from the tray. Ask him to give you a clue by telling you the beginning letter of the missing item.

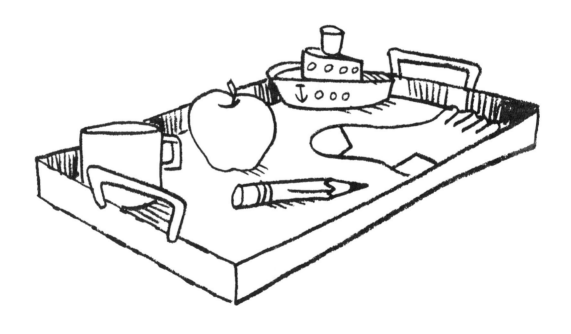

HIDDEN HANDS

◁▷◁▷◁▷◁▷

Hands can't talk, but they can still tell you things.

The 5 senses play a vital role in the life of a child. In this activity, the sense of touch is used.

To introduce this activity, show the child 5 objects (for example, apple, ball, feather, ribbon, and sock), and have the child

say what the objects are. After the objects are properly identified, cut a hole in the box that is large enough for the child's hand to fit through. Place the objects inside the box. Then ask the child to reach inside, grasp an object, and describe what she is holding while saying what the beginning letter sound of the object is.

For a variation, place 5 objects in the box without showing them to the child. Then ask him to feel, describe, name, and identify the beginning letter sound of the object.

PLEASE PASS THE PANCAKES

◁▷◁▷◁▷◁▷

It doesn't take much to make eating pancakes a learning experience.

Caution: This project requires adult supervision.

Here's an easy way to help children learn letters as they have fun preparing breakfast.

Pour some pancake batter into a pan. (A large pancake will give the child more space to write on.) Have the child arrange blueberries in the shape of a letter on the pan-cake. The child might make one

of his initials or another favorite letter. In place of blueber-ries, other kinds of small berries or diced fruits, such as straw-berries, peaches, or apples, can be used.

YAK-A-SAK!

◁▷◁▷◁▷◁▷

Creating new sentences from random sentence parts is a hilarious way to practice building sentences.

Sentences are made up of 2 basic parts: the subject, or naming part (for example, red, juicy tomatoes) and the predicate, or telling part (are growing in the garden).

Before beginning this activity, think of 10 simple sentences, and write each of them on a separate strip of paper. Cut the strips of paper between the naming parts and the telling parts so that each sentence is cut in 2 pieces. Label 2 paper bags as shown. Place all of the naming parts in the correct bag, and place all of the telling parts in the other bag. Next, have the child pick 1 sentence part from each sack and combine them to make a sentence. Prepare yourself for some silly sentences!

For additional creative fun, invite the child to draw pictures of the silly sentences with pencils or crayons.

What You'll Need
- paper
- blunt scissors
- pen or pencil
- 2 paper bags
- crayons (optional)

HEY! A SURVEY!

◁▷◁▷◁▷◁▷◁▷◁▷

Take a tally of friends, neighbors, and family.

What You'll Need
- paper
- pencil
- clipboard or cardboard and large paper clip
- string or yarn

For a simple survey, create a check-off tally sheet with 2 columns. Decide with the child whether he wants to ask a yes/no question (Do you like chocolate ice cream?) or a 2-choice question (What do you like better, dogs or cats?). If he's decided to ask a yes/no question, label the top of one row "Yes" and the other "No." For a 2-choice question, label the top of each row with one of the choices. Clip the tally sheet on a clipboard or to a piece of cardboard with a paper clip. Tie the pencil onto the clipboard with yarn so the child won't be walking around holding the pencil. The child can then survey family members, friends, and neighbors and record the results on the sheet. When he's finished with his survey, count up the rows together, and see what the results are. For more of a challenge, help the child come up with a community-issue question for a neighborhood survey, such as "Do you think we need a stop sign at the corner?" or "Do you think dogs should always be on leashes?" Create a tally form, and accompany the child to survey the neighbors!

Marble Rolls

◁▷◁▷◁▷◁▷

Beautiful designs can be made by rolling marbles in paint.

Caution: This project requires adult supervision.

With this activity, the child will be developing fine motor skills—both by using a clothespin to pick up the marble and by tilting the pan to make the marble move.

Pose a riddle to the child, and have him guess what the answer is. Say, "I am thinking of something round that begins with an *M* sound, can be rolled, and sometimes is used in playing games. What is it?" After the child responds that the object is a marble, tell him that marbles can also be used in art. Follow these simple steps.

What You'll Need
- aluminum pie pan
- paper to fit bottom of pan
- tempera paint
- marble
- clothespin
- container for small amount of paint

1. Put a piece of paper, sized to fit, in the bottom of an aluminum pan.

2. Pour enough paint into a small container so that a marble could be completely submerged in it.

3. Have the child put the marble in the paint.

4. Using a clothespin, the child can pick up the marble from the paint and drop it onto the paper in the pan.

5. Tilt the pan from side to side, causing the marble to roll in different directions.

6. Remove the marble from the pan.

7. When the painting is dry, remove it from the pan. A design will be printed on the paper, and it will be ready for display.

Note: For a younger child, use a box and an old tennis ball (since marbles can be a choking hazard). Emphasize the sound of the letter *T.*

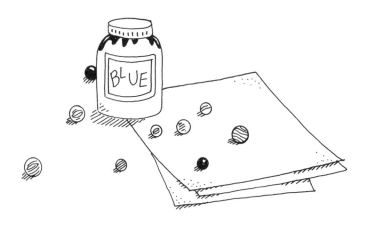

WINDOWS TO THE WORLD

⊲▶⊲▶⊲▶⊲▶⊲▶⊲▶

Make a window picture, and open the windows to see outside!

What You'll Need
- stiff paper
- scissors
- small pieces of drawing paper
- crayons or markers
- tape

The adult can create the building for the child's window views. Make the building from stiff paper. Cut a number of windows in it. Make the windows by cutting squares or rectangles on 3 sides so that the windows can open and close. The child then creates all the outside views by drawing pictures of outside things on pieces of paper just slightly larger than the window openings. The child can draw trees, animals, sky, clouds, and other things that we see when looking out a window. (The child can look outside a window for research!) Help the child tape the pictures behind the windows. The child can then open and close the windows to reveal the outside views.

READ THE PAPER

⊲▶⊲▶⊲▶⊲▶⊲▶⊲▶

Introduce the child to the local newspaper.

This activity will make children feel grown up as they look for words in a newspaper.

What You'll Need
- newspaper

Point to a word in a newspaper headline, and ask the child to find the same word somewhere else on the page. If necessary, point to the story or paragraph in which the word can be found. To begin, find proper names, since words that begin with capital letters are easier to spot. For a bigger challenge, help the child read the words that he finds.

CROSSED WORDS

◁▶◁▶◁▶◁▶◁▶◁◁▷

Make a crossword puzzle for two by playing this word-linking game.

Begin by marking off a square that contains 15 boxes down and 15 boxes across, like the one shown here. Graph paper works best, but if you don't have any, use a ruler to draw the lines on a piece of blank paper. Outline the box in the center of the puzzle so it stands out.

Next, choose a theme for the puzzle together, such as food, animals, and so on. Begin by thinking of 1 word that fits in the chosen category, and write the word on the page, 1 letter per box. The first word must have at least 1 letter that goes through the middle box. Then have the child think of a word within the category—the tricky part is that every word must share a letter with a word that's already on the page. Continue taking turns until neither you nor the child can think of any more words that will fit on the graph. See how close you both come to filling the puzzle.

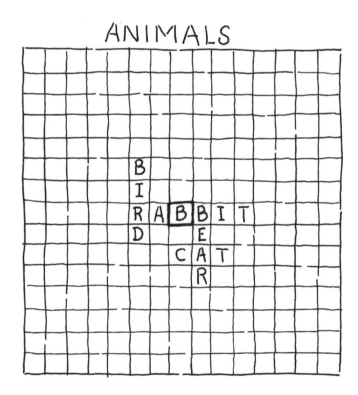

ANIMALS

VEHICLE TALLY

◁▶◁▶◁▶◁▶◁▶◁▶

Keep track of cars and trucks with a graph and tally!

What You'll Need
- tally sheet
- clipboard
- pencil

Divide the tally sheet into 3 to 5 columns and attach it to a clipboard. Take the clipboard and pencil with you to a park or the sidewalk near your house—somewhere it is easy to watch cars driving by. Ask the child to predict what kind of vehicle will pass by most often. Label each of the columns (pictures are best). The child can choose the column categories. The child might choose vehicle types (truck, car, motorcycle, van) or car colors (yellow cars, blue cars, red cars). Write down predictions of which vehicles the child expects to see most and which he expects to see least. Then let him keep track of the sightings by tallying the passing cars in the correct columns. When one of the columns is all checked off, stop the tally and check against the predictions. For a further challenge, take the same tally at different times of the day or on different days, and compare all the tallies to see if the results are the same or different.

SOLVE THE PROBLEM

◁▶◁▶◁▶◁▶◁▶◁▶

Step into a story and be a problem solver.

What You'll Need
- favorite story or book

Read a book together, but stop the story at the height of a problem. Then ask the child to describe what he might do in a similar situation. Encourage him to give reasons and explain his choices.

In Another Tongue

◁▷◁▷◁▷◁▷

The child can expand his horizons with this multicultural language activity using counting words.

Learn to count to 10 in a language other than the one you use every day. Use a dictionary of the language chosen for correct pronunciation, or look for the words in books from the library.

English	Spanish	Japanese	Russian
one	uno	ichi	odin
two	dos	ni	dva
three	tres	san	tre
four	cuatro	shi	cheteri
five	cinco	go	pyat
six	seis	roku	shest
seven	siete	shichi	sem
eight	ocho	hachi	vosem
nine	nueve	ku	devyat
ten	diez	ju	desyat

Rhyme Time!

Jolly Jim is a jumping jack,
a jumping jack,
a jumping jack.
Jolly Jim is a jumping jack;
he jumps up and
down with glee.
Jolly Jim pops into his box,
into his box,
into his box.
Jolly Jim pops into his box,
and says, "You can't catch me."

BIG BUBBLES

◁▷◁▷◁▷◁▷

Bubbles are fascinating—and you can learn something from them.

To demonstrate comparison words and the sounds of word endings *er* and *est,* try making bubbles to show the concepts of big, bigger, and biggest.

Take a medium plastic bowl, and fill it ¾ full with water. Add a small amount of dish soap and food coloring. Demonstrate the fine art of blowing bubbles by putting one end of a straw into the liquid and blowing gently into the other end. Then have the child try it.

Have the child blow a bubble, then a bigger bubble, and, finally, the biggest bubble he can make. As the bubbles appear at the top of or over the container, take a piece of paper, put it over the container, and make an instant print of the bubble. If you use different colors of bubble mixtures, you can add those bubble prints to the same sheet of paper. When finished, look at the bubble prints with the child. Ask him to show you the big, bigger, and biggest bubbles.

What You'll Need
- mixing bowl
- water
- dish soap
- food coloring
- straws
- white paper

MUD PAINTING

◁▷◁▷◁▷◁▷

Mud painting is messy but, oh, so much fun!

What You'll Need
- smock or old clothes
- plastic containers
- dirt
- water
- paper
- cardboard
- aluminum foil
- large and small brushes

Can you paint with mud? The child can experiment with muddy mixtures to answer this question and also to determine what consistency of mud paints best. Let the child mix dirt and water in plastic containers to different consistencies, then experiment with mud painting. The child can also explore painting with different kinds of brushes and on different kinds of surfaces.

CAPTURE THE WIND

◁▷◁▷◁▷◁▷◁▷

Make a wind catcher and invite the wind to come and play!

What You'll Need
- circle of stiff paper or paper plate
- markers
- nontoxic white glue
- glitter or glitter glue
- blunt scissors
- ribbons
- yarn

Caution: This project requires adult supervision.

Invite the child to decorate a circle of stiff paper using markers and jazz it up with glitter and glue or glitter glue. (Adults: Glitter glue should not be used by children under age 3. If using glitter, be watchful—glitter can be dangerous if it gets in children's eyes!) When the decoration is complete, the child can glue ribbon strips to the bottom of the circle so they hang down. Cut 3 pieces of yarn to the same length. Make 3 holes in the circle, and thread a piece of yarn through each hole. Tie a knot in the yarn underneath the bottom of the circle. Tie the tops of the 3 strands of yarn together. Hang the wind catcher outside to catch the wind. To simplify, the child can use masking tape and several paper party streamers (about 3' long). Have the child observe how the strips dance with the wind.

WASH-DAY WORDS

◁▷◁▷◁▷◁▷◁▷

Kids can learn beginning sounds by folding towels and T-shirts.

What You'll Need
- clean laundry

Make helping out around the house a game of matching beginning sounds. As you and the child fold and sort clean laundry, have the child name each item and then say another word that begins with the same sound: *socks/silly, jeans/jump, towel/toy.*

REBUS RECIPE

◁▷◁▷◁▷◁▷◁▷

Read and follow a rebus recipe, and end up eating a yummy treat.

What You'll Need
- measuring cup
- paper
- marker
- ½ cup peanut butter
- ¼ cup honey
- 2½ cups puffed wheat
- spoon
- bowl
- waxed paper

Make a rebus recipe chart for a peanut-butter and puffed-wheat treat that shows and tells the directions with words and pictures. Use the example shown, or make up your own rebus. After washing his hands, the child can make the snack!

Following the picture directions, the child can measure the peanut butter, honey, and puffed wheat; mix the ingredients; roll the dough into balls; and place the balls on waxed paper. Then it's time to taste the delicious treat!

SMART ART

◁▷◁▷◁▷◁▷◁▷

Visiting an art museum with a child can be an enlightening experience on many different levels.

Expand a child's world—and practice beginning sounds—by visiting an art museum and studying the paintings and sculptures found there.

Select a particular gallery in the museum that you think the child would enjoy seeing. If a certain painting or sculpture attracts the child's attention, go to that piece of art. Look at it together, and have the child describe it to you. Ask him to find something in the painting that begins with a certain letter, or name a letter and ask the child to identify an object in the artwork that begins with that letter. Tell the child the name of the artist who created the artwork.

When you are at home or at the library, see if you can find a book about the child's favorite artist, or find a book that contains a photo of a painting the child likes, perhaps one seen at the museum.

JUMPIN' JIMMINY

◁▷◁▷◁▷◁▷

**The child will practice spelling words frequently used in reading
and writing while jumping from X to X.**

What You'll Need
• masking tape
• list of spelling words

Place masking tape *X*s in a path around the room. Have the child stand behind the first *X*. Explain that the object of this game is to jump from one *X* to another until the child reaches the end of the path. Begin by reading words for the child to spell, focusing on words the child uses frequently. Some examples may include: *the, come,* and *said.* For a correctly spelled word, the child jumps ahead one *X*. The child does not move if he has spelled the word incorrectly. As the child jumps forward, start reading harder words, possibly words from a school spelling list. For spelling especially difficult words correctly, you may offer the child two jumps ahead. So get ready, get set, spell, and jump!

For an interesting twist, have the child use each spelling word correctly in a sentence.

TOE TALK

◁▷◁▷◁▷◁▷

Draw tiny toe faces and gather toes together for a talk!

The adult and child can each draw faces on the bottoms of each other's toes using washable markers. The adult and child (or two children) can then sit on the floor, feet to feet, and make up conversations for their

What You'll Need
• washable markers

toes to have with one another. For a variation, have knee-to-knee talks, elbow conversations, and finger chats, too!

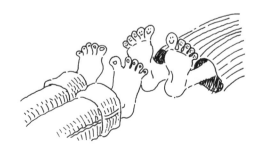

ALPHABET BRACELET

◁▷◁▷◁▷◁▷

Children will find this initial-letter search charming.

What You'll Need
- construction paper
- blunt scissors
- masking tape
- household objects

Here's an opportunity for children to wear the alphabet on their wrists.

Cut out the letters *A* through *F*, approximately 1½" high, from various colors of construction paper. (Older children may use blunt scissors to cut letters drawn by adults.) Put masking tape loosely around the child's wrist with the sticky side out. Choose one of the construction-paper letters. Have the child find an object in the house that begins with that letter. When the object is found, the letter may be put on the bracelet. Continue until all of the letters are on the bracelet.

Also try searching for objects outside, or use a different group of letters.

NOW I KNOW MY ABCs

◁▷◁▷◁▷◁▷

Singing the "Alphabet Song" can be a visual as well as a musical experience.

Use music to make learning the alphabet fun. Sing the "Alphabet Song" with the child until he is familiar with it. You might also play one of the many recordings of the song. Place the stack of letter cards facedown on the table, but in alphabetical order. Sing the "Alphabet Song" slowly. Have the child pick up and show each letter card as you sing its name in the song.

What You'll Need
- letter cards for the alphabet
- recording of the "Alphabet Song" (optional)

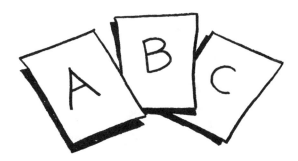

Alike & Unalike

◁►◁►◁►◁►

Tell what's the same and what's not!

What You'll Need

- household items (salt and pepper shakers, sock and shoe, spoon and fork, etc.)

Take turns finding and telling one similarity and one difference for two items. The adult can start the game by suggesting two different items and challenging the child to name a way they are alike and a way they are not alike. Begin with easy matches such as a shoe and a sock, salt and pepper shakers, a spoon and a fork. As the child becomes familiar with the game, take turns thinking up two items to pose to one another. Increase the challenge as you go by choosing items whose similarities are not so easily visible, such as a bucket and a sponge, or a pencil and a computer.

Phone Fun

◁►◁►◁►◁►

Believe it or not, talking on the phone can be educational.

Children will feel grown up making a telephone call to share their word skills with a friend or relative.

What You'll Need
- telephone
- word cards

Review a set of word cards that the child has learned. Help the child call a favorite adult friend or relative on the telephone and read the words that he knows. Prepare the adult ahead of time so that he offers plenty of praise and encouragement.

RING!!

SOFT PRETZEL LETTERS

◁▷◁▷◁▷◁▷

Twist some dough to make letters—and pretzels.

Caution: This project requires adult supervision.

Measuring, stirring, mixing, and kneading are the procedures the child will use to make soft pretzels. These tasks can be fun for a child, and the result will be something that she will enjoy eating.

With the child's help, measure 1½ cups of warm water, 1 tablespoon of sugar, 1 teaspoon of salt, and 1 packet of yeast. Ask the child to pour the ingredients into a mixing bowl and stir. Add 4 cups of flour to the other ingredients, and mix thoroughly. The child can remove the dough from the bowl and knead it on a floured tabletop. Kneading the dough until it is smooth, the child will be using all of her hand and finger muscles. As the child is kneading the dough, discuss the different possible types of pretzel shapes you could make.

When the kneading is completed, pull off a piece of dough and shape it to make several letters (perhaps the initials of the child's name). Place these shapes on a baking sheet lined with aluminum foil. Brush the pretzel letters with a beaten egg and sprinkle with coarse kosher salt. Bake the letters at 425°F for 12 to 15 minutes, or until they are golden brown. Let cool before eating. Exercise proper safety around the stove. Do not allow the child to come in contact with the heated baking sheet.

What You'll Need
- measuring cups/spoons
- water
- sugar
- salt
- 1 packet yeast
- mixing bowl
- big spoon
- flour
- baking sheet
- aluminum foil
- egg
- pastry brush
- kosher salt

THREE KIND MICE

◁▷◁▷◁▷◁▷

*Become a new Mother Goose (or Father Gandor) while twisting
old story lines into something new!*

What if the mice were described as
kind instead of blind? Maybe they
wouldn't have had their tails cut off
if they had been able to see.
What if the old woman in
the shoe bought a
condo instead? Maybe her children would
have behaved better with a nicer place to live.

Read a variety of rhymes together. Then
help the child create new twists on the story
line. Invite the child to make a small book of
new nursery rhymes to share with others.

What You'll Need
- nursery rhymes
- paper
- pencil

SUITCASE SPECIALS

◁▷◁▷◁▷◁▷

Packing for a trip? These suitcase specials are a must.

What You'll Need
- suitcase
- objects that begin
  with the letter *S*

Planning and going on a trip is an enjoyable experience
for most children.

The task in this activity is for the child to find things in
the home that begin with the letter *S* and can be packed
in a suitcase. Items might include socks, sandals, soap, a
swimsuit, or a sweater. See what items the child selects.
You may have forgotten one of those items on your list.

SANDBOX TOYS AND PLAY

◁▷◁▷◁▷◁▷

Make sandbox toys out of common household items.

Caution: This project requires adult supervision.

Make these sandbox toys for hours of sand fun! They will help the child practice her manual dexterity. Although the adult should make these toys, wherever possible, let the child help.

1. Use a hammer and large nail to punch holes in a plastic margarine tub to make a colander.

2. Cut a soda bottle in half. The child can use the top half as a funnel, while the bottom can be used as a sand container.

3. Cut a milk jug to make a scoop.

Children can also use foam egg cartons, ice-cube trays, plastic bottles, old pots and pans, scoops, wooden spoons, sieves, sifters, slotted spoons, cake pans, a garlic press, cookie cutters, and rolling pins in the sandbox.

What You'll Need
- plastic margarine tubs
- 20-ounce plastic soda bottles
- plastic milk jugs
- hammer
- large nail
- wood block
- heavy-duty scissors
- knife (adult use only)

My Name Is Adam

◁▷◁▷◁▷◁▷

**Here's a challenging game that encourages fast thinking
and learning the alphabet.**

This alphabet chant game requires the child to think of a name, a place, and an object that begin with the same letter of the alphabet. Start the game at the beginning of the alphabet with the letter *A*. For example, you might begin by saying, "My name is Adam, I come from Alabama, and I like apples." Then invite the child to repeat the chant, replacing each *A* word with an appropriate word that starts with *B*. Then take another turn, moving into *C* words. See how many letters in the alphabet can be turned into chants.

Increase the difficulty of the game by clapping to set a beat. Each time a new sentence is chanted, the child must speak on the beat without stopping to take extra time to come up with the right words.

ABC Action

◁▷◁▷◁▷◁▷

A, B, C, D, E, F, *Gee*, it's fun to pantomime action words with this up-and-at-'em action activity.

What You'll Need
- paper
- pencil
- crayons or markers

What do the words *run, skip, climb, eat, plant, fly,* and *sing* have in common? They are action words, or verbs. Make a list of action words together with the child, then ask the child to choose a word from the list to pantomime. After she has acted it out, write the word on a piece of paper, and invite the child to illustrate the action by making the first letter perform the action. For example, a child may make the *s* in *sing* look as if it is singing or the *r* in *run* appear to be running.

 # Nonsense Rhymes

◁▷◁▷◁▷◁▷

The child will use knowledge of letter sounds when making up silly nonsense words and rhymes.

Begin by offering a simple word, then invite the child to create a nonsense word that rhymes with it. For example, *jat* is a nonsense rhyme for the word *cat,* and *rish* is a nonsense rhyme for the word *fish.* Next suggest words with more than one syllable.

After the child has become comfortable making up nonsense rhyming words, make the activity more challenging by providing a sentence to be "nonsensically" transformed. Invite the child to turn as many words in a sentence as possible into a nonsense word that rhymes with the word it will replace. For example, the sentence "A caterpillar crawled on a tree" could be "nonsensically" transformed into "A fraterpillar jawled on a cree."

DUCK, DUCK, CATEGORIES

◁▷◁▷◁▷◁▷

Try this twist on the familiar game Duck, Duck, Goose by using categories.

Have players sit in a circle on the floor. Then the player chosen to be "it" selects a category, such as food, and proceeds around the circle tapping players on the head, naming an object in the category—a different object for each head tapped. When an object is named that does not fit in the category, the player whose head has just been tapped stands up and the chase is on! "It" tries to run around the circle and sit in the empty space before being tagged by the tapped player. If "it" makes it successfully, the other player becomes "it" and play starts over, using the same category. If "it" is tagged, she retains the role of "it" and a new game (with a new category) begins.

SIDEWALK STEP

◁▷◁▷◁▷◁▷

A letter patch helps teach alphabetical order one step at a time.

Draw a path of 6 blocks on the sidewalk. If you wish to play indoors, make the path on a long sheet of butcher paper or the blank side of a roll of wrapping paper. Write the letters *A* through *F* in order on the path spaces.

Shuffle the letter cards and ask the child to take the first one. If the card says *A,* the child steps into the first space

and puts the card on the space. If not, the child must keep drawing until she picks an *A,* putting unused cards at the bottom of the pile. Repeat the activity with the letters *B* through *F.* You can also repeat the game using other sets of letter cards.

BACKWARD IT SAY

◁▷◁▷◁▷◁▷◁▷

Take turns trying to say a simple sentence backward! Backward sentence simple a say to trying turns take!

This tricky word game is an intriguing way to develop memory and aids the ability to see the parts and whole of a sentence. You may want to have paper and pencil handy. Begin by saying a simple 3-word sentence. Then invite the child to say it backward. Then have the child say a simple sentence, and you say it backward. Work up to 4 words and, eventually, 5-word sentences. For a challenging variation, say a sentence backward, and invite the child to turn it around.

John is name my.

What You'll Need
• paper (optional)
• pencil (optional)

RUB-A-DUB-DUB

◁▷◁▷◁▷◁▷◁▷

Rub-a-dub-dub objects with a specific sound to make a piece of art.

What You'll Need
• paper bag or cardboard box
• newsprint
• pencil

Take a nature walk with the child. Bring along a bag or box, newsprint, and a pencil. While walking, ask the child to look for objects that have a target sound, such as long *e*. The child should place each of these objects in the collection bag until she has at least 5 items. They can be 5 of the same kind of thing or all different, as the child chooses. Help the child arrange the objects on a flat, hard surface. Then cover the collection with newsprint, and invite the child to rub over the top carefully with the long side of the pencil. The result will be an interesting print. Invite the child to complete the print by labeling each object on the paper. You may wish to mat the prints and display them in a prominent place.

POETRY FUN

◁▷◁▷◁▷◁▷

Inspire the young reader by exploring humorous poetry and having fun at the same time.

Read a number of funny poems together. Invite the child to predict the words that will rhyme or the words that will complete the lines. Discuss which rhymes are the funniest. Then have the child choose one poem and practice reading it aloud, adding gestures and voices when appropriate. Encourage the child to make the gestures as funny as possible.

What You'll Need
• collection of humorous poems

MAY I SERVE YOU?

◁▷◁▷◁▷◁▷

Properly prepared, playdough can become a dreamed-up dinner!

What You'll Need
• playdough
• rolling pin
• cookie cutters
• garlic press
• plastic tableware
• paper plates
• old magazines (optional)
• blunt scissors (optional)
• nontoxic white glue (optional)
• construction paper (optional)

The child can use simple utensils to create pretend foods out of the playdough. The "meals" can be served on paper plates on a table surrounded by stuffed animals or willing adults—or both! The child can plan a whole menu for the meal or stick to one specialty dish. For more food preparation play, the child can turn the pretend kitchen into a restaurant with menus for the guests. To make the pretend menus, the child can cut pictures of food from old magazines and glue them onto folded construction paper sheets.

SENSE-A-TIONAL POEM

◁▶◁▶◁▶◁▶

This irresistible form of poetry helps budding poets understand the body's senses.

What You'll Need
- paper
- pencil

Introduce the body's 5 senses: tasting, hearing, smelling, seeing, and touching. Talk about how each of these senses helps the child appreciate the world. Think of a topic or idea that could be described by the senses, such as food, a season, or an event (carnival, birthday, holiday). Share the example of the poem's format below. Then share the example poem. Have the child create a poem using the same format.

Line 1:	color of topic or idea	Winter wears white and gray.
Line 2:	tastes like	It tastes like ice on the tongue.
Line 3:	sounds like	It sounds like whispers in the night,
Line 4:	smells like	Yet it smells cool and clear.
Line 5:	looks like	It looks like a fairyland in the dark,
Line 6:	feels like	And sends shivers to all who feel its chill.

DYE JOB

◁▷◁▷◁▷◁▷

Fold, dip, and dye to make pretty paper!

With a few simple ingredients the child will transform white paper towels into decorative works of art! Have the child fill each section of a muffin tin halfway with water using a plastic pitcher. With adult help, the child can add a few drops of food coloring to each section to make different colors.

The child next folds a paper towel into small squares or triangles and dips each corner into a different color. The paper towel is then unfolded and laid on the newspaper to dry.

ONCE UPON A PROP

◁▷◁▷◁▷◁▷

Spark cooperative tale-telling with a bagful of commonplace props.

Fill a bag or pillowcase with a small assortment of commonplace items. The child can help choose the items. When the story bag is ready, reach into the bag and, without looking, choose one of the items. Begin a story using the prop as part of the plot! Then invite the child to take a turn, asking her to close her eyes, pick a prop, and make up the next part of the story, weaving the prop into it. Continue taking turns picking a prop and adding it to the story until the last prop is chosen, signaling time to make up the story ending (which includes the last prop, of course).

DIVING DEEP FOR NOUNS

◁▶◁▶◁▶◁▶◁▶

See and write about what's at the bottom of the sea while studying nouns.

What You'll Need
- 5" × 40" white construction paper (or two 5" × 20" strips taped together end-to-end)
- crayons

Help the child fold the strip of white construction paper back and forth to create an 8-page accordion-fold book. Set the book aside. Sing the song "There's a Hole in the Bottom of the Sea" with the child. Then count how many nouns are in the bottom of this sea together. Name them: *hole, log, bump, frog, fly, wing, flea.* Invite the child to complete the accordion-fold book by humorously illustrating all of the nouns in the song. After the illustrations are finished, have the child unfold the pages of the book, one by one, to show each illustration as you both sing the song again.

MOOD MATCH

◁▶◁▶◁▶◁▶◁▶

What makes people happy? What makes them sad? Try to make a match.

Gather an assortment of pictures cut from magazines of people expressing a variety of emotions. Gather an equal number of pictures of places, events, and things. Invite the child to match the happy, sad, frightened, or angry people with pictures that show something that might have caused the person to feel that way. Encourage her to explain why she made the choices she did.

What You'll Need
- pictures of people with different facial expressions and pictures of places, things, or activities cut from magazines

RACING CARS

◁▷◁▷◁▷◁▷

Create a simple board, and play a counting race game with cars.

Make a racetrack by drawing 2 or more columns (depending on the number of players) of 20 squares. Draw a finish line at the end. Each player chooses a column on the racetrack and a toy marker. Then take turns rolling the die, counting the dots on the die, and mov-

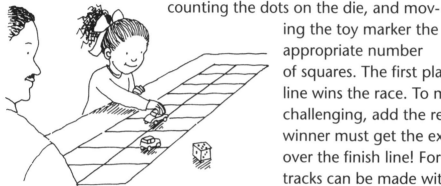

ing the toy marker the appropriate number of squares. The first player to cross the finish line wins the race. To make the game more challenging, add the requirement that the winner must get the exact number to cross over the finish line! For a variation, race-tracks can be made with curving or round tracks instead of straight rows.

PICTURE PLATES

◁▷◁▷◁▷◁▷

Present children with a full plate of beginning sounds.

In this activity, children use paper picture plates to work on beginning sounds.

First, help the child look through old magazines and find 5 or 6 pictures of objects, each of which is a different color (a red car, a green field, a blue pen, a black building, an orange vegetable, and so on). Cut out the pictures, and glue or tape each one onto a paper plate. Stack the plates. Ask the child, "Can you find a picture of something green?" Have the child find the green picture. Then identify the object, and say a word that has the same beginning sound. Continue through the entire stack of plates.

WAGON WORK

◁▷◁▷◁▷◁▷

*You can take anything with you along this path—
as long as you've got your wagon!*

What You'll Need
- ball of string or yarn
- wagon

Lay out a path with the ball of string for the child to follow by pushing or pulling a 4-wheeled wagon. Have the child maneuver the wagon along the path, pulling or pushing, depending upon the direction of travel needed. Have the child start with an empty wagon, but as she masters the task, lay out objects along the path for her to discover and put into the wagon. Later the child can move the string to make a different pathway. If there is more than one child, the children can take turns pulling each other on the pathway (supervise this closely and be sure the path is on a grassy area).

ROCK & CLAY CREATURES AND THINGS

◁▷◁▷◁▷◁▷

Turn rocks into creatures with features using a little bit of clay.

What You'll Need
- rocks
- stones
- plasticine clay
- cardboard

The child can create animals, people, martians, and monsters out of rocks using clay to add features or to hold smaller pebbles in place. The clay can be used to create legs, horns, eyes, ears, tails, or anything the child can think up. The creatures can be made to lay flat on cardboard or to stand on

their own. To simplify the activity, invite the child to explore creating rock sculptures by combining the clay with rocks to make interesting shapes, unusual things, and pretty designs.

GOING TO THE ZOO

◁▷◁▷◁▷◁▷

You can create an exciting zoo and help your child's writing at the same time with this activity.

What You'll Need
- stuffed animals
- 3" × 5" index cards
- pen or pencil
- empty boxes
- blunt scissors
- tape

Help the child collect a variety of stuffed animals. Then help the child write each animal's name on an index card. Next, take several empty boxes and cut out a window in each box. Place each animal in a box, and have the child tape the card with the animal's name under the window.

For a more challenging activity, help the child include background information about the animal. Extend this activity by writing directions for visitors and creating a "map" of the zoo with a list of the animals they will see.

 # BODY PARTS MIX-UP

◁▷◁▷◁▷◁▷

Mix and match to make unusual creatures and critters.

Cut out pictures of people and animals from old magazines. Then cut the pictures further to create an assortment of heads, legs, wings, arms, torsos, and tails. Ask

What You'll Need
- magazine pictures of people and animals
- blunt scissors
- paper
- nontoxic white glue

the child to reassemble the body parts to make new creatures and then glue them together on a sheet of paper. He can then talk about or describe what he has invented, or he can make up stories about these new creatures!

WHERE DID THEY GO?

◁▷◁▷◁▷◁▷◁▷

Paint letters with water on a sunny day, then see what happens.

What happens on a sunny day when there's water on the sidewalk? Let the child find out.

On a bright, warm day, take the child outside. Give her a paintbrush and a container partly filled with water. Find a safe and sunny cement surface (such as the sidewalk), and have the child "paint" letters of the alphabet. The child will be amazed at how quickly the letters disappear.

COOKIE-CUTTER WORDS

◁▷◁▷◁▷◁▷◁▷

Here's a tasty way for the child to practice spelling theme-related words.

Caution: This project requires adult supervision.

Set out prepared cookie dough on a surface covered with flour (so the dough doesn't stick) while discussing words related to a particular theme. Roll the dough flat, and carefully cut it into letters. Have the child spell these theme-related words by arranging the cookie-dough letters on a cookie sheet. Invite the child to decorate the cookies with sprinkles before you bake them in the oven. Once the cookies have cooled, remove them from the cookie sheet with the spatula, and place them on waxed paper or a paper plate. Review the spelling of each word before enjoying the tasty spelling treat.

STOP & GO STORIES

◁▶◁▶◁▶◁▶◁▶◁

Stop and go stories are a fun way for the child to focus on words during a narration.

Invite the child to tell a story. The child can retell a favorite story or fairy tale, or make up a story. Before the child begins, explain that during the story you will be giving stop and go directions, and the child must stop telling the story the moment you utter the word "stop." The child may not continue the story until you say "go." As soon as you say "go," the child must begin the story right where she had stopped with the very next word that follows the last word she said, even if that means beginning in the middle of a sentence. Challenge the child to tell the story from beginning to end without losing her place in spite of all the stop and go directions.

PICTURE READING

◁▷◁▷◁▷◁▷

This activity is sure to help a beginning reader get excited about reading.

What You'll Need
- illustrated book
- self-adhesive notes

Choose an illustrated book that has words the child uses when talking or playing. Each page of the book should have just 1 or 2 words. A book the child is already familiar with and enjoys, such as a book about toys or animals, would be particularly useful.

Cover one of the words on a page with a self-adhesive note. Have the child describe the illustration. Then remove the note, and compare the child's description of the illustration to the text. If the child used a word that is a good description but different than the word in the book, discuss how different words can sometimes be used to describe what is happening in an illustration.

NIGHT SOUNDS

◁▷◁▷◁▷◁▷

Listen carefully and quietly for nighttime noises.

Sit quietly together in a darkened room, and listen to the nighttime sounds in the house. Share ideas and talk about what might be making

What You'll Need
- tape recorder (optional)

each sound, whether it is also heard in the day, and if it sounds the same in the day. Nighttime sounds can also be listened to and explored sitting quietly in the backyard. To carry the exploration further, record some of the various nighttime sounds together to listen to again during the daytime.

WORD BUILDING BLOCKS

◁▷◁▷◁▷◁▷◁

Show how 1 letter can grow into 3 words.

A word-square box demonstrates how to build on single letters and letter groups to make new words.

On a sheet of paper, draw a box at least 4" × 4" and containing 16 squares. Show the child how to build words: Write the letter *A* in the second box from the left in the top row. In the second row, write the *A* in the second box and add a second letter to make a 2-letter word—for example, *AT.* In the third row, repeat the *A* and *T* and add a third letter to make a 3-letter word—for example, *RAT.* In the fourth row, repeat the *R, A,* and *T* and add a fourth letter to make a 4-letter word—for example, *RATE.*

Continue making 16-square boxes with other letters in the top row. Help the child make new words to complete the rows in the box. Other possible progressions include *A, AN, ANT, WANT; E, BE, BEE, BEEF; I, IT, KIT, KITE;* and *O, NO, NOT, NOTE.*

MAKING AN IMPRESSION

◁▷◁▷◁▷◁▷◁

Use playdough to make a good impression!

The child can explore impression making using different kinds of household objects. Gather an assortment of items for the child to press into the playdough to make impressions. After experimenting, the child can search for other objects that might make interesting indentations. The child can explore the various impressions each item makes, create impression designs, or even make impression patterns using the tools. Discuss the shapes and impressions with the child.

Alphabet Nitty Gritty

◁▷◁▷◁▷◁▷

Who says reading is rough? Only when fingers do the walking.

Some children learn better through activities that concentrate on touch. Cut letter shapes out of sandpaper. Invite the child to trace each letter with his finger while saying which letter it is.

What You'll Need
• sandpaper
• blunt scissors

Question Day

◁▷◁▷◁▷◁▷

Have fun asking who, what, where, when, why, and how.

What You'll Need
• paper
• pencil

Children are naturally curious and ask a lot of questions. Take time out and help the child write a list of questions to which she would like to know the answers: "When is dinner?" "Why is it raining?" "Where does a turtle live?"

Title the list "Questions I Have." Call attention to the beginning letter of the word *question.* Explain to the child that the letter *Q* will always be followed by the letter *U.*

When all the questions are written down, show her what is at the end of each question (a question mark). Ask the child to make a question mark. Next, point out the words that are used for asking a question (*who, what, where, why, when, how*). Have the child underline these "question words." Review the *Q* sound in the word *question.*

WIGGLE WORMS

◁▷◁▷◁▷◁▷

Worms can do wonders when you want to try the letter W *sound.*

What You'll Need
• chenille stem
• pencil

This art activity can be used to draw attention to the beginning sound of the letter *W*. Show the child how to make a "worm" by winding a chenille stem around a pencil. Slide the "worm" off the pencil, and invite the child to make the worm crawl around as you count to 10. Before you reach 10, the child must say a word that begins like *worm*.

DON'T SAY WHAT YOU SEE!

◁▷◁▷◁▷◁▷

This picture-description activity challenges the child to find the right words to convey meaning.

SIZE 5½

Together create 15 to 20 picture cards of common animals or objects. The cards can be simple drawings on index cards or pictures cut from old magazines and glued or taped onto the cards. Put the cards in a shoe box.

What You'll Need
• 3"×5" index cards
• crayons or markers
• old magazines
• blunt scissors
• clear tape or glue
• shoe box

Invite the child to pull out a card and, without naming the animal or object, describe what is pictured. Make sure the child keeps the card hidden from your view. You are now allowed 5 chances to guess the name of the animal or object on the card. After the answer has been given, it is your turn to pick a card, describe what is pictured, and ask the child to guess its identity.

PAPER WARDROBE

◁▶◁▶◁▶◁▶◁▷

Dress up in newspapers and bags, and go out on the town!

What You'll Need
- large brown paper bags
- newspaper
- blunt sissors
- large paper clips
- tape
- stapler
- markers

Large brown paper bags and newspaper can be cut and folded to create skirts, shirts, and vests to inspire dramatic play. The child can decorate the paper clothing with markers or wear the wardrobe as is.

Paper Bag Hula Skirt: Cut open a large brown paper bag and cut the bottom off. Fold 1 long edge down approximately 1 inch to make a waistband. At the other long side, cut slits in the skirt, stopping several inches short of the waistband. Secure the skirt on the child's waist with a paper clip.

Paper Bag Vest: Cut open a large brown paper bag and cut the bottom off. Cut armholes in the appropriate places and cut out a V neck. The child can fringe the bottom for a fancy vest.

Newspaper Poncho: Cut a vertical and a horizontal slit (approximately 10 inches long) in the middle of a large sheet of newspaper. The slits will allow the child to slip the paper over her head. Tape the end of each slit with masking tape to prevent tearing.

Newspaper Hula Skirt: Fold a sheet of newspaper 4 times to make a 2" waistband. For the skirt, tape together 2 sheets of newspaper. Cut slits from one long side, stopping several inches from the other side. Fold down the uncut end 1" to make it stronger. Take the skirt and insert the folded end into the fold of the waistband. Staple along the length. Fasten the skirt on the side with a large paper clip.

BAG-O-BOOKS

◁▷◁▷◁▷◁▷

*Share and discuss favorite books and stories with the child
in this contagious activity.*

What You'll Need
- backpack
- favorite books
- self-adhesive notes
- pencil

Invite the child to select a few favorite books she has either read or wants to read and put them in a backpack. Encourage the child to read the book and attach self-adhesive notes on the books with comments. The child may wish to comment on which book was a favorite, which books were written by a favorite author, and which books had interesting illustrations. The child may also tag a favorite page in each book or a story event that was particularly funny or interesting.

After the child has finished reading the bag-o-books, it is your turn to read and make comments. After you have finished reading the books, discuss the comments. Encourage the child to send the bag-o-books on to a friend, sibling, or another adult, and have each of the readers make comments.

 # KEEPING A STORY IN ORDER

◁▷◁▷◁▷◁▷

*Learn the importance of sequence in a story while documenting events
through pictures and words.*

What You'll Need
- favorite book
- large sheets of paper
- pencil
- markers or crayons

While the child reads the book, invite her to keep track of all the key events in the story, listing them in sequence. Help the child plan how to illustrate each of the major events in the story. Then on a large sheet of paper, draw enough boxes to hold all the events. Draw the boxes in rows from left to right. Number the boxes. Now invite the child to draw the events in the boxes, and write a short sentence that describes the event portrayed in each box. Then retell the story.

MOUSE IN A BLOUSE

◁▷◁▷◁▷

Bet you can't play Mouse in a Blouse without laughing. Ready, set, try it!

What You'll Need
- paper
- pencil
- crayons

Invite the child to draw animals dressed in clothes. The only rule is that the animal's name must rhyme with the name of the clothing. How about a goat in a coat? A kitten wearing a mitten? A dog in clogs? Or try to hold back a giggle when you see a mouse in a blouse or ants in pants! Have the child think of a title for each dressed animal.

PENCIL, CRAYON, MARKER

◁▷◁▷◁▷

Here's an activity that exercises hands and minds.

Writing with 3 different instruments will give children plenty of hand exercise.

In a row at the top of a sheet of paper, draw a small pencil, a crayon, and a marker. Write the letter *P* next to the pencil, *C* next to the crayon, and *M* next to the marker. Make up a sentence that contains a word that

What You'll Need
- paper
- pencil
- crayon
- marker

begins with *P, C,* or *M.* For example, you might say, "I went to the store and I saw potatoes (or crackers or milk)." Ask the child to use the writing tool whose name has the same beginning letter as the word to write that letter in the correct column.

STACK AND CRUSH

◁▶◁▶◁▶◁▶◁▶

Jump into the fun of preparing boxes for recycling!

What You'll Need
- large assortment of empty cardboard grocery boxes from cereal, cookies, macaroni and cheese, etc.

Take a box and demonstrate how to crush it by jumping on it. Invite the child to do the same with various boxes. Then encourage him to make piles of two or three boxes and crush them all at once. When all the boxes are crushed, ask the child to help you sort them by size. Together, make one big pile, placing the largest boxes on the bottom and the smallest on top. Let him knock over and rebuild the pile as often as he likes. When he is done playing with the boxes, ask him to help you put them in an appropriate container. Take the child with you to a recycling bin or center, and explain to him the benefits of being environmentally responsible.

WATER VIEWER

◁▶◁▶◁▶◁▶◁▶

Make a water viewer, and view what's underwater!

Caution: This project requires adult supervision.

What You'll Need
- milk carton
- heavy clear plastic wrap
- rubber band

Cut the top and bottom off an empty washed milk carton. Help the child place heavy clear plastic wrap over one end and secure it in place with a rubber band. The child can submerge this end in a pond and look through the open

end to view underwater happenings more easily. (Adults should always supervise children around water!) If there is no pond nearby, the child can use the water viewer in a bathtub or wading pool, placing small toys or pebbles underwater to be viewed.

MORSE CODE

◁▶◁▶◁▶◁▶◁▶

Once the child knows this spelling code, dots and dashes blossom into words!

Explain to the child that in 1838 Samuel Morse created a special code that was named after him. In his code, a dot is a short tap and a dash is a long tap (with more time in between taps, that is). People used this code to send messages before telephones or radios. Morse designed his code so that the letters in the alphabet used most often have the shortest signals.

Begin by asking the child to choose a vocabulary word from a school spelling list or one the child wants to learn to spell. Then invite the child to tap out the correct spelling of the word on her knee. Have the child use a short tap for dots and a longer tap for dashes.

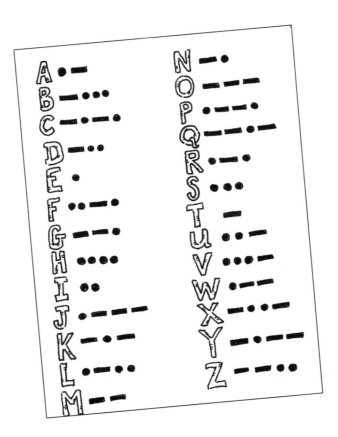

DONKEY DE-TAILS

◁▷◁▷◁▷◁▷

"Pin the Tail on the Donkey" is more than a party game when it includes letter identification.

What You'll Need
- brown wrapping paper
- marker or pen
- blunt scissors
- construction paper
- clear tape
- scarf for blindfold

Make a favorite children's game a learning experience.

Draw a donkey shape on a large sheet of wrapping paper, or use a ready-made game. Cut donkey tails out of construction paper, and print a letter on each tail. Put a piece of tape on each tail.

Blindfold the child and have him pin the tail on the donkey. If the child is playing alone, have him pin several tails on the

donkey. Otherwise, have each child pin one tail on it. When all the tails are on the donkey, have the child (or children) identify the letter on each tail and say a word that begins with the sound the letter represents.

STICK UPS

◁▷◁▷◁▷◁▷

Forming words from mixed-up letters is an exciting and educational way for the child to learn story vocabulary.

Select an interesting word from a favorite book or story, and collect magnetic letters to make that word. Use a safe working surface to display the letters, such as a magnetic board, refrigerator door, front of a washing machine, or metal file cabinet. Then scramble the letters. Next, invite the child to unscramble the letters to create the

What You'll Need
- magnetic letters
- magnetic surface
- favorite book or story

known word. You may want to provide clues to help the child guess the word. Continue the activity with more words from the story.

GOGGLES FOR GIGGLES!

◁▷◁▷◁▷◁▷

Goggles lead to silly parts to play!

Create goggles and half masks using a portion of an egg carton. Cut 2 adjoining egg cups from the egg carton—be sure to include the portion bordering either side. Measure and staple a length of yarn to each outer side so the goggles can be slipped on and off. Cut holes in the bottom of each cup so the child can look through the goggles. The child can decorate the goggles and use them for dramatic play. For variety, one egg cup can be used to make a mask that just goes over the nose (be sure to cut some air holes).

What You'll Need
- egg carton
- blunt scissors
- yarn
- stapler
- markers

COLOR SORT

◁▷◁▷◁▷◁▷

Mix and match and sort an array of colored squares.

What You'll Need
- construction paper (various colors)
- blunt scissors
- clear contact paper

You and the child can cut the construction paper into small color squares. The child can sort the squares into color groups by choosing categories. He can then record choices or make a design by placing squares on the sticky side of a piece of clear contact paper.

Place a second sheet of clear contact paper on top to seal the color record. For more challenge, the child can place the color squares in order, explaining the reason for the choice of ordering.

MEMORIES

◁▷◁▷◁▷◁▷

Make a keepsake album of a special field trip.

What You'll Need
- camera
- photographs
- paper
- glue or clear tape
- pen
- hole punch
- string

A field trip can be a rewarding experience for a child. In this activity, a lesson on language can be incorporated into the experience.

Select a special place to visit with the child—for example, a zoo, a farm, or a circus. While on this trip, have the child take photographs. (Your assistance may be needed with the camera.) After the film has been developed, the child can paste or tape the photos on paper. Allow space for captions.

Have the child dictate a sentence to describe what happened in each photo. Write this description below each photo so the child sees the process of sounding out letters and putting them in written (printed) form. Punch holes in each page and, using string, tie the pages together to form a book. Save a special photo for the cover, then decide on a title for the book, and write it on the cover. The child now has a special book about a special trip.

WASTEPAPER BASKETBALL

◁▷◁▷◁▷◁▷

The child will enjoy hooping it up with this mock basketball activity!

What You'll Need
- wastebasket
- masking tape
- old magazines
- blunt scissors

Mark the floor with masking tape at 2 distances from the wastebasket; for example, one masking-tape mark might be at 4 or 5 feet from the basket and another could be at 7 or 8 feet.

Explain to the child that sometimes two letters combine to form one sound, such as *sh* or *th.* Next have the child flip through old magazines to find pictures of objects that begin or end with these "blended" sounds. Cut these pictures out. Place each picture that begins with the sound at the closer mark to the wastepaper basket. Place each picture that ends with the sound at the farther mark. The child can then choose a picture, say the word, and then crumple the paper up and toss it from the appropriate line, trying to make a basket. One point is scored for short shots, two points for long shots.

SWEATIN' TO THE ALPHABET

◁▷◁▷◁▷◁▷

Time to exercise! Have the child help you with a new exercise routine.

To develop a routine, ask the child to think of some ways to exercise. Give the child a letter, and have him think of an exercise move for that letter. For example, *B* could stand for *bend, J* for *jump, H* for *hop, T* for *touch toes, S* for *stretch,* and so on. Do the exercises together. Very active children—and their parents—can benefit greatly from this activity.

EDIBLE LETTERS

◁▷◁▷◁▷

Start your day off right with a bowl of alphabet cereal.

Letters are found in many places, and food is no exception.

Buy a box of alphabet cereal, and pour some in a bowl. Ask the child to sort through the cereal to find the letters that make her name. The child can arrange these letters on the table. Say each letter as it is placed to emphasize letter awareness. After this activity, enjoy a bowl of cereal.

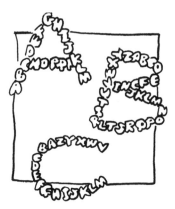

 # WOULD YOU BELIEVE IT?

◁▷◁▷◁▷

This game fosters imaginative thinking while the child responds to "what if" situations.

Make up an interesting "what if" situation, and invite the child to act out a response. The following are some suggestions:

What if a bird flew in the window and started playing with your toys?

What if it started raining in your house?

What if you ate a hamburger that tasted like pizza?

Have the child dramatize or explain what actions might be taken if a particular instance occurred. How would the child react to the particular instance?

FLOATING BOATING

◁▷◁▷◁▷◁▷

Can you make a boat that floats?

What You'll Need
- aluminum foil
- tub or sink
- water
- buttons, paper clips, or pennies (optional)
- modeling clay (optional)
- paper (optional)
- crayons (optional)

What shape works best when building a boat? What shapes don't work? Why? These are questions the child can tackle while creating boat shapes out of common materials. The child can experiment with aluminum-foil boat building by bending, folding, scrunching, and crumpling the foil. Boats can be tested in a plastic tub or sink filled with water. After a shape has been created that successfully floats, the experiment can be taken one step further. The child can test out how much weight a boat can carry before sinking. Pennies, paper clips, or buttons can be used for weights. The child can add one item at a time, keeping track of how many it takes to sink a boat. The number can be recorded using crayons to color in squares in a bar graph. The difficulty of the activity can be increased even further by inviting the child to create floating boat shapes using modeling clay. (Always supervise children around water and when they handle small objects, which could be choking hazards.)

PICTURE DICTIONARY

◁▶◁▶◁▶◁▶◁▶◁▶

Make a special book for a special person.

What You'll Need
- old magazines
- 28 sheets of 8½" ×11" construction paper of various colors
- blunt scissors
- glue or clear tape
- marker
- hole punch
- yarn

Have the child design a "picture dictionary" filled with pictures of things that are of interest to him. For example, if the child likes sports, use several old sports magazines for this project.

Write both the capital and lowercase form of one letter of the alphabet in the upper right corner of each of 26 sheets of construction paper. Give the child an old magazine and blunt scissors, and ask him to look for and cut out pictures of things that begin with each letter of the alphabet. Help the child glue or tape a picture on the correct letter page. When all or most of the pages have pictures on them, help the child make a front and back cover with the remaining 2 sheets of construction paper. Punch holes on the left side of each page, then bind the pages together with yarn.

GOING CRACKERS

◁▷◁▷◁▷◁▷◁▷

*There's a whole menagerie of creatures—and sounds—
in a box of animal crackers.*

In this activity, children practice both sorting and identifying beginning sounds.

Have the child put animal crackers into groups according to kind of animal. Then ask him to identify each kind of animal and say  the letter that stands for the beginning sound in its name. Have the child write each beginning letter on a sheet of paper, or write each letter yourself and have the child copy it. Finally, have the child place each animal cracker on the paper next to the beginning letter of its name.

PICTURE TALK

◁▷◁▷◁▷◁▷◁▷

A picture tells a thousand words...with a little help!

The child can draw a story and then talk about it to share it! For brightly colored picture stories, soak colored chalk in sugared water. The child can measure several tablespoons of sugar into a bowl of water, stir it, and add the chalk to the bowl. Soak the chalk 10 minutes. The child can then draw a colorful picture story on paper and tell about it. For another way to explore picture and story drawing using chalk, pour a little white or light-colored tempera paint into a small container. The child can dip the colored chalk (not presoaked) into the paint before drawing with it on dark-colored construction paper. The lines will be the same color as the chalk but will be edged with the light-colored tempera paint.

SINK & FLOAT

⬦▷⬦▷⬦▷⬦▷

Check it out: What will sink and what will float?

What You'll Need
- sink
- water
- variety of common items (foam cup, sponge, marble, button, thread spool)

Caution: This project requires adult supervision.

Gather together an assortment of household items for experimenting (beware of choking hazard if items are small). Everyone should wash their hands before playing in water. Invite the child to explore some of the items in and out of water, enjoying the feel of the water  and observing that some things stay up and some go down to the bottom. After the child has had some exploration time, all the items can be gathered together once more (and new items added), and the child can predict which items will sink and which will float. The child can sort the items into the 2 categories and then test out the predictions.

WHAT'S SILLY?

⬦▷⬦▷⬦▷⬦▷

Listening for what's silly in a story gives the child the experience of listening actively with purpose.

Make up a story that includes 3 or 4 nonsensical things, and tell it to the child. For example, you might say, "I slept late and didn't get out of bed until noon. I would have slept later but the hooting of the owls woke me up. As soon as I got out of bed, I took my shoes off and went into the bathroom to brush my face and wash my teeth. When I was finished, I put the soap back in the soap dish and put fresh toothpaste on my toothbrush."

After you finish telling the story, ask the child to name as many silly things in the story as possible. After that, the child may enjoy taking a turn telling a story with some silly things for you to catch.

STAR MOBILE

Star light, star bright, the first star the child sees tonight will be from this attractive mobile.

What You'll Need
- sturdy paper
- scissors
- aluminum foil
- markers
- masking tape
- heavy string
- clear tape

Cut a piece of sturdy paper into a large star shape, cover it with aluminum foil, and write the word *star* on it. Then cut several small star shapes, covering each with aluminum foil. Next invite the child to find other examples of words with the letter pattern *ar* and have him write each of these words on a piece of masking tape. Invite the child to attach the masking tape to the smaller star shapes—one word per star. Use clear tape to tape pieces of heavy string to the top of each small star. Complete the mobile by taping the smaller stars to the larger one as shown in the illustration.

Invite the child to make other mobiles using shapes and words that contain the following letter patterns:

bird	*ir*
letter	*er*
horse	*or*
purse	*ur*

BOOKS OF A FEATHER

⊲►⊲►⊲►⊲►

Compare two books from the same genre to see why they are favorites.

What You'll Need
• 2 favorite books from the same genre, such as fairy tales, fantasies, biographies, etc.

Encourage the child to read or reread both books. Then have the child make a list of the characteristics in each book. Discuss with the child how the characteristics are alike. How are they different? Which book did the child like better? Are the characters in each book similar? Do the books have similar story lines?

 # STORY STEW

⊲►⊲►⊲►⊲►

Inspire original storytelling by incorporating common household objects.

Choose 5 to 7 common but unrelated household items, and lay them on a table. Challenge the child to make up and tell a silly story that includes each of the items! Encourage the child, as he is inventing the story, to add or take away items in order to make the story better, just like a stew!

What You'll Need
• 5 to 7 random household objects (such as a sock, mixing spoon, saltshaker, hat, yarn)

After the child has created a story, suggest that he act out that story, using the items as props.

PAINTING WITH NATURE

◁▷◁▷◁▷◁▷

Make your own paints—with nature!

What You'll Need
- fruits or vegetables and other natural items (beets, blueberries, purple cabbage, spinach, red onion skins, walnut shells, coffee grounds, marigold or dandelion flowers)
- pots
- water
- pot holder
- brush
- paper
- white cotton twine
- scissors
- newspaper
- nontoxic white glue (optional)

Caution: This project requires adult supervision.

Paints in a multitude of colors are easily available at any local art store, but what did people do before they could buy paints at the store? They made their own! Make natural dyes by simmering beets, berries, onion skins, or the other items listed at left until the water turns color. Remove the vegetables, then reserve the water, and let it cool. (The vegetables can be saved for soups, the fruit for pudding, and the onion skins tossed away!) The child can help with the cooking by placing the items in the pot (one fruit or vegetable per pot) and adding the water.

After the colored water has cooled, the child can use it to paint on paper or to dye cotton twine. To dye the twine, let it soak in the vegetable dye for an hour, and then set it to dry on newspaper. As a further activity, the child can make several colors of twine and then use the naturally dyed twine for a collage.

OPPOSITE DAY

◁▶◁▶◁▶◁▶

Say just the opposite of what you mean in this contagiously funny activity.

Declare the day, "Opposite Day." Think of what you want to say, and then say the opposite. For example, if you want to say "Hello" to someone, you would instead greet them with "Goodbye." If you wanted to thank someone for turning off the light, you would say, "You're welcome for turning on the dark."

MUSIC LOOKS LIKE THIS

◁▶◁▶◁▶◁▶

Happy, sad, fast, or slow? Listen to music, take your brush, and go!

What You'll Need
- tape player
- several cassettes
- paper
- paint
- brushes

Gather together several musical selections that express different moods or tempos. Play one of the pieces. Ask the child how the music makes him feel. Encourage the child to share feelings in words or with movement. Then invite the child to paint to the music, painting the way the music makes the child feel. Afterward, or at another time, play a different selection and paint again.

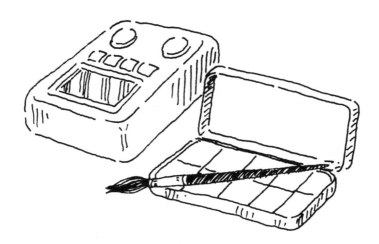

CARDBOARD SHAPE FAMILY

◁▸◁▸◁▸◁▸◁▸◁▸◁▸

Turn circles, squares, and triangles into sisters, brothers, fathers, and mothers.

What You'll Need
- cardboard
- blunt scissors
- nontoxic white glue
- fabric scraps
- yarn
- markers

Cut cardboard into a variety of sizes of circles, squares, triangles, and rectangles. The child can use the shapes to create the members of his family. The child might choose to make very simple bodies, gluing only a circle onto a rectangle or triangle, or he may favor more sophisticated people, using a square for a body, a circle for a head, a triangle for a hat, and skinny rectangles for arms and

legs. Honor all choices! After the child has created the people, fabric scraps can be glued on for clothing, yarn can be glued on for hair, and faces and other details can be drawn with markers. The child can then tell about the family members and can also create stories and dialogue.

Fun Fact
Having an imaginary friend is common and normal for children. It usually indicates a rich imagination and a fondness for pretend play rather than some sort of socialization problem.

WHEEL ALONG

◁▷◁▷◁▷◁▷

Find 2 wheels and a pole, and explore how things roll!

The child can experiment with wheels and axles using common household items. Gather assorted items together to get the child started. The child can choose which things to use for wheels and what to use for the axle and can then secure the wheels to the axle with plasticine. The child can create 2 or 3 different kinds of wheels and axles and experiment to see which vehicles roll best, farthest, and fastest.

What You'll Need
- plasticine clay
- assorted household items for wheels and axles: pencils, straws, thread spools, paper plates, plastic coffee-can lids

SAY IT IN A LETTER

◁▷◁▷◁▷◁▷

Write a letter, and send it to someone dear, whether far or near!

What You'll Need
- paper
- pencil or markers
- envelope
- stamp
- tape recorder (optional)

Invite the child to write a letter to a grandparent, relative, friend, or neighbor. The child can dictate the letter to you, or he can write independently and use invented spelling or pictures to write down ideas if the correct spelling is not known. The child can fold the letter, put it in the envelope, seal it, and put a stamp on it. After you or another adult addresses the letter, the child can decorate the back of the envelope. When the letter is signed, sealed, and ready to go, take a walk together to the nearest mailbox, and drop it in! For a variation, next time send a tape-recorded letter. The child can share adventures and news by recording the news and sending off the tape.

The child might also enjoy expressing an opinion in a letter to a local official about a community issue, such as a park cleanup or animal rescue.

TIC-TAC-TOE A WORD

⊲►⊲►⊲►⊲►⊲►⊲

Try this new twist on the popular children's game.

What You'll Need
- paper
- felt-tip pens
- self-adhesive notes

Make a tic-tac-toe board similar to the one shown below. The spaces should be relatively large, at least 1½" × 1½". Next decide on 9 words, perhaps theme-related words (such as foods, animals, favorite story characters) or recently learned vocabulary words, and write them in random order in the spaces.

Draw an *X* on 5 self-adhesive notes, and draw an *O* on 5 different self-adhesive notes. The game is then played as in regular tic-tac-toe, except here the player must say the word in the box he chooses and use it in a sentence before covering it with a note. Help the child sound out the word and recognize the letters. The first player to cover 3 words in a row—either across, down, or on a diagonal—wins the game.

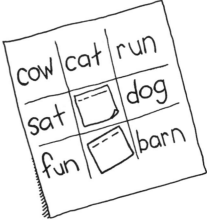

 # BUBBLE BABBLE

⊲►⊲►⊲►⊲►⊲►⊲

Blow some bubbles, and practice the B sound.

What You'll Need
- liquid soap
- water
- large plastic container
- drinking straw

Use bubble-blowing to help the child practice beginning sounds.

Make a bubble solution by pouring soap and water into the container, using ¼ cup of soap to 1 quart of water. Invite the child to blow bubbles with the straw. Each time he blows a bubble, say a word. Have the child say a word that begins with the same sound.

MELT-AND-EAT COLLAGES

◁▷◁▷◁▷◁▷

Create edible artwork that transforms in the oven!

Caution: This project requires adult supervision.

Butter the bread and place it buttered-side down on the cookie sheet. Invite the child to use the scissors to cut out different shapes from the cheese and cold cuts. After she has produced a collection of shapes, encourage her to use the pieces of cheese and cold cuts along with the tomato bits to create a "collage" on the bread. She can make a face, a building, or simply an abstract work of art. Butter additional pieces of bread and let her produce more creations. Place the creations in the broiler until the cheese melts. Remove the cookie sheet and let the child observe the results. Make sure she doesn't touch the cookie sheet or the food while it is hot. When the food has cooled sufficiently, put her creations on a plate and let her eat them.

What You'll Need
- plastic knife
- butter
- bread
- cookie sheet
- potholder
- cheese slices
- sliced cold cuts
- chopped tomato
- clean, blunt scissors
- broiler
- plate

Riddle Time!

Q: How do you ask for tiny green vegetables?
A: Pass the peas, please.

WAXED-PAPER WINDOW

◁▷◁▷◁▷◁▷◁▷

Turn a pretty collage into a see-through window.

What You'll Need
- flat nature items
- waxed paper
- ribbon (optional)
- yarn (optional)
- crayon scrapings (optional)
- iron
- paper towels
- pinking shears

Caution: This project requires adult supervision.

The child can collect flat nature items and arrange them on waxed paper. Ribbon, yarn, or crayon scrapings can also be added for extra decoration. When the child has finished assembling the design, the adult can iron a second sheet of waxed paper on top to create a sealed nature window. (Tip: Place paper towels under the waxed paper so the wax isn't ironed into the ironing-board cover!) The child can also create designer bookmarks. Have him place all the lovely materials in long, rectangular areas on the waxed paper. When this has been ironed together, the adult can cut the edges with pinking shears to make the bookmarks extra special.

PALINDROME PALS

◁▷◁▷◁▷◁▷◁▷

The child will want to back up and start again with this wacky activity that puts spelling in forward motion.

Explain to the child that a palindrome is a word that is spelled the same forward or backward. Some examples are *mom* and *toot*. Invite the child to see how many palindromes he can come up with. Use the following clues to help the child get started: another name for father *(dad)*; sound made by a baby chick *(peep)*; sound made by a bursting balloon *(pop)*; body part for seeing *(eye)*; time in the middle of the day *(noon)*.

CROSSWORD PUZZLES

⬦▷⬦▷⬦▷⬦▷⬦▷

Across, down, this way and that, crossword puzzles make spelling old hat.

What You'll Need
• graph paper with large squares
• pencil

Invite the child to create a crossword puzzle using spelling words you and the child have chosen. The words may be from a list of words the child has had difficulty spelling in daily writing, a spelling list from school, or new words the child wants to learn to spell. Help the child make the words fit on the graph paper, going across or down. Cross as many words at the letters they share as possible. On a separate sheet of paper, assist the child in making a blank puzzle to match the one he already created. Then, help the child think of a clue for each word and write those on the bottom of the paper. Be sure to add numbers to the boxes and the clues. The child should then color in the boxes that will be empty. When the puzzle is finished, pass it on to another person to solve.

Activity Twist

Extend this activity by turning the answer page on the original graph paper into a word search. Have the child fill each empty square with a letter, surrounding the words already there. A friend can then search for the newly hidden words.

PREDICTION FUN

⬦▷⬦▷⬦▷⬦▷⬦▷

This activity will engage the child in creative thinking while making predictions for an unfamiliar story.

Begin by reading the book and thinking about where the child can make predictions. Be sure that the illustrations do not give away the answers! Plan to pause at certain points and ask the child to make a prediction. Accept all answers before continuing with the story. Be sure to enjoy the child's surprises and creativity in making predictions. Then invite the child to read the book for enjoyment.

What You'll Need
• book that is unfamiliar to the child

LISTENING WALK

⊲▶⊲▶⊲▶⊲▶⊲▶⊲◀

Describing everyday sounds engages the child's attention while enhancing language development.

What You'll Need
- paper
- pencil

Go on a listening walk with the child around the neighborhood, or even just around the house. Before you start, have the child write down all the sounds on a piece of paper that might be heard while walking. Then go on the walk.

Walk quietly together. Don't talk. Just listen carefully. Write down all the sounds you hear. When you return, check the list. How many items on the list did the child hear while walking? What did the child hear that was not on the list? Ask the child to describe each sound that was heard on the walk.

For a creative challenge, invite the child to make up a story that includes some or all of the sounds on the list.

SHADOW PLAY

⊲▸⊲▸⊲▸⊲▸⊲▸⊲▸

Create shadow shapes, and watch them dance!

Hang a sheet on a line outside on a sunny day (or create an indoor line, and shine a light on the sheet). The child can stand in front of the sheet so that his body casts a shadow on it. Encourage the child to experiment with shadow shapes. Can the child make a tall, skinny shape? A tiny, round

What You'll Need
• clothesline or cotton twine
• clothespins
• sheet

shape? A fat, wide shape? A shape with holes in it? How does the shape change as the child moves closer and farther from the sheet? For a variation, play different kinds of music, and have the child invent shadow dances.

WEATHER CHART

⊲▸⊲▸⊲▸⊲▸⊲▸⊲▸

This chart will help you keep a record of your local weather.

What You'll Need
• construction paper of various colors to make weather symbols (for example, yellow to make a sun, white to make clouds, blue for raindrops)
• blunt scissors
• monthly calendar (with the days of the week spelled out)

Children are curious about the weather: What makes it rain? Why is it sunny?

Help the child make an assortment of weather symbols—a sun, clouds, raindrops, etc. Each day, he can place the appropriate weather symbol on the calendar square for that day. Have the child go outside or look out the window and observe the weather conditions. Is it sunny, cloudy, or rainy? Discuss the weather each day, then let the child select the appropriate weather symbol.

By using a calendar every day, the child will learn to recognize and read the days of the week. He will also learn how symbols represent words.

LETTER LINE

◁▷◁▷◁▷◁▷

Using clothespins to learn beginning sounds keeps kids from getting out of line.

Children can work on beginning sounds by hanging
letter cards and objects from a line.

Stretch a piece of string across a secluded corner of
the house, and secure it on both ends. Collect several
objects that can be hung from the line, such as a sock,
napkin, mitten, letter, paper plate, and towel. Next,
make letter cards containing both the capital and lowercase forms of the beginning letter of each chosen item.

What You'll Need
- string
- objects described at left
- index cards
- marker or pen
- plastic clothespins

Have the child choose an object and hang it on the line. Then have him find the
letter card that shows the beginning sound of the object's name and hang it next to
the object. When the child has hung all the objects and matching letter cards along
the line, have him name each object and the beginning sound of its name.

DOGGIE, DOGGIE

◁▷◁▷◁▷◁▷

*Defining words is not so r-r-r-rough when the child is engaged
in this dog-and-bone game.*

What You'll Need
- 8 to 12 bone-shape paper
  cutouts
- markers

Write vocabulary words on bone-shape cutouts. Sit
on the floor facing each other to play the game
"Doggie, Doggie, Where's Your Bone?" While one
player chants, "Doggie, doggie, where's your bone?"
the other player sits with the bones
turned over so that the writing
is facedown. When the
"doggie" finishes the chant, he picks up one of the bones
and reads the word. If the "doggie" can correctly read
the word, he keeps the bone, and play continues. If not,
it's the next player's chance to be the "doggie."

MOOD DANCE

◁▷◁▷◁▷◁▷◁▷

Make up mood movements for happy, sad, and mad dances!

Invite the child to create different dances to express different kinds of moods. The child can choose one mood and make up a dance. Encourage the child to imagine and

What You'll Need
• music

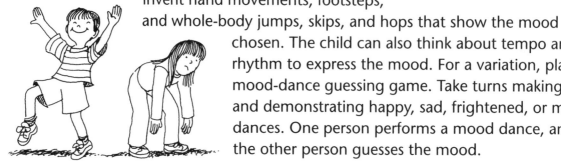

invent hand movements, footsteps, and whole-body jumps, skips, and hops that show the mood chosen. The child can also think about tempo and rhythm to express the mood. For a variation, play a mood-dance guessing game. Take turns making up and demonstrating happy, sad, frightened, or mad dances. One person performs a mood dance, and the other person guesses the mood.

WORD EMPHASIZING

◁▷◁▷◁▷◁▷◁▷

Change the meaning of a sentence by emphasizing a different word.

Discuss the different ways of conveying meaning when using the same sentence. Make up a simple sentence, and have the child repeat the sentence, emphasizing a different word each time. Talk about how the meaning of the sentence changed each time a different word was emphasized.

Tongue Twisters!
Terrible Tommy tickled Terry's tiny toes.
No one knows Noah's nose like Noah knows Noah's nose.

BLOCK PARTY

◁▶◁▶◁▶◁▶

Kids' earliest toys can become three-dimensional learning tools.

What You'll Need
- set of building blocks with letters
- paper
- marker or pen

Here's an activity that makes children's play with building blocks even more instructive.

Print a word on a sheet of paper. Have the child find the blocks with the letters that spell the word and arrange them in order. Words to start with are *cat, dog, boy, top, big, fan, run, jump, play, ball,* and *girl.* As the child progresses, you might list words with a theme, such as animal words or family words. You might also have the child suggest the words.

HANDY GIFT WRAP

◁▶◁▶◁▶◁▶

Here's an easy way to personalize your gift-wrapping paper.

Relatives and friends will love this special handprint wrapping paper.

Lay out a large sheet of thin or regular paper and several bottles of tempera paint. Let the child select the colors of paint that he wants to use. Ask him to tell you the beginning letters of the colors selected—for example, *R* for red, *P* for purple.

What You'll Need
- large sheet of thin or regular paper
- tempera paint
- paintbrush

Ask the child to name the part of the body that begins with an *H* and can be used to make prints with paint. (Answer: hand.) Next, take the colors of paints the child selected, and brush paint on the child's palm with a paintbrush. While doing this, reinforce the *H* sound of the word *hand.* When the child's hand is painted, have him press the hand all over the paper to make colored prints.

APPLE STAR PRINTS

◁▷◁▷◁▷◁▷◁

What's inside an apple? Just seeds? Try this activity, and you'll be surprised.

What You'll Need
- apple
- knife (to be used by adult)
- washable tempera paint
- paper towel
- clean foam meat tray
- paper
- pen or marker

Caution: This project requires adult supervision.

The child will learn the short vowel *A* in this arts-and-crafts activity.

Cut an apple in half, making the cut parallel to the stem. Ask the child to examine both halves of the apple. Point out how the exposed seed formation at the apple's core is in the shape of a star. Remove the seeds, and have the child dip the inner (skinless) side of the apple into a shallow tray of tempera paint. (This works best if a small amount of paint is put on a wet paper towel placed on a foam meat tray.)

After the paint is applied to the apple, help the child print several "stars" on white paper. As the child is making these prints, have him say the word *apple*. When the prints are finished, label the picture "Apple Stars." Point to the letter *A* in the word *apple* to make the connection between the printed letter and its correct sound.

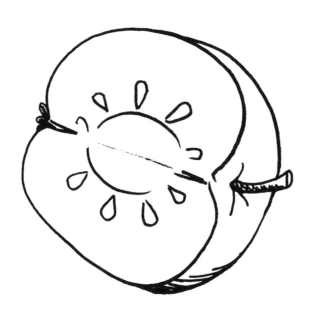

COOKING QUESTIONS

◁▷◁▷◁▷◁▷

What's the best way to cook an egg?

What You'll Need
- egg
- bowl
- variety of mixing tools (hand beater, spoon, fork, whisk, jar for shaking)
- nonstick electric frying pan
- pot holder
- spatula
- plate
- cheese (optional)
- chopped vegetables (optional)

Caution: This project requires adult supervision.

Challenge the child to figure out what would taste best, and try it out! After washing hands, the child can crack an egg in a bowl and experiment with different tools to figure out what mixes best. The child can then decide whether to fry the egg, make a flat omelet, or scramble the egg. The adult must supervise the child as the egg is cooked in an electric frying pan. For a variation, include cheese or chopped vegetables. Put the egg on the plate, and let the child eat it!

REPORT CARDS

◁▷◁▷◁▷◁▷

Make a mock report card to see if characters in favorite stories and books make the grade.

On a folded piece of construction paper, invite the child to make a report card for grading a story character. Include the following areas to be graded: helpfulness, attitude, sense of humor, completing assignments, following rules, and being on time.

What You'll Need
- construction paper
- felt-tip pen

The report card is not complete until the child "grades" the character in each of the selected areas. The child may even find it necessary to request a conference with the character's parents. If so, this should be noted on the report card, too.

A Story to Be Told

◁▶◁▶◁▶◁▶◁▶◁▶

Make a new story every time you "read" a picture book.

What You'll Need
• picture book
• paper
• pencil

A child needs to be able to interpret or "read" pictures, since sight recognition of words is very limited at a young age. By looking at pictures, stories can be understood—or imagined.

Select a picture book without written text, and look at it with the child. After going through the book, ask the child if anything seemed to be missing. When the child responds that there aren't any words, suggest that you can add them and write the story together.

Ask the child to look carefully at the pictures and tell you what he thinks is happening. As the child is describing a picture, write his story on a piece of paper. Ask the child to name different beginning letter sounds of the words in his story. For example, if the story involves a monkey, ask the child, "What letter does the word *monkey* begin with?" You can take this even further by asking, "What does a monkey like to eat?" When the child answers "bananas," ask him what letter the word *bananas* begins with.

When finished, sit back and enjoy reading the whole story with the child. A new interpretation of the pictures may be made another day.

HARK! I SEE BARK!

◁▷◁▷◁▷◁▷

Record and remember trees with bark rubbings!

What You'll Need
- thin paper
- crayons

Peel the paper off several crayons, and go out bark hunting! The child can choose the trees to record and the crayon color to record them with. Hold the paper against the tree as the child makes the rubbing. The child can make rubbings on different kinds of trees and compare the unique impressions they make. As a variation, the child can make building rubbings, recording impressions of different materials (stone, wood, stucco, cement) and comparing them.

Activity Twist

Collect scraps of bark, rocks, seashells, pinecones, etc. Press some of these natural items into plasticine or playdough. Observe the impressions created. Use a magnifying glass for extra fun. Can you match the items to their impressions?

ALPHABET NOODLES

◁▷◁▷◁▷◁▷

What letters are most frequently found in a box of alphabet noodles? Try this activity and find out.

When grocery shopping, go down the pasta aisle. Select a box of alphabet noodles. Many phonics activities can be done with them.

What You'll Need
- box of alphabet noodles
- bowl

In this particular activity, empty the alphabet noodles into a bowl. Have the child group the noodles by letter (all of the *A*'s, *B*'s, *C*'s, and so on). When this task is completed, help the child determine whether any letters of the alphabet are missing, which letters are the most common, and so on.

CATS AND DOGS

⊲►⊲►⊲►⊲►⊲►⊲►

Follow a 4-legged friend in this simple board game.

What You'll Need
- pictures of a cat and a dog
- poster board
- die and markers from board game
- marker or pen

Here's a board game that teaches children the letters C and D.

Make a board game with 2 paths of 12 squares each. Put a picture of a cat at the end of one path and a picture of a dog at the end of the other. Write the letter C in several squares of the path to the cat and other letters in the rest of the squares. Write the letter D in several squares of the path to the dog, using other letters in the rest of the squares.

Two players take turns rolling a die and moving markers along their paths. If a player on the cat path lands on a C, he continues. If not, the player loses a turn. The player on the dog path continues only if he lands on a D. Play until one player reaches the end of a path.

EMBARRASSING MOMENTS

◁▷◁▷◁▷◁▷

Everyone has a memory that brings back a red face or a chuckle.
Use that to inspire some great writing.

What You'll Need
- paper
- pencil

Begin by telling the child about an embarrassing or scary experience you had. Perhaps you went to school with 2 different socks on. Maybe the teacher caught you not paying attention in class because you were talking to a friend. Talk about embarrassing things that the child has experienced. Then have the child write about the event, making it as humorous as possible.

ABC CUPS

◁▷◁▷◁▷◁▷

It's sort of satisfying to put objects into their very own letter cups.

What seems like a simple sorting exercise reinforces a child's vocabulary and the ability to identify letters.

Mark 3 plastic drinking cups with the letters *A, B,* and *C* (1 letter per cup) using a permanent marker. Collect several small objects whose names begin with each of these letters, such as an animal cracker, toy airplane, and an acorn for the letter *A;* a ball, bandage, and bean for the letter *B;* and a playing card, piece of candy, and a cotton ball for the letter *C.*

What You'll Need
- marker
- 3 plastic drinking cups
- small objects as described at left

Put the items in random order on a table, and ask the child to put each object in the cup with its beginning letter on it. Discuss the names of the objects as the child completes the activity. Repeat the activity using other letters and objects.

FISHING FOR LETTERS

◁▷◁▷◁▷◁▷

Bait that hook, and cast your line. See what fish letters can be caught.

What You'll Need
- construction paper
- blunt scissors
- marker or pen
- paper clips
- dowel rod
- string
- magnet

Here is an opportunity for a child to go fishing—for letters.

Using several sheets of construction paper, cut out 26 fish shapes. Write 1 letter of the alphabet on both sides of each fish. Affix a paper clip to each fish. To make the fishing pole, take a dowel rod and tie a piece of string onto one end. At the end of the string, tie a magnet. To set the atmosphere for this activity, place the paper fish in a bathtub, dish pan, or inflatable swimming pool. (They should not contain water.)

The task for the child is to use the fishing pole to catch a fish. The magnet will attract the paper clip on each fish. When a fish is caught, have the child pull it gently off the magnet and say the letter.

PILLOWCASE PICKS

◁▷◁▷◁▷◁▷

A prize awaits the participant when the pillowcase is filled.

In addition to a pillow, have the child find other objects in your home that begin with the letter *P.*

Show the child a pillowcase. Ask what goes inside a pillowcase. The child should respond with "pillow." Ask the child to make the sound of the *P* in the word *pillowcase.* Give the child the pillowcase and have him find and place different objects that begin with the letter *P* inside it (for example, pen, pencil, piece of popcorn, paintbrush).

What You'll Need
- pillowcase
- objects that begin with the letter *P*

When the child has collected every item he could identify, put them on the table and review the items. As you are talking with the child, use as many *P* words in your conversation as you can. When you are finished, give the child a prize of peanuts or a pear (or anything else that begins with the letter *P*) for the successful completion of this activity.

NAMES IN THE NEWS

◁▶◁▶◁▶◁▶◁▶◁▶

Extra! Extra! Read all about it! Your name is in the news.

What You'll Need
- old newspapers
- blunt scissors
- blank paper

Ask the child to search through an old newspaper to find one set of the letters that make up his first name. When the letters are found, have the child cut them out and arrange them to spell out the name on a blank piece of paper. Remember that the first letter needs to be a capital letter.

For an extra challenge, ask the child to find the letters of his middle and last names as well. This activity may be repeated by searching for and using different types, sizes, and colors of print.

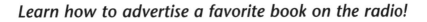

RADIO ADVERTISING

◁▶◁▶◁▶◁▶◁▶◁▶

Learn how to advertise a favorite book on the radio!

Invite the child to reread a favorite book. Discuss what the child likes about the book and what makes it outstanding. Then help the child create an ad appropriate for reading on the radio. It should truly "sell" the book to listeners. Write down the ad. Then have the child practice reading it into a tape recorder until it is ready to be shared.

What You'll Need
- favorite book
- paper
- pencil
- tape recorder

SINGING MY OWN SONG

◁▷◁▷◁▷◁▷◁▷

Create new lyrics to old songs!

Sing familiar songs with simple melodies, such as "Row, Row, Row Your Boat" or "Mary Had a Little Lamb." After singing the song, change the words to make up entirely new stories and sing them to the familiar tunes. The new songs can be silly or serious, make-believe or real. To get the child started, invent a new verse about the child and sing it to one of the old familiar tunes. For example, "Row, Row, Row Your Boat" can be changed to be a song about the child eating dinner. Then invite the child to make up the next verse.

Activity Twist

Make up songs for special transition times (hand washing, going outside, cleaning up, nap time). For example, use a peppy tune like "Jingle Bells" for clean-up time. "Pick up the blocks; pick up the blocks; pick up the blocks today. Oh what fun it is right now to put them all away." Or, you and the child might like to try making up a nap song to a quiet, gentle tune like "Hush Little Baby."

COLOR CLUES

◁▷◁▷◁▷◁▷◁▷

Color your world with color names.

In this activity, the child learns to read the names of various colors.

Print a color word (*red, blue, green*) on an index card using a marker of that color (in other words, use a red marker for *red,* blue marker for *blue,* etc.). After the child has mastered associating the words with the matching colors, make another set of word cards. This time use a black marker. See if the child can match these word cards with the appropriate color.

LET THE SUN SHINE

◁▶◁▶◁▶◁▶◁▶◁▶

Follow the winding path, and review the letter S.

What You'll Need
- construction paper
- pen
- crayons or markers
- blunt scissors
- glue
- poster board
- die and markers from board game

Construct your own board game to practice the beginning sound of the letter *S*.

Draw 10 to 15 circles, each with a diameter of about 1½", on construction paper. Ask the child to decorate these "suns" with crayons or markers. Cut them out and paste them on a piece of poster board to form an *S*-shaped path.

Play a game by taking turns moving markers along the path according to the roll of the die. Each player must say a word that begins like the word *sun* in order to leave his marker on a circle. The game ends when one player reaches the end of the path.

VOCABULARY DANCE

◁▶◁▶◁▶◁▶◁▶◁▶

Learn new action words to create a dance!

Play a favorite tune. Ask the child to join you as you create a special dance to go along with the song. Start with simple movements and instructions, such as "run" and "jump." Gradually make the dance more complicated by adding new words, such as "leap," "twirl," and "stretch." Make

What You'll Need
- CD or cassette tape player
- favorite CDs or cassette tapes

sure to model the appropriate movements that go along with the new words. After the child has become comfortable with a variety of movements, add directional cues as well. For example, say, "Run forward, jump back, twirl around this way, twirl around the other way, leap to this side, leap to that side." If the child indicates an inclination to take the lead, you can then follow his movements and describe what he is doing.

Puff, Puff, Toot, Toot!

◁▷◁▷◁▷◁▷◁▷

*Music and movement are an ideal and fun way for the child
to learn sound words.*

Sing the following chorus of the familiar song "Down by the Station" together. Then have the child repeat the words that imitate sounds in the song, such as *puff* and *toot*. Invite the child to mimic the sounds, emphasizing expression and body language, such as shuffling feet or moving the arm up and down while making a fist to simulate the motion that makes the sound *toot, toot*. Sing "Down by the Station" again, but this time have the child act out the sound words. Point out that more meaning is added to words when expressive voices and actions are used. Follow up by having the child list other sound words she knows.

"Down by the station early in the morning,
See the little puffer bellies all in a row.
See the stationmaster turn the little handle,
Puff, puff, toot, toot,
Off we go!"

For an additional challenge, research the names for train cars. Find out what a puffer belly looks like and what it was used for.

SCRAMBLED LETTERS

◁▶◁▶◁▶◁▶◁▶◁▶

Even kids who don't like eggs will have fun with this "egg-citing" activity.

Sorting letters into egg cartons is one way to recognize letter likenesses and differences.

Cut off the lids of the egg cartons so that you have 3 bottoms with 12 hollow sections each. With a marker, print a letter on the bottom of each section, with A to I in the first carton, J to R in the second carton, and S to Z in the third carton. (Since you'll have more hollow sections than letters, some sections will remain blank.) Using construction paper, cut out 26 circles approximately 1" in diameter and print 1 letter of the alphabet on each. Put the letter discs in a small container and mix them. Have the child take the discs out one at a time and put each into its matching egg-carton section.

CLIFF-HANGERS

◁▶◁▶◁▶◁▶◁▶◁▶

The child will enjoy reading a good cliff-hanger while practicing reading and comprehension skills.

Read a "cliff-hanger" story into a tape recorder. Then have the child listen to the tape and read in the book along with it. This will help the child follow and understand the text. After each chapter, stop the tape recorder, and invite the child to predict what will happen next. Discuss that prediction together. Then have the child read the next chapter to find out if the prediction is correct. Continue the activity until the book is finished. This activity can last for a few days if the book you choose has a lot of chapters.

SUN SHAPES

◁▶◁▶◁▶◁▶◁▶◁▶

Next time there's a sunny day, try making these sun-bleached prints.

What You'll Need
- collection of familiar objects (such as a pencil, ruler, marker, and paper clip)
- dark-colored construction paper
- marker or pen

This activity blends science and phonics.

On a sunny day, help the child collect some objects that are easily recognizable by their shapes—for example, a pencil, ruler, marker, and paper clip. Discuss the beginning letters and sounds of those objects.

Next, ask the child to select a piece of dark-colored construction paper. Then take the collected objects and the paper outside. Place the paper on the ground, in direct sunlight, and have the child arrange the objects on the paper. (You may need to place some heavy stones on the edges of the paper if it is a windy day.)

Approximately one hour later, instruct the child to remove the objects from the paper. Ask the child what she sees, and discuss what happened to the paper. As each image is identified, have her use a marker or pen to write the beginning letter under each image left under the object (*P* for *pencil,* *M* for *marker,* *R* for *ruler,* and so on).

TRACKING DOWN WORDS

◁▷◁▷◁▷◁▷

Create a story from words found on a walk,
and provide an opportunity for verbal expression.

Take a walk outside together to track down words. Bring
a pen or pencil and paper along, and search for words
that are displayed in easy view, such as on a street sign or
a billboard. Write down 10 to 20 of the words you discover. When you return, encourage the child to make up
a story or narration using the words that you collected
together. This activity will also enhance the child's observation and imagination skills.

The inquisitive child will also enjoy searching for 10 to 20 words found inside the
house, or even in just one room!

What You'll Need
• pen or pencil
• paper

TRACING LETTERS

◁▶◁▶◁▶◁▶◁▶◁▶

Cut out paper letters, and help set a pattern for learning.

Using patterns to create letters will improve a child's dexterity.

Draw and cut out several letter shapes from poster board, such as *A*, *P*, and *T*. On a sheet of paper, write a word that can be formed from the letters, for example, *PAT* or *TAP*. Have the child arrange the letter shapes that will form the word and then trace around them with a crayon or marker to write the word.

What You'll Need
• poster board
• paper
• blunt scissors
• marker or crayon

VOCABULARY SEED PACKETS

◁▶◁▶◁▶◁▶◁▶◁▶

Little seeds of knowledge can grow into a garden of information with this vocabulary-rich project.

What You'll Need
• seed packets
• 3" × 5" index cards
• markers
• glue

Have the child look at some real seed packets. Then invite the child to design a seed packet for something she'd like to grow. The plant the child chooses could be real or imaginary. Have the child draw a colorful picture of the plant on the front of an index card and label it. Help the child write a descriptive sentence about the plant on the back. The sentence may tell what the plant looks like, explain how or when to plant the seeds, suggest tools needed to do the planting, or remind the grower of foods that can be made from the harvested plant.

The child might also enjoy keeping a seed diary. Have the child wash, dry, and then glue seeds from fruits and vegetables onto cards. With your help, the child can then label the cards with the name of the seed, date eaten, and comments.

ODDS AND ENDS WEAVING

◁▷◁▷◁▷◁▷◁▷

Weave together a medley of things for fun and display!

What You'll Need
- blunt scissors
- yarn
- ribbon
- string
- nature items (feathers, twigs, thin leaves, etc.)
- cardboard

The child can cut pieces of yarn, ribbon, and string, and weave them together using a homemade loom. Nature items such as feathers and twigs can also be collected to weave in, creating an abstract weaving out of found and collected objects. Make a loom out of cardboard by notching the edges on either end, as shown. Wrap a piece of yarn around the board through the notches, and then tie it tightly in the back to

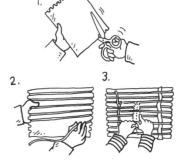

create the loom. More notches can be spaced closer together or fewer notches farther apart to make it easier or more challenging for the child to weave ribbons, yarn, and string over and under the yarn strings with her fingers.

FUNNY DAYS

◁▷◁▷◁▷◁▷◁▷

The calendar will never be the same with this fun day-renaming activity.

Before beginning this activity, look at a calendar together with the child and point out the following: the month and year, days of the week, numbers for the days, and special events. After setting out poster board and markers, invite the child to

What You'll Need
- calendar
- poster board
- markers

design a calendar for one week, like the example shown here. Have the child create new names for the days of the week based on her scheduled activities or how she feels about a particular day. For example, if the child plays soccer on Saturdays, she might rename it Soccerday; the child's favorite day might be renamed Funday.

CUP PUPPETS

◁▷◁▷◁▷◁▷

Make pop-up puppets for peekaboo stories!

What You'll Need
- stiff paper
- blunt scissors
- crayons or markers
- nontoxic white glue
- unsharpened pencils
- 2 to 3 polystyrene cups

The child can make the puppets by drawing characters on stiff paper and cutting them out. Glue the characters to the eraser ends of the pencils. The adult can then pierce a hole in the bottom of each cup, and the child can insert the blunt ends of the pencil puppets. The child holds the puppet inside the cup. A puppet is pushed out of the cup to come onstage and is slipped back into the cup to go offstage. Encourage the child to make up stories for the puppets to act out. For added challenge, have the child make up stories with more than one character—one cup can be the stage for up to 3 puppets!

Activity Twist

Still more cup puppets! This time, cut familiar characters from wrapping paper, gift cards, or magazines. You can also cut props for the puppets (ball, purse). Jazz up the miniature stages by drawing scenery all around the cups with colored markers.

RHYME BOX

◁▷◁▷◁▷◁▷

Rhyme with real things!

What You'll Need
- box
- 4 to 8 pairs of small objects that rhyme (i.e., fork/cork)

Create a rhyme box filled with pairs of real objects that rhyme—like *fork/cork, clock/rock, ring/string, duck/truck, box/socks.* Gather up 4 to 8 rhyming pairs and place them in a box. Invite the child to explore the items in the box and talk about the name of each item. Then play a rhyming game

together. The child closes his eyes, reaches into the box, and pulls out an item. The child looks at the item, names it, and then checks the box to find the rhyming partner. The child takes it out of the box also. Then the adult takes a turn. Continue playing until all the rhyming partners have been found and put together. The child can also spread out all the items in the box and work independently to match up the pairs.

DRESS FOR SUCCESS

◁▷◁▷◁▷◁▷

Clothes make the child—or at least the child's phonics knowledge—in this start-the-day activity.

As the child gets dressed in the morning, play a beginning-sound guessing game using at least 3 items of his clothing.

What You'll Need
- several items of clothing

   Start this way: "Now it's time to put on something that begins like the word *party.*" (Answer: pants.) Have the child guess each piece of clothing before putting it on. This game can also be played at bedtime using a night-gown, pajamas, robe, or slippers.

TRAVEL POSTER

◁▶◁▶◁▶◁▶◁▶

*Visit faraway countries, interesting cities,
or other travel destinations without leaving home. Here's how.*

What You'll Need
• old magazines
• blunt scissors
• scrap art materials
• poster board
• glue
• markers

Help the child think of words that can describe nouns. Explain that these descriptive words are called *adjectives.* Next invite the child to make a travel poster that encourages her friends to visit a new place. The travel destination may be a place the child has actually visited or a place she would like to travel to one day. It may be a country, state, city, or specific tourist attraction.

To make the travel poster, look through old magazines, and help the child cut out pictures of sights a traveler would want to see while visiting a chosen destination. The child could also make inviting pictures from scrap art materials. Glue the pictures on the poster board. Remember, the pictures should describe the location in a way that would motivate others to travel there. Once the pictures have been placed, have the child write phrases using colorful adjectives that describe the destination. Find a place where the poster can be easily seen, and put it on display.

SYLLABLE BUGS

◁▶◁▶◁▶◁▶◁▶◁▶

Creepy, slimy bugs have invaded this syllable activity. Watch out!

What You'll Need
- egg carton
- blunt scissors
- chenille stems

To make insect models out of egg cartons, first separate the egg cups by cutting the carton apart. Next ask the child to think of an insect, perhaps a butterfly or a caterpillar. Help the child determine how many syllables are in the word by clapping your hands together as you say each part of the word: *cat-er-pil-lar*. Then write each syllable of the insect's name on an egg cup, one syllable per cup.

Use short pieces of chenille stems to attach the cups together. Bend and twist additional chenille stems, poking them through the cups, to create antennae, wings, or other features that you and the child would like to add to make the insect look complete. For continued syllabic fun, choose from these other insects: beetle, bumblebee, hornet, centipede, and grasshopper.

SPLATTER PAINTING

◁▶◁▶◁▶◁▶◁▶◁▶

Sprinkle, splatter, and scatter colorful drips and drops!

Beware—this is a very messy project! This can be done outside (on a calm day) or inside. If inside, spread out plenty of newspaper on the floor, and tape it down. Place paper in the middle of the newspaper, and tape it down. Set the bowl filled with paint on the newspaper. The child can dip a brush into the paint and then, from a standing position, splatter and sprinkle paint drops. After exploring with the paint, encourage the child to experiment.

What You'll Need
- newspaper
- tape
- large sheet of white paper
- tempera paint
- plastic bowls
- brush

What happens if the brush is shaken softly? What happens if it is shaken harder? Does the child notice a difference if paint is sprinkled from high up or down low?

LOTS OF PUPPETS AND MUPPETS!

◁▷◁▷◁▷◁▷

Puppets and muppets parade some more... puppets to make by the score!

Lunch Bag Puppets: The child can draw a face on a paper bag with markers. When the face is finished, the child can stuff the bag with crumpled newspaper. Insert a paper-towel tube in the bottom of the bag and scrunch the end of the bag around the tube. Secure the tube to the bag by tying a piece of yarn around it. The tube then becomes the handle by which the child holds the puppet. (The child might also want to glue yarn on top of the bag for hair.)

Spoon Puppets: Gather together several old wooden spoons. The child can turn these into stick puppets by drawing faces on the backs of the spoons with markers.

Stick Puppets: The child can cut out pictures of people or animals from a magazine or make their own pictures and cut them out. Glue the cut-out pictures to stiff paper. The child then glues these people and animals to a strip of cardboard, which is used as a handle.

What You'll Need
Lunch Bag Puppets:
- lunch-size paper bag
- newspaper
- markers
- paper-towel tube
- yarn
- nontoxic white glue (optional)

Spoon Puppets:
- old wooden spoons
- markers

Stick Puppets:
- old magazines
- paper (optional)
- markers
- stiff paper
- cardboard
- blunt scissors
- nontoxic white glue

WHAT'S HAPPENING HERE?

◁▷◁▷◁▷◁▷◁▷

Observe, notice, note, and discuss!

Share a graphic picture from a storybook, magazine, or poster with the child. Encourage the child to look at the picture, make observations, and draw conclusions based on visual clues. Ask questions to spark discussion. Here are some discussion questions to start with: Who do you think these people are? What are they doing? What would you do if you were there? How do you think the little boy/girl/dog feels? What do you think will happen next? How can you tell? Did something like that ever happen to you? What does this picture remind you of?

WALKIE-TALKIE

◁▷◁▷◁▷◁▷◁▷

Make a walkie-talkie, and engage in telephone talk!

What You'll Need
• 2 empty cans
• electrical tape
• large nail
• hammer
• twine

Use electrical tape to tape the top of each can—to smooth down any sharp edges. The adult or child (with adult supervision) can make a hole in the bottom of each can using a hammer and a large nail. Insert the ends of the twine into each of the holes of the cans. Tie a large knot in the end of the twine on the inside of each can to hold it in place. The adult and child (or 2 children) can then each take one of the cans and walk away from each other until the line is taut. Using the cans as both a telephone receiver and a mouthpiece, start your walkie-talkie conversations!

CAREERS FROM A TO Z

◁▷◁▷◁▷◁▷◁▷

Consider careers—from acrobat to zoologist—in this alphabet game.

What You'll Need
- large sheet of paper or poster board
- marker or pen

Here's a project that relates to the question, "What do you want to be when you grow up?"

Help the child make a poster illustrating various careers. Begin with the letter *A,* and ask the child to think of a career whose name begins with that letter, such as astronaut. Have the child write the letter and draw a picture of an astronaut. Continue through the alphabet, skipping letters that do not bring an easy response.

MELTDOWN

◁▷◁▷◁▷◁▷◁▷

How fast will ice melt? Let's find out!

Here's an activity that will help the child discover what it takes to melt objects: heat! The child can place the same number of ice cubes into 4 self-sealing bags and then carefully seal each bag. The child can then choose a different part of the room or

What You'll Need
- ice cubes
- small self-sealing bags

house to place each bag. One can be put in a sunny window, one near a radiator, one in the refrigerator, and one can be held between two warm palms! Have the child predict which cubes will melt the quickest and which the slowest—then observe the results.

Activity Twist

Have fun with an ice race! Pour the same amount of water into differently shaped plastic containers—for example, square storage containers or cookie molds. Freeze the water. Pop out the ice shapes on a tray when they are frozen solid. Guess which shapes will melt first or last. Why?

COOKIE CORNER

◁▷◁▷◁▷◁▷◁▷

Here's an educational way to enjoy a batch of fresh-baked cookies.

Children can learn about letters as they eat their favorite snack.

Ask the child to help you mix a batch of cookie dough. Cookie dough from a mix, frozen dough, or

What You'll Need
- cookie dough
- letter cookie cutters
- baking sheet
- decorative icing in tubes

refrigerated rolls of dough work just as well. Roll the dough out. Have the child use cookie cutters shaped like letters to cut the dough. After baking and cooling the cookies, help the child decorate each cookie by tracing the shape of each letter with decorative frosting in a tube.

Put the cookie letters out on a plate. Play an easy game of "I Spy," taking turns giving clues, such as, "I spy a letter that begins the word *apple.*" Each cookie letter may be eaten after it has been correctly identified.

LETTER PUZZLES

◁▷◁▷◁▷◁▷◁▷

The alphabet won't seem so puzzling to children who master this activity.

What You'll Need
- heavy paper or poster board
- colored markers or crayons
- blunt scissors

A letter puzzle can help children improve hand-eye coordination as they learn letter recognition.

Write 2 or more letters on a piece of heavy paper or poster board. Make the letters so they are two-dimensional; in other words, draw each letter in outline form, letting the child color the inside portion of the letters. Cut the paper into several puzzle pieces. Have the child put the puzzle together and name each letter. You can make increasingly difficult puzzles, eventually using the entire alphabet.

Turnaround Sounds

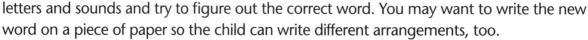

Turning around sounds enhances the child's listening skills with a little help from phonics.

Rearrange the letters of a word to make it into a different word. For example, the word *spoon* can be rearranged to *snoop, star* can be changed into *rats,* and *charm* can be changed into *march.* Think of a word that can be rearranged, and tell the child the new word along with a clue to the original word. You may say, "If you turn around the letters and sounds, you can eat with a 'snoop.' What is the word?" Invite the child to rearrange the letters and sounds and try to figure out the correct word. You may want to write the new word on a piece of paper so the child can write different arrangements, too.

 # Beginning Sound Baseball

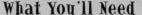

Even children who aren't power hitters can score a home run in this game.

Use this indoor or outdoor activity to teach children the fundamentals of base running in baseball and to help them practice beginning sounds.

First, set up 4 bases in an approximate diamond shape. At each base, put several toys whose names begin with a *B* sound—for example, a ball, a bat, a beanbag, a bear, and blocks. Mix in some

toys whose names do not begin with a *B* sound—for example, a car, a doll, and a horse. Explain to the child that, to make a home run, she must go to each base in order and pick up a toy whose name begins like the word *baseball.* When the child reaches home plate, she must name each object.

How Does My Shadow Grow?

◁▶◁▶◁▶◁▶◁▶◁▶◁▶

Sunny days make great shadows—at noon, 1:00, and 2:00!

Sunny days and shadows are a perfect combination for outside investigation and experimentation! Go outside together on a sunny day and look for shadows. The child can make shadow records by placing paper on the ground on top of intriguing shadow shapes and tracing the shapes with a crayon or tracing the shapes on cement with chalk. The adult can hold the paper down while the child draws. To add to the shadow exploration, the child can observe and record morning, noon, and dusk shadows. Find a sunny place on the pavement, and take turns tracing each other's shadows in the morning. Trace around where feet are placed so you can each step into the same position the next time you measure. Come back and retrace both shadows at lunchtime and again in the afternoon. How are the shadows different? How did

they change? For a variation, the child could place a teddy bear or a toy in the sun and trace the changing shadows during the day. Or to create a simple shadow to trace, the child can put a tall stick or ruler in a coffee can filled with soil or stones.

What You'll Need
- paper
- crayons
- chalk
- teddy bear or other toy (optional)
- coffee can (optional)
- stick (optional)
- stones or soil (optional)

What Can It Be?

◁▷◁▷◁▷◁▷

A letter can be used to form many things. See what you can make.

It's good to stimulate a child's creativity. Here's one fun way to do it.

Draw a large letter (capital or lowercase) on a piece of paper. Ask the child to create an object based on the letter's shape (for example, the letter *O* can be made into a wheel, the letter *V* into an ice cream cone). Label the drawing. See how many objects the child can create with different letters. When the project is completed, show the drawings to other family members to see if they can find the letter.

Magic Words

◁▷◁▷◁▷◁▷

Put a magic spell on some familiar words and turn them into new words. Just say "Abracadabra!"

Pose the following question to the child: How do you turn a cap into a cape? The answer: With magic! A magic *e*, that is. Show the child how adding an *e* to some words will "magically" turn them into other words.

Next invite the child to put a magic spell on words such as *tub* and *cub,* turning them into the new words *tube* and *cube.* Ask the child to think of other words that could fall under the same spell. You may want to suggest the following words to get the child started: *tap, her, cut, kit, rip, rob,* and *can.*

WEATHER WONDERINGS

◁▶◁▶◁▶◁▶◁▶◁▶

Play a weather wardrobe game.

What You'll Need
• magazine pictures of people

Gather together an assortment of magazine pictures that show people dressed in clothing or engaged in activities for a variety of weather conditions. Then take turns describing a weather condition to one another. For example, the child can describe the condition: It's very chilly, and rain is coming down. The adult can pick a picture that shows the appropriate clothing or activities for that weather and explain the choice.

WORD HANG-UP

◁▶◁▶◁▶◁▶◁▶◁▶

Sometimes letters and words are just hanging around.

What You'll Need
• old magazines
• letter cards
• clothes hanger
• plastic clothespins

Help children enjoy unusual methods of putting letters together to make words.

Think of several easy words, such as *dog, cat, bird, car, jet, cup, pig,* and *boy.* While searching through old magazines, find and cut out a picture of each one. Put a clothes hanger on a doorknob. Display the first picture. Instruct the child to find the letter cards that spell the word and clip them onto the hanger with clothespins.

WHAT WOULD YOU DO?

◁▷◁▷◁▷◁▷◁▷

Share the solution with a display of dramatic action!

Take turns making up imaginary situations, and challenge one another to act out what one might do. These are some possible situations to get you started:

- What would you do if 5 lions walked into the kitchen while you were eating lunch?
- What would you do if you woke up in the morning and discovered you'd been sleeping in a tree?
- What would you do if the cat came to the kitchen table and asked for breakfast cereal?

CHECKING LICENSE PLATES

◁▷◁▷◁▷◁▷◁▷

Search for license plate letters while you travel by car.

What You'll Need
- paper
- pencil

To pass the time when traveling in the car, give the child a sheet of paper with the alphabet printed on it in capital letters.

Have the child call out the letters that she sees on the license plates of other cars and then cross off those letters on the sheet of paper. Travel time will go by more quickly when the child is involved with this activity, and she will be exposed to reading mixed combinations of letters and numbers.

PICTURE DICTIONARY

◁▷◁▷◁▷◁▷

This dictionary provides the child with a powerful tool for alphabetizing, spelling, and learning new words.

What You'll Need
- clear tape
- several 18" × 6" strips of construction paper
- markers

Invite the child to make a picture dictionary of new spelling words. Choose the words from a school spelling list or from words the child wants to learn to spell. Help the child tape the 18" × 6" strips of paper together, end to end. Fold the long strip back and forth, accordion-style, creating about 3 sections to each 18-inch strip. Make sure there are 26 pages and a cover. Then have the child decorate the book cover.

Next, the child should write one letter of the alphabet, from *Aa* to *Zz*, on each page. The child can then write the spelling words on the appropriate page. You may want to help the child alphabetize the words before they are written in the picture dictionary. Finally, help the child write a definition and draw a colorful illustration for each entry.

FAMILY NEWSLETTER

◁▶◁▶◁▶◁▶◁▶◁▶

*Start a new family tradition that benefits everyone,
especially if family members live far apart.*

What You'll Need
- pencil
- paper
- envelope
- stamp

Invite the child to create a newsletter that has one or more short articles about family events. The newsletter can be as simple as one page written in pencil or as elaborate as a booklet done on a computer, complete with special fonts and art. Then have the child send the newsletter to a relative, along with a list of other relatives' addresses and the route the newsletter should take after the first relative reads it. Make sure the final address belongs to the child. A note asking all recipients to add their news to the newsletter should also be enclosed.

When the newsletter returns to the child, she should replace the information in the old newsletter with new information. Then the child can send it off again, following the same route as the first edition of the newsletter, and instructing family members to replace their previously circulated information with new information. This way everyone gets the latest family news without having to write individual letters to family members.

BOWLING FOR SCHOLARS

◁▶◁▶◁▶◁▶◁▶

Children who know their letters can bowl a perfect game.

What You'll Need
- 10 empty plastic soft-drink bottles
- masking tape or self-adhesive labels
- marker
- large beach ball or plastic ball

This activity combines bowling and letter identification.

Put a strip of masking tape or a self-adhesive label on each bottle, and print a different letter on each one. Set the bottles up in a row, and have the child roll the ball toward the "pins."

Ask the child to identify the letter on each pin she knocks down. If the child identifies the letter correctly, the pin stays knocked down. If the child cannot identify the letter, the pin is set back up. Continue playing until all pins have been knocked down and all letters correctly identified.

BEASTLY BABBLE

◁▶◁▶◁▶◁▶◁▶

Imagine the tales animals might tell!

Use animal pictures as a spark for creative interpretation and tale-telling. Cut out pictures of a variety of animals from magazines, and paste them onto a piece of construction paper. Share the pictures, and encourage the child to consider what the animals in the pictures might say if they could talk. The pictures can be labeled with the child's ideas and then later bound into a book, if desired.

What You'll Need
- magazine pictures
- blunt scissors
- nontoxic white glue
- construction paper
- crayons or markers

PICK A PUMPKIN

⬦▶⬦▶⬦▶⬦▶⬦

You don't have to wait for autumn to create an educational pumpkin patch.

Make learning the sound of the letter *P* fun by creating a pumpkin patch. Help the child draw and cut out several pumpkins from orange construction paper. Place the pumpkins around the room. Ask the child to gather pumpkins from the "patch" by saying a word that begins like *pumpkin* each time she picks up a pumpkin.

What You'll Need
• orange construction paper
• pencil
• blunt scissors

FRESH LEMONADE

⬦▶⬦▶⬦▶⬦▶⬦

Nothing tastes better than a glass of fresh lemonade you make together.

On a warm summer day, nothing is better than a glass of freshly squeezed lemonade. The squeezing, stirring, and pouring of the ingredients provide great muscle-developing skills.

Ask the child to place each lemon half on top of the juicer and squeeze it. You may need to place the juicer over a small bowl so the child can work more easily. As the child is squeezing the lemons, talk about what sound she hears in the beginning sound of the word *lemon*.

After the lemons have been squeezed, empty the juice into a pitcher.

What You'll Need
• 2 lemons, cut in half
• juicer
• spoon
• water
• measuring cup
• 1 cup of sugar
• ½ gallon pitcher

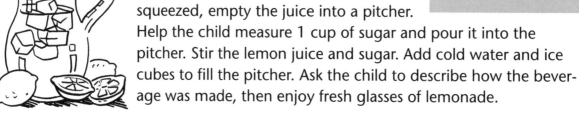

Help the child measure 1 cup of sugar and pour it into the pitcher. Stir the lemon juice and sugar. Add cold water and ice cubes to fill the pitcher. Ask the child to describe how the beverage was made, then enjoy fresh glasses of lemonade.

BACKWARD ALPHABET

◁▶◁▶◁▶◁▶◁▶

If walking backward is difficult, try talking backward.

Invite the child to say the alphabet forward from *A* to *Z*. Use a watch with a second hand or a stopwatch to time the child. Then have the child say the alphabet again, but this time in reverse, *Z* to *A*. Time this, also. Continue this several times in a row to see how fast the child can say the alphabet, forward and backward.

NUMBER RIDDLES

◁▶◁▶◁▶◁▶◁▶

Inventing riddles can be a humorous way for the child to put critical thinking skills to use.

Invite the child to make up a number riddle and try to stump you. Begin by sharing examples of number riddles. Then encourage the child to invent a new one. Here are 3 trusty traditional number riddles:

What has 4 legs but never walks? (A chair.)
What has 4 legs and barks? (A dog.)
What has 8 legs, 2 arms, 3 heads, and wings? (A man riding a horse carrying a canary.)

CAT AND MOUSE

◁◀▷◀◁▶◁▷

Here's a chance for the child to feel like the "big cheese."

What You'll Need
• letter cards

Here's a game that will challenge a child to move quickly and quietly.

Have the child imagine that he is a mouse and that you are a cat. The "mouse" must take the "cheese"— a letter card— without getting caught by the "cat."

Sit in a chair. Place a letter card on the floor behind you. Close your eyes, and wait for the child to take the card. If you hear him, say, "I hear a mouse." If you speak before the child has picked up the card, he must take your place on the chair, and you must try to take the card. If the child takes the card without getting caught, he must name a word that begins with the letter on the card. The child then keeps the card, a new card is laid down, and the game is repeated. The player who successfully takes the most cards wins.

STEPS IN A PATH

◁◀▷◀◁▶◁▷

Take these "steps" to learn letters and sounds.

Let the child explore the many possibilities of this activity.

Write a capital *A* on one side of a sheet of paper and a lowercase *a* on the other side. Do the same for each letter of the alphabet. Spread the sheets of paper on the floor like stones, and see how the child uses these materials. She can arrange them in alphabetical order or make a long path and say each letter as she steps on it.

What You'll Need
• 26 sheets of paper
• markers

MONTH AT A GLANCE

⊲►⊲►⊲►⊲►⊲►⊲◁

The child will practice using and learning new nouns
while creating this lively calendar.

Help the child make a calendar for one month by drawing a
7 × 5-square grid on a piece of poster board. Have the
child write the name of the
month and the days of the week
on the calendar. Remind the
child that names of days are
proper nouns and should begin
with capital letters. Help the
child number the days from 1 to
28, 29, 30, or 31. Make the calendar lively with cutouts
and pictures to mark special days and events.

What You'll Need
- poster board
- felt-tip pens
- old magazines
- construction paper
- blunt scissors
- glue

FEEL & SORT

⊲►⊲►⊲►⊲►⊲►⊲◁

Feel and touch, then sort and such!

What You'll Need
- variety of materials with
different textures: bark,
buttons, metal washers,
cotton ball, fabric
scraps, aluminum foil,
rock, sandpaper

Gather together an assortment of items that have different textures. The items should all be large enough so
that none can be swallowed. The child can use her fingers, hands, and even face to feel the texture of the
items and sort them into simple
categories, such as smooth/rough
or soft/hard. For more challenge,
invite the child to do
the sorting with her
eyes closed and by touch alone, putting smooth
things on one side and rough things on the other.
For a variation, provide 2 of each texture.

SNAP LETTERS

◁▶◁▶◁▶◁▶◁▶◁▶

Instead of using those clothespins on a clothesline,
try snapping them on pictures.

This activity reinforces 8 different beginning sounds.

Take a piece of lightweight cardboard and, using a compass, draw and cut out a circle approximately 8" wide. Use the pen to divide the circle into 8 equal sections, as if it were a pie. Next, cut out pictures of familiar objects from a magazine (for example, ball, pen, fish, dog, carrot, hat, shoe, apple). Make sure that each picture is small enough to fit into 1 section of the circle and that no 2 objects begin with the same letter. Glue or tape the pictures in place.

On the opening end of each snap clothespin, write a letter that matches the first letter of the object in each picture (in our example, the letters *B, P, F, D, C, H, S,* and *A*). Ask the child to take each lettered clothespin and snap it onto the section of the circle that has an object that begins with the same letter. Continue until all the letter matches are made.

If the child has difficulty with certain letters, focus on those letters the next time you do this activity. (Hint: You can use the back of the circle to repeat this activity with a new set of letters.)

PASS-ALONG STORY

◁▷◁▷◁▷◁▷

*This evolving tale-telling activity encourages
fanciful thinking and comprehension.*

Create a pass-along story with the child. Choose an object to be the "pass-along" and to represent the story that gets passed along from person to person. The pass-along can be a stone, a stuffed animal, or a potato. You may even want to start the story about the object that is being passed along.

For example, let's say you choose a potato as the object you want to pass along. Then you would think of a story idea that would include the potato or even be about the potato. You might begin, "Once upon a time a farmer dug up a magic potato, and the potato started to talk." After telling only a little bit of information, "pass along" the object (in this case the potato) to the child. Now it's up to the child to make up the next part of the story. Continue until you're both satisfied with an ending.

SYLLABLE TALLY

◁▷◁▷◁▷◁▷

*The child will enjoy rhythmic play while practicing breaking
words into their sound parts.*

Teach the child the following simple chant, and have her clap on each syllable as you say the chant: "Word, word, I know a word. How many syllables has my word?" Then suggest a word, and invite the child to guess how many syllables by clapping them out while saying the word. Then repeat the chant together again. This time invite the child to suggest a word for you to clap out in syllables.

PLANT MAZE

◁▶◁▶◁▶◁▶◁▶◁▶

Even when the going gets dark, plants will find a way to light!

Plants always grow toward sunlight. Here's an activity for the child to test a plant's determination to find the light. The child can fill a small pot with soil and plant 2 or 3 lima beans in the soil an inch or so deep. The child can place the pot in a sunny place, water the soil, and keep it moist until the beans begin to grow and sprout. After the plant has begun to peek above the soil, the child can place it inside a plant maze. Help the child create the maze by cutting a hole (approximately 3 inches in diameter) in one side of the box. Cut 2 pieces of cardboard to fit inside the box, making 2 walls. Cut a hole in each wall on opposite sides. Place the walls inside the box. When the maze is ready and the plant has sprouted, the child can place the plant in the box in the section farthest away from the outside hole. Let the child close or cover the box. Place the plant maze in a sunny place, and check the plant regularly to keep it moist. Within days the plant will find a way through the maze and out to the light! To add to this activity, the child can grow 2 lima bean plants in full sunlight. After the plant has leafed out, the child can cover 2 or 3 of the leaves with aluminum foil for a week so that they do not receive sunlight. Watch what happens!

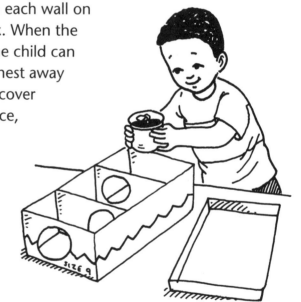

Fun Fact
The letter y can be either a consonant or a vowel. In year, it's a consonant. In happy, it's a vowel.

BLOWING BEAUTIFUL BUBBLES

◁▷◁▷◁▷◁▷

Everyone loves blowing bubbles—blow away!

Make bubble solution by combining 8 tablespoons of liquid detergent, 1 tablespoon of glycerin, and 1 quart of water in a tub or basin. The child can experiment with different tools (bubble wand, berry basket, cardboard tubes, can with both ends removed, etc.) and investigate what makes the best bubbles and why. (Make sure the can does not have any sharp edges!) The child can explore which tool makes the biggest bubble, the smallest bubble, the longest bubble, the strongest bubble, the most bubbles, and even the prettiest bubble!

What You'll Need
- tub or large, flat basin
- liquid detergent
- glycerin
- tablespoon
- bubble wand
- berry basket
- cardboard tubes
- can with both ends removed
- 6-pack plastic rings
- coated wire clothes hanger

LETTER PATTERNS

◁▶◁▶◁▶◁▶◁▶

Children can match letters even if they can't identify them.

What You'll Need
• 2 sets of letter cards

Even before children can identify letters by name, they can recognize their shapes.

You'll need 2 matching sets of letter cards. Randomly select 3 letter cards from one set, and place them in a row on a table. Give the child the other set of cards, and ask her to find the matching letter cards and lay them down in the same order. Increase the difficulty by making a series of more letters.

LID O'S

◁▶◁▶◁▶◁▶◁▶

What letter can you print with a lid? Dip one in paint and find out.

The child will learn all about *O*'s in this colorful activity.

Ask the child to help you find and collect lids of various sizes, then pour some paint into several small containers. Have the child guess what letter will be made when the lid is pressed on the paper. (Answer: *O*.)

What You'll Need
• collection of lids of various sizes
• tempera paint
• small containers
• paper

Next, select a lid and dip its edge into the paint. Press the lid onto the paper. As the child prints the letter on a sheet of paper, ask her what letter is being made. Make several prints with that lid, then have the child select another lid that will make a bigger or smaller letter *O* and make prints with those. When the prints are dry, ask the child which letter *O*'s are capital letters and which ones are lowercase letters—and why.

Seed Farming

◁▶◁▶◁▶◁▶◁▶◁▶

Cultivate seeds to eat!

What You'll Need
- seeds for sprouting (alfalfa, mung bean, radish)
- jar
- water
- cheesecloth
- rubber band

Sprout seeds for a lunch salad or sandwich or to steam for a dinner vegetable. The child can measure a spoonful of seeds into a jar and then fill the jar with lukewarm water. The seeds should sit overnight in the water. In the morning, place a piece of cheesecloth over the top of the jar, and secure it with the rubber band. The child can then pour out the water, while the seeds stay secure in the jar. The child can then fill the jar with fresh water, jiggle the jar to rinse the seeds, and pour out the fresh water. Then have the child refill the jar with water. The seeds should be rinsed several times a day. In a day or two the seeds will begin to sprout. Within a few days, the seeds will have sprouted and be ready to eat!

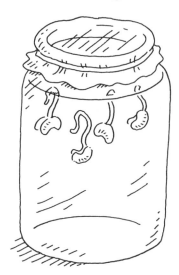

Word Wall

◁▶◁▶◁▶◁▶◁▶◁▶

Let words be a positive experience and a memory booster for the child with this creative activity.

Hang several large sheets of paper on a wall. Place a variety of markers nearby. Explain that the child is going to fill the papers with words about books she has read, such as quotes, authors' names, titles, and so on. Remind the child how powerful punctuation can be. For example, if she really likes an author, the child might write the author's name and follow it with an exclamation point instead of a period.

What You'll Need
- large sheets of paper
- masking tape
- markers
- favorite books

Spoonful of Beans

◁ ◀ ◁ ◀ ◁ ▶ ◁

Pour carefully, and guess how many beans a spoon can hold!

What You'll Need
- small plastic pitcher
- dry beans
- soup spoon

Caution: This project requires adult supervision.

The child pours dried beans from a small plastic pitcher into a soup spoon, trying to get as many beans as possible in the spoon before any spill. As soon as the first bean spills, the child stops pouring. Observing the spoonful of beans, the child guesses how many beans are in the spoon. The spoonful of beans is then spilled out onto the table and counted to check the prediction. After counting, the child can put all the beans back into the pitcher and take a second turn—aiming for a higher number! To continue the exploration, the child can experiment by using different kinds of beans or different sizes and shapes of spoons and comparing the results. (Adults should supervise this activity, especially with younger children. Small beans can be a choking hazard.)

Activity Twist

Enhance the child's predicting powers by creating a graph for guesses. Make a grid on paper with a marker. Print numbers across the top of the grid, and draw an X in the square of the number of poured beans the child predicts. Now lay out the beans across the graph and count them. Was the guess high? Low? Exact? See if the child pours the same number of beans the next time. Keep checking the graph for a visual reference.

STRETCH-A-WORD

◁▶◁▶◁▶◁▶◁▶◁▶

In this activity, the child exercises the body and the mind for the sake of spelling.

Tape 9 pieces of colored paper on the floor to make a 3 × 3-foot grid large enough for the child to stretch out on. Write the letters *a, b, d, f, m, n, p, s,* and *t* in the grid's construction-paper squares. The letter *a* should be in the middle.

What You'll Need
• 9 pieces of colored construction paper measuring 12" × 18"
• masking tape
• markers

To play the game, say a 3-letter word that has the short vowel *a* sound, such as *fan* or *nap.* Have the child spell the word by putting his feet on the first letter, the left hand on the second letter (which will always be *a*), and the right hand on the third letter.

For a more challenging game, have the child spell 4- or 5-letter words, using both hands, both feet, and even his head!

CONSONANT CANS

◁▷◁▷◁▷◁▷

Mix the clatter of household items with a variety of letter sounds.

What You'll Need
- large coffee cans
- plastic lids
- marker

Children will learn beginning sounds with this grab bag activity.

First, make sure the coffee cans have no sharp edges. Print a consonant letter on the top of the can lid. Have the child look for objects that have names beginning with that letter. For example, for the letter *P*, the child might find a peanut, postcard, pen, paper clip, and penny. Put the lid on the can, shake it up, and take turns removing and naming the items. Create cans with other letters.

TELL A SONG

◁▷◁▷◁▷◁▷

Tell a song story and guess the song.

Play a song guessing game together by retelling the stories of familiar songs. Take turns retelling song stories for the other to guess. Use new words to tell the story of a song you normally sing together. For example, a song question might be: "What song is about a little girl who brings a fluffy white pet that goes 'baa baa' to her school?" To give an extra hint to the person trying to guess the song, the person telling the story can hum some of the tune of the song.

Zoo

◁▷◁▷◁▷◁▷

***Every child likes to act like an animal sometimes,
and this game actively encourages it.***

What You'll Need
- sheet of paper
- marker or pen

Children's natural love of animals can be channeled into wordplay that helps develop reading skills.

On a sheet of paper, print the word *ZOO* in capital letters. Ask the child to identify the first letter of the word. Say the word together several times.

Talk with the child about trips to the zoo, or zoos he may have seen on TV or in movies, and encourage the child to think about some of the animals he saw there. Whenever the child mentions a specific animal, ask him to identify the beginning letter of the animal's name. Make a list of all the animals the child names, then show him the list and say, "Can you find the ____?" Read one of the animal names on the list, and see if the child can find that word.

For more fun, take turns acting like zoo animals, such as an elephant, monkey, gorilla, lion, and bear, as the other player guesses the animal's identity and identifies the word on the list.

WORD STAIRS

◁▷◁▷◁▷◁▷

Enhance a child's ability to build words, step by step.

Begin by writing a word across the bottom of a piece of paper. To build the next step in the word stairs, help the child think of a word that ends with the same last letter as the first word. The new word should be written vertically on the paper as shown. The third word must begin with the same first letter as the second word and should be written across the page. Continue this process until a staircase of words has been created from the bottom to the top of the paper. Use a large piece of paper, and challenge the child to see how high he can build a staircase.

CREATING A CHARACTER

◁▷◁▷◁▷◁▷

An imaginative child will enjoy becoming a favorite character for a day!

Invite the child to choose a favorite character from a well-liked book. Help the child find descriptive passages in the book that tell about that character. Then

invite the child to decide how that character would dress and act. For example, a very old lady might wear a shawl, use a handbag, and walk slowly while using a cane. Have a dress-up day when the child dresses up as the character of his choice and reads portions of the story aloud.

For further challenge, invite the child, while in character, to write a letter to another character from the story.

CREASE, CRUMPLE, CRIMP & CURL

◁▷◁▷◁▷◁▷◁▷◁▷

Fold and fashion fanciful paper-strip sculptures.

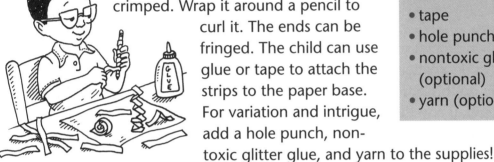

Provide a paper base and an assortment of precut construction paper strips in a variety of colors. Encourage the child to try different ways to use the paper to create a three-dimensional sculpture. The paper can be bent or folded, pleated or crimped. Wrap it around a pencil to curl it. The ends can be fringed. The child can use glue or tape to attach the strips to the paper base. For variation and intrigue, add a hole punch, nontoxic glitter glue, and yarn to the supplies!

What You'll Need
- construction paper
- blunt scissors
- unsharpened pencil
- nontoxic white glue
- tape
- hole punch (optional)
- nontoxic glitter glue (optional)
- yarn (optional)

RED-LETTER DAY

◁▷◁▷◁▷◁▷◁▷◁▷

Teach a child the alphabet in less than one month.

What You'll Need
- red pen or pencil
- paper

Devoting a day to one letter helps focus a child's learning. At the beginning of the day, assign a letter to look for. Write the letter in red, and display it in the kitchen. Ask the child to look for it in the home—on cans and boxes in the kitchen, in magazines and newspapers, on television. Each time the child finds the letter, he writes it in red on a sheet of paper.

AWAY WE GO

◁▷◁▷◁▷◁▷

Making a travel brochure will get anyone in the mood to travel!

This activity can be used to plan a trip or to serve as a record of a vacation. If creating the brochure before a trip, use the library to gather information about the destination. You can also go to a travel agency to pick up some sample brochures. Then help the child create his own brochure that might convince someone else to choose that destination as a vacation spot.

If you want to do this activity after the child has been to a particular place, you and the child can collect information while on the trip. Invite the child to create the brochure by using postcards or photographs collected on the trip.

CHOW DOWN

◁▷◁▷◁▷◁▷

Explore a character's likes and dislikes in this activity that's sure to make you hungry.

Have the child look through a collection of favorite books and select one with a main character he is particularly fond of. Invite the child to explain why he likes the character. Then help the child plan a meal for that character. Start by cutting out pictures of various foods from old magazines. Then tape the pictures to a paper plate to show what will be served. If the character is an animal, help

the child research the kind of food that animal eats. The child may also wish to create a just-for-fun menu that is sure to whet his favorite character's appetite.

THREE THINGS STORIES

◁▶◁▶◁▶◁▶

Put people, places, and things together in new and unusual ways!

What You'll Need
- magazines
- blunt scissors
- nontoxic white glue
- white paper
- paper bags
- marker

Gather an assortment of pictures of people, places, and things cut from magazines. Mount each picture on a separate piece of white paper. Include as wide a variety of subjects as possible. After all the pictures are cut, mounted, and gathered, invite the child to sort the pictures into 3 piles: 1 for people, 1 for places, and 1 for things. Take 3 paper bags and label 1 for people, 1 for places, and 1 for things. Open the bags and stand them up in a row. When the pictures have been sorted, place each of the piles into the appropriate paper bag. Take turns choosing a picture from each category and telling ways the 3 pictures go together. The reasons can be realistic or entirely fanciful! To encourage fantasy, you can start the game by giving examples of how the first 3 things might go together in a story. After the storyteller has explained the ways the pictures go together, the listener can ask 3 questions of the teller to elicit more details. To simplify the game, use only 2 categories: people and places or people and things.

WHAT'S DOT?

Start with one dot to create a whole picture!

What You'll Need
- stick-on dots
- paper
- crayons
- blunt scissors

Place one stick-on dot anywhere on a piece of paper. Let the child decide what the dot will become and then draw the rest of the picture around the dot. (The dot could be an animal head, the tip of someone's hat, a ball that children are throwing, etc.) If he enjoys this activity, on another day give the child a paper with a small hole in it as a picture challenge. Cut out a hole approximately 1 inch in diameter anywhere on the paper—or have the child tell you how big to cut the hole and where. Invite him to draw a picture around the hole, incorporating the hole into the picture any way he likes. (For instance, it might be a hole a worker is digging, the open mouth of a bear, the moon, or part of a design.)

A, B, See It!

Grab a pencil and a notebook, and take the child on a walking field trip to explore words.

Write a letter of the alphabet on the top of a piece of paper in a notebook. Give the notebook to the child and have him name the letter and indicate the sound for the letter. Next take the child on a letter walk, outside if possible. Instruct the child to look for words that begin with the letter on the paper. Then have the child copy the words into the notebook.

What You'll Need
- notebook
- pencil

WALKING WAYS

◁▶◁▶◁▶◁▶◁▶◁▷

Traipse and tramp to tell a tale!

Invite the child to act out walking in a variety of manners to communicate different ideas. Together with the child, think up a variety of situations, and take turns acting them out. Here are some examples to start with:

- Walk as if it's pouring rain.
- Walk as if you're in a great hurry.
- Walk as if you can't wait to get to the park.
- Walk as if you don't want to go somewhere.
- Walk as if you're being followed by a bear.
- Walk as if you're on the moon.

To make the activity simpler, invite the child to walk across the room the way a cat, dog, mouse, duck, or elephant might.

WHAT WILL IT BE?

◁▶◁▶◁▶◁▶◁▶◁▶

Follow directions to discover the mystery object.

What You'll Need
- paper
- crayons

This drawing task involves giving directions to the child and seeing if he can follow them to form an object. The concepts of left to right, top to bottom, straight, and down will be reinforced.

Think of an object and give step-by-step directions to the child to create it. For example, here is how you might give directions to draw a rectangle or square:

1. Draw a straight vertical line on the left side of your paper.

2. Draw a straight vertical line on the right side of your paper.

3. Draw a straight line on the top of the paper, connecting the top of the line on the left to the top of the line on the right.

4. Draw a straight line on the bottom of the paper, connecting the bottom of the line on the left to the bottom of the line on the right.

After the child follows these directions, ask him what has been made. As the child's ability to follow directions grows, increase the complexity of the object to be drawn. See if you can direct the child to draw letters of the alphabet without naming them in advance.

Rhyme Time!

Tick, tock, tick, tock,
happily sings
Grandfather clock.
It's time for work,
it's time for play.
Tick, tock, tick, tock,
Grandfather clock
sings all day.

DEEP DIRT DIGGING

◁▷◁▷◁▷◁▷

Get down and dirty, and explore what's deep below!

A sunny day, old clothes, and an open dirt area are a perfect combination for muddy exploration. The child can use the digging tool to shovel dirt into a plastic tub, then add water for a muddy mix. The mud can be strained. The child can pour water into the hole as part of the play. When the play is over, the child can scoop the mud back into the hole and pat it back down.

What You'll Need
- old clothes
- rubber boots
- digging tool (child-size shovel, trowel, old spoon)
- strainer
- pail
- plastic tub
- water

WHAT'S IN IT?

◁▷◁▷◁▷◁▷

Read the packaging to learn what you'll find inside.

What You'll Need
- food packages—cans, boxes, and bags

All kinds of words are found on food packaging. Select a few of those items from your food cabinet. Ask the child to try to determine what is inside the bag, box, or can. The child may be asked what kind of soup or fruit is in a particular can, what type of cereal or cookie is in a box, or what type of chip is in a bag. Ask the child to look at the lettering on the package and, using letter sounds, sound out the word.

At an early stage of reading development, the illustrations on the package can be used as clues for sounding out and recognizing the words. Before you know it, the child will be able to do a food inventory for you.

CAN YOU TIPPLEFIZZY ME?

◁▶◁▶◁▶◁▶

Play a word-detective game.

One person chooses a common word (*water, cat, shoes*), keeping it a secret. Then he makes up a sentence using *tipplefizzy* to substitute for the secret word. ("I'm thirsty, I want a glass of tipplefizzy.") Use *tipplefizzy* in as many different sentences as possible until the other person can guess what word *tipplefizzy* is being used for!

HOP, HOP-A-RALLY

◁▶◁▶◁▶◁▶

The child can hop to rhyming success with this interactive hopping activity.

See how many times the child can hop on one foot while practicing rhyming. Begin by chanting this rhyme: "Chickety, chickety, chop. How long before I stop?"

After you finish the chant, ask the child to name words that rhyme with *chop* and *stop.* Have the child hop once for each rhyming word. How long can he hop?

ALPHABET PHOTO ALBUM

◁▷◁▷◁▷

*Neighborhood adventurers and photography enthusiasts
will find this activity eye-opening.*

What You'll Need
- camera
- scrapbook or photo album

This is an exciting outdoor activity that helps children learn the alphabet—as well as operate a camera.

Get a camera (a disposable one will do), and go on a walk through the neighborhood or a nearby town or city with the child. Ask him to look for each letter of the alphabet on many different street signs and store signs. Take one picture of each letter found. You might want to show the child how to use the camera so he can help. Don't try to get the whole alphabet in one outing.

Develop the pictures, and help the child put them in a scrapbook or album in alphabetical order. Enjoy one or two more outings in which you look for the specific letters you're missing to complete the set.

Hink-Pink!

Q: How does an elephant take a shower?
A: With its nose hose.

MIX 'N' MATCH LETTERS

◁▶◁▶◁▶◁▶◁▶◁◁▶

*Encourage young artists to create this collage of letters
while learning new spelling words.*

What You'll Need
• old magazines
  and newspapers
• scissors
• clear tape or glue
• wallpaper

Before beginning this activity with the child, cut out a wide
assortment of letters from old magazines and newspapers.
Next, help the child tape or glue the letters to spell out words
on sheets of patterned wallpaper to make creative collages. If
you'd like, choose a particular theme, such as sports or flowers, and help the child brainstorm theme-related words.

PEANUT BUTTER PLAYDOUGH

◁▶◁▶◁▶◁▶◁▶◁◁▶

Make, mold, and munch playdough!

What You'll Need
• peanut butter
• powdered milk
• honey
• measuring cup
• measuring spoons
• wooden spoon
• bowl

Start by washing and drying hands thoroughly! The child can
then help to measure the ingredients into the bowl and mix
them up. Combine ½ cup peanut butter with ½ cup of powdered milk and ½ teaspoon of honey (have extra
powdered milk available in case dough is
too sticky). When the dough
is malleable, the child can
experiment with it—making
shapes and sculptures. And
fingers can be licked, too!

Activity Twist

For more peanut butter play, the child can roll pinecones first in a dish of peanut butter
and then in a dish of birdseed. Help the child tie these great feeders to trees or bushes
visible from a window. Then, wait for your feathery visitors to arrive! For even more fun,
help the child identify the birds in a field guide, and then draw pictures of them!

TELEPHONE DIRECTORY

◁▷◁▷◁▷◁▷

Find names beginning with different letters using an old phone directory.

What You'll Need
- old telephone directory
- blunt scissors
- envelope

One place where many letters are found is a telephone directory.

Show the child an old telephone directory, and look through it together. Explain what is in a telephone directory. A good introduction to the directory is to look for and cut out the child's last name or a friend's name. Using blunt scissors, the child can also cut out names beginning with each letter of the alphabet. (You can use boldfaced names for easier cutting and viewing—or cut out groups of 5 or more consecutive names.) Have the child recognize that names always begin with a capital letter, that a telephone directory lists last names first, and that the book is arranged in alphabetical order. After the names are cut out and every letter has been found, place these cuttings in an envelope, saving them for "Telephone Directory II" on page 512.

INGENIOUS INVENTOR

◁▷◁▷◁▷◁▷

Be creative! Design a new invention.

New products are added to the market practically every day, but what might a child like to create? Emphasizing the sound of the short *I*, have the child pretend to be an inventor.

What You'll Need
- Collection of scrap items

Talk about what an invention is and what items in the home have been invented. Discuss how those inventions have helped us.

Give the child a collection of scrap items, and see what "invention" he can create. When the invention is finished, talk about it. What is it? How does one use it? What will it do? How will it help us?

TIC-TAC-TOE RHYMES

◁▷◁▷◁▷◁▷◁▷

Tic-tac-toe, three in a row!

Here's a way to play this classic game while learning to recognize letters and rhyming words.

Make a game card by dividing a sheet of drawing paper into 9 squares (3 rows of 3 squares). Help the child draw or color the following pictures inside the squares: a hat, mouse, boy, peach, car, goose, tree, boat, and dime. Divide a second sheet of paper into 9 squares. This time, the child should draw or color a cat, house, toy, beach, jar, moose, bee, coat, and lime inside the squares and then cut these squares apart with blunt scissors.

To play, shuffle the picture cards. Players take turns picking a card and matching it to a rhyming word on the game board. If a player makes a correct match, he puts a board-game marker on the square. The first player to get 3 markers across, down, or on a diagonal wins the game.

CATEGORY COMPILATION

◁▷◁▷◁▷◁▷◁▷

Turn category creation into a challenge game!

One player thinks of and names a category. The next player then tries to come up with 5 things that would fit in that category. Start off with familiar themes, such as colors, animals that make good pets, or yummy desserts. Increase the challenge by choosing category topics that are a little broader, such as kinds of weather, sounds animals make, kinds of shoes, etc. Next, see if the child or other players can "Name That Category!" Take turns creating lists of similar objects or things, and have the other players come up with the major classification. For example: tyrannosaurus rex, brontosaurus, pterodactyl—"dinosaurs." Now put on your thinking caps. Personalize items for a specialized category: mustard, ketchup, relish—"toppings you like for hot dogs!"

KNOCK, KNOCK, NONSENSE

▷◁▷◁▷◁▷◁▷

Explore consonant sounds while sharing favorite knock-knock jokes.

Teach the child the formula for knock-knock jokes while sharing some of your favorites. Then invite the child to make up knock-knock jokes using words spelled with the consonant digraphs *sh, ch, wh, th, ph,* and *gh.* You may wish to start with the cheetah and gopher jokes shown here. But be warned: Telling knock-knock jokes is contagious.

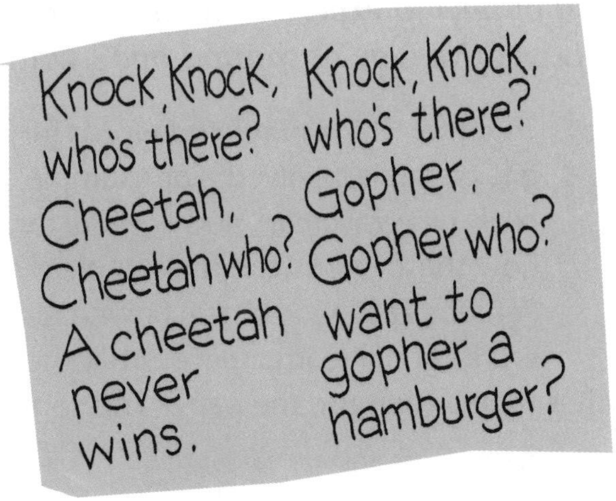

Knock, Knock,
who's there?
Cheetah,
Cheetah who?
A cheetah
never
wins.

Knock, Knock,
who's there?
Gopher.
Gopher who?
want to
gopher a
hamburger?

BONDED

◁▷◁▷◁▷◁▷◁▷

The object of this activity is to bond together a word, forward and backward.

Begin by choosing a vocabulary word from the child's school spelling list or one the child wants to learn to spell. Make 3 vertical columns on a piece of paper. Write the chosen word down the left column, one letter atop the other. Next, write the same word backward, last letter first, down the right column. Then take turns trying to "bond" the columns of letters together by adding whatever letters you or the child can think of in the middle column to spell words across. See if you can fill the middle column. The following example is for the word *horse.*

WRAPPING IT UP

◁▷◁▷◁▷◁▷◁▷

Instead of buying expensive wrapping paper, try this creative way of sharing one's writing.

What You'll Need
• paper
• markers
• ribbon

Together, think of related words for a holiday in which gift-giving is involved. For example, you may list *caring, cook, career woman,* and *cheerful* for Mother's Day. Plan how these words can make a pleasing pattern on paper. Perhaps each word has its own color or a special shape. Work carefully on paper so that the words are not smudged as the child writes them. Then use the paper and some ribbon to wrap a gift.

ALL ABOARD THE TRAIN

◁▶◁▶◁▶◁▶◁▶

Turn boxes into buses, and tour the town!

What You'll Need
- chairs or boxes
- paper plate
- stuffed animals
- paper
- markers

The child can become a bus driver, train conductor, or an airplane pilot by using a few simple props. Trains, planes, or buses can all be easily imagined and created using large cardboard boxes alone or along with chairs. If the child is using boxes, they can be decorated to look like a taxi, car, plane, train, etc. A paper plate can be a steering wheel. Stuffed animals become passengers. Tickets and signs can be made with paper and markers. The child can then transport people and animals around the city, state, and nation! If the child shows continued interest in vehicle play, check out some library books on transportation. The child can look at the pictures to learn more about different vehicles and to get fresh ideas for dramatic play!

IT'S ALL IN A NAME

◁▷◁▷◁▷◁▷◁▷◁▷

Sentences can be captivating, especially when they involve one's own name!

Begin by having the child write his name on a piece of paper. Then have the child think of one descriptive word that starts with each of the letters in his first name. Each word should tell something about the child. Next have the child use the words to write a self-descriptive sentence. For example, if the child's name is Martin, he might choose the following words:

What You'll Need
• paper
• pencil

Magical
Amazing
Red-haired
Ticklish
Interesting
Nice

MIME TIME

◁▷◁▷◁▷◁▷◁▷◁▷

In this activity, children will take on the role of mimes to act out verbs for an audience.

What You'll Need
• strips of paper
• pencils
• envelope or box
• white gloves
• top hat

Have children write an action word (verb) on a slip of paper. Invite them to share the words they wrote. Then have them place the slips of paper in an envelope or box.

Next invite one child to take on the role of a mime, slipping on white gloves and a hat. Explain that a mime is an actor who mimics or pantomimes people, animals, or events. The mime can use hand and facial gestures, body movements, and props, but cannot speak. Instruct the mime to pick a slip of paper from the box, and act out the action. Invite children to guess the action. The first person who guesses the verb becomes the next mime.

LOVABLE LOLLIPOPS

◁▶◁▶◁▶◁▶◁▶◁▶

*Learn about **L** words while you make some lovely lollipops.*

Caution: This project requires adult supervision.

What could be better than a lovely homemade lollipop? Follow this simple recipe, exercising due caution when working around the stove. Note that all cooking and handling of hot foods should be done by an adult.

With the child's help, put 2½ cups of sugar, ½ cup of water, and 1 cup of light corn syrup into a saucepan. Ask the child to stir this mixture until blended. Place a candy thermometer into the saucepan. Stir this mixture over medium heat until it boils and the thermometer reaches 280°F. While doing so, the child can prepare the waxed paper. Have him lightly grease the waxed paper with margarine and then place the lollipop sticks on the paper. Make sure the sticks are not too close to each other.

While both of you are working, talk about the different *L* words that appear in this activity: *lollipop, liquid, light, lightly, lovable, lovely, ladle, luscious*. When the temperature of 280°F is reached, remove the liquid from the heat, and add color if desired. Using a ladle, pour the mixture over the tops of the sticks on the greased waxed paper. Let cool, and then enjoy a lollipop.

What You'll Need
• sugar
• water
• light corn syrup
• measuring cups
• saucepan
• wooden spoon
• candy thermometer
• waxed paper
• margarine
• paper lollipop sticks
• ladle
• coloring (optional)

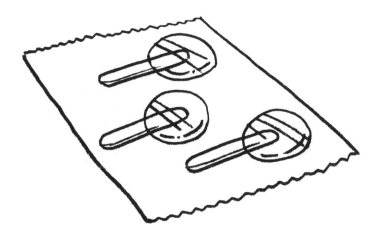

PLENTY OF PASTA

◁▶◁▶◁▶◁▶

This clever approach to writing new sight words will have the child practically glued to the paper.

What You'll Need
- alphabet pasta
- heavy paper
- glue

Invite the child to use alphabet pasta to write new vocabulary words. Help the child select pasta letters and arrange them in order to spell words. Next, the child may glue the letters on heavy paper. When the glue is dry, the child can trace the letters with his fingers and say the words. Encourage the child to use the words in sentences, too.

 # PLANT PARTS SALAD

◁▶◁▶◁▶◁▶

Make a root, stem, leaf, flower, and seed salad!

What You'll Need
- salad ingredients
- bowl
- salad servers
- plates
- salad forks

Go shopping together for the ingredients for the plant parts salad. Explain to the child that you will need one of each kind of plant part for the salad. The child can make the choices! At the market, point out several items in each category (one category at a time). The child can choose a root part from among carrots, radishes, or parsnips; a stem from celery or leeks; leaves from spinach or lettuce; flowers from cauliflower or broccoli; and seeds from sunflower or sprouted alfalfa. Purchase the ingredients, and come home and make the plant parts salad together! For a variation, make a tree salad, using only things that grow on trees as ingredients!

BOX BOUNCE

<⊳⊳⊳⊳⊳⊳⊳⊲

Here's a game that tests coordination and quickness—both mental and physical.

What You'll Need
• small box
• rubber ball

Play a ball game that will keep children active and improve their coordination while they learn letters and beginning sounds.

Show the child how to catch the ball using the box. Bounce the ball for the child to catch. If he catches it, the child must say a word that begins with the letter *A.* When the child catches the ball a second time, he must say a word beginning with *B.* Continue through the rest of the alphabet.

LOOK AT ME

<⊳⊳⊳⊳⊳⊳⊳⊲

Watch what happens when you talk into a mirror.

Mirrors are fascinating to children. This activity allows them to see what lip and mouth movements occur when different words are spoken.

What You'll Need
• mirror

Tell the child various words and have him repeat them while looking in a mirror (for example, *dog* for a *D* sound, *button* for a *B* sound,

milk for an *M* sound, *pat* for a *P* sound, *tooth* for a *T* sound, and so on). As each word is said, ask the child if his lips touched (as when saying words that begin with *B, M,* and *P*). And where was "Mr. Tongue"? Was he touching the front teeth, on the roof of the mouth, or hiding inside?

Ask the child to think of other words that begin with a particular letter and say them to the mirror, seeing if his mouth formations are the same for each letter sound.

RAIN PAINTING

◁▶◁▶◁▶◁▶◁▶◁

Can rain paint? It can with a little help from a child!

Caution: This project requires adult supervision.

What You'll Need
• powdered tempera paint
• sprinkle jars
• paper

Invite the child (with supervision) to sprinkle a few colors of powdered tempera paint on paper. It's time to let the rain create a picture with the paints. (Adults should be careful that children do not inhale paint powder.) The child can set the paper outside on the ground on a drizzly day, weighing down each corner with a rock, and leaving it outside for a few minutes. If the rain is more than a drizzle, the child (with a raincoat and rain hat on!) can stand in the rain and hold the paper for a moment or two before bringing it back indoors to dry.

BUMPING, BOUNCING BALLS

◁▶◁▶◁▶◁▶◁▶◁

Not just for sport, balls are also learning tools!

Bouncing balls are not only fun for games and sports, they can be wonderful scientific tools as well. The

What You'll Need
• variety of balls such as tennis ball, table-tennis ball, foam ball, football, rubber ball

child can gather a bunch of balls together and make a variety of predictions about them. Predictions can include which balls will bounce and which won't, which balls can be tossed the highest, which balls can be thrown or rolled the farthest, and which balls will float or sink. Encourage the child to make one kind of prediction at a time and then test out that prediction on all the balls. For a further puzzler, invite the child to think about what happens when a ball loses its air. If a flat ball is available, have the child test that out, too!

Natural Letters

◁▷◁▷◁▷◁▷

Your environment is a source for many letter shapes. How many can you find?

Many letters of the alphabet can be seen if one looks closely at different objects.

Inside the house, is the letter *H* visible if you look at the legs of a chair? Do you see a *Y* when looking at the branches of a plant? Outdoors, can you see an *L* by looking at the side of the steps? Can you see an *A* in the frame of your swing set? See how many letters you can find in your environment.

Story Pizza

◁▷◁▷◁▷◁▷

Slice, mix, sort, and arrange pieces of a story as you create a delicious story pizza.

What You'll Need
• pie pan
• cardboard
• pencil
• blunt scissors
• markers

Trace around the bottom of the pie pan on the cardboard, and cut the circle out. Pretend that the circle is a large pizza. Invite the child to imagine what toppings the pizza would have on it and how it would look, smell, and taste. Then cut the cardboard pie into 3 equal slices. Discuss with the child events at the beginning, the middle, and the end of a favorite story. On each piece of pizza, have the child draw a picture or write at least one sentence that tells about an event in the story. Then have the child put the slices of pizza in the pie pan in the correct order, working clockwise, while retelling the story.

Cut new story pizzas into more and more slices—4, 6, or 8—and have the child list events in more detail on each slice.

SHINY PENNIES

◁▷◁▷◁▷◁▷

Experiment and explore penny polishing!

Prepare 3 solutions: vinegar and salt, lemon juice, and soapy water. The child can predict, test, and tell which solution will clean the pennies best. The child can dip the pennies in the solutions and then scrub them with cotton swabs. Let them dry on paper towels. After testing, invite the child to share ideas on why one solution works the best. Explain that the vinegar and salt caused a chemical reaction that dissolves the copper oxide that darkens the penny. The child can experiment further by testing to see if the vinegar and salt solution will clean other kinds of coins, as well as other small materials.

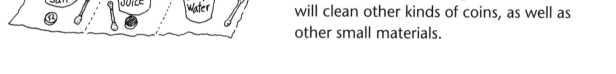

> ## What You'll Need
> - 3 plastic cups
> - vinegar
> - salt
> - lemon juice
> - soapy water
> - pennies
> - cotton swabs
> - paper towels

ECHO ME, ECHO ME

◁▷◁▷◁▷◁▷

In this easy, listening exercise, the child will be your echo and repeat everything you say.

Begin by asking the child to be your echo—that is, repeat everything you say. Start out by saying 2 or 3 words at a time for the child to echo. Then move up to sentences, first short sentences and then long sentences. Try experimenting with nonsense sounds, and invite the child to try to repeat those sounds. Then trade roles and invite the child to make up words, sentences, and sounds for you to echo!

SAY IT ANOTHER WAY

Find new words to say the same thing.

Take turns making statements and challenging one another to say the same thing in another way. For example, "I went to the park to play"—"I skipped to the grassy place to have fun" or "The dog is hungry"—"Our pet wants food." To simplify, invite the child to replace one descriptive word with another. For example, ask the child to find another word to explain that a cookie tastes good (*yummy, delicious, great*) or that it would be fun (*neat, super, exciting*) to go to the park.

LABELING FRUIT

Here's an appealing activity using some of your favorite foods.

What You'll Need
- seed catalogs
- blunt scissors
- paper
- glue or clear tape
- index cards
- pen or pencil

In this activity, children learn to read the names of assorted fruit with the help of their corresponding pictures.

Ask the child to find pictures of different kinds of fruit in old seed catalogs, and let him cut them out with blunt scissors. Glue or tape these fruit pictures in a column on the left side of a sheet of paper.

Make cards on which you print the names of the selected fruits, one fruit per card. Spread out the cards, and ask the child to place the correct card next to the picture of that fruit. Encourage the child to match the printed word to its picture by sounding out the beginning letter of the fruit word and the fruit picture.

ORCHESTRA IN ONE

◁▷◁▷◁▷◁▷

One child, 5 instruments, lots of music!

Caution: This project requires adult supervision.

Kazoo: The child can fit a piece of waxed paper over the end of a paper-towel tube and secure it with a rubber band. To make the kazoo easier to handle, cut the tube to make it shorter.

    Maraca: The child can bend and staple closed one end of a paper-towel tube. He can next fill the tube halfway with beans (or buttons or washers), and then bend the other end over and staple it closed. The child can paint the maraca. (Beware of choking hazard.) This tube can also be shortened before filling with beans.

    Tambourine: Punch 5 or 6 holes around the edge of a paper plate. The child can attach small bells with chenille stems that are threaded through the holes.

    Drum: An empty oatmeal container becomes a drum. Have the child glue on yarn or add stickers for drama!

    Jangle Anklet: String bells on a piece of yarn or sew them to a strip of elastic. Tie the yarn onto the child's ankle or wrist, or sew the ends of the elastic strip together so the child can easily slip it on and off without help.

    Orchestra in One: The child taps on the drum with one foot, wiggles the jangle anklet with the other foot, waves the tambourine in one hand, shakes the maraca in the other, and hums on the kazoo—all at the same time!

What You'll Need
- waxed paper
- cardboard tubes
- rubber band
- stapler
- dry beans
- paint and brush
- paper plate
- hole punch
- bells
- chenille stems
- empty oatmeal container
- yarn

STORY STAND-UPS

◁▶◁▶◁▶◁▶

Creating story stand-ups is a wonderful opportunity for the child to construct and convey meaning through language.

Invite the child to make stand-up drawings of characters from a favorite story for easy dramatization and retelling. First have the child fold index cards in half. Then draw the characters on one outside half of the cards, one character per card. Each character will now be able to stand up. Invite the child to use the stand-up characters to dramatize character interaction while narrating the story.

What You'll Need
• large blank index cards or construction paper
• crayons or markers

WHAT DOES IT MEAN?

◁▶◁▶◁▶◁▶

Listen, then listen again to find a word's meaning.

Choose a word or word phrase that the child is not familiar with for this sleuthing game. Tell him the word, but do not explain what it means. Then use the word in a sentence that gives a clue to the meaning of the word. Continue to make up new sentences using the word in different ways until the child is able to figure out what it means! Start off with easy words or word phrases (for example: *supper, stocking*). Increase the difficulty by using less concrete words, such as *lazy,* where the meanings can be guessed from the context.

MATCH THAT PICTURE!

◁►◁►◁►◁►◁►

In this activity, the beginning reader will practice comprehension while matching words with pictures.

What You'll Need
- any picture book with many illustrations
- paper
- pen or pencil

Before reading the book aloud, look at the illustrations and discuss them with the child. Invite the child to point to and name interesting objects in the illustrations. Then read the story aloud to the child while he looks on. Have the child find words in the text that match the objects in the illustrations. If there are illustrations without matching words, list the words on a piece of paper and discuss their meaning.

To encourage creative thinking, read a story with no pictures. Then help the child determine what illustrations might be used in the story.

MAPPING THE STORY

Mapping a story after reading it aids in understanding story structure.

What You'll Need
- book with several different settings
- paper
- pencil
- crayons or markers

Have the child read the book. Then ask the child to write down where the story begins and every location described in the book. Help the child make a colorful map of all the different places the book describes, label-

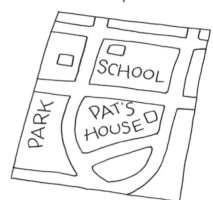

ing each location (school, someone's house, park, and so on). For an additional challenge, suggest the child add arrows showing the route the main character takes to go to these locations.

PLANT A ROOT WORD

Learning root words has never been more fun than in this planting activity.

Write a root word on a cup, and then fill the cup with dirt. You may want to use one of the following root words: *fold, do, view, hurt,* or *season.* Invite the child to draw and cut out 3 to 5 flowers from construction paper. Help the child glue the paper cutouts onto craft sticks to make them sturdy. Have the child add ending letters (such as *ing* or *er*) or beginning letters (such as *un* or *pre*) to each root word to make new words, writing a new word on each flower. Finished flowers should be "planted" in the cup of dirt. Invite the child to make additional cups of flowers.

What You'll Need
- polystyrene cups
- markers
- dirt
- construction paper
- blunt scissors
- glue
- craft sticks

GOOEY GLOP

◁▷◁▷◁▷◁▷◁▷

Half the fun of this letter activity is mixing up the gooey dough.

Caution: This project requires adult supervision.

Children can make three-dimensional letters with this homemade modeling dough.

Mix 2 cups salt and ⅔ cup water in a saucepan. Heat until almost boiling. In a separate bowl, mix 1 cup cornstarch and ½ cup cold water. Pour it into the hot salt-and-water mixture and mix. Let it cool.

Have the child use the Gooey Glop to shape letters that stand for the beginning sounds of words. The child can work with the dough on a kitchen counter or a plastic surface. Store the dough in a plastic bag, and reuse it.

What You'll Need
- 2 cups salt
- water
- 1 cup cornstarch
- measuring cups and spoons
- saucepan
- stove
- large bowl
- plastic bag

SIMON SAYS SOUND ALIKE

◁▷◁▷◁▷◁▷◁▷

*Simon says that the words **listening** and **learning** start alike.*

Play a version of "Simon Says" that focuses on beginning sounds in words. If "Simon" makes a correct statement, the child should follow the given directions. If "Simon" makes an incorrect statement, the child should not.

For example, if you say, "Simon says *finger* and *football* begin alike; wiggle your finger," the child should follow the directions and wiggle her finger. However, if you say, "Simon says *tongue* and *nose* begin alike; stick out your tongue," the child should not follow the directions because the statement is incorrect.

DIRT COMPARISONS

◁▷◁▷◁▷◁▷

Explore dirt for a muddy scientific experience!

Gather dirt from 3 different places, and bring it home for comparison. A garden, a vacant lot, and a wooded area have different kinds of dirt. The child can scoop a cupful of dirt into an empty can with a taped edge or a box, labeling each to remember where it came from. To puddle-test the 3 kinds of soil, place each kind on a different plate, and form into a shallow volcano shape. The child can add a spoonful of water to each hill of dirt. Then watch what happens to the water, and compare the differences. (Sand and potting soil can be puddle-tested, too!) To further test each kind of soil, the child can add enough water so each soil type can be formed into a mud ball. The mud balls can be compared and observed as they dry. Be sure the child washes hands thoroughly when done.

What You'll Need
• 3 cans
• marker
• spoon
• 3 old plates
• jar of water

STRANGE STRIPES

◁▷◁▷◁▷◁▷

Have you ever seen a striped strawberry?
In this "strange" art activity, anything is possible.

What You'll Need
• corrugated cardboard
• blunt scissors
• large sheet of white construction paper
• poster paints
• paintbrush

Review words with the consonant cluster *str* as in *stripe, strawberry,* and *street.* Then set out corrugated cardboard and blunt scissors, and cut out a large strawberry. Invite the child to paint the corrugated side of the cutout. Turn the wet cutout over, and press it against a piece of white paper. The result is the print of a striped strawberry. Encourage the child to label the artwork.

WET & WILD!

◁▷◁▷◁▷◁▷

Squeeze, squirt, and scoop the water!

Caution: This project requires adult supervision.

What You'll Need
- 2 large dishpans or bowls
- large sponge
- baster
- dish detergent
- plastic measuring cups
- wire whisk
- scoops
- squeeze and spray bottles
- funnel
- containers
- ladles

The best way to introduce water play is to start with a few of the items listed at left; too many objects in the water may create confusion. Young children have a tendency to try everything at once if the tub is full, rather than working in an organized way and slowly acquiring skills. (Always supervise children around water.) These are great outside activities, so have the child put on a bathing suit and splash away! (If you decide to do this inside, make sure to place the dishpans on a thick towel or newspaper to lessen the mess.)

1. On one day, place the sponge, baster, and 2 pans outside. Fill 1 pan with water. Encourage the child to move the water from 1 container to the other with the sponge and then with the baster.

2. Another time, fill ⅓ of the dishpan with water, and put in 5 drops of dish detergent. Add the measuring cups, the wire whisk, and the scoops. As your child pours, stirs, and measures, bubbles will begin to appear on the surface of the water, creating interesting effects.

3. For a different activity, fill ⅓ of the dishpan with water, and give the child a squeeze bottle (an empty dish-detergent bottle) and a spray bottle. Have the child fill the bottles and spray the water back into the dishpan.

4. On another occasion, fill ⅓ of the dishpan with water and give the child a funnel, containers, scoops, and ladles.

ALPHABETICAL SHOPPING

◁▷◁▷◁▷◁▷◁▷

From apples to zucchini, the grocery store has everything. What can you find?

What You'll Need
- paper
- pen or pencil

Try this alphabetical shopping activity. It may take some extra time.

Before going grocery shopping, ask the child to help you put your shopping list in alphabetical order. If the list is short and you don't mind doing a little extra walking, locate the items in the store in alphabetical order.

If your shopping list is long, shop as you normally do, but let the child cross off each item from the list as you locate it.

 # DANCE STREAMERS

◁▷◁▷◁▷◁▷◁▷

Swirl and sway with streamers, and dance away!

The child can hold and wave dance streamers, using them to explore movement and dance. To make the dance streamers, cut the centers out of 2 plastic lids so they are hoops; be sure there are no sharp edges. The child can help tie several long strips (2 to 3 feet) of crepe paper onto each hoop. The child can use the streamers, holding one in each hand, or experiment with movement using just one. Encourage the child to try different kinds of movements. The child can move slow or fast, with big movements or little ones. For greater challenge, add music to the mix!

What You'll Need
- 2 plastic lids
- scissors
- crepe paper rolls
- music (optional)

CLOUD PICTURES

◁►◁►◁►◁►◁►◁►

Find a cat or a car in a cumulus cloud.

Looking for images in cloud formations is a great creative exercise. With a little extra effort, you can also turn it into a lesson in beginning letters.

On a day with many clouds in the sky, go outside with the child and talk about them, noting how they sometimes look like animals or objects. Take turns pointing out clouds and saying what you think they resemble.

While outside, or when you get back inside, ask the child to re-create some of the cloud objects she saw by drawing them with white chalk or crayon on blue construction paper. Encourage the child to describe the cloud drawings to you, then print the beginning letter of the object that the cloud resembles in the upper-right corner of the page.

SOAPY SIMILARITIES

◁▷◁▷◁▷◁▷

Different kinds of soap are all good for cleaning, but are they all the same?

What You'll Need
- different types of soap (bar soap, liquid detergent, soap flakes)
- plastic containers filled with water (one for each type of soap)
- spoon
- eggbeater

Gather up several different kinds of soaps. Invite the child to play! Then think up categories in which to compare the soaps and test out how they measure up. Some things the child might test are:

Which soap makes the most bubbles in water? Which will float in water? Which dissolves the best? Which is the most slippery? Which washes hands best?

ACTION FIGURES

◁▷◁▷◁▷◁▷

Cartoon characters provide lots of opportunities to be exposed to common and proper nouns.

What You'll Need
- poster board
- crayons or markers

Discuss the child's favorite cartoon and action characters from TV and the movies. Invite the child to draw these characters on a large piece of poster board. Then have the child write the name of each character above the corresponding drawing. Below the drawing, have the child write what kind of creature the character is. While looking at the pictures, point out the differences between common nouns and proper nouns.

MISCHIEF MAKERS

◁►◁►◁►◁►

*A little word mischief will add just the right amount of intrigue
and excitement to vocabulary building.*

What You'll Need
- large index cards or self-adhesive notes
- markers
- clear tape

Help the child make labels for different objects in the room, such as doors, cabinets, computers, and so on. Have the child stick or tape the labels beside or on the corresponding objects. After a few days, secretly mix up some of the labels. Then tell the child that the labels have been moved by a mystery mischief maker, and encourage him to return them to their correct places.

LETTER PALMS

◁▶◁▶◁▶◁▶

Here's a new way to "read palms" that children are sure to enjoy.

Surprise children with a "palm tree" made out of newspapers.

Roll a sheet of newspaper to the center of the sheet. Then add a second sheet so that its edge is at the center of the first sheet. Continue rolling the two sheets together, and put a piece of tape around the base to keep the tube from unrolling. Next, cut halfway down the tube you have made. Make 3 or 4 more similar cuts. Carefully pull up on the paper, and a "palm tree" will form.

What You'll Need
- newspapers
- tape
- blunt scissors
- letter cards
- paper clips

Ask the child to randomly select a card from a stack of letter cards. If the child can name a word with that beginning letter, she can clip the card to one of the paper palm fronds. Continue until the child has clipped on several cards.

IMAGINARY SNOW

◁▶◁▶◁▶◁▶

Create clouds and snow with silky, fluffy, puffy white foam!

What You'll Need
- plastic tablecloth
- shaving cream
- waterproof smock
- plastic animals or cars

Spread a plastic tablecloth over a table, and spray it with mounds of shaving cream. Put a smock on the child, and invite him to mold and mush and slosh the foamy cream, enjoying and talking about the texture. (Remind the child not to rub his eyes with foamy fingers.) The child can form the foam into puffy clouds, snowy mountains, or imaginary white worlds. Or he can make patterns and designs in it. Plastic animals, cars, and other toys can be used for active story-making. On a warm summer day, this activity can be done outside in a bathing suit!

STAR TREK

◁▷◁▷◁▷◁▷◁▷

There's a whole universe of fun in this alphabet board game.

What You'll Need
- construction paper
- poster board
- marker or pen
- blunt scissors
- glue or clear tape
- die and markers from a board game

Invite the child to play a letter identification game with an outer-space theme.

To prepare the game board, cut 15 to 26 star shapes and 1 moon shape from the construction paper. Paste or tape the stars in an S-shaped path on the poster board, with the moon at the end. Write letters in random order on the stars.

To play the game, take turns throwing the die and moving markers along the star path. In order to continue along the path, the player must name the letter on each star she lands on. If the player does not name the letter correctly, she must go back to the beginning of the path. Continue until one player reaches the moon.

PREFIX SLIP

◁▷◁▷◁▷◁▷◁▷

Create a bevy of different words with this charming approach to prefixes.

Help the child cut 2 horizontal slits in the rectangle of paper, just above and below the center and slightly toward the right. The slits should be about 4 inches long and 2 inches apart. Then have the child write a prefix in the space to the left of the slits, as shown. Common prefixes include but are not limited to: *un, re,*

What You'll Need
- 5" × 8" rectangle of heavy paper or poster board
- scissors
- markers
- 12" × 3" strip of paper

dis, pre, de, and *ex.* Help the child brainstorm a list of words that can be added to the prefix to form a new word. Write these words on the strip of paper. Explain that by pulling the strip through the slits, the child can make and read new words with the designated prefix.

Try making a different type of game. This time write a common word to the left of the slits and different suffixes on the paper strip.

LINES AND DOTS

◁▷◁▷◁▷◁▷◁▷

*Here's a game that adds a touch of competition to
a simple connect-the-dots activity.*

What You'll Need
- marker or pen
- sheet of paper
- colored pencils or crayons (a different color for each player)

In this activity, children practice making the kind of precise strokes that are necessary to "draw" letters.

Make a grid of dots approximately 1 inch apart on a sheet of paper. Taking turns, each player draws a single line from one dot to another using the writing utensil with her assigned color. The goal for each player is to complete a square in her color.

Take turns drawing lines and making squares until no more squares are possible. At the end of the game, use the different colors to count up how many squares each player completed.

TEN QUESTIONS

◁▷◁▷◁▷◁▷◁▷

*While enjoying this game of questions and answers,
the child will develop sentence sense.*

What You'll Need
- small objects
- box or bag
- notebook paper
- pencil

Place an object, such as a hairbrush, inside a bag. Invite the child to ask questions about the object in the bag in an effort to discover its identity. Write each question on a piece of notebook paper,

pointing out the capital letter at the beginning of each sentence and the question mark at the end, before answering them. A maximum of 10 questions can be asked before the object is revealed; however, at any time during the question-and-answer exchange, the child can try to guess the object. If the child correctly identifies the object, a new object is placed in the bag, and play is continued.

In-Basket

◁▷◁▷◁▷◁▷

A-tisket, a-tasket—here's a beginning-sound basket!

What You'll Need
- index cards
- marker or pen
- small basket

Here's an "office" activity that encourages children to practice letter sounds.

Make letter cards by writing a large letter (for example, *B, D, G, S,* and *T*) on each of several index cards. Give the child one card (for instance, the letter *B*), and have her say a word that begins with the same letter (such as *bed*). After giving a word with the correct beginning sound, the child drops the card into the "in-basket." If the child's word does not have the correct first-letter sound, put the card aside, and continue with the other cards.

More Tall Tales

◁▷◁▷◁▷◁▷

Sometimes it's fun to exaggerate—the bigger the better!
This activity helps develop a young writer's imagination.

What You'll Need
- paper
- pencil
- book of tall tales (optional)

Many tall tales, such as those about Pecos Bill or Paul Bunyan, are built on the theme of settling the West in America. They rely on exaggeration (also called hyperbole), as well. For example, the horse Widow-Maker could buck as high as the moon.

Read some tall tales together that contain a lot of pictures. Discuss exaggeration and give examples, such as "I'm so hungry I could eat a horse" and "It's so hot I'm melting." Invite the child to make up and write down other examples. This can be kept in a book of writing ideas that can later be incorporated into other writing.

REVAMPING OLDIES

◁▶◁▶◁▶◁▶

*The child can revamp a favorite song by creating new words to sing
in place of the existing verses.*

This is an opportunity for the child to reinterpret a favorite song and compose new
verses for it. For example, the child may want to change the words for "Mary Had a
Little Lamb," to "Sally had a little bear, little bear, little bear. Sally had a little bear, and
it was brown as mud." "Twinkle, Twinkle, Little Star" may be transformed into "Wiggle, wiggle, little worm. Under the ground, there you squirm."

Once the new verses have been created, invite the child to sing the newly composed version of the song.

CHAIN OF LETTERS II

◁▷◁▷◁▷◁▷

This activity helps mend missing links in alphabet identification.

Gluing strips of paper to make a chain is a great exercise for hand-eye coordination.

Cut 26 strips of paper measuring approximately 6" long and 1" wide. Write both the capital and lowercase forms of a letter on each one: *Aa, Bb,* and so on through the alphabet. Help the child make a paper chain by gluing or taping the first strip of paper into a circle. Continue to glue the strips into circles, one linked with the next, to make a chain. When the chain is finished, ask the child to name the letter on each link.

What You'll Need
- construction paper
- blunt scissors
- glue or clear tape
- marker or pen

TELEPHONE DIRECTORY II

◁▷◁▷◁▷◁▷

Forgot a telephone number? This directory can help.

What You'll Need
- names cut out for "Telephone Directory" activity on page 483
- sheet of paper
- glue or clear tape

Have the child use the names in the envelope that were cut out for "Telephone Directory." The object now is for the child to organize these names in alphabetical order. (It may be easier for the child to spread all the names on the floor or table.)

When the names are arranged in alphabetical order, have the child begin with the *A* name, and glue or tape it onto the paper. Proceed through the alphabet. The names can be arranged as in a real telephone directory—in columns, proceeding from top to bottom and left to right.

NEWS OF THE DAY!

◁▷◁▷◁▷◁▷◁▷

Explore main ideas as the child writes headlines for a day's events and activities.

Recall the events the child was involved in on a particular day, and discuss the most important and the most memorable. Which event or events would other people want to know about?

Page through a newspaper together. Point out the headlines to the child. Explain that a headline is used to provide a glimpse of what's in the article and to entice the reader to read the article.

What You'll Need
- newspaper
- magnetic letters
- magnetic surface (such as a refrigerator door or metal pan)

Display magnetic letters on a magnetic surface. Let the child manipulate the letters freely for a few minutes, then invite the child to arrange the letters to create a headline describing one of the events of the day you discussed earlier.

For an additional challenge, point to a particular headline in the newspaper and ask the child to guess what the story is about. See how accurate the child and the headline are.

BOOK REVIEW

◁▶◁▶◁▶◁▶◁▶

The child will practice critical reading skills while preparing a book review.

What You'll Need
• book the child has not read

Invite the child to read a new book. Discuss with the child all the things she liked and did not like about the book. Make a list of the likes and dislikes. For a more challenging activity, encourage the child to write a short review of the book based on the list. Have the child share the review with you for further discussion.

For an alternative project, read the child a long book with chapters. Read a little at a time. When the book is finished, you and the child can each write a short review of it. Compare your reviews.

ALPHABET ACTIVITY BOOK

◁▶◁▶◁▶◁▶◁▶

C is for creating. Make an alphabet book filled with activity ideas.

Help the child create an alphabet book. Begin by punching one or two holes in each letter card and using the yarn to tie the cards together in order. Go through the letter book and have the child suggest an activity for each letter; for example, *A* (ask a question), *B* (bat a ball), *C* (cook a meal), *D* (dig a hole). Suggest that the child draw and color a picture to illustrate each activity. Later, the child can choose a page and perform the activity.

What You'll Need
• letter cards for the entire alphabet
• hole punch
• 18" of yarn

WORD SEARCH II

◁►◁►◁►◁►

While learning to spell new words,
the child will create a puzzle to challenge others.

Provide a list of words that you would like the child to learn to spell. Then have the child write the words randomly on the graph paper, one letter per square. The words can go across, down, or diagonally on the paper. Although some words may also share letters if they cross, make sure there are plenty of blank spaces.

When all of the spelling words have been written on the graph paper, have the child write any letter in each blank space so that the entire grid is filled. Then have the child share the word-search puzzle with a friend, asking the friend to find the spelling words and circle them.

BUG BANQUET

◁►◁►◁►◁►

Feed the bugs—maybe they like chocolate, too!

Most everyone knows the favorite foods of people and some animals, but what do bugs eat? The child can perform an experiment to find bugs' culinary delights. Invite the child to make predictions about food bugs might like. The child can then place small amounts of food outside (not too close to the

house!) where the child has seen bugs. The bugs may need time to find the food, so check several times during the day to see which foods seem most popular.

Asparagus to Zucchini

◁▷◁▷◁▷◁▷

Plant an alphabet garden from asparagus to zucchini.

What You'll Need
- vegetable seeds
- pots and soil (if planting indoors)
- tape
- craft sticks
- marker
- paper

Planting a garden encourages a child to develop responsibility, especially if she agrees to water and care for the plants.

Take the child to the store to help select different vegetable seeds to plant in your garden. Ask the child, "What vegetable begins like the word *buy*?" (Answers: *beans, beets,* or *broccoli.*) Then have the child point to that vegetable's seed packet. Continue giving other beginning-sound clues for other vegetables. Purchase the seeds. If you don't have an outdoor garden, purchase some large pots and soil to use for planting indoors.

On your trip home, discuss how you and the child will begin planting. Ask the child, "What vegetable did you select that begins with the letter *B* (or other letters, depending on which vegetables were selected)?"

At planting time, read the seed-packet planting directions to the child, then have her tell you what steps are necessary for planting these seeds. After the seeds are planted, save the packet and tape or otherwise secure it to a craft stick. Have the child write the beginning letter of that vegetable on the stick with a marker, then place this stick by the planted seeds.

Make a simple chart on which the child can place an *X* each day that the vegetables were cared for and watered. This encourages and reinforces responsibility on the part of the child.

Good luck with the garden, and enjoy eating those special vegetables.

STORY OPPOSITES

◁▶◁▶◁▶◁▶

*Invite the child to demonstrate good listening skills
by turning a story into its opposite.*

Take turns creating opposite versions of the
same story. Begin by telling a simple story and
then invite the child to retell the story, changing
as many things as possible to their opposites.
You may want to offer suggestions to get the
child started. In the story "Cinderella," for example, you might tell of how the shoe did not fit.
After the child has taken a turn, discuss any
other opposites that could be added to the
story. Then invite the child to make up or read a
story for you to change, or give the child
another attempt at a new story.

TELL ME THREE REASONS WHY

◁▶◁▶◁▶◁▶◁▶

Share personal preferences, and back them up with reasons why!

Take turns making up preference questions for each other, such as "What do you like
better on your pizza, sausage or pepperoni?" "Do you like red or blue better?" "What's
more fun, jumping or hopping?" The questioner chooses the question. The person
answering reveals a personal preference, but she also has to give 3 reasons for that
choice! Pass time quickly on a long car ride or while waiting for food at a restaurant by
playing this game! In a restaurant, use menu items to make up preference questions.
In the car, base the preference questions on things outside—the weather, dogs, birds,
bicycles, toys in a yard. Make the game more challenging by trying to come up with
more reasons why. Can you come up with 6, 7, or 8 reasons instead of 3?

CARROT CONVERSATION

◁▷◁▷◁▷◁▷◁▷

Here's an activity to brighten kids' eyes and polish their sound skills.

While children are enjoying a healthy snack, they can practice beginning sounds.

Use the carrot peeler to make thin, curly carrot slices. As the child munches on the carrot curls, take turns saying words that have the same beginning sound as the word *carrot: cat, car, corn, can, come, kitten, kite, kettle, keep.*

For more advanced children, write the letters *C* and *K,* and point out that both letters can stand for the beginning sound in *carrot.* Then write each word that you named under the appropriate beginning letter.

> **What You'll Need**
> • carrots
> • carrot peeler
> • paper
> • marker or pen

SHARED READING

◁▷◁▷◁▷◁▷◁▷

One of the best memories you can give a child is sharing a favorite book together.

> **What You'll Need**
> • favorite book that is comfortable for the child to read aloud

Begin by reading aloud the first page of the book. Then have the child read the second page. Continue taking turns until the entire book is read. If the book is long, take turns reading paragraphs or half pages. Make the reading fun, and help the child with any unknown words when necessary.

Tongue Twisters!

Will Wanda Walrus wash Willy Weasel's wagon with warm water?

SHAPE, PAINT & BAKE COOKIES

◁▶◁▶◁▶◁▶◁▶

Make captivating cookies that are lovely to look at and tasty to eat.

What You'll Need
- purchased sugar-cookie dough or your favorite recipe already prepared
- rolling pin
- cookie cutters
- 2 egg yolks
- 4 small containers
- food coloring
- clean brush
- cookie sheet
- spatula
- pot holders
- raisins or chocolate morsels (optional)

Caution: This project requires adult supervision.

Wash hands first! When cookie dough is ready, have the child help you roll it out and cut out shapes with cookie cutters. Now it's time to paint the cookies! Make cookie paint by mixing the egg yolks with a little water and dividing it into 4 containers. Add a drop or two of food coloring to each container. Invite the child to paint the cookies before baking. For a variation, add a topping, such as raisins or chocolate morsels. Follow the recipe directions, and bake!

INVISIBLE PAINTING

◁►◁►◁►◁►◁►◁►

Watercolors reveal the invisible drawing.

Use the candle to draw a pattern or scene on a sheet of paper. The wax drawing will be almost invisible. Ask the child to paint the entire sheet with a watercolor. As the paint dries, the pattern or scene will appear. Encourage the child to draw or simply scribble on other sheets of paper with the candle. Then let her paint those sheets and reveal her invisible creations. On other sheets, use the dark marker pen to write out

What You'll Need
• white wax candle
• white paper
• watercolor paints
• brush
• marker

the names of simple objects, such as *apple, bottle,* or *cat*. Then use the candle to draw a picture of the object. Encourage the child to use her detective skills to find the invisible object that goes with the word you've written on each sheet.

PICTURE THIS

◁►◁►◁►◁►◁►

Draw one picture, tell two stories!

Take turns drawing pictures to use for story starters. When a picture is finished, the person who drew it (adult or child) tells about the picture and makes up a story to go with it. Then the listener makes up an entirely different story about the same picture! For more challenge, instead of drawing 2

What You'll Need
• paper
• markers or crayons

separate pictures, take turns drawing 1 picture together! Plan out what will be in the picture and who should add what where, or just take turns making additions to the drawing. When the cooperative picture is done, use it as a story starter for 2 different tales.

THE SAME & DIFFERENT

▷◁▷◁▷◁▷

Play this game to develop the child's ability to perceive relationships and make comparisons.

Name any 2 items, and invite the child to tell 1 way in which the items are similar and 1 way in which they are different. Begin with easy comparisons, such as a cat and a dog, and increase the difficulty as you go along. Answers for easy comparisons will be more obvious while the more-difficult comparisons will require some creative thinking.

For example, the child might suggest a dog and cat are similar because they both are animals but are different because one meows and the other barks. For a comparison of a star and a television, the child might suggest they both glow or you can look at both of them, but one is close and the other is far away.

Accept all answers that make good connections, as there are no right or wrong answers.

 # TORN-PAPER PICTURES

◁▷◁▷◁▷◁

Make beautiful paper pictures using only colored paper and glue.

The child can make decorative collage designs by tearing construction paper into big and little shapes. Help the child discover the technique that works best for tearing paper by encouraging experimentation with thumb positioning. For a variation, include wrapping paper and tissue paper. Glue the paper pieces on a fresh sheet of paper to create a unique collage. For further exploration, share with the child pictures that artists have made using torn paper. Two children's book illustrators who use torn paper are Patricia Mullins and Candace Whitman. Illustrators who cut paper and use it as part of their collage art include Ezra Jack Keats and Eric Carle.

What You'll Need
• construction paper
• nontoxic white glue
• wrapping paper (optional)
• tissue paper (optional)

WHAT I SAW

◁▷◁▷◁▷◁▷

Tell all about what happened without words!

Invite the child to tell about something he did—but do it without talking. The child can report about an afternoon adventure, visit, or walk, and all that happened and was observed—but tell the tale without words! Challenge the child to report observations through pantomime. To simplify, allow the child to use one-word clues to help communicate each pantomime action.

WHAT'S THAT I SEE?

◁▷◁▷◁▷◁▷◁▷

Spy an object, and see who can "detect" it.

Play an I Spy game by giving clues that include beginning sounds. For example: "I spy something white; it is in the kitchen; it begins like the word *rabbit*." After the child answers correctly (refrigerator), give clues for another object.

 # ACCUMULATING MEMORIES

◁▷◁▷◁▷◁▷

Share observations by creating a cooperative cumulative list!

After a trip to the market, a visit to the park, or just a backyard adventure, have one person report one thing she observed. The other person then repeats the first observation and adds another. For example: We saw a caterpillar; we saw a caterpillar and a worm; we saw a caterpillar and a worm and the blue sky. Keep taking turns and adding observations, and see how long a list you each can remember and repeat! When the list gets too long, start another one with observations about a different adventure, and see how long that list can get! To play another version of this game, take turns naming 3 things you each observed. Then take turns seeing how many of these 6 named things each person can remember!

PROP PROMPTING

◁▷◁▷◁▷◁▷

Use story props for friendly hint helpers in storytelling.

What You'll Need
• props related to stories

After sharing a favorite story, fairy tale, or nursery rhyme, provide the child with some simple props that relate to the story or rhyme. Place the book along with the props in a place where the child is free to dramatize and act! The child can use the props as prompters for retelling and acting out the story or rhyme.

BUILDING WORD STEPS

◁▷◁▷◁▷◁▷

See how many words you can use to describe a single object.

A child's vocabulary and use of descriptive phrases can be enhanced with this activity. Ask the child to say a letter (for example, *B*) and then think of an animal or object beginning with that letter (for example, *ball*). For the next step,

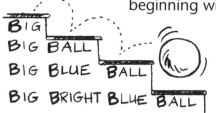

have the child add a word that begins with *B* to further describe the ball (for example, *big ball*). Add a third step with yet another *B* word (for example, *big blue ball*). Continue with as many steps as the child is capable of making.

CALL OUT AND DO

◁▷◁▷◁▷◁▷

Hop, skip, and jump to the music!

What You'll Need
• radio or tape player and taped music

This activity is for those children who can do the activities listed below. The adult will be the caller, and the child will be the doer. Set the activity to music for lots of fun! Select a radio station that has a variety of music selections or use a musical tape. Call all the activities listed in random order: gallop, skip, jump, hop, leap, crawl, stomp, fall, spin, run, roll, skip, squat, bend, stoop. To make it more challenging, give the child a sequence of steps, such as squat, crawl, and roll. Have the child do them in sequence several times. Then change the sequence of steps.

Papier-Mâché Pulp Play

◁▶◁▶◁▶◁▶◁▶◁

Make papier-mâché pulp and mold away!

What You'll Need
- bowl
- water
- newspaper
- electric beater
- wheat paste
- wire rack
- paint
- brush

To make the pulp, fill a large bowl halfway with water. Add newspaper torn into strips, and soak the strips overnight. Beat the mix to a pulp, then squeeze out excess water. Add wheat paste a little at a time. Beat again until smooth. The child can help with tearing the newspaper, squeezing the water out of the mash, and adding the wheat paste. When the pulp resembles clay and is smooth, the child can mold it. To speed up drying time, hollow out the middle of the piece by turning it over and scooping out some material from the bottom. Molded pieces can be placed on a wire rack to dry. Allow plenty of drying time, and turn the pieces occasionally to keep them from getting moldy. When the pieces have dried thoroughly, the child can paint them.

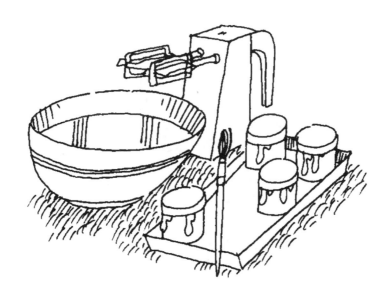

FREQUENT WORD SEARCH

◁▷◁▷◁▷◁▷◁▷

Kids will find some words appear over and over again.

What You'll Need
- word cards
- crayons
- magazine page with words

What words are used most frequently? This is the time for the child to find out.

Think of a word that you believe is used frequently (for example, *the*). Give the child a card with this word on it, a crayon, and a magazine page. Every time the child sees the word on the magazine page, she should put a circle around it.

Search the entire page. When finished, count how many times the word was used. Remind the child the word might begin with a capital letter.

Choose another word (for example, *on*). Give the child the word card, and, using a different crayon, have her circle this word on the magazine page. Then count and tally. See which word was used more frequently. Try searching for and counting words the child thinks are used a lot.

LACY LETTERS

◁▷◁▷◁▷◁▷◁▷◁

Letters of the alphabet get ruffled in this fun art project.

What You'll Need
- poster board
- pen or pencil
- blunt scissors
- tissue paper
- glue

Children will be delighted with this easy, pretty way to decorate letters.

First, outline and cut out a letter from poster board. Next, cut squares of variously colored tissue paper. Make each square approximately 10" × 10". Show the child how to put a square of tissue paper over a finger and then squeeze it around the finger to form a ruffled shape. Make several ruffles, then put a spot of glue on the bottom of each one and glue them on the letter.

Display the letter on the refrigerator, and have the child identify it each time she opens the refrigerator door. Make additional lacy letters to add to the collection.

ALL ABOUT ME

◁▷◁▷◁▷◁▷◁▷

Be an author! Here's a chance to write an autobiography.

What You'll Need
- crayons
- paper
- hole punch
- yarn or O-rings

What better way for a child to express himself than by writing a book?

Ask the child to draw a picture of himself and write his name below the picture. Other pages to be added to the book may be about family, friends, favorite foods, toys, books, colors, or places to visit. When the child has drawn these pictures, write a caption sentence about each page; for example, "My favorite food is _____." Say the letters as you are writing so the child associates them with their sounds.

Help the child make a special cover for this book. Assemble the book by punching holes along one side of each page. Yarn or O-rings can then be used to bind the book. On the back cover, date the book. It will become a keepsake. Try making a new book every month or two to see how the child's ideas, art, and spelling ability change from one time to the next.

BOX O' SOCKS

◁▷◁▷◁▷◁▷

Laundry day is awash with this sorting activity that engages the child in critical thinking.

What You'll Need
- box or laundry basket
- socks

Collect socks in a variety of sizes, colors, patterns, and types. Check out some used clothing stores if you need a wider variety. Place them in a box. Then have the child sort the socks into several specific categories. For example, sort first by color, then by size. Next try sorting by function, such as socks for a baseball player, soccer player, snow skier, or maybe a ballerina. Invite the child to think of new categories for sorting socks. See how many different sorting ideas the child can come up with.

 # SNOWY DAY FUN

◁▷◁▷◁▷◁▷

Warm up a snowy day with this activity by finding various ways to have fun in the snow.

Read the book or story aloud together. Discuss all kinds of ways to have fun in snow. One way is to make a snow person. Help

What You'll Need
- a book or story featuring snow
- dark paper
- pencil
- white glue
- scissors
- construction paper

the child make a snow person on paper by drawing its outline on dark paper with a pencil. Fill in the outline with white glue. Allow the glue to dry. Cut various items from construction paper, such as a hat, a broom, and gloves, and glue those in place. You may want to create a whole snow family on the paper. Label them with names, by role, or by other characteristics.

Enchanted Power Cape

◁▷◁▷◁▷◁▷

Make playtime magic with an enchanted power cape!

What You'll Need
- piece of fabric (approximately 1 yard square)
- fabric crayons
- nontoxic fabric glue
- ribbons
- rickrack
- lace
- glitter

The child can make an enchanted power cape by decorating a large square of fabric. The child can color the square with fabric crayons or glue on pieces of lace, rickrack, and ribbon. When the child is finished, tie the two ends of the cape around her shoulders. This cape then transforms the child into a power being who can imagine and perform enchanted feats.

Activity Twist

Provide materials (wallpaper samples, construction paper, glitter glue, markers, scissors, stapler) for the child to create and decorate "power" crowns. Encourage the child to share these with special friends and relatives or favorite stuffed animals, who can think good or clever thoughts while wearing them.

Letter Sculptures

◁▷◁▷◁▷◁▷

The artistic shapes of the alphabet are just around the bend in this activity.

Simple sculpting becomes a hands-on learning experience in this engaging activity. Help the child make a long, flat base, measuring about 3" × 12", out of clay. When that's done, ask him to make letter shapes out of the chenille stems, spelling his name by standing the shapes in the clay.

What You'll Need
- clay
- chenille stems

PICTURE POCKETS

◁▶◁▶◁▶◁▶

*Poking through pockets produces plenty of practice with
the letter P in this activity.*

What You'll Need
- purse with pockets
- magazines
- blunt scissors

Children have fun as they search through a purse with pictures of objects beginning with the letter *P*.

Find an old purse or wallet with several pockets and compartments. Cut pictures from magazines of items beginning with *P*. Put a picture in each pocket of the purse. Instruct the child to find one picture at a time and name it. For an extra challenge, have the child find new pictures of objects that begin with the letter *P* to put into the picture pockets.

 # BUBBLEGUM WORDS

◁▶◁▶◁▶◁▶◁▶

Every dentist will like these absolutely cavity-free bubblegum activities!

What happens when you take one end of the bubble gum you are chewing and pull on it? It stretches! The same thing can happen to words. Words can get longer when extra letters are added to the beginning or the end. Write the word *and,* and show how to stretch it to make the words *hand* and *handcuff.* Then invite the child to stretch his own words from *and.* Use a children's dictionary if necessary.

LETTER RIDDLES

Just a few minutes to spare? Try a letter-riddle game.

While traveling or shopping or during spare time, play a riddle game that begins, for example, by saying: "I am thinking of the letter that has the beginning sound of *ball*. What letter is it?"

This activity provides many opportunities for riddles. A more challenging approach to the riddle concept is to present a series of clues. For example: "I am thinking of something that begins with a *B*." Allow the child to guess the answer between each successive clue. Continue with more clues: "I am thinking of something that is round; I am thinking of something that goes up very high and may be different colors; I am thinking of something that bounces."

Keep giving clues until the child guesses the object in mind. For a further variation, reverse roles and have the child give the clues. This activity helps develop the child's thinking skills as you progress from general to specific clues.

SURF'S UP!

A smart whale can help alphabet surfers challenge the waves.

What You'll Need
- large sheet of art paper
- crayons or colored markers (including blue)
- piece of gray poster board
- blunt scissors
- glue or clear tape
- craft stick

Here's a whale of a game that makes identifying different letters fun.

On a large sheet of paper, draw ocean waves. Make at least 10 wave peaks. At the top of each wave peak, write a letter. Have the child color the ocean blue. Next, ask the child to draw the outline of a whale on a piece of gray poster board. Cut it out, and glue or tape the whale to a craft stick.

To play the game, ask the child to make the whale travel over the waves. In order to go from one wave to the next, the child must identify the letter on the wave. If the child misses a letter, he must go back to the beginning.

THAT'S HAPPY, THAT'S SAD

◁▶◁▶◁▶◁▶◁▶◁▷

Play a storytelling game with happy, sad, silly, and mad options.

What You'll Need
- poster board
- blunt scissors
- marker
- brad

Make a spinner for the game using poster board: Cut a square, and draw a large circle on it. Then cut out a pointer also. Divide the circle into 4 sections using a marker. Draw either a happy, sad, angry, or silly face in each section. Attach the pointer to the center of the circle with a brad pierced through both pieces.

Now it's time to start the storytelling! Take turns spinning the spinner to tell a story. The first person spins and starts the story. If the spinner lands on the sad face, something that is sad must happen in that part of the story. If the spinner lands on the silly face, something silly has to happen! Continue spinning and adding to the story until the story starts winding down. One person can then end the story. Another option for ending the game is to decide ahead of time how many turns each player will have.

Revealing Sentences

◁▷◁▷◁▷◁▷

Exercise creative and critical thinking while using one word as an anchor to create an entire sentence.

What You'll Need
• pencil
• paper

Choose a word that represents a person, place, or thing. The word should be plural unless it is someone's name. Invite the child to make a sentence using the letters of the word to determine the first letter of each word in the sentence. The chosen word should be the first word of the sentence.

For example, if the word chosen was *cars*, the sentence could be: *Cars are really super.* A sentence for *cats* might be: *Cats are timid sometimes.* A sentence for *Jim* might be: *Jim is messy.*

CARS ARE REALLY SUPER

Story Cards

◁▷◁▷◁▷◁▷

Use magazine pictures to elicit entertaining tales!

Encourage the child to choose pictures of assorted subjects, such as people, animals, places, foods, shoes, etc., from magazines. Have him cut out 10 to 12 of the pictures. Glue each picture onto a separate piece of paper to create the story cards. When the glue is dry, turn the papers facedown and spread them out. Ask the child to turn over 3 of the story cards and make up a story that includes all 3 pictures.

What You'll Need
• magazines
• blunt scissors
• paper
• nontoxic white glue

You can also use the story cards for cooperative storytelling. One person chooses a card from the facedown cards and begins a story about that picture. The next person chooses another card and makes up the next part of the story, incorporating that picture. Keep going until there are no more cards or you're tired of the story.

Activity Twist

For a twist, use the cards to make a storytelling flip book. Sort the cards into 3 groups: people or animals, things, and places. Attach them to cardboard backing with brads.

LEAF PRINTING

◁▷◁▷◁▷◁▷◁▷

Remember and record lovely leaves with painted prints.

What You'll Need
- different types of leaves
- poster or tempera paint
- brush
- paper
- paper towel
- rolling pin

The child can paint the underside of a leaf and then place it, paint-side down, on paper. Place a paper towel on top of the leaf, and have the child gently roll the rolling pin over the paper towel and leaf to make the print. Then lift the paper towel and leaf carefully. Try this with a few different types of leaves, and have the child examine them. How are the leaves the same? How are they different? Which leaf is the prettiest?

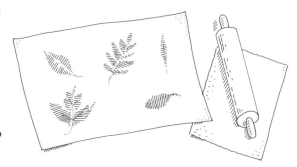

RED LIGHT, GREEN LIGHT

Follow the traffic signals on the road to higher learning.

◁▷◁▷◁▷◁▷◁▷

What You'll Need
- set of letter cards
- red and green construction paper
- blunt scissors
- glue

This simple game utilizes children's understanding of traffic signals.
Cut red and green dots out of construction paper, and glue them at the top of each letter card. Make about a third of the dots red and the rest green. Shuffle the cards. Have the child go through the cards one at a time and identify the letter on each card that has a green "light" (dot). When the child comes to a card with a red "light," his turn is over. Players can continue taking turns in this manner.

Activity Twist
You can also play the game with letter cards made of red and green circles cut from construction paper.

LET'S TELL A STORY!

⬦▶⬦▶⬦▶⬦▶⬦

Encourage the young storyteller to share a favorite story.

What You'll Need
• any favorite fairy tale

Invite the child to choose a favorite fairy tale that she would like to read to an audience. Encourage the child to read it aloud several times to you. Then have the child tell the story in her own words without thinking about the author's exact words. Discuss gestures that would add interest to the telling and would help the listeners understand the story, such as waving a magic wand or sprinkling fairy dust. Finally, encourage the child to rehearse in front of a mirror before sharing the story with an audience.

 # LEGENDARY LISTS

⬦▶⬦▶⬦▶⬦▶⬦

Invent fanciful categories, and fill them with imaginary listings.

Take turns creating categories and challenging one another to name real or pretend events, ideas, or items that fit into them. Encourage the child to have fun and be creative when making the list! Some examples of categories you might suggest for one another are:

What You'll Need
• pen or pencil
• paper

important items to take along on a trip to Mars; new holidays that should be invented; unusual ways to use a paper cup; new flavors of ice cream that might be created. For further fun, turn a fanciful list into a fiction story!

LITTLE WORD SEARCH

◁▷◁▷◁▷◁▷

Show how little words can grow to be large ones by adding letters.

In this activity, children learn reading skills by recognizing a small word in a longer word.

Write a row of words. Start with a small word and then write two longer words that contain the small word. Ask the child to underline the "little" word in each longer word, then tell how the longer words are different. Encourage advanced children to read as many words as possible. Start with the following word rows:

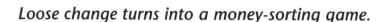

up pup puppy
an and hand
it bit bite
jump jumped jumping
play plays replay

 # TAKING IT TO THE BANK

◁▷◁▷◁▷◁▷

Loose change turns into a money-sorting game.

Cut a slit in the top of each lid. Write "1¢: penny," "5¢: nickel," "10¢: dime," and "25¢: quarter" on the different index cards, and tape one to each tub. Pour out the loose change in front of the tubs and show the child which coins go into each tub. Ask her to sort the remainder of the change, and help her count how many of each kind of coin there are in the piles. Then ask the child to "take the money to the bank" by placing the coins in the

appropriate tubs. Keep the tubs in an area to which she has easy access. Any time you have collected a pile of spare change, give the child the coins, and let her repeat the exercise. Open the tubs occasionally to make sure the contents are consistent.

WORD-A-DAY

◁▷◁▷◁▷◁▷

Learn new words every day of the week with this "drip-dry" method.

String a clothesline across one corner of the room, and clip clothespins along the line. Next, write interesting theme-related words on index cards. Choose words such as *caterpillar, cocoon,* and *butterfly* (from a science project), or *square, circle,* and *triangle* (from a math lesson on shapes). Place the words in the clothesline pouch.

Each day, invite the child to pick a word from the pouch. Help the child say the word, use it in a sentence, and illustrate it when applicable. Then have the child clip the new word to the clothesline to review later.

PATTERN PLAY

◁▷◁▷◁▷◁▷

Improve the child's spelling abilities with this creative approach to analyzing spelling patterns.

List words spelled with a similar pattern, and invite the child to discover how they are alike. For example, the words *took* and *cook* have the spelling pattern *ook,* and the words *night* and *light* have the spelling pattern *ight.*

Next, ask the child to form each letter in the pattern by bending and twisting chenille stems. Then make chenille-stem letters to add to the pattern in order to spell new words with the same pattern. How many words can the child spell with the same spelling pattern?

Johnny's Hammer

◁▷◁▷◁▷◁▷

Hammer away at syllable identification while singing.

Chant the first verse of the following rhyme, "Johnny's Hammer," with the child. At the end of the first verse, have the child name a word with one syllable. Then chant the second verse together. This time the child must name a word with two syllables. Continue in this manner for verse three.

Johnny builds one hammer, one hammer, one hammer. Johnny builds one hammer all the day long.

Johnny builds two hammers, two hammers, two hammers. Johnny builds two hammers all the day long.

Johnny builds three hammers, three hammers, three hammers. Johnny builds three hammers all the day long.

Seed Taste Test

◁▷◁▷◁▷◁▷

Take a seed taste test, and tell which seeds taste best!

What You'll Need
- variety of edible seeds (sunflower, peanuts, sprouts, popped corn, coconut)
- small paper plates
- unbreakable magnifying glass

Wash hands first! Gather together a variety of seeds that can be eaten as food. Invite the child to observe and compare the seeds. The child can use the magnifying glass for careful observation, noting differences in size, shape, and color. Then the child can eat the seeds and note the differences in taste! Discuss with the child which seeds he likes best and which seeds he likes least.

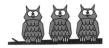

Create-o-Saurus

Create your very own noun with this word-origin activity.

What You'll Need
- paper
- crayons

Write the words *brontosaurus, tyrannosaurus,* and *stegosaurus* on a piece of paper. Then ask the child: What do all these words have in common? (They are all dinosaurs and nouns, and they all contain the word part *saurus.*) Explain that *saurus* means large lizard. Encourage creative thinking by having the child create and draw new dinosaurs and name them. Remind him to use the word part *saurus* in the dinosaur name.

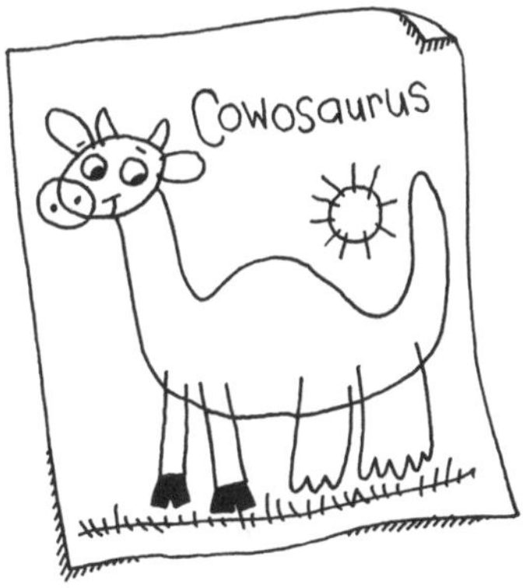

Snack Patterns

Turn a snack treat into a tasty pattern-making feat.

What You'll Need
- celery sticks
- cream cheese
- spoon
- paper plate
- raisins, pretzel sticks, peanuts, or other topping

After washing hands, the child can spread cream cheese on celery sticks with the spoon. The child can then use raisins and pretzel sticks to make pattern decorations on top. The child can make simple patterns (raisin-pretzel-raisin-pretzel-raisin-pretzel) or more complicated ones (raisin-raisin-pretzel-raisin-raisin-pretzel). A third topping (such as peanuts) can also be added to encourage more sophisticated pattern making.

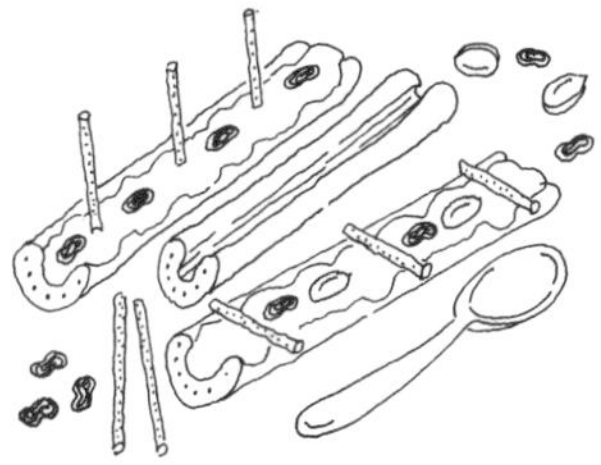

Activity Twist

Encourage the child's observation powers by studying patterns in faces. Talk about placements of the eyes, nose, mouth, and ears. Provide peanut butter or icing to spread on crackers or cookies. Offer grapes, pineapple chunks, apple wedges, and other fruit selections for the child to design delicious face patterns. When you're done, eat them!

GOOD GREEN GROWTH

◁▷◁▷◁▷◁▷◁▷

What do plants need? Are sun and water necessary?

What You'll Need
- 4 plastic cups
- potting soil
- newspaper
- lima beans or grass seed
- label tape or marker
- paper bag
- watering can
- paper and pencil (optional)
- penny, pebble, and button (optional)

The child can perform an experiment to find out what the essentials of plant growth are—what a seed needs not just to sprout, but to grow into a healthy green plant. The child will be testing whether a seed can grow without light, without soil, without water, or if it must have all three. The child can start the experiment by filling 3 of the cups with soil and 1 with a crumpled newspaper. Plant a lima bean in each one. The child can then place the cups on a windowsill and put a paper bag over 1 of the cups with soil. Help the child make labels using label tape or write on cups with a marker. Label the bean planted in newspaper "no soil." Label the bean under a paper bag "no sun." Label one of the remaining beans "no water." Label the last one, "soil, sun, water." The child can now water each of the beans except the one designated "no water." (Make sure the "no sun" plant gets covered up after watering!) The child can check the plants daily and continue to add water to 3 of the plants to keep them moist during the duration of the experiment (a couple of weeks). Invite the child to predict and observe which beans grow into plants.

To increase the challenge, the child can chart the results or draw his observations. To continue this activity, after the child has determined that it takes soil, water, and light for good green growth, the child can plant different items (a penny, a pebble, a button) and provide each with soil, water, and light. The child can predict which will grow.

BAKERY NOUNS

◁▷◁▷◁▷◁▷

Munching a bunch of sugar cookies is a yummy way for the child to learn about nouns! See for yourself.

What You'll Need
- prepared cookie dough
- paper
- pencil
- cookie cutters
- cookie sheet
- oven

Caution: This project requires adult supervision.

If possible, visit a bakery to look at the shaped sugar cookies. Point out that bakers bake cookies in many shapes, such as stars, circles, hearts, squares, and diamonds. Explain that the names of the cookie shapes are called nouns. Follow up by inviting the child to cut out some cookies using

cookie cutters with prepared cookie dough. Then have the child write the noun that names the cookie shape on a piece of paper. Next bake the cookies for the child, following the package directions. Once the cookies have cooled from the oven, enjoy a tasty snack.

WHAT'S WHOSE JOB?

◁▷◁▷◁▷◁▷

Play a guessing game about who does what.

Gather together pictures of professionals at work or in different uniforms that show what their jobs are. Put all the pictures into a bag or box. Take turns pulling a picture out of the bag or box. The person who has chosen a picture looks at it but doesn't let the other person see it. The adult or child who has chosen the picture then

What You'll Need
- pictures cut from magazines or simple drawings showing people in different professions
- bag or box

tells about the person's job and what kind of tasks that person does, without mentioning the name of the job or the profession. The other person guesses the profession from the description. After playing, invite the child to share more ideas about different jobs people have.

COMICAL MAGNETS

◁▶◁▶◁▶◁▶◁▶◁▶

Turn Sunday funnies into refrigerator story magnets.

To make these magnets, choose a comic strip that demonstrates obvious action. Cut apart each of the comic panels, and glue them onto a piece of cardboard or the back of a cereal box cut to size. Place a strip of magnetic tape on the back of each to turn the comic squares into magnets. The child can put the pictures in sequence on the refrigerator and make up original stories to tell using the pictures. The child can

What You'll Need
• Sunday funnies
• blunt scissors
• nontoxic white glue
• recycled cardboard
• magnetic strips

also rearrange magnets into new action sequences and make up different stories. For a variation, make refrigerator magnets using stickers or canceled postage stamps that the child can use for magnetic sorting.

ALPHABET TALES

◁▷◁▷◁▷◁▷◁▷◁▷

Weave an alphabet tale with a group of friends.

What You'll Need
- paper
- marker or pen

Children put the alphabet to good use in this group activity.

Alternating turns with one or more friends or parents, the first child names a word beginning with the letter *A,* the next person picks a word beginning with a *B,* and so on. To complicate the exercise, the words should combine to tell a story. For example: *Alice bakes cookie dough every Friday.* See if you can use the entire alphabet. As the story evolves, you can write it down and read it when completed.

BIG LETTER, LITTLE LETTER

◁▷◁▷◁▷◁▷◁▷◁▷

Confusion over capitals? Create a color code.

What You'll Need
- paper
- marker or pen
- crayons

Help children practice recognizing the capital and lowercase forms of letters.

Draw a circle and divide it into 6 equal parts. In the top 3 parts, write the capital letters *A, B,* and *C.* In the bottom 3 parts, write the lowercase letters *c, a,* and *b.* Ask the child to find each matching capital and lowercase letter and shade the 2 parts with the same color.

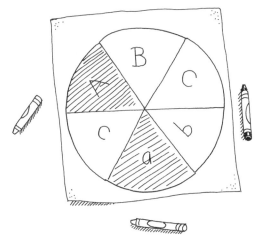

For all knowledge and wonder (which is the seed of knowledge) is an impression of pleasure in itself.

—Francis Bacon

SWING AND SLIDE

◁▷◁▷◁▷◁▷◁▷

Swings, slides, and jungle gyms! The playground is an exciting place.

A child's play environment is important for his muscle development. This area can also be a learning environment.

On a sunny day, take the child to the playground. As you approach the play area, ask, "What can you go back and forth on that begins like the word *sweater*?" (Answer: swing.) Next ask, "What can you go down that begins like the word *slim*?" (Answer: slide.) Give the child similar riddles for the other equipment found at the playground (a see-saw, jungle gym, sandbox, obstacle course, tunnel).

As you are going from one area of the playground to another, ask the child to think of words with different beginning-letter sounds that describe different ways to get from one place to another—for example, *jump, walk, skip, gallop, hop, run.* See if the child can think of additional words, telling you the beginning-letter sounds of each one. Have fun at the playground!

INTERACTIVE JOURNAL

◁▶◁▶◁▶◁▶

Share daily events by writing notes to each other in this interactive journal.

Explain that in this journal you and the child will both be writing notes or letters to each other, describing daily events and asking interesting questions. If the child is a beginning writer, encourage him to draw pictures when he does not know how

What You'll Need
- notebook
- pencils
- colored pencils (optional)

to spell a word. Begin the journal by sharing details about your day. End your entry by asking questions about the child's day. Invite the child to do the same, and continue alternating entries.

To vary the writing, colored pencils can be used, or the activity can take on a particular form, such as a simile poem (see page 300).

BALL-TOSS RHYMES

◁▶◁▶◁▶◁▶

Test a child's verbal skills with a bouncing rubber ball.

What You'll Need
- rubber ball

Rhyming words are an effective way for a child to develop listening skills and acquire the ability to make new words.

Think of a simple rhyming word, such as *hat.*

As you throw, bounce, or roll the ball to the child, say the word *hat.* The child, after receiving the ball, is to say a rhyming word (for example, *cat, fat, mat, sat, rat, pat*) before returning the ball to you. Repeat moving the ball back and forth and saying a rhyming word. If the child cannot think of a new word, have him say *hat.* Then it's up to you to give a rhyming word.

BEANBAG TOSS

◁▸◁▸◁▸◁▸◁▸

Ready, set, toss! Where did that beanbag land?

What You'll Need
- old shower curtain or plastic tablecloth
- marker
- beanbag

This is a good activity for an energetic child.

Find an old shower curtain or tablecloth. On an unprinted side, write the letters of the alphabet in scrambled order. Make the letters fairly large, but try to spread them out so that they are at least a few inches apart and cover most of the surface. Place this alphabet sheet on the floor. Give the child a beanbag (see "Beanbags" on page 279 for directions on how to make one), and ask him to toss it onto the sheet from several feet away. Have the child say the name of the letter closest to the spot where the beanbag lands.

To vary the activity, call out a letter first, and then tell the child to try to throw the beanbag so it lands on that letter. Or, instead of saying a letter, say a word, then have the child identify the beginning letter and try to toss the bag on that letter.

Little, Liddle, Loddle

⬦▶⬦▶⬦▶⬦▶⬦

Changing one word a little at a time is a fun way to learn how to analyze the parts and sounds of words.

Explain to the child that you will both take turns changing a word, 1 sound at a time. Then choose a word that has 2 or more syllables. Take the first turn, and change 1 sound. Then invite the child to try and change another sound in the word. Continue to change the word, sound by sound, until you are both satisfied that the word is quite different than the original. Use the following example to get you started.

bubble, rubble, ripple, triple, triplet, tripping, sipping, skipping, skipper

What Is the Letter?

⬦▶⬦▶⬦▶⬦▶⬦

Give a child a "feel" for the letters of the alphabet.

Another way for a child to experience letters is for you to "write" a letter on the child's back by slowly tracing it with your finger. Capital letters are probably the easiest to identify. Ask the child to guess the letter. She will have to concentrate on your motions and strokes to determine the correct letter. For an advanced child, spell out simple, 3-letter words. Have the child guess the 3 letters and, if possible, determine the word.

NEWS FLASH

◁▷◁▷◁▷◁▷

Invite the child to be a news anchor, recalling events from a favorite story.

Begin by choosing a story the child has read and is familiar with. Then help the child select and organize information, which is an important reading skill needed to retell a story as a newscaster. Next, invite the child to report the events of the story from the point of view of a news reporter.

What You'll Need
• pen or pencil
• paper

How would the reporter describe what happened? What would the headline of the story be? Can the child retell the major events of the story as if they were being broadcast on the evening news?

FRUITFUL FUN

◁▷◁▷◁▷◁▷

Children learn the names of fruits in this mouth-watering activity.

What You'll Need
• various fruits
• package of fruit string (available at grocery stores)

In this activity, children review fruit names as they work on beginning letters.

Name a fruit, such as an apple, and hold up a real apple. Have the child form the fruit string into the shape of the letter *A* for the word's beginning sound. Take turns naming other fruits, such as a banana, peach, pear, watermelon, apricot, cantaloupe, nectarine, orange, and berries. Start with common fruits, and hold up examples of each. For an added challenge, have the child describe each fruit as it is named, or give clues for each fruit instead of naming it.

Watching Beans Grow

◁▷◁▷◁▷◁▷

Plant a bean, then watch and record its growth.

What You'll Need
- lima bean
- soil
- jar or can
- watering can
- paper
- crayons
- yarn
- scissors
- nontoxic white glue
- craft stick (optional)

The child can plant a bean in a can or jar of soil, set it in a sunny place, water it, and make sure the soil stays moist. A lima bean grows very quickly. The child can record the growth in drawings, making a picture each day of what the plant looks like. At a later time, the pictures can be mixed up, and the child can lay them out and put them back in order according to the growth pictured. The child can also record the growth of the plant by measuring it. Starting when the bean plant appears above the surface of the dirt, the child can measure the plant with a piece of yarn. Each day the child can cut a piece of yarn the same height as the plant. The lengths of yarn can be glued on paper in a row next to one another, charting the growth of the plant. For more challenge, a craft stick that has inches or centimeters marked on it can be inserted in the soil. The child can note how tall the plant is each day and (with help from an adult) color in squares on a graph to represent the height, thus graphing the growth.

TELL IT TO ME

◁·◁▷·◁▷·◁▷·◁▷

Illustrate a story and author it, too!

What You'll Need
- paper
- markers or crayons
- pencil

After the child has drawn a picture for a story, invite her to dictate the words that tell the story. The words can be written down on the top or bottom of the picture or on a separate piece of paper. Encourage the child's storytelling with questions to elicit story details such as: What did he do next? Then what happened? Did she have any pets? What did his mother say? How did he feel? When the story is finished, read it back to the child. Ask if the story has been recorded correctly or if there are any other details the child wants to add or change. For more challenge, encourage the child to write the words for her story. The child can use invented spelling or lines and scribbles. After the child has "written" the story, have her "read" it aloud.

CITY SEARCH

◁·◁▷·◁▷·◁▷·◁▷

Where can you visit today? Search the map for a clue.

Write the letters of the alphabet at the top of a large map of your state of residence. Locate the town or city where you live, and place an X there. Have the child search for cities or

What You'll Need
- state map
- marker or pen

towns that begin with the same letter of the alphabet and circle those locations when he finds them. At the top of the map, where the alphabet is written, cross off letters that represent towns or cities that have been located.

Top Ten List

◁▷◁▷◁▷◁▷

Making lists is a popular and fun way to motivate a reluctant writer.

Invite the child to think of something he enjoys doing, such as staying in bed. The child should create a list of the top ten reasons to do that. Then he can create a list of reasons to do the opposite, such as in these examples.

<table>
<tr><td>What You'll Need
• paper
• pencil</td></tr>
</table>

Ten Reasons to Stay in Bed

It's a school day.

I haven't studied for spelling.

My toe hurts.

My turtle will be lonely if I go.

My friend is sick.

It's meat loaf day at school.

My pinkie hurts.

My dog will be lonely if I go.

It's raining outside.

I want to watch television.

Ten Reasons to Get Out of Bed

It's a school day.

I need to study for spelling.

Mom will tell me to wash dishes if I stay home.

My turtle wants to hibernate.

My friend is coming over.

It's brownie day at school.

Dad will tell me to clean the house if I stay home.

My dog just wants to sleep anyway.

I can go out and see a rainbow.

Mom unplugged the television.

Activity Twist

While the child writes one version of a top ten list, write your own amusing list of reasons why you should or should not stay in bed. Compare lists for added enjoyment.

HEAR THE BEAT

◁▷◁▷◁▷◁▷◁▷

Listen for the beat in the sounds of a day!

The child can listen to music and try to find the beat—then he can clap to it or tap to it to get familiar with it. To take the activity further, the child can listen for beats going on around him naturally—the sounds of people walking on a sidewalk, a construction worker hammering, the clothes in a dryer thumping. Encourage the child to listen for those beats and try to tap and clap to them also!

What You'll Need
• music

SPIDER MAN

◁▷◁▷◁▷◁▷◁▷

Fans of creepy, crawling creatures will enjoy making fuzzy spiders.

What You'll Need
• cotton balls
• 18" to 24" length of yarn
• clear tape
• blunt scissors
• construction paper
• nontoxic white glue
• pen
• poster board or butcher paper

Invite children to play a board game that uses their ability to recognize like and different letters.

First, make a spider game piece for each player. Use a cotton ball for each spider's body, and tape 8 short pieces of yarn to its bottom for legs. Glue 2 construction-paper eyes on the top of the cotton ball. For the game board, draw a path of squares on the poster board or a sheet of butcher paper. At the end of the path, draw a spider web. In each square, write a pair of letters, sometimes the same (*B, B*) and sometimes different (*E, F*). Players take turns moving a spider to each square on the path and telling whether the letters on the square are the same or different.

STILL-LIFE PAINTINGS

◁▷◁▷◁▷◁▷

Look carefully, and paint what you see!

Invite the child to paint a picture of a vase of flowers, a potted plant, or other natural items that the child can look at and study while painting. Assemble the still life with the child. Share picture books with paintings of still lifes by artists whose styles are very different. Help the child understand that all the artists started by looking at the things they painted, but they all had a different way of seeing. Encourage the child to look closely at the still life you've created together and to paint it as he sees it.

What You'll Need
• flowers or potted plant
• paper
• paint
• paintbrushes
• water

MAIL CALL

◁▷◁▷◁▷◁▷

All the mail starts with the letter M in this make-believe mailbox activity.

What You'll Need
• shoe box
• marker
• old magazines
• blunt scissors

Help the child practice recognizing the beginning sound of the letter *M*. Print a large *M* for *mailbox* on the shoe box. Then invite the child to look through magazines for pictures of objects whose names begin with *M*. Help the child cut out the pictures and "mail" them by putting them into the *M* box.

Lost and Found

◁▷◁▷◁▷◁▷

Where, oh where, has my favorite storybook character gone?

What You'll Need
- storybooks
- poster board
- crayons or markers

Place a collection of favorite storybooks on a reading table or in another quiet reading area in the house, and provide ample time for the child to browse through the books before you begin this activity.

Tell the child that a character in one of the storybooks is lost, and invite the child to make a "lost and found" poster for that character. Let the child pick the character who is lost. Encourage the child to describe the lost character before beginning to draw. Explain that the reader will want to know who is lost, what the character looks like, and anything else about the character that would help identify that character. Invite the child to return to the book area, if needed, to look for pictures of the selected character or to double-check information.

As the child works on the poster, make sure he includes information about what should be done if the lost character is found. Encourage creative thinking and spontaneity as the child creates the poster.

Ice-Cream Syllables

◁▷◁▷◁▷◁▷

Scoop up a triple-decker treat when you make your own ice-cream syllables.

What You'll Need
- blunt scissors
- construction paper
- pencil
- nontoxic glue

Cut out triangle-shaped cones and round ice-cream scoops from construction paper. Write root words (such as *end, cap,* and *vent*), prefixes (such as *un* or *pre*), which go before a root word, and suffixes (such as *ed* or *ing*), which go after a root word, on the scoops.

Next, invite the child to make triple-decker syllable treats by combining the scoops and gluing them on top of the paper ice cream cone to make a word. Challenge the child to see if he can use the new word in a sentence.

For an extra challenge, have the child make up or write a story including 4 different ice-cream–cone words, each used in its own sentence.

EVENT HANGERS

◁▶◁▶◁▶◁▶

Understanding cause-and-effect relationships in reading is made simple with this creative activity.

What You'll Need
- clothes hanger
- paper
- clear tape
- favorite story
- markers
- old magazines
- blunt scissors
- glue
- poster board
- hole punch
- yarn

Cover the hole in a hanger (but don't wrap the hook!) with blank paper. Use tape to hold the paper firmly in place. Set the hanger aside for now.

Begin by having the child read a favorite story. Then invite the child to draw a picture on the paper-covered hanger that shows an important event in the story. Next have the child draw pictures or cut out pictures from old magazines that show what caused the event to happen. Glue the pictures on poster board. When glue is dry, cut out the shapes. Help the child punch a hole in the top of each shape and in the bottom of the paper-covered hanger. String yarn through the holes, tie the yarn, and hang the cutouts from the clothes hanger. Put the hanger on display so others can see it.

Activity Twist

As a variation, have the child draw or find pictures to illustrate what happened before and after the event pictured on the hanger, and attach them as well.

TELEVISION TALKS

◁▶◁▶◁▶◁▶

Don't just watch; watch and talk!

Talk to the child about the programs or videos the child watches to make the TV viewing active. The adult can ask questions such as: What do you think will happen next? What do you think about what he did? Do you agree with that? Ask questions after the program also. What did you see? What would you have done if you were there? What did you like? What didn't you like? Why?

HAMBURGER HELPER

◁▷◁▷◁▷◁▷

Add some educational ingredients to your next hamburger meal; kids will relish it.

What You'll Need
- ground meat
- buns
- other items used to make a hamburger meal

Caution: This project requires adult supervision. Wash hands well with soap and water *before* handling the food and *after* handling the hamburger meat.

Helping with a hamburger meal is a great way for children to learn not only the steps in meal preparation, but beginning sounds in words as well.

Have the child help you prepare a meal of hamburgers, starting with making the patties. As the two of you work, discuss each food item you are using: meat, salt, pepper, bun, mustard, ketchup, pickles, beans, and so on. Have the child name other words that begin with the same sound as the name of each food item. Using the word *meat,* for example, the child might respond with the words *map, man, mouse, make,* or *mind.*

WHAT'S IN THE BOX?

◁▷◁▷◁▷◁▷

Play a mystery guessing game using descriptive hints!

Take turns choosing a mystery item to put in a shoe box. Choose common objects, such as a spoon, a block, a toy car, etc. The person who has chosen the object describes how

What You'll Need
- shoe box
- assorted common items

the object is used—without telling what it is. The other person guesses what the object is! To make the game more challenging, have the child think of an object and describe it!

HUMPTY DUMPTY'S FALL

◁▶◁▶◁▶◁▶◁▷

Experiment with is and are *while answering questions about favorite nursery rhyme characters.*

Invite the child to act out traditional nursery rhymes, such as "Jack Be Nimble," "Three Blind Mice," "Jack and Jill," and "Humpty Dumpty." Pause from time to time to ask the child how the character or characters feel. Have the child answer the questions using the verbs *is* or *are.* After several responses, ask if the child sees a pattern for using *is* and *are.* Explain that singular subjects name one thing and plural subjects name more than one thing. The verb *is* is used with a singular subject: Humpty Dumpty is sad when he falls off the wall. The verb *are* is used with a plural subject: Jack and Jill are hurt when they tumble down the hill.

TELL ME A STORY

◁▷◁▷◁▷◁▷◁▷◁

Here's one way to get applause whenever you tell a story.

Use verbal storytelling to practice listening for beginning sounds. Ask the child to listen for words that begin with a particular sound (such as the *B* sound) as you tell a simple story. For example: "I went outside and took my bat. I picked up a ball. I ran around the bases." Have the child clap each time she hears a word that begins with the chosen sound and then repeat that word.

 # OLYMPIC DISTANCES

◁▷◁▷◁▷◁▷◁▷◁

This event challenges you to beat your own record!

Pick a spot in the yard or park from which the child can safely throw the various objects suggested at right. Mark the craft sticks with different colors to represent each object she'll be throwing. Ask the child to throw each one as far as she can, and use the craft sticks to mark how far each one traveled. Encourage the child to note the distance and then retrieve all of the objects. Challenge her to beat her "record" by throwing each object again. Talk to her about the different objects and why some are easier or more difficult to throw long distances. Return to the yard or park from time to time for additional attempts. Make sure to cheer and applaud the child whenever she succeeds in breaking one of her old records.

What You'll Need
- plastic flying disk
- tennis ball
- wiffle ball
- marble
- craft sticks
- colored markers

ABC Order

◁▷◁▷◁▷◁▷◁▷

*A little word processing on the computer will add pizzazz
to this ABC order activity!*

What You'll Need
- computer with word-
processing program

Invite the child to type words from a spelling list into the computer. Show the child how to highlight and move a word to a new location on the page. Then ask the child to put the words on the list in alphabetical order. The final product can be made to look creative by changing the type to a large, decorative font before printing.

Hole-Punched Letters

◁▷◁▷◁▷◁▷◁▷

Here's a creative way of writing letters that's a "hole" lot of fun.

This activity engages children's hands while helping them match beginning sounds with letters and objects.

From a sheet of regular white paper, cut the following shapes: a cup, a fish, and a boat. Write the letters *C, F,* and *B* on a separate sheet of paper, and ask the child to tell you which letter stands for the beginning sound in each shape's name.

What You'll Need
- blunt scissors
- white paper
- marker or pen
- hole punch
- construction paper (pick a dark or bright color)
- nontoxic glue

Show the child how to use a hole punch to make holes in a sheet of paper, then instruct the child to use the hole punch to make the letter for the beginning sound of each object's name directly on the cup, fish, and boat shapes. You may need to fold the paper to reach all the holes. Paste each shape with its hole-punched letter on a sheet of colored construction paper.

BACKPACK BOOKS

◁▷◁▷◁▷◁▷

Backpack books bring characters to life as the child practices telling the story from a character's point of view.

Have the child keep the book and the stuffed animal in a backpack. Encourage the child to take it when going somewhere or for use at bedtime. Invite the child to read the book to the stuffed animal. Another time, have the child pretend to be the stuffed animal, reading to you in the animal's "voice."

Add writing materials to the backpack, and invite the child to create letters or notes to and from the characters in the story.

What You'll Need
- favorite book
- backpack or school bag
- stuffed animal that relates to the book
- pencil (optional)
- paper (optional)

SPORTS HEROES

◁▷◁▷◁▷◁▷

This creative reading and recording activity is for sports fans of all ages.

What You'll Need
- book about a favorite sports figure
- newspapers or magazines with information about that person
- notebook
- pencil

Read together through a book about a favorite current-day sports figure. Then scan the newspapers or magazines for additional information about that person. Invite the child to start a notebook to record facts or statistics about the sports figure. Encourage the child to add to it regularly.

My Hand Is Grand

◁▶◁▶◁▶◁▶◁▶◁▶

Contemplate the marvelous mysteries of just one little hand!

Trace the child's hand on construction paper with a marker. Then, invite the child to think about and list things that can be done with a hand. Record the child's ideas on paper. Give clues to encourage new kinds of thinking. Reread the list together, and keep adding to it. Challenge the child to continue to come up with more ideas! For a variation, challenge the child to demonstrate 5 different ways to use a hand to make noise, to touch someone, to hold things, etc.

What You'll Need
- construction paper
- markers
- paper
- pencil

Activity Twist

Turn the child's ideas into a personalized song. Begin by adapting the old favorite "If You're Happy and You Know It." Instead sing, "If Owen's happy and he knows it, let him clap his hands." Or, "If Owen's mad and he knows it, let him shake his fist."

ANTONYM CHECKERS

◁▷◁▷◁▷◁▷

**Use opposites in this challenging game of checkers,
and see how many kings you can crown.**

What You'll Need
- 24" × 24" poster board or cardboard square
- crayons
- checkers or large red and black buttons
- masking tape

This game is played much like the game of checkers, except that in order to be "crowned" a player must land on a space with an antonym corresponding to the word on the checker. For example, a player must move a checker marked *pretty* toward the red space marked *ugly* (the antonym of *pretty*). When it lands on that space, it can be crowned. As in the original game, the player with the last remaining checker wins.

Begin by making a checkerboard. Draw a grid of 8 squares by 8 squares on a piece of poster board or cardboard. Color the spaces red and black, alternating the colors as you go. Print the following words in the red squares on the first row of each player's home side: *big, sad, ugly, well.* Before starting the game, invite the child to select the color of checkers she would like to use as game pieces.

Next, make 2 sets of game pieces. For each set, mark the game pieces by putting a piece of masking tape over each checker and writing one of the following words on each: *little, small, tiny, happy, joyful, glad, pretty, lovely, beautiful, ill, sick, unhealthy.* Then set the checkers on the red squares at each end of the board, and you're ready to go. Change the words periodically for continued play.

WHERE DID I GO?

◁▷◁▷◁▷◁▷

This simple guessing game will stimulate thinking skills while the child learns about interesting places.

Begin by describing a place you have visited and the things you did there without naming the place. Then invite the child to guess where you have been. If the child is unable to guess, give her more clues. Continue until the child guesses correctly or until you have given 10 clues.

After finishing, invite the child to describe a place that she has visited and see if you can guess where it is, using the same technique.

WORD LETTER MATCH

◁▶◁▶◁▶◁▶◁▶◁

Look for clues to solve this game, matching capital and lowercase letters.

Knowledge of lowercase letters is necessary for reading printed materials. This activity helps the child recognize letters in lowercase form.

What You'll Need
• index cards
• pen or marker

On index cards, write simple words, such as *cat, ball, fish, mat,* and *cake,* in capital letters. Write the same words on a second set of cards in lowercase letters. Have the child sound out the words and match the cards with the same word.

FUNNY, FOOLISH, FALSE

◁▶◁▶◁▶◁▶◁▶◁

This statement-making activity enhances a child's understanding of the way language can be used.

What You'll Need
• strips of paper
• pencil
• small paper bag

Write words that describe different kinds of statements on strips of paper. These descriptions can include words such as *funny, silly, foolish, true, exaggerated, false,* and *wise.* Discuss with the child the meaning of these words, then put the strips of paper into a small paper bag. Pick a piece of paper from the bag, and make a statement that can be identified or labeled by the word written on the card. For example, if you pull out a strip of paper with the word *silly* written on it, you might say, "Bears wear shoes." Next, invite the child to do the same thing. Take turns pulling pieces of paper out of the bag until all the words have been chosen.

TAKE STOCK OF A ROCK

◁▷◁▷◁▷◁▷

There are so many ways to look at a rock!

What You'll Need
- rocks
- paper clips
- yarn
- blunt scissors
- balance scale
- bucket of water
- unbreakable magnifying glass
- paper (optional)
- pencil (optional)

Invite the child to collect rocks and then look—really look!—at them. The child can measure, compare, describe, and draw the rocks. The rocks can be measured by finger lengths, paper clips, or with pieces of yarn cut to the length of each rock. The weights of the rock can be compared using a balance scale, and they can be ordered by weight. Their textures can be compared using fingers or even cheeks (gently!). They can be examined dry and wet. Examine them even more carefully using a magnifying glass.

BIRD WATCHER

◁▷◁▷◁▷◁▷

"I spy a big, black crow." Children are observers of nature in this indoor/outdoor activity.

Teach the child to spell *bird,* and introduce her to the study of these fascinating creatures.

What You'll Need
- marker or pen
- several sheets of paper
- colored pencils or crayons

Print the word *bird* on a sheet of paper, and have the child copy it. On a walk in the neighborhood or in a park, tell the child to watch out for birds, pointing out and describing the different ones she sees—for example, "a robin redbreast sitting in a tree" or "a big, gray pigeon eating crumbs on the sidewalk." Tell the child the names of any birds that you know.

At home, display the word *bird* that the child wrote. Ask the child to draw and color pictures of the birds she remembers from the walk.

Tennis Ball & Aluminum Cans Bowling

◁▷◁▷◁▷◁▷◁▷◁▷◁▷

See how many cans you can knock down with one roll!

What You'll Need
- 15 empty aluminum soda cans
- small beans
- masking tape
- old belt
- tennis ball
- marker (optional)

Caution: This project requires adult supervision.

Fill the aluminum soda cans half full with beans; the child can help if supervised carefully (beans can be choking hazards). Place tape over the holes in the tops of all the cans—tape them well. Have the child arrange the cans in a triangle. Put down the belt for a throw line, about 3 to 4 feet from the cans. Have the child use the tennis ball to bowl. Move the belt closer or farther away, depending on the child's skill level. It is important that the child be successful in knocking down the cans, so it is better to start closer and move back. If the tennis ball does not knock the cans over, pour out some of the beans to make them lighter or try a heavier ball. To make this more challenging, put numbers on the cans, and keep track of the points the child makes each time he knocks over the cans. You can make each can a point or, if the child can add, put a different number on each can.

COOKIE COUNTING

Make five raisin cookie designs!

What You'll Need
- refrigerated cookie dough
- plastic knife
- cookie tray
- raisins

Caution: This project requires adult supervision.

After washing hands, the child can help cut and place cookie dough on a cookie tray. When all the cookies are placed on the tray, the child can make raisin designs on top. Challenge the child to count out and use 5 raisins for every cookie, but to make a different design for each cookie! Bake the cookies according to package directions.

COMICAL COMICS

Kids can have fun with phonics by focusing on the funnies.

Reading the comics is a great way to introduce children to newspapers.

What You'll Need
- comic strip from newspaper
- blunt scissors

Read several comic strips with the child. Point out simple words as you read. Have the child choose a favorite strip and tell it in her own words. Then cut out the strip, and cut the strip into its parts. Mix the pieces up. Have the child arrange the pieces in order and tell the story. Don't worry if the pieces are not in their original order, as long as the child tells the story in a logical way.

MILLIONS OF CREATURES!

◁▶◁▶◁▶◁▶◁▶◁▶

Creating a list of creatures encourages research that is guaranteed to fascinate.

There are millions of creatures in the world—insects, birds, animals, and reptiles. How many creatures can the child name? Begin by asking the child to write down or dictate the names of all the creatures that come to mind. See how many creatures the child can list.

Keep the list in an accessible place so that new animals can be added easily as the child notices or thinks of them. Encourage the child to discover "unlisted" animals while outside, watching TV, or reading.

To learn more about creatures, take the child on a trip to the library. Spend a few hours looking at children's encyclopedias or other children's books.

COOKED AND UNCOOKED

Find out whether food tastes different when it's chopped, cooked, or mashed.

Caution: This project requires adult supervision.

Prepare one food several different ways, and let your child take a taste test. Does cooking change the flavor? Does size or shape make a fruit taste different? Does a shredded vegetable taste the same as an uncut vegetable? The child can make predictions and then test them out. First, make sure everyone washes their hands! Peel and core an apple, then invite the child to help you cut up the apple into small pieces. She can then put the pieces into a pot that contains a small amount of water. Cook the apple slowly, until it is mushy. While the apple is cooking, cut a second apple into slices to be eaten raw. When the cooked apple is soft enough, let the child mash it with a potato masher.

> **What You'll Need**
> • apples
> • vegetable peeler
> • plastic knife
> • pot
> • water
> • potato masher
> • bowl
> • spoon
> • blender
> • cutting board
> • other vegetables (optional)

Spoon the fresh applesauce into a bowl, taste, and compare it to the raw apple slices. Encourage the child to describe the differences, including how each one tastes. To make the activity more difficult, you can also include any of the following in the test: grated apples, uncooked applesauce, or fresh apple juice. For uncooked applesauce, put apple slices in a blender and blend with a little bit of water.

For a variation on this comparison activity, use carrots. They can be diced, sliced, curled, shredded, cut in sticks, or eaten whole. They can be steamed in chunks or cooked with a little water, then mashed or pureed. They also can be juiced.

TELEPHONE TALK

◁▶◁▶◁▶◁▶◁▶

Consult, confer, and converse with pretend people!

What You'll Need
- toy telephone
- large cardboard box
- child-size chair
- notepad
- pencil

With the help of a toy phone and a pretend phone booth, the child can improvise and act out imaginary conversations.

The child can dramatize phone calls to real or pretend people or animals. The child might also want to call characters from favorite stories! A pencil and notepad can be used for taking messages. A large cardboard box can be turned into a telephone booth by standing it on its side and placing a child-size chair inside.

To give this activity an added challenge, provide a "phone book" or cards with names or pictures and phone numbers for real or pretend people or animals. The child can read the numbers and dial them on the play phone.

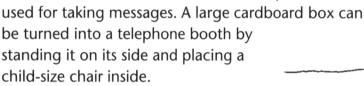

Hinkie-Pinkie!

Q: How did the car get a dent?
A: In a fender bender.

LEFT OR RIGHT

⊲►⊲►⊲►⊲►⊲►⊲►⊲►

Use your hands and letter sounds to learn the difference between left and right.

A prerequisite for reading is to be able to differentiate between left and right, since the reading process requires a left-to-right progression. The concepts of left and right can be confusing for a child, but with a little help from painted hands, a memory association can be made.

What You'll Need
• red and blue tempera paint
• paintbrush
• white paper
• ribbon (optional)

Use a paintbrush to paint the palm of the child's right hand red. Emphasize the beginning sound of *right* and *red.* Then make an impression of that painted hand on a piece of white paper. Next, use blue paint to make a similar impression using the child's left palm. After the child's hands are washed and the handprints are dry, she can practice matching both hands to the prints. To further assist the child, a red ribbon may be tied around the right wrist and a blue ribbon around the left one.

STEPPING STONES

◁▷◁▷◁▷◁▷

Practicing beginning sounds can sometimes become a balancing act.

What You'll Need
• large, flat stones
• letter cards

In this activity, children improve balance and dexterity as they practice beginning sounds outdoors.

In the yard or a park, find several large, flat stones and arrange them into a path. (Or you can find an existing stone path.) Make sure the child can step from one stone to the next without difficulty.

Put a different letter card on or beside each stone. Tell the child that in order to step on each stone, she must say a word that begins with the sound the letter stands for. If the child gives an incorrect answer, she must return to the beginning of the stone path.

INVENT YOUR OWN MACHINE

◁▷◁▷◁▷◁▷

Explore what makes machines work, and invent a new one!

The child can examine some simple nonelectrical machines, such as a manual eggbeater, a can opener, or a tricycle, and make observations and comparisons. The child can also look at pictures of machines in books, catalogs, or magazines and talk about what the machines can do and how people use them. Encourage the child to imagine a new kind of machine and what it might do. Let her create a machine by using an assortment of the items listed at right. The child can decide how it works, what it does, and what it is named.

What You'll Need
• simple nonelectric machines
• cardboard tubes
• paper plates
• small boxes
• chenille stems
• aluminum foil
• junk from the hardware drawer
• nontoxic white glue
• books (optional)
• catalogs (optional)
• magazines (optional)

One-Piece Puzzle Match

◁▷◁▷◁▷◁▷◁▷

Mix and match one-piece puzzles and parts.

What You'll Need
- construction paper
- blunt scissors
- 2 large manila envelopes

The child or adult can create several one-piece puzzles by folding construction paper in half and cutting or tearing a shape out of the center of each of the papers. Using the same color of paper for all the puzzles, make 3 to 8 puzzles. (Make 3 for a toddler, more for an older child.) Place all the center pieces into 1 pile, and mix them up. Next put all the puzzle frames into a second pile, and mix them up! The child can try to fit the centers into the frames by finding the middle part that fits. For added challenge, use large stencils to cut letter shapes out of the center of pieces of paper, and have the child try to match each letter with its frame. Try creating a puzzle for each letter of the child's name! Store the frames and holes in 2 separate envelopes.

Roller Painting

◁▷◁▷◁▷◁▷◁▷

Create a paint roller, and roll out a painting.

What You'll Need
- cardboard tubes
- empty cans
- tape
- cardboard
- yarn
- string
- blunt scissors
- nontoxic white glue
- shallow pan
- paint
- paper

The child can use assorted cylinders to make a variety of rollers, print with each of them, and compare the printed results. Remove the labels from the cans. Cover the edges of the can with tape to avoid cuts. The child can make rollers by gluing cardboard shapes onto the empty cans; by gluing pieces of string or yarn on an empty can or cardboard tube; and by cutting or punching holes in a cardboard tube. After the glue is dry, dip finished rollers in a tray of diluted paint, and roll them on paper to make designs.

VEGETABLE PRINTS

◁▷◁▷◁▷◁▷◁▷◁▷

What better way to learn about vegetables than to make art prints with them.

Vegetables such as peppers and onions have distinctive aromas. In addition, they have distinctive shapes and textures.

Pour some tempera paint onto several foam meat trays. Show the child some vegetables, and see if she can identify them. Then ask, "What letter does the word *vegetables* begin with?" Cut portions of the vegetables so that the child can handle them.

What You'll Need
- tempera paint
- clean plastic foam meat trays
- vegetables (such as pepper, mushroom, broccoli, cauliflower, radish, carrot, onion, potato)
- construction paper
- marker

Have the child select a cut vegetable, then tell you the name of the vegetable and its beginning letter. Next, instruct the child to dip the cut vegetable into the paint and "print" it on the paper. Continue with different vegetables and paints.

When the prints are dry, ask the child, "What type of food beginning with the letter *V* was used to make all the prints?" Discuss the shapes and characteristics of each vegetable as the child points to its print and says its beginning letter. Have the child write that letter under each vegetable print with a marker.

PRETEND HIKE

◁▶◁▶◁▶◁▶

Create a picnic path inside, and follow the trail!

What You'll Need
- pillows
- newspaper
- picnic lunch
- backpack
- cardboard tube (optional)
- blunt scissors (optional)
- rubber band or string (optional)

The child can create a pretend mountain path in the home. Turn pillows into hills to climb, a chair into a large tree to walk around, newspapers into a stream to jump over—we don't want wet feet! The child can map out the mountain path, then pack a lunch to carry in a backpack on the trek. The child can follow the path to a designated mountaintop and then eat the picnic lunch or snack there.

For more fun, make a pair of binoculars to add to the child's hiking gear so she can look for birds and bears along the way and check out the view from the mountaintop. Cut a cardboard tube in half across the middle, and fasten the halves side by side with a rubber band or some string. For lively hiking, make up a song about everything the child sees along the way.

SECRET SIGHTS

◁▶◁▶◁▶◁▶◁▷◁▷

Play a camouflage game.

What You'll Need
- 3 or 4 common household items
- tape

Take turns hiding items in the open for the other person to find. Choose several common items, such as a wooden spoon, a small box, a bar of soap, or a polystyrene grocery tray. Both adult and child note and agree on the items to be used for the game. After one person leaves the room, the other hides all the items. The items are hidden in full view, not under beds or inside boxes. A wooden spoon might be taped to the side of a wooden cupboard so the colors make it hard to spot. It is hidden in sight—not out of sight! After all the items are hidden, the first person tries to find them. Then choose new items and play again.

 # A RING OF THINGS

◁▷◁▷◁▶◁▷◁▶◁▷

Create loop books out of pictures of things that go together.

If possible, have the child punch holes in the corner of the index cards to serve as the pages of the book. Otherwise, the adult should punch the holes. The child chooses categories for the looped books, such as dogs, red things, baby animals, hats, or things the child likes to eat. After selecting a category, the child searches magazines for pictures that fit the category. The pictures can be cut or torn out and glued onto the individual cards. All the cards in one category are looped together with a ring. After a looped book has several pages, encourage the child to share the book with others, telling them about what is in it and why these things go together. Looped books can be ongoing—the child can continue to add pictures. The child can also add to them by drawing on the cards, putting stickers on them, or even taking photographs of items that fit in the category!

What You'll Need
- index cards
- hole punch
- old magazines
- nontoxic white glue
- blunt scissors
- large key ring or binder ring or shower curtain ring
- crayons (optional)
- stickers (optional)
- camera (optional)

SOCCER IS A KICK

◁▶◁▶◁▶◁▶◁▶◁▶

*Young children can play an educational version of their big sisters'
and brothers' favorite game.*

What You'll Need
- marker
- kraft paper
- adhesive tape
- soccer ball or large ball that bounces

In this activity, children can practice their soccer skills—and learn a new word.

Make a soccer "goal" by writing the word *kick* with a marker in large letters on a 3' × 3' piece of kraft paper. Tape the sign on a wall in a gym, basement, or recreation room.

Ask the child to identify the initial letter in the word and its beginning sound. Say the word, and have the child demonstrate the action of kicking the ball. Tell the child to stand several feet back from the kick sign and kick the ball toward it. Each time she hits the "goal," the child can shout, "Kick!"

Rhyme Time!

What says the little duck with a yellow back?
The little yellow duck says quack-quack-quack.
What says the friendly brown cow when she looks at you?
The friendly brown cow says moo-moo-moo.
Does your calico kitten say bow-wow-wow?
No, your calico kitten says meow-meow-meow.

OVER, UNDER, AROUND, AND THROUGH

◁▷◁▷◁▷◁▷◁▷

Create a dot city and then draw a path over, under, and around the dot town!

What You'll Need
- paper
- paint
- paintbrush
- markers

The child can make different colored dots and splotches on a large piece of paper using paint and a paintbrush. When the painting has dried, the child can use a marker to draw a path through the dot

town going over, under, and around the dots and splotches. Create a challenge for the child by providing directions for the child to follow while creating the path. For example, the adult can suggest that the child go around the blue dot, under the green splotch, and above the yellow dot.

PUZZLE PEEKER

◁▷◁▷◁▷◁▷◁▷

Turn pictures into puzzles with a puzzle peeker.

Make a puzzle peeker by cutting 5 to 8 horizontal strips in a piece of paper to about 1½" from the edge. Place the puzzle peeker on top of a picture that your child has not yet seen. Ask her to pull one strip back at a time and try to guess what the picture is. To increase the challenge, place the puzzle peeker on top of a complex picture!

What You'll Need
- paper
- blunt scissors
- picture from a book or magazine

EGG CARTON COUNT

◁▷ ◁▷ ◁▷ ◁▷

Make a more-or-less comparison counter for intriguing math play.

Caution: This project requires adult supervision.

What You'll Need
- 3 egg cartons
- masking tape
- tempera paint
- paintbrushes
- 2 kinds of counters (paper clips, buttons, acorns, beans)

Make a comparison container using 3 egg cartons. Remove the tops of the cartons, and tape the bottoms together to create 2 rows of 18. The child can paint the rows different colors. When the paint has dried, the comparison container can be used to play a predicting game. (The counters should be large enough to avoid a choking hazard, or an adult should supervise carefully.) Using 2 different kinds of counters, the child can place a small handful of 1 kind of counter in 1 pile and a small handful of the other kind of counter in another pile. Observing the 2 piles, the child then predicts which pile has the most items and gives a reason for his prediction. To check, the child lines up the 2 different piles of items in the 2 rows of the comparison container. To make the game more challenging, the child can also predict how many items are in each pile!

PRETZEL PRACTICE

◁▷◁▷◁▷◁▷◁▷

Pretzel sticks can provide a great impromptu lesson on letter formation.

What You'll Need
• pretzel sticks

Not only are pretzels a tasty snack, but children can use them to form letters without making a mess.

Ask the child to wash her hands, then show her how to use pretzel sticks to form letters, including breaking them in half to form some letter parts. Start with simple stick letters, such as *E, I,* and *T.* You might progress to making all the letters in the alphabet. Say each letter as the child makes it, and also have her name each letter frequently.

IMAGINARY KINGDOM

◁▷◁▷◁▷◁▷◁▷

Invent and design an imaginary land and locale.

The child can depict an imaginary place that she would like to visit and create a map showing what goes where. Encourage the child to imagine and describe the details of the fantasy place: the people and animals that live there, the homes they live in, and the kinds of trees and flowers that grow there. The child can create the background of the map by painting with watercolors on wet paper. (The paper is either dipped in water first or sponged on both sides with a wet sponge.) When the paint has dried, the child can draw in the details of the land with markers, showing where the people live, where the houses are, and where the animals roam.

What You'll Need
• watercolors
• paper
• sponge
• bowl of water
• paintbrush
• markers

ENVELOPE PUPPETS

◁▷◁▷◁▷◁▷

An imaginative child will love creating these animated story puppets.

What You'll Need
- 6½" × 9½" manila envelopes
- blunt scissors
- markers
- glue or clear tape
- arts and crafts scraps

Set out all materials. Use as many envelopes as the number of puppets you and the child intend to make. To make a puppet, carefully cut off the top flap of a manila envelope. This open end will be the bottom of the puppet. Invite the child to draw a face on the envelope. Have the child glue or tape odds and ends of arts and crafts scraps on the envelope to create a puppet resembling a character from a favorite story or book. The child can make puppets for every character involved in the story she wants to tell.

Have the child put her hands inside the envelope puppets. Encourage the child to use the finished puppets for retelling the story or for other dramatic play.

For an additional activity, help the child create a puppet stage. Paint a cardboard box with poster paints, and use it as the setting of the story.

WHAT'S IN A NAME?

◁▷◁▷◁▷◁▷

Here's an art project that adds a new dimension to letter shapes.

Children will enjoy decorating their own and others' names with many colors and textures.

Start with the child's name. Write it in large, outlined letters on a sheet of construction paper or poster board. Brainstorm with the child to come up with different ways to decorate each letter—for example, with pictures and designs made with paint or markers, or perhaps with cut-up bits of fabric glued to the paper.

After doing her own name, have her make decorative names for friends and family. Encourage the child to personalize the decorations by using pictures, designs, and colors that remind her of each person.

What You'll Need
- markers
- construction paper or poster board
- paint
- paintbrush
- bits of fabric
- glue

ONE-SYLLABLE ALIEN

◁▷◁▷◁▷◁▷

An alien visits Earth to teach young earthlings about one-syllable words.

What You'll Need
- masking tape
- markers
- box or backpack
- index cards
- pen or pencil

Pretend that an alien lands its spacecraft at the child's school or home. It has come to collect objects to take back to a faraway planet. The alien, however, only collects objects that have one-syllable names. Invite the child to collect one-syllable objects, label them with masking tape, and place them in a backpack or box for easy transporting. Then, using index cards, have the child make a list of more one-syllable words, in addition to the objects in the backpack, for the alien to take back to its faraway planet. How many words does the child know?

WOOD-SCRAP SCULPTURE

⬦▶⬦▶⬦▶⬦▶⬦▶⬦

Build and construct creative sculptures with wood scraps.

What You'll Need
- newspaper
- wood scraps (often free at lumberyards)
- sandpaper
- plastic goggles
- nontoxic white glue
- tempera paint
- paintbrush

Caution: This project requires adult supervision.

Start by spreading newspaper over the construction area. Gather together all the wood pieces so the child can sort through and choose just the right ones (the adult should check the wood for splinters). Provide sandpaper and goggles so the child can sand the wood if he chooses. The child can then glue wood pieces together to make an abstract or symbolic sculpture. After the glue dries, the child can choose to paint the sculpture or leave it natural.

TONGUE TWISTERS

⬦▶⬦▶⬦▶⬦▶⬦▶⬦

Try out this tongue twister, and see who gets tongue-tied first.

Say the following tongue twister, "Peter Piper," slowly to the child.

Peter Piper picked a peck of pickled peppers;
A peck of pickled peppers Peter Piper picked.
If Peter Piper picked a peck of pickled peppers,
Where's the peck of pickled peppers Peter Piper picked?

Invite the child to repeat the tongue twister. Ask the child what she noticed about the words. Stir up some fun by having the child repeat the tongue twister over and over, saying it faster each time. Then have the child name other things Peter could have picked that would begin with the same letter. Use the new words in the tongue twister.

When you're finished with that one, give some more tongue twisters a try. See how fast you can say them.

Rubber baby-buggy bumper.
Three tall tree tops.
How much wood would a woodchuck chuck if a woodchuck could chuck wood?
He shells and she sells seashells by the sandy seashore.

FUNNY-BONE TICKLE

◁▶◁▶◁▶◁▶

This game is sure to tickle your funny bone as actors do their silliest dramatizations of common words.

Begin by making a list of homographs. Homographs are words that are spelled the same but have different meanings, such as *bark*. Sometimes homographs, like *dove* or *wind,* can be pronounced in different ways depending on their meaning. You may wish to begin with these and the following examples and then add your own: *batter, ring, plant, brush.*

What You'll Need
• paper
• markers

   Here's how to play: One player chooses a word from the list and tries to make the others laugh by pantomiming one definition of the word, using impersonations and funny gestures. The first player who guesses the word gets to choose the next word.

WORD FACTORY

◁▶◁▶◁▶◁▶

This game teaches children to construct simple words.

What You'll Need
• 36 blank index cards
• marker or pen

Play a game that challenges a child to put letters together to make words.
   Make a letter card for each letter of the alphabet.

Make 2 extra sets of the letters *A, E, I, O,* and *U.* Give each player 6 cards to start. Work with the child to create words using as many of the 6 letters as possible. Have the players take turns making words. After spelling a word, a player may draw as many new cards as she used.

PAINT A STORY

◁▶◁▶◁▶◁▶

Young artists can practice making a picture that helps tell a story.

What You'll Need
- paper
- paint
- paintbrush

Invite the child to create a picture of a story. However, instead of creating an illustration for a known story, have the child paint a made-up story that you narrate.

The child should illustrate each action or event as it is being told, adding more and more details to the picture to match the story.

MAILING TUBES & BALLS

◁▶◁▶◁▶◁▶

Pick which ball fits in each tube.

Store the balls with the mailing tubes in a basket. (Note: If you cannot find mailing tubes, PVC pipe works well.) At first, have the child pull out a tube and choose which ball will roll through it. As the child develops skill at accurately selecting a ball and tube of the correct size, have her place a smaller tube inside a larger tube and again select a ball to see if it will roll through both tubes.

What You'll Need
- 3 or 4 mailing tubes with different diameters
- various balls: table-tennis ball, small rubber ball, tennis ball
- large basket

LETTERS IN THE MAIL

◁▷◁▷◁▷◁▷

Open your own post office to reinforce letter recognition.

What You'll Need
- letter cards
- crayon or marker
- 6 blank envelopes
- 6 shoe boxes
- drawing paper

Children can learn letters and increase their dexterity by creating their own "mail."

Hold up a letter card. Have the child use a crayon or marker to write the letter on an envelope and on the side of one of the shoe boxes. Ask the child to draw a picture of an object whose name begins with the letter on the envelope. Show the child how to fold the drawing, put it into the envelope, and seal the envelope (or put the flap inside the envelope).

Follow the same procedure until you have 6 different drawings in 6 envelopes, each one representing a different letter, and 6 shoe boxes, each one with a matching letter on its side. Shuffle the 6 "letters" and have the child "mail" each one in the appropriate shoe box. The next day, the child can receive her mail, further reinforcing letter recognition skills.

ROLLING, ROLLING, ROLLING

◁▷◁▷◁▷◁▷

Predict what happens when you use cars and ramps to roll.

The child can create a ramp by setting one end of a piece of cardboard on a shoe box or block and the other end on the floor. To make the ramp more secure, the child can tape the two pieces together. Invite the child to gather a group of toy cars and other round or rolling toys to test. The child can guess which will roll the farthest and make guesses as to how far each will roll—to couch, under couch, to TV. A large piece of paper (even newspaper will do) set in front of the ramp can be used to record both guesses and actual roll distances. Predictions can be marked on the paper with one color of crayon, and results can be marked in a different color.

What You'll Need
- cardboard
- shoe box or block
- masking tape
- toy cars
- marbles
- paper
- crayons

DRAMATIC DIORAMA

◁▷◁▷◁▷◁▷◁▷◁▷

Use this activity to bring a favorite story to life!

Read a favorite story aloud, and discuss the illustrations together. The more vivid and exotic the illustrations are, the better. Use the illustrations to inspire a diorama, which is a three-dimensional representation of a scene, and make the diorama together.

Begin by choosing one long side of the inside of the shoe box to be the bottom when the box is turned on its side. Decide what color the bottom should be, and get construction paper to match that color. For instance, if the ground will be made up of grass, use green construction paper. If it will be water, use blue construction paper. You can also draw or color on the construction paper to add different elements, such as a sidewalk or path. Then cover the remaining sides with blue construction paper for the sky. If appropriate, the child can draw clouds or birds in the sky.

What You'll Need
- a favorite illustrated storybook
- shoe box
- construction paper
- scissors
- glue
- markers or crayons
- paint
- paintbrush
- clay

To construct the inside, turn the shoe box on its side, with the side you chose for the bottom down. Talk with the child about what should be included in the diorama: trees, grass, buildings, cars, boats, and anything else you think of. Invite the child to use construction paper, markers or crayons, and paint to create these objects. Use clay to fashion any people or animals you want to include. Display the diorama next to the book it illustrates. Then use the diorama when retelling or rereading the story.

COLOR WORDS

◁▷◁▷◁▷◁▷

Making books about color is a fun and productive way for the child to reinforce color words.

What You'll Need
- picture book showing color words
- paper
- pencil
- paints
- paintbrush

Find a favorite book that talks about colors, and read it aloud together. Then read the book again, pointing out the color words on the pages. Talk about how the illustrator and/or author used color and words to show what the words, such as *red,* mean. Together, write down some ideas and pictures that might appear in a book. Then invite the child to use paints to make that book.

NAMES, NAMES, NAMES

◁▷◁▷◁▷◁▷

Get out your markers, and write a stack of labels for items around the house.

Set out index cards, stickers, or sentence strips and a box of markers. Invite the child to make labels for objects (nouns) in the house, such as furniture, a computer, items on a desk, and so on. Encourage the child to use a dictionary for

What You'll Need
- 3" × 5" index cards, stickers, or sentence strips
- markers

the correct spelling of the noun before writing it. Then have the child display the labels on or beside the objects they name.

MONEY ART

◁▷◁▷◁▷◁▷◁▷

Here's an interesting way to "make" some money.

The child will be using small hand muscles as she is making rubbings of different coins and learning about them at the same time.

Show the child a penny, nickel, dime, and quarter. Say, "I am thinking of a word that begins like *mouse* and describes all of these coins. What word is it?" (Answer: *money.*) Discuss with the child the colors and sizes of the coins. Ask, "What beginning letter sound do you hear in the words *penny, nickel, dime,* and *quarter*?" (*P, N, D,* and *Q.*)

What You'll Need
- penny
- nickel
- dime
- quarter
- crayons
- thin or regular paper

Have the child select a crayon and a coin. Put a sheet of thin or regular paper over the coin, and instruct the child to rub the crayon over the paper where the coin is. This will create an imprint of the coin. Repeat this with the other coins. When all of the money has been rubbed, have the child match the coins to the coin imprints and write the beginning letter of each coin next to the corresponding crayon imprint.

WHAT THE SUNDAY FUNNIES REALLY SAY

◁▷◁▷◁▷◁▷

Make up new stories for old funnies!

What You'll Need
- Sunday newspaper comics
- white self-adhesive labels
- pen

Place white self-adhesive labels inside the word balloons of the Sunday funnies. The child can look at the sequence of pictures of a comic and make up a story to go along with the sequence. The child can dictate the words that each character says while you write the words in the bubbles. Read the new story back to the child, or have the child read the story to you.

HOW BIG AROUND?

◁▷◁▷◁▷◁▷

They are this tall, but how big around are they?

What You'll Need
- yarn
- blunt scissors
- apple, potato, radish, pumpkin, watermelon (or other fruits and vegetables on hand)

It's common to measure how short, tall, long, or wide something is, but not how big around! Measuring the circumference of various fruits and vegetables can lead to surprising results when the round distances are spread out into flat lengths and compared to one another. The child can use yarn for measuring. Long pieces of yarn can be precut to make the measuring easier. The child can measure around the fruit or vegetable with the yarn and cut the yarn to that size. She can then line up the strips and compare them.

MACARONI LETTERS

◁▶◁▶◁▶◁▶

There's no cheese, but lots of pasta, in this recipe for hand-eye coordination.

What You'll Need
- 18" length of yarn
- uncooked macaroni

Tasks such as threading pieces of macaroni on a string can help a child improve hand-eye coordination, which is necessary for learning to read and write.

Tie a knot at the end of a length of yarn, and show the child how to string macaroni on it. When the string of macaroni is complete, tie a knot at the other end. Ask the child to make different letters by laying the string of macaroni on a tabletop and forming letter shapes.

BATTER UP

◁▶◁▶◁▶◁▶

See if students of beginning sounds can hit a home run.

Sports lovers can play baseball as they learn beginning sounds.

Make picture cards by gluing or taping pictures of simple objects onto index cards. Place the pictures around the room or yard in a baseball-diamond pattern. Have the child walk or run from home plate to first base.

What You'll Need
- index cards
- old magazines
- glue or clear tape
- scissors

At first base, ask him to name the object on the picture card and say a word that has the same beginning sound. If the child's word has the correct beginning sound, he goes on to the next base.

Let the child continue until he reaches home plate and scores a "home run." Play the game again using new picture cards or actual sports items.

WORD SORT

◁▶◁▶◁▶◁▶◁▶◁

This sorting activity is a creative way of putting information in order, a skill necessary for reading.

What You'll Need
• pencil
• index cards

Begin by creating with the child a list of 20 to 30 words. You may choose words randomly from a storybook. The child may even want to include words he is particularly fond of.

Write the words on index cards. Then invite the child to make up categories and to sort the word cards into those categories. The child may sort the words by first letter, by last letter, or by meaning, such as things that grow, things that fly, and so on. Encourage the child to choose one category and tell a story using all the words in that category.

Invite the child to sort the words into categories such as by number of letters in a word, number of syllables in a word, and so on.

Mix & Fix & Fizzle & Drizzle

⬦⬦⬦⬦⬦⬦

Make painting more interesting by making the paint first!

What You'll Need
- clear vinegar
- baking soda
- cornstarch
- corn syrup
- measuring cup
- measuring spoons
- bowl
- spoon
- jar lids
- food coloring
- brush
- paper

Make homemade watercolor paints by using clear vinegar, baking soda, cornstarch, and corn syrup. The child can help with the measuring and mixing and, of course, with the painting! Mix ¼ cup clear vinegar and ¼ cup baking soda in the bowl. Wait for the fizzle to stop, and then add ¼ cup cornstarch and 2 teaspoons corn syrup. Stir. Pour the brew into empty jar lids, add a few drops of food coloring to each, and stir. The paints can be used immediately, or the child can wait until they dry to paint with them, adding a little water to the brush.

 # Apron or Apple

⬦⬦⬦⬦⬦⬦

*Here is a challenge to determine if **A** words have long or short sounds.*

Old catalogs are good sources for pictures of specific objects. Find some that the child can use for this activity.

What You'll Need
- old catalog
- blunt scissors
- apron
- apple

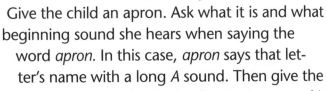 Give the child an apron. Ask what it is and what beginning sound she hears when saying the word *apron.* In this case, *apron* says that letter's name with a long *A* sound. Then give the child an apple, and ask what beginning sound is heard when saying *apple* (the short *A* sound). Give the child a catalog to find things that have long *A* sounds (for example, *alien, ape, angel*) and short *A* sounds (*ant, ax, animal*). If the object has a long *A* sound, place it by the apron, and if it has a short *A* sound, place it by the apple.

HUNG OUT TO DRY

◁▷◁▷◁▷◁▷

Come join the three little kittens in their search for sentence order.

Read or chant the familiar nursery rhyme "Three Little Kittens" with the child.

> Three little kittens have lost their mittens,
> And they began to cry,
> "Oh, mother dear, we sadly fear
> That we have lost our mittens."
> "What! lost your mittens, you naughty kittens!
> Then you shall have no pie.
> Mee-ow, mee-ow, mee-ow.
> No, you shall have no pie."

Choose 1 or 2 sentences from the rhyme. Write each word of the sentence or sentences on individual cards, and mix up the cards. Then have the child arrange and hang the cards on the clothesline in sequential order to make complete sentences.

Pop, Pop, Popcorn!

◁▷◁▷◁▷◁▷◁▷◁▷

Put the child's senses through a vocabulary test with this popping good activity.

Begin by making some popcorn together. Invite the child to describe what he sees, hears, and smells while you are popping the popcorn. Cut some construction paper into small squares, and record the words the child uses on paper squares yourself, or ask the child to write down the words. Feel free to snack on some of the popcorn while you and the child brainstorm for other words that describe or are associated with this treat. Don't forget to include words about how the popcorn tastes.

What You'll Need
- popcorn
- popcorn popper
- construction paper
- blunt scissors
- pencil
- threaded needle

Write those words on the paper squares as well. Some words you might want to include are *salty, crunchy, pop, hot, white, munch,* and *yummy.*

Next help the child use the needle to string some of the popcorn with the words on paper squares to create a decorative word bank. Display the completed popcorn-and-word strand in the room for a day or so to review the words. Then remove the popcorn from the strand, and take it outside for birds to enjoy.

WORDS LIKE MY NAME

◁▷◁▷◁▷◁▷

Help a child find words that begin with the same first letter as his name.

What You'll Need
• old magazines
• blunt scissors
• sheet of paper
• glue or clear tape

Have the child become aware of words that begin with the same letter as his first and/or last name.

Give the child blunt scissors and some old magazines (those with a lot of advertisements and big print will work best). Talk about the first letter in his name, and begin the search for words in the magazine beginning with that same letter. After the words are found and cut out, they may be pasted on paper. Read the chosen words aloud. Keep emphasizing that the words also have the same beginning sound as the child's name.

LETTER LADDER

◁▷◁▷◁▷◁▷

The sky's the limit in this letter-identification game.

Use a ladder to show a child's progress in letter identification.

On poster board or butcher paper, draw a ladder with 6 or 7 rungs. (Make the space between each 2 rungs large enough to display a letter card.) Place a letter card on each rung. Challenge the child to move up the ladder by identifying the letter on each rung.

What You'll Need
• poster board or butcher paper
• marker or pen
• letter cards

LETTER TILES

◁▷◁▷◁▷◁▷◁▷

In this word-building game, the child creates letter tiles to spell out words!

Help the child make 3 sets of letter tiles from index cards for the consonant clusters *gr, br,* and *fr.* Then make 3 sets of tiles for each individual letter of the alphabet, from *a* to *z.* Next invite the child to build words with the consonant clusters and letter tiles. Encourage the child to build 2 words at a time, making sure that the words have at least 1 consonant cluster in common, as shown. Then challenge the child to build 3 words at a time. Continue building words until all of the consonant clusters are used up.

ON THE GO

◁▷◁▷◁▷◁▷

Use those spare moments in the car to keep the child reading and writing (and busy!).

What You'll Need
- clipboard
- paper
- pencil

The child can see a lot of words—on signs, billboards, in store windows—as you go on errands, take short trips, or travel to and from school. Keep a clipboard, paper, and pencil in the car. As you travel, have the child copy the names of the stores you frequently go to. Keep the list, and invite the child to practice reading and writing the names. Once the child is familiar with the names, have the child list the places in the order that you will go. For more challenging directions, add street names to the list.

SHOPPING FOR CLOTHES

◁▷◁▷◁▷◁▷

Dread shopping? You won't when you try shopping this way.

Shopping for clothes with a child can be fun—and educational—when both of you know what you want.

On the way to the store, talk about different clothing items that you might find. When the child names a certain article of clothing (pants, for example), ask him, "What beginning letter sound do you hear?" (Answer: *P.*) Continue in the same manner for other clothing items, such as a coat, jacket, socks, and so on.

Identify the articles you want to find. When you enter the children's clothing department, knowing what needs to be purchased, ask the child to help you find the item(s). When you return home, have the child take the items you purchased out of their bags, identify the items, then tell you the beginning sound for each one.

MYSTERY MAZE

◁▷◁▷◁▷◁▷◁▷

Go through a mystery maze to find and learn the lowercase m.

The child learns several reading skills in this fun activity.

Design and draw a maze with a pen on a piece of paper, as illustrated in the accompanying drawing. Place a capital *M* at the start and a lowercase *m* at the end of the maze.

Ask the child to take a pencil and begin at the capital *M* to follow a path that reaches the lowercase *m* at the end.

The purpose of the maze is for the child to learn the lowercase *m* and to relate the letter to its sound, as in the word *maze.* In addition, by using those beginning and ending points, the child will be working through the maze going from left to right, reinforcing the directions used in the reading and writing process.

DOES IT DISSOLVE?

◁▷◁▷◁▷◁▷◁▷

Become a scientist to find out what dissolves!

Invite the child to be a scientist and make predictions about what substances can be dissolved in water. Then experiment to find out if your predictions are correct. Gather materials together with the child. Start by adding sugar to a bowl of water to show the child what *dissolve* means. The child can then examine each item, look at it, touch it, and predict whether or not it will dissolve in water. The child can then test the items, one by one!

What You'll Need
• bowls of water
• spoon
• variety of objects (salt, pepper, sugar, pebbles, ice cubes, laundry detergent, polystyrene foam, oil, marbles, lima beans)

BLUE RIBBON

◁▷◁▷◁▷◁▷◁▷

Hip, hip, hooray! You'll be cheering, too, for the heroes in this rewarding activity about characters.

What You'll Need
• blue and yellow construction paper
• blunt scissors
• 2 blue-ribbon streamers
• clear tape
• markers

FIRST PLACE! YOU'RE A WINNER! FUNNIEST DOG! HERO! YOU'RE NUMBER 1!

Discuss different ways to describe a person or an animal that has accomplished an outstanding achievement. Then invite the child to design and create a blue-ribbon award for a favorite story character. Explain that the award may be for kindness, hard work, courage, or any other action or quality the child thinks is noteworthy. Create the ribbon from construction paper and blue-ribbon streamers. Suggest that the child print the name of the character and the reason the award was given on the ribbon.

PRETTY PRINTED PATTERNS

◁▶◁▶◁▶◁▶◁▶◁

Create colorful patterns and designs with sponge shapes.

What You'll Need
- sponges
- scissors
- adding-machine tape
- tempera paint
- plastic trays
- water bowl
- paper towels (optional)

Cut sponges into simple shapes, such as circles, squares, triangles, or stars, for sponge painting. Unroll a strip of adding-machine tape. Pour 2 or 3 colors of paint into shallow trays. Dip a sponge into the water, then into the paint. The child can make random sponge painting decorations on the paper strip or can experiment and explore shape and

color patterns. Several finished strips can be taped to the bottom of a wire hanger to make a simple decorative mobile. For a BIG variation of the activity, cut shapes out of huge sponges and invite the child to make BIG sponge painting decorations and designs on a strip of white paper toweling.

THE ALPHABET GAME

◁▶◁▶◁▶◁▶◁▶◁

You will love this ABC order game of wits and laughs.
It's great for a rainy day or a long trip.

Invite the child to think of a word that begins with each letter of the alphabet. You may want to limit the search to a particular theme, such as words used in a current science study about insects or names of cities and states the child has learned in social studies. Have the child start with *A* and go in order. How far into the alphabet can the child go?

If the child is unable to think of a word that starts with a particular letter, suggest choosing a word that contains that letter.

WATER, WATER EVERYWHERE

◁▷◁▷◁▷◁▷◁▷

A child can make quite a splash while learning the letter W.

What You'll Need
- marker or pen
- sheet of paper
- plastic and paper cups of various sizes and shapes

This activity lets a child practice words that begin with the letter *W.* It also gives you an opportunity to discuss one of our most important natural resources.

Write the word *water* on a sheet of paper. Have the child copy the word and name other words that begin with the same sound—for example, *wash, walk, warm, worm.*

Take plastic and paper cups outside, and have the child collect water from several sources, putting each into a different container. Possible sources include an indoor faucet, an outdoor faucet, rainwater, and pond water. Also, have the child put an ice cube from the freezer into a cup and see what happens to it.

Discuss the various sources of water and which ones contain clean or dirty water. Have the child display the water samples with the word *water* that she wrote, then talk about how we use water every day.

JUST LIKE ME

<⊳<⊳<⊳<⊳<⊳

Look and see what's the same as me!

What You'll Need
• magazines

Look through magazines together, and find pictures of people to investigate. Choose one person in a picture to look at. Then invite the child to tell something about that person that is the same as the child and something that is different. For example, the child might say, "He is the same as me because he has a shirt with buttons, and I have a shirt with buttons. He is different than me because he is a grown-up, and I am a kid." Or, "She is the same as me because we both have brown hair, but we are different because she is outside, and I am inside." After the child has taken a turn, take a turn yourself! For a variation, play the game outside while taking a walk, at a park, or even while watching TV. Note passersby or TV characters, and take turns quickly thinking of ways they are the same as or different than each of you.

FAIRY-TALE CHALLENGE

<⊳<⊳<⊳<⊳<⊳

In this activity, different versions of fairy tales are discussed.

Read aloud the 3 versions of the same fairy tale together. Then discuss the beginnings. Compare how the retellers started the stories. Did they all start with "Once upon a time"? Did some have short sentences and some have long? Did some make the beginning serious and others start with humor? How do the illustrations differ?

What You'll Need
• 3 versions of one fairy tale, such as "The Three Bears" or "Cinderella"

Continue by discussing the rest of the story. Invite the child to compare illustrations, portrayals of the characters, how the story ends, and so on.

ABC Flips

◁▷◁▷◁▷◁▷

Flip the letter card. This activity is self-correcting.

What You'll Need
- index cards
- marker
- lowercase alphabet cards

Capital letters are the first set of letters that a child learns. Next come the lowercase letters. Capital letters serve as the point of reference in this activity, which is intended to help the child learn lowercase letters.

To make a flip card, fold a 3" × 5" index card in half so the card stands up. On the exposed surface, write a capital letter. Write the matching lowercase letter on the half covered by the capital letter flap. Make a card for each letter of the alphabet.

Stand up the flip cards so the child can see all of the capital letters. Give the child the lowercase alphabet cards one letter at a time, and have him place each card by the matching capital letter on the flip card. The child can lift the flap to see if the lowercase letter matches the one that he selected.

Acting Out Musical Stories

◁▷◁▷◁▷◁▷

Listen and retell a story using music and action, not words!

Share a recording of story-based instrumental music with the child. Talk briefly about the story before listening to the music. Then listen together, sharing reactions to the story portrayal. Listen a second time, inviting the child to act out the story to the music. For a variation, invite him to listen to instrumental music that doesn't illustrate any specific story. Let the child invent his own story and act it out in movement to the music.

What You'll Need
- instrumental music that tells a story, such as *Peter and the Wolf* or *The Nutcracker Suite*
- tape recorder or CD player

SAY A WORD

◁▶◁▶◁▶◁▶◁▶◁▷

Spin the arrow, and learn to say a new word.

What You'll Need
- compass
- lightweight cardboard
- marker or pen
- scissors
- brad fastener

Use a compass to draw a circle 8" in diameter on a piece of cardboard. Then draw lines to divide the circle into 6 equal sections. At the center point of the circle, make a small hole with the scissors. Cut out a simple arrow about 3" long and 1" wide from another piece of cardboard to use as the spinner. Put a brad fastener through the middle of the arrow and the center of the wheel. Next, write a single letter in each of the 6 sections of the circle. The child spins the arrow on the wheel and says a word that begins with the letter in the section where the arrow comes to rest.

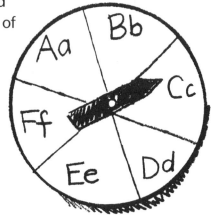

To make this activity more challenging, increase the number of sections. For the child who can read, in addition to saying a word beginning with a particular letter, the child should also spell the word.

 # LETTER SELF-PORTRAIT

◁▷◁▷◁▶◁▶◁▷

Help a child make a revealing life-size self-portrait.

Do this project to personalize a child's study of letters.

Find a large sheet of paper that is sturdy and a few inches longer than the child's height. Put the paper on the floor, have the child lie on it, and trace around him. Have the child color the "self-portrait" with crayons or markers and print his name at the top.

What You'll Need
- large sheet of heavy kraft paper
- crayons or markers

Encourage the child to add distinguishing characteristics of dress, hairstyle, and so on. Write the first letter of the child's name, and have the child draw pictures of toys whose names begin with that letter.

FREEZE DANCING

◁▷◁▷◁▷◁▷

Dance, prance, jump, and hop, then turn off the music, freeze, and stop!

What You'll Need
• music

Play music or sing a song for the child to dance to. The child can also jump, hop, skip, sway, or move to the music in any way. Explain to the child that while the music plays he should keep moving, but as soon as the music stops he must freeze and become a statue! As soon as the music begins again, the frozen statue melts back into motion. To make the game more challenging, encourage the child to imagine and report on the kind of statue he has frozen into each time the music stops.

BOUNCING WORDS

◁▷◁▷◁▷◁▷

Try bouncing words. It can be more fun than using a ball.

Whenever you have a few minutes, whether you're at home or traveling in the car, try this quick activity involving "bouncing" words from one to another.

Say a word, such as *ball*. The child then says a word that begins with the same first letter, such as *bat*. Continue bouncing new words back and forth to each other until neither of you can think of any more words. Then try a new letter. You can also have someone keep count to see how many words you come up with for each letter.

SEEDS I SEE

⊲►⊲►⊲►⊲►⊲►⊲►

Search for seeds in everyday foods!

What You'll Need
- seeds
- stiff paper
- nontoxic white glue
- markers or crayons
- index cards

The child can save the seeds found in fresh fruits and vegetables and start a collection. Let the child wash and dry the seeds, then glue them onto stiff paper to make a chart. Next to each glued seed the child can draw a picture of the food in which the seed was found. To make a seed-matching game, the child can glue 1 of each kind of seed to index cards. A picture of the food is drawn on the back of the paper for self-checking. A second picture of the food is drawn on another paper square. The child can match the seed cards to the picture cards, turning over the seed cards to check the matches.

Activity Twist

Create an interesting seed picture or collage by gluing the dried seeds to construction paper. Look closely at the different textures of the seeds—watermelon seeds make a great beard, and apple seeds are cute freckles! What else does the child see?

ALTERNATIVE ART CANVAS

◁▶◁▶◁▶◁▶

Create a variety of effects by drawing on different materials.

Lay out sheets of different materials on a table. Encourage the child to draw or scribble on each one. Talk to him about the feel and appearance produced by each one. For example, say, "That makes an interesting picture when you draw on the shiny aluminum foil!" or "The waxed paper doesn't work very well as something to scribble on, even when you press hard, does it?" Ask the child which effects he likes best and give him additional sheets of the materials that produce those effects. In addition, invite him to use paints on the materials. Talk about the different looks and textures produced by tempera paints and watercolor paints. Display the artwork in an area where he can admire it easily and often.

What You'll Need
- sheets of various materials, such as construction paper, brown paper bags, cardboard, aluminum foil, and waxed paper
- crayons
- paints (tempera, watercolor)
- paintbrush

STOP AND GO

◁▶◁▶◁▶◁▶

Whether you're going fast or slow, you'll have to freeze on command.

Use any tune you like to sing a variety of movement commands to the child. For example, "Spin, spin, spin!" or "Jump, jump, jump!" Model the appropriate action and encourage her to mimic you. Once she becomes comfortable with the movements, occasionally "freeze" and call out "Stop!" After she has "frozen," too, call out "Go!" and resume your movement. You can also introduce variations in speed. For example, "wiggle, wiggle, wiggle, slower, slower, slower" or "run, run, run, faster, faster, faster." Also, try introducing combinations of movements, such as "hop and turn, hop and turn." If she shows interest in reversing roles, permit her to be the leader, and follow whatever commands she gives. If she simply models the commands without saying them, say the appropriate words for her as you do whatever she is doing.

GOOD VIBRATIONS

⊲▶⊲▶⊲▶⊲▶

Use only your breath to make fun sounds!

Vibrations produce sounds. The child can make vibrations with columns of air and change the sounds by changing the columns. Encourage the child to experiment (noisily) by blowing into the different items and noticing the different kinds of sounds that can be achieved. Extend the challenge by asking the child to make different sizes and shapes of tubes with paper and observe how the sounds change as the tube is changed.

What You'll Need
• cardboard tubes
• variety of narrow-necked plastic bottles
• straws
• paper

THE LOCAL SCENE

⊲▶⊲▶⊲▶⊲▶

Create a mural of the neighborhood highlights.

What You'll Need
• large paper
• crayons or markers
• disposable camera (optional)

After taking a research tour of the neighborhood, the child can try to recall as many details as possible and draw them on large paper. The adult and child can then take another walk through the neighborhood to see if there are any important buildings, trees, houses, or other street details that the child wants to add. For more challenge, the child can make a mural or a map of the area, drawing the location of the buildings, roads, and sidewalks. The child can also use a camera to record neighborhood scenes. The child can use the pictures when drawing the mural, as a reference for map making, or as a separate activity, for sequencing. To sequence the pictures, the child can line them up in the same order as the buildings on the block.

PUMPKIN PIE

◁►◁►◁►◁►◁►◁►◁►

Here's the best kind of recipe for kids—simple, healthy, and delicious.

What You'll Need
- colored pencils or crayons
- drawing paper
- pie plate
- pie crust
- can of pumpkin and other ingredients for pumpkin pie

Have fun with the letter *P*—and reward yourselves with some pumpkin pie.

Ask the child to draw and color a picture of a pumpkin. Ask him to identify the beginning sound of the word *pumpkin.* Show the child how to write the letter *P* on his drawing.

Explain that a pumpkin pie can be made with pumpkin from a can. Prepare a frozen, refrigerated, or homemade pie crust. Show the child a pumpkin-pie recipe (most cans of pumpkin include one on the label), and go through each step together. Let the child help add ingredients and mix the pumpkin-pie filling.

STORY PLAY

◁▷◁▷◁▷◁▷

Stuffed animals and simple stories combine perfectly to give the child an opportunity to develop simple scripts.

Ask the child to gather a variety of stuffed animals. Then share a simple story with the child, and discuss how that story can be acted out with the stuffed animals. Make a list of characters together, and plan which animal will play which character. Help the child write the story in script form. For rehearsal, read the script aloud while the animals act out the story. Revise the script as necessary until the performance is perfected. Prepare the play, and share it with others.

When the child has the play just right, suggest he use a cardboard box for a backdrop, creating scenery by painting different scenes on each side.

CATERPILLAR MENU

◁▷◁▷◁▷◁▷

This delicious activity just may become a favorite for the child.

Have you ever seen a caterpillar eating a leaf? It seems like the caterpillar will go right through it, eating anything in its way! Read a favorite book about food together with the child. Write all the food words found in the book on the index cards. Which of these foods do you think a caterpillar would like to eat?

Read the book again. This time match the words on the cards to the pages where they appear in the book. Invite the child to arrange the words in the same order they are found in the book. Then together create a menu for a caterpillar, listing all the foods from the book the child thinks the caterpillar might like to eat.

PLAYFUL DEBATING

◁▶◁▶◁▶◁▶◁▷

***Debating is a test of wits and knowledge
and an energetic way to practice verbalizing ideas.***

Choose a topic for a playful debate with the child. You might debate about which is tastier—chocolate or vanilla ice cream? Or what's more fun—hiking or soccer?

Take turns offering reasonable arguments to support your side of the debate. You may want to have a third party listen to each of your reasons and judge which ideas and information are the strongest and most on target.

LETTER SEARCH

◁▷◁▷◁▷◁▷

Have fun looking at pictures to find special hidden letters.

This activity allows a child to look for hidden letters and then make a word out of them.

Take a picture from a magazine or travel brochure. Using a pen or marker, hide some letters in the photograph by blending all or parts of them into the lines, curves, and shapes of objects in the picture. Ideally, the letters must be written so that they are visible, yet thin enough so that the child's search will be somewhat challenging.

One way to start is to use the letters in the child's name. Try capital letters first and then lowercase letters. Give the child the picture and have him search for the letters in his name. When the letters are found, ask the child to say each one and show where it is.

What You'll Need
- pictures from a magazine or travel brochure
- pen or marker

CAN YOU SEE MY FACE?

◁▷◁▷◁▷◁▷

Turn twigs and leaves and odds and ends into found faces!

Gather assorted natural and household items. Challenge the child to arrange items on a piece of paper to create a face. To make it easier to begin, suggest that he start by picking an item to use for a nose, and then ask him where to place it on the paper. If the child has difficulty, have him look at the shape and position of your nose. After that, it's a simple matter of picking eyes and a mouth. Other features can also be added. After a face is finished, take turns making changes by replacing parts of the face with different items.

What You'll Need

- assorted household and nature objects, such as: bottle caps, buttons, rubber bands, twigs and leaves, paper

ARTIST STUDY

◁▷◁▷◁▷◁▷

Observe an artist's work, and work like that artist!

What You'll Need

- group of children's books illustrated by one artist or book of reproductions of a famous artist's paintings

Gather together several children's books illustrated by the same artist. After reading the stories, look at the pictures together, and talk about the artist's style. Encourage the child to share ideas about that artist's work. What is similar about the pictures in all the books? What colors does the artist like? Are the lines thin or big and bold? Discuss with the child the media the artist uses to make pictures (watercolor, acrylics, chalk, etc.). After making observations about the artist's style, invite the child to make a picture in the same style! The child can make a picture using the same technique.

SOCK WALK

◁▷◁▷◁▷◁▷

Go searching for seeds without looking for them!

What You'll Need
- large pair of old socks
- newspaper
- jar or pot
- soil
- water
- unbreakable magnifying glass
- plastic bag (optional)
- rubber band (optional)

Invite the child to put on an old pair of socks over his shoes. Then take a walk together in the yard, a garden area, or a local park. After returning home, the child can take off the socks, lay them on a newspaper, and carefully look over all the odds and ends that have stuck to the fabric. There may be some seeds stuck to the socks! Use a magnifying glass to examine the seeds more closely. Cover the work area with newspaper, and invite the child to prepare a planting pot for the seeds by filling a jar or pot with soil. The child can plant everything that looks like it might be a seed by poking holes in the soil, inserting the seeds, and then gently covering them with soil. Have the child place the pot in a sunny place, add a little water, and watch to see what grows. (What grows will depend on the season.) To help the seeds germinate, the child can create a greenhouse by covering the pot with a plastic bag and sealing it with a rubber band.

GOING ON A TRIP

◁▷◁▷◁▷◁▷

Pack your bags and get ready to go on a trip to learn about nouns.

Think of a place to go on an imaginary trip. Then have the child pack her "bags." Begin by listing items to pack. For example, start with something that begins with the letter *A,* such as an apple. Then have the child repeat the first item and add something that begins with *B.*

Play continues until the end of the alphabet is reached. If the child is unable to find an object that starts with a particular letter, skip to the next letter. Remind the child that the name of each item packed for the trip is a noun. For an additional challenge, see how many of the nouns packed for your imaginary trip the child can remember.

MAKING SENTENCES

◁▷◁▷◁▷◁▷◁▷

Unscramble words to make sensible sentences.

What You'll Need
• index cards
• pen or marker

The child will actually make a complete sentence, including punctuation, in this challenging activity.

Make and then scramble word cards, each containing one of the following words: *cat, fat, mat, sat, A, on,* and *a.*
Also make one card with a period (.) on it. Have the child take the cards and arrange them to make a sentence.

In this activity, attention is being called to beginning a sentence with a capital letter, ending the sentence with a period, and arranging words to make a complete thought: *A fat cat sat on a mat.* The child is using his knowledge of letters and sounds, combining them to make words, and then using those words to make a sentence.

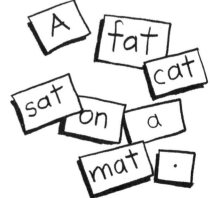

BRIGHT IDEA

◁▷◁▷◁▷◁▷

The child will be caught hook, line, and sinker with this bright idea for reviewing nouns and verbs.

What You'll Need
• large paper
• crayons

Explain to the child that some words in our language can be both a noun and a verb. For example, write the word *fish*. The word can be a noun that names an animal that swims in the water. It can also be a verb that means to drop a line with a hook in the water so one is able to catch the scaly animal. Write the word *slide.* Ask the child what the word means when used as a noun. When is it used as a verb?

Set out paper and crayons. Invite the child to make a poster or banner by writing and drawing words that can be either a noun or a verb, such as *fish, slide,* and *paint.* Invite the child to think of other words to add to the poster.

For a fun and challenging way to use words that are both a noun and a verb, help the child write a sentence that contains both forms.

HELLO/GOOD-BYE

◁▷◁▷◁▷◁▷

Hello, horse; good-bye goat!

In this activity, the child is asked to recognize the beginning sounds *H* and *G*. Say a series of words that begin with *H* and *G*, such as *hat, girl, head, horse, gate, garden, hand, goat,* and *house.* Have the child say "hello" each time you say a word that begins with *H* and "good-bye" each time you say a word that begins with *G*.

GOOD NEWS, BAD NEWS

◁▷◁▷◁▷◁▷

Good news, bad news stories are fun to create and often produce a lot of laughter.

Create a good news, bad news story together. Each person takes a turn telling something good that happened followed by something bad. The next person must continue the story by adding the next good thing followed by the next bad thing.

For example, the first person might start by saying, "I found a magic stone in the park. That was good. I lost it on the way home. That was bad." The second person might then continue with, "My friend found my stone. That was good. He wouldn't give it back. That was bad."

SPLASH YOURSELF!

*Writing down descriptive words about oneself is a fun
and creative way to learn about who we are!*

What You'll Need
- pencil
- paper
- markers or crayons
- old magazines (optional)

Begin this activity by having the child brainstorm descriptive words about who she is—such as *smart, kind,* and *fun*—and write them on a piece of paper. Next, have the child write her name in the center of a piece of paper. Have the child use markers or crayons to create a "splash" of words or pictures that describe herself. This can be extended to include words or pictures cut out from magazines.

For variation, have the child make an acrostic poem with her name. She can find a descriptive word starting with each of the letters in her name.

ONE BY ONE

*How can you change a bug into a pup in 6 easy steps?
Play this challenging word game, and find out!*

Write the word *bug* on a piece of paper. Now make a new word by changing one letter. Perhaps you will change the *u* to an *a* to make the word *bag.* Continue the game in this way to see how many new words the child makes before ending up with the word *pup.* For continued play, try using other words to start and finish with.

What You'll Need
- paper
- pencil

GRANDMOTHER'S SUITCASE

◁▷◁▷◁▷◁▷

Exercise those memory muscles with this cumulative list story!

Start this cumulative list story by saying, "Grandmother is coming to visit. In her suitcase she will pack her pajamas." Explain to the child that he is to repeat everything you say and add one more item for Grandmother's suitcase. For example, the child may say, "Grandmother is coming to visit. In her suitcase she will pack her pajamas and a toothbrush."

Take another turn, and then invite the child to take another turn. Continue to repeat the original verse as well as each additional item Grandmother packs up to bring for a visit. How long of a list can be remembered?

ALPHABET ILLUSTRATION

◁▷◁▷◁▷◁▷

Alphabet art lets young illustrators stretch their creative muscles.

This activity is a great way to reinforce the idea of beginning letters.

Suggest a letter, and explain to the child that he should paint a picture that contains items whose names begin with the letter. For example, an *S* picture might contain sand, a sea, a sidewalk, a sun, and a sailboat. A letter *B* picture might contain a bus, buildings, birds, balloons, and a bench. When the child completes the picture, encourage him to point out each item with the chosen letter.

What You'll Need
• washable paints
• paintbrush
• paper

BLOW OR NO?

◁▷◁▷◁▷◁▷

Carry out a blowing test to find out what objects are blown best.

What You'll Need
• assorted small objects (crumbled aluminum foil, penny, paper clip, bottle cap)
• cardboard tubes
• straws

Caution: This project requires adult supervision.

Gather an assortment of small items for the blow test. (Supervise carefully— small objects may pose a choking hazard.) The child can predict

which items can be moved easily by blowing and then experiment by blowing them! After testing, the child can sort the items into categories. To test further, add a cardboard tube and a straw. The child can blow through the tube and the straw to test if either changes the results.

Invented Words

◁▷◁▷◁▷◁▷

The child will Zam! Pow! and Whammy! into spelling with this awesome cartoon-lover's activity.

What You'll Need
- comic strips
- scissors
- crayons
- construction paper

Review comic strips together, reading and enjoying the action. Look for words made up by the writer or artist that express actions or feelings. Have the child cut out the action words and study them to discover the interesting ways in which they are spelled.

Next, have the child make up his own comic words. Invite the child to make a cartoon with the invented words by writing the words in large, colorful letters on construction paper.

Invite the child to create his own comic strip by drawing favorite or made-up characters to accompany the comic words.

PRINTED ALPHABET

◁►◁►◁►◁►◁

Below are the alphabet's letters in their common printed forms. Children are taught this "ball and stick" style in the primary grades, so it's important for parents to introduce this style to their preschoolers.

Aa Bb Cc Dd Ee
Ff Gg Hh Ii Jj Kk
Ll Mm Nn Oo Pp
Qq Rr Ss Tt Uu Vv
Ww Xx Yy Zz

MOST COMMON WORDS

◁▶◁▶◁▶◁▶◁▶◁▶

These are the 150 most commonly used words in the English language. The first 100 make up about 50 percent of all written language. Therefore, it is important that the child learn to recognize all of the words in this list and eventually learn how to say, write, and define them.

1. the	31. but	61. some	91. find	121. name
2. of	32. not	62. her	92. long	122. good
3. and	33. what	63. would	93. down	123. sentence
4. a	34. all	64. make	94. day	124. man
5. to	35. were	65. like	95. did	125. think
6. in	36. we	66. him	96. get	126. say
7. is	37. when	67. into	97. come	127. great
8. you	38. your	68. time	98. made	128. where
9. that	39. can	69. has	99. may	129. help
10. it	40. said	70. look	100. part	130. through
11. he	41. there	71. two	101. over	131. much
12. was	42. use	72. more	102. new	132. before
13. for	43. an	73. write	103. sound	133. line
14. on	44. each	74. go	104. take	134. right
15. are	45. which	75. see	105. only	135. too
16. as	46. she	76. number	106. little	136. means
17. with	47. do	77. no	107. work	137. old
18. his	48. how	78. way	108. know	138. any
19. they	49. their	79. could	109. place	139. same
20. I	50. if	80. people	110. years	140. tell
21. at	51. will	81. my	111. live	141. boy
22. be	52. up	82. than	112. me	142. following
23. this	53. other	83. first	113. back	143. came
24. have	54. about	84. water	114. give	144. want
25. from	55. out	85. been	115. most	145. show
26. or	56. many	86. called	116. very	146. also
27. one	57. then	87. who	117. after	147. around
28. had	58. them	88. oil	118. things	148. form
29. by	59. these	89. its	119. our	149. three
30. words	60. so	90. now	120. just	150. small

PHONOGRAMS

⟨▶⟨▶⟨▶⟨▶⟨▶⟨▶⟨▷

The following list contains some of the most commonly used phonograms (and the symbol representing the sound of the key vowel) in the English language. A phonogram is a series of letters that is consistantly used to form words. The child should study this list in order to learn the many different words derived from the same sounds.

-ace (ā)
face
lace
race
brace
grace
place
space
trace

-ad (ă)
bad
dad
fad
had
lad
mad
pad
sad
glad

-ail (ā)
bail
fail
jail
mail
nail
pail
rail
sail
tail
snail
trail

-ain (ā)
gain
main
pain
rain
brain
chain
drain
grain

plain
sprain
stain
train

-ake (ā)
bake
cake
fake
lake
make
rake
take
wake
brake
flake
shake
snake
stake

-ame (ā)
came
fame
game
name
same
tame
blame
flame
frame
shame

-an (ă)
ban
can
man
pan
ran
tan
van
bran
plan
than

-and (ă)
band
hand
land
sand
bland
gland
grand
stand
strand

-are (ā)
bare
care
dare
fare
rare
scare
share
spare
square
stare

-ave (ā)
cave
gave
rave
save
wave
brave
crave
shave

-eak (ē)
beak
leak
peak
weak
sneak
speak
squeak
streak

-eat (ē)
beat
feat
heat
meat
neat
peat
seat
cheat
treat
wheat

-ell (ĕ)
bell
cell
fell
sell
tell
well
yell
dwell
shell
smell
spell

-ent (ĕ)
bent
dent
lent
rent
sent
tent
vent
went
scent
spent

-ight (ī)
fight
knight
light
might
night

right
tight
bright
flight
fright

-ill (ĭ)
bill
dill
fill
gill
hill
ill
pill
will
chill
drill
grill
skill
spill
still
thrill

-ing (ĭ)
king
ring
sing
wing
bring
cling
sling
spring
string
swing
thing

-ink (ĭ)
link
pink
rink
sink
wink
blink

drink
shrink
stink
think

-ip (ĭ)
dip
hip
lip
rip
sip
tip
zip
chip
clip
drip
flip
ship
skip
trip

-ock (ŏ)
dock
lock
knock
rock
sock
tock
block
clock
flock

-old (ō)
bold
cold
fold
gold
hold
mold
old
sold
told
scold

-ot (ŏ)
cot
got
hot
jot
lot
not
pot
rot
spot

-ow (ou)
bow
cow
how
now
sow
vow
brow
chow
plow

-ow (ō)
know
low
row
tow
blow
flow
glow
show
slow
snow

INDEX

Critical Thinking